THE
DAY YOU
WERE BORN

THE DAY YOU WERE BORN

A Journey to Wholeness through Astrology and Numerology

LINDA JOYCE

CITADEL PRESS
Kensington Publishing Corp.
www.kensingtonbooks.com

CITADEL PRESS BOOKS are published by

Kensington Publishing Corp.
850 Third Avenue
New York, NY 10022

All Kensington titles, imprints, and distributed lines are available at special quantity
discounts for bulk purchases for sales promotions, premiums, fund-raising, educational,
or institutional use. Special book excerpts or customized printings can also be created
to fit specific needs. For details, write or phone the office of the Kensington special
sales manager: Kensington Publishing Corp., 850 Third Avenue, New York, NY
10022, attn: Special Sales Department, phone 1-800-221-2647.

CITADEL PRESS and the Citadel logo are Reg. U.S. Pat. & TM Off.

First Citadel printing: August 2003

10   9   8   7   6   5   4   3   2   1

Printed in the United States of America

Cataloging data may be obtained from the Library of Congress

0-8065-2467-7

ACKNOWLEDGMENTS

Any great effort is never completed alone. There are always those who contribute along the way. I am fortunate to say that I have many people to thank for my being able to write *The Day You Were Born*. First and foremost I would like to thank my sister, Paula Wesselmann, who ignited my desire to write by asking me to coauthor a novel she was working on. We learned together how to write, but the real lesson was how to share, how to put aside one's ego for the betterment of the project and the goal. This we did easily because we had a relationship based on faith, love, and support. When you have these ingredients, anything and everything is possible. To my parents I would like to say thanks for the gifts of courage, creativity, and a passion for life, truth, and knowledge that they imparted to me. My mother taught me through her own achievements that anything was possible, never to accept defeat or no for an answer; if something doesn't work, there is always another way. My father was the "idea" man, he could take a thought and turn it inside out, upside down, place it on its back, sideways, or all ways at once. With this kind of training there's no such thing as getting stuck; you persevere and you come up with something new. To them both I say thank you with all my heart. To my sister Camille, who died when I was sixteen, I also say thank you, for I know she was one of the spirits guiding my thoughts through this project. When you have heaven and earth working to get the job done, it happens.

There have been many wonderful teachers in my life, and I'd like to mention four of them. To my sixth-grade teacher, Mr. Kleinback, I owe a special thanks for the gift of "specialness" he gave me. He made me feel as if I had something wonderful to offer the world. At the University of Arizona I encountered Dr. Caponi, who opened my mind and challenged me through the world of Italian literature, which was my major. He guided me, but never limited my own concepts, and for that I will forever be grateful.

As an astrologer I owe a great deal to Michael Lutin, *Vanity Fair*'s outrageously wonderful astrologer. He not only accepted my unique approach to astrology, but introduced me to his own. Together, learning and discovering became magic, and I progressed in the field because of his support and guidance. Michael is also responsible for introducing me to yet another teacher, one whom I know only through his work, Robert Langs. His book *The Listening Process* and its ideas transformed the way I thought forever. He taught me how to be in the "now."

The teachers closest to me are my children. From my son Michael, I learned how to confront and let go. I couldn't bend his will, so I surrendered to it and accomplished through love what can never be done through control. Jordana has inspired me with her strength and her great compassion for others. She has within her, naturally, so many of the talents I have struggled so hard to achieve.

Friends are the honey of life, and I've been blessed with many. I would like to thank Monty Renov for all the books he gave me that provided the exact thought or concept I needed to explore at that moment and for the time he spent discussing and challenging my ideas, helping me refine and make them more clear. A special thanks to Patricia Reed, who pushed me out into the world as a young astrologer, helping me put together my first classes and lecturers. The many friends who have believed in me: Alan Rothschild, Maureen Mutchler, Helen Tobin, Carol McGowan, Zahavit Paz, Juli Huss, Elvira Kock, Sharon Smith, and Judith King. I would also like to thank those who didn't believe I would ever publish a thing; they added to my determination to succeed. I owe a special thanks to my agent, Patricia Collins for guiding me in the presentation of my work to the publishers, and to Tracy Bernstein, my editor at Kensington Zebra. She had the courage and insight to undertake this difficult and controversial job. She allowed me to develop the book according to my own point of view, and for that I will always be grateful. And last but not least I would like to thank my *Ego* and *Spirit* for struggling with my will to get the job done.

"One's relative position in the universe controls viewpoint."
—Albert Einstein

A PRAYER FOR THE JOURNEY

*D**ear Lord, please guide me on my journey, helping me to keep an open mind and heart so that I may go beyond my limitations and see your divine plan. Help me recognize the truth, find the strength to implement that truth into the daily tasks of my life, and experience the faith that will be demanded to transcend my illusions and desires so that I may live with love, peace and unity.*

Contents

Prologue

The Day You Were Born was a journey that challenged every thought and concept I ever held dear. As I followed the zodiac through its cycle of becoming, I realized I had changed and that the change had been triggered by new ideas. See the world and yourself differently and the seeds of change will take root. As with most journeys, I was not aware of what lay ahead as I began to write my book. Halfway through the project I stopped, deciding I should sell it before I continued. The year it took to get an agent, do the proposal, and sign the deal seemed inconsequential at first, that is until I returned to the writing. I noticed immediately that something had changed, something magical had joined the project. The book began to speak to me, and I'm ever so grateful I listened. Originally I intended to share *my* point of view with you, the reader, but as I began to do more research on the famous people of the signs, they started to tell me what each sign was about. The more I surrendered to my ancient teachers, the more the universe stepped in and took charge. Life became so synchronistic that I began to live each sign and its challenges in my own life. In Gemini I had to face my fear of intimacy. In Cancer I was asked to be courageous and strong, in Virgo a stranger on the street approached me for help, and I had to give to the unknown. Books were given to me; they seemed to jump into my hands at bookstores or libraries. Whatever I needed appeared without effort. Even the movies helped out. Each film I saw depicted the struggle of the sun sign I was working on. It was as if the universe was my teacher and everything I did, everywhere I turned, it found a way to teach what had to be said. I discarded any previous views I had had of sun signs and entered each one with an open mind. I've been an astrologer for fifteen years, and I felt as if I knew nothing. The ideal of each sun sign is what emerged, not the mistakes and failed approaches of the masses. I realized that astrology has based so much of its views on what usually happens, not on what could or should. Only a few among us are capable of meeting the requirements that each sun sign demands. But without it being stated, there is no role model, no symbol above us to which we can aspire. Our ideals shape our visions and our actions, and they can play an important role in our success if we know how to use them. Through the words and voices of the many great souls who have lived and struggled with the consciousness of the sign, this book was put together. It may not sound like anything you have heard before, and for that I am grateful. It's time for the world to readjust its consciousness and ideals. I hope *The Day You Were Born* aids that goal. My voice is the synthesizer of the many voices of the past and the now, joined together to present to you a new and exciting approach to your journey. You'll see how the struggle between life's duality, represented by Ego and Spirit, is within us all, and in everything we do. Balance these two worlds of heaven and earth, your spiritual quest and your earthly mission, and you will not only feel empowered, but find a new meaning to life. I hope that you will read the whole journey, because each sign is part of a process that is constantly in progress in your life. Understanding is a powerful tool; understanding yourself is the key to success in both worlds. Without a doubt, writing *The Day You Were Born* has been my spiritual mission in life. I hope through reading it, you can find yours, too.

CHAPTER ONE

The Formula

Like a seed that holds the potential of a life waiting to unfold, the day you were born contains the secret of your destiny. All of your talents and challenges are coded in the dynamics of that special day. Through understanding your birthday number and your sun sign you will get a glimpse of the greater picture. If you have the desire to change your life for the better, the power and the insight gleaned from numerology and astrology will give you a chance to recreate yourself in your own image. It's never too late to cast off the unnecessary restrictions and habits imposed upon you by parents, partners, children, or life itself. Your conditioned responses are what keep you from evolving and really experiencing life. If you feel stuck, or if there's an area of your life that constantly brings you pain—pay attention. It's not just fate or bad luck that's the cause. Chances are, you're a major part of the problem. You are responsible for where you are right now. Every choice you have ever made has led you to this moment. If what I've just said upsets you, you're not looking at the whole picture. Because it also means *you* have the power to *change* your life. Know yourself, and life becomes an exciting journey, not an obstacle course traveled by a blind man.

Throughout our lives, we seek adventure, gather experiences, and learn through trial and error, always striving to complete the process of individualization: the formation of a well-balanced and independent being. However, few of us *ever* achieve this goal, and most of us certainly don't by the time we reach the point of committing to a serious relationship!

If that last word just turned you to stone, please don't panic. You *can* learn to be happy with yourself and with another person. You see, whatever parts of you haven't developed—ego, sensitivity, or boundaries, (to name a few examples)—you will seek to find in someone else. We attract what we need, not what we want. We expect the *other* person to give us—even to *be*—what we don't have. Call it projection, or simply using someone else as a crutch, but as long as a particular energy is unused in *you,* you will be attracted to it in someone else. For example, the need for balance can bring together an intellectual snob and an oversensitive, emotional mate. They will probably drive each other crazy—if they are not aware of why they are together. However, with a little self-awareness, the snob can learn to manifest and respect his or her emotions, and the oversensitive mate can become more analytical. When this happens, each has become a well-balanced, independent person.

Life is nothing less than a creative force, an act of becoming rather than a static state of being. Everything you do, from the first breath you take, is part of the process of creation. Yet we often try to hold on to and crystallize emotions, events, and things. Change or evolution makes us feel out of control, so we resist it. Resistance brings tension and stress. Change inevitably does come, only now it's through crisis. If we can learn to go with the flow, to trust in ourselves and have faith that life is not just chaos and happenstance, that there is meaning and reason for everything that happens to us, and that we are part of that meaning and reason, then we can meet both the challenges and the triumphs without losing our purpose, our identity, or our centeredness.

For many thousands of years, the Eastern world has viewed life as the play of opposites, the interaction of yin and yang, the passive and aggressive, the visible and the invisible forces of life. This basic duality is symbolic of heaven and earth, of spirit entering the physical body and creating life. From the moment we are born these two energies, the material and the ethereal, are in conflict. From the beginning we are souls fraught with struggle. The Ego is yang energy. It rules the physical and material world. It desires luxury, pleasure and things of the senses, in other words, anything it can possess. It is selfish, dominating and impatient. Spirit is yin energy. It finds its expression in philosophy, art, music, and faith. It seeks love, virtue, and peace, not power over people, or positions of status. Spirit sees itself as part of the greater picture, and so it is patient and enduring.

These contradictory forces, Spirit and Ego, yin and yang, are competitive and can be destructive if *you* don't take charge. You must be like a good leader, who pulls divergent people and talents together to work harmoniously for the betterment of the whole. Our growth requires that we *direct* all our thoughts and actions, instead of allowing them to battle for or hide from the spotlight. An equal dose of Ego and Spirit are necessary for a successful life journey. In fact, the tension of their opposition is exactly what is necessary to propel us forward. That means both must be acknowledged and respected.

Imagine life without Ego. For starters, it's dangerous. Ego protects you; it knows how to navigate through the maze of the desires, greed, and needs of others. It does this through the illusion of separateness. Ego distracts others from your truth, keeps them at a safe distance, and allows you a freedom to proceed toward your goals without having to do battle unnecessarily.

Problems arise when *you* believe the counterfeit to be real. When this happens, the way is lost and so is your real identity. Ego acts from fear; the world it rules is not eternal. Its power comes from your allowing it to maintain a hold on your thoughts and actions. Those seduced by pleasure empower it, for whatever we give our attention to, we strengthen. Choosing to follow Ego alone keeps you tied to the wheel of fortune, reacting to events rather than consciously rising above them. Ego is limited to the physical body. When it encounters an obstacle, it either tries to dominate and destroy, or it grovels and surrenders. Ego's only options are victory or defeat, not the learning process along the way. With this linear view of life, events themselves take on a powerful importance; success based on results becomes the only thing of value. However, Ego's success does not last; nor is it satisfying.

Spirit is yin in nature. It rules love, faith, and unity. It offers the ethereal things of life like beauty, hope, sharing, and understanding. With Spirit, the cold, competitive existence of the *real* world is softened by feelings, inspiration, and dreams. Unlike Ego, Spirit is eternal; it is not limited by physical boundaries and thoughts of the impossible. Spirit emphasizes the process, not the end result. When Spirit encounters an obstacle, it vanquishes it through faith and love. Spirit joins with the obstacle, surrounding it and molding it to its purpose, accepting it. Spirit does not know fear, and so Ego, and the limitations and feelings of separateness it brings with it, are left behind. Spirit dwells in the hearts of heroes. It is what propels them to accomplish the seemingly impossible with an ease others envy.

Spirit life is a spiral, returning to the source but always ascending. It transcends the weight of consciousness through the divine spark of intuition, that eternal source of power and energy available to us all. Your personal challenge is to balance Ego and Spirit, to create a new perspective and see yourself as the creator of your world, to know that you have the power and the ability to accomplish so much more than you have ever imagined.

In Taoism, man is believed to be the mediator between heaven and earth, between yin and yang. Our ability to establish and maintain a balance between these two worlds or energies depends largely on our spiritual, mental, and physical health. The farther we are from our center, the greater our imbalance. Imbalance directly contributes to failure and discontent.

If happiness and wisdom depend on the balancing of opposites, then determining the duality that exists within and seeking its reconciliation should be our priority. The spiritual quest has always been the struggle to return to this center of being. T. S. Eliot said, "It is necessary to go a long way, through many difficulties, to find a place one has never left." Helping the reader find that place he has never really left is the goal of *The Day You Were Born*.

The journey home to unity and love is rarely achieved without pain and suffering. The universe routinely challenges your choices. If you are isolated, life will demand you open the door. If your sense of self is weak, life will do its best to toughen you. Most of us avoid situations that make us uncomfortable. However, avoiding problems only makes them grow. Treat the wound, and you allow it to heal.

Growth is painful. Think about it. For most of us, our first physical encounter is a slap on the bottom, a necessary slap that helps us begin the process of breathing—of taking in and letting go of the life force. All life is learning how to receive and how to give, how to hold on and how to let go. When you learn to do both, you are capable of making conscious choices, not just reacting to situations.

Your inner voice has all the answers you seek. Listen to it, and the choices you make will be correct for you. Face your obstacles with courage, faith, and self-confidence, then the more you listen, the stronger you will become.

There's something magical in a birthday. No, it's not the presents or the cake or the friends wishing you well. The magical part of your birthday is that it represents the union of heaven and earth—the day spirit descended into matter and got the whole karmic wheel of fortune spinning again. Ego and Spirit once again begin to compete for attention. The race is on. How long will it take you *this time,* (I'm coming from the position that you've been here before) for consciousness to emerge and for the true meaning of life to become apparent? The starting gate is the day you were born, symbolically embedded in your sun sign and birthday number is your personal life purpose and the strategy you have chosen to accomplish it.

The Day You Were Born takes the reader on a journey beginning in Aries and ending in Pisces. Each sign of the zodiac has both a spiritual and earthly lesson; each lesson prepares the way for the next. It is important to learn each lesson well before moving on. When we skip a step in our journey, we create a weak link and a potential for crisis. Everything we need to know for peace and happiness is included in this journey. You are the navigator; astrology and numerology are your maps. These ancient disciplines are energies that unite at your birth, creating a challenge through their need for balance and integration. This is revealed in your personal formula. Your will, your goal, and your consciousness of this challenge are tools that can help you succeed. As you progress through the lessons of each sign you learn to use everything in life to your advantage: grief, emotions, strength, hope and even despair become objectified so that you can direct them to help you proceed and become strong along your path. Intention is the centering factor and it determines whether you move closer toward unity and Spirit, or toward identifying with Ego and separateness. The Lakota Indians call this choice the Red and the Black Road. The Red Road leads inward toward Wakan

Tanka, or Great Spirit, and the Black Road keeps you away from God, and toward a world of separateness, pain and sorrow.

Through exploring the *formula* in *The Day You Were Born* you learn that your birthday number is your point of view, the attitude you bring to your environment. Your sun sign describes the environment your point of view will encounter, the people, places, and kinds of events that you must learn to use with proper intent. This is done not by dominance or passivity, but through expressing your truth with courage. Of course, if you don't understand yourself, your truth, or your point of view, you will have no ability to resist others pulling you into their perspective, their truths, their lives, and you will waste your precious time living someone else's choices. *The Day You Were Born* will help you recreate your life around your *own* destiny. It's time to be the center of your world.

Chaldean Numerology and the Planets

Pythagoras, the famous sixth century B.C. Greek mathematician said, "Numbers contain the secret of all things." The ancients believed in the power of numbers. To them, numbers were not just quantities. Numbers represented an evolving pattern of nature. The ancients believed that through contemplation of the pattern, a person could gain self-awareness, harmony, and spiritual growth.

You can determine the number of the day you were born by taking the single digit of your birthday, or if there are two digits, adding them together. For example $21 = 3$; $29 = 11 = 2$. Zero always adds intensity. Add zeros to any number and it becomes more powerful. Each number represents certain qualities that express themselves in the personality of the person with their birthday numbers. Later, we will associate the number with a planet and combine it with your sun sign. For now, simply read the description of your birthday number.

At the end of each introductory paragaph, you will find brief passages explaining how the energy of the number may be expressed when either Ego or Spirit dominates your personality. Neither situation is ideal; both, when they act independently, impede your life journey. Spirit tends to ignore the mundane world; it denies Ego. If Spirit rules to the exclusion of Ego, your soul is left unprotected and your body weakens. Others take precedence and before long, you have forgotten who you are and where you should be.

If Ego ignores the needs of Spirit, your world is small and selfish. You want instant gratification; consequences are unimportant. Power and control are at the fore of your world. Separateness, loneliness, and greed are your companions. Obstacles seem insurmountable.

However, when Spirit and Ego are balanced, life is harmonious. You discover your true identity, keep to your true path, and are able to help and inspire others.

One/Sun (1, 10, 19, 28) Leo/Yang/Masculine

PURPOSE: To take the best that you are and present these qualities to the world in a form of talent, creation, and principles, so that you can receive recognition for your efforts. The courage you use to risk and expose yourself in the face of tough competition gains you your place at the center of your world, the kingdom you have created.

Ones, like the sun, ruler of **LEO,** know how to shine, even when clouds block their view. Eternal optimists, they believe in themselves and their confidence is contagious. Hardworking, persistent, and unyielding, their ego is strong and so is their desire for freedom. *Ones* love a challenge; difficult people and projects get their attention. They need resistance to test themselves, and a good dose of discipline is welcome, too. Authority issues are a source of problems, so don't try to tell them what to do. This attitude is what makes their childhood often very difficult. They meet their own unyielding selves and learn through experience the unjustness and limitations of an unbending will. Their hearts are big and filled with love, and yes, love affairs can easily lead them astray. They give the best parties because they love people and having a good time. Whether on stage captivating an audience or the center of attention at the local pub, they know how to make themselves important. They need to be first and the best. Adoration is never taken for granted, though. It must be earned, and toward that endeavor they will use every tool they have, including persistence, charisma, and patience. If you're a *One* who sits on the sidelines and shies away from a challenge, then your mission is to risk yourself. You're not going to feel really alive until you take your place in the world. *Ones'* duality is expressed by their need for privacy. They have a shadow side, a place where parts of themselves are hidden from the public eye. *Ones* share their whole truth with only a few trusted souls. Their challenge is the balance of independence and the need to risk themselves. Their fear is losing their identity in an intimate relationship. *Ones* are not complicated. They will give you everything, but first you must give them what they need—respect and attention.

IF SPIRIT TAKES THE LEAD: Ones in whom Spirit reigns seek high purposes and lofty causes. Their principles are strong. They don't give an inch where truth and justice are concerned. Their tendency is to lose themselves in a grand cause. In fact, they might not have a life except through that cause. The opposition they encounter is there to teach them to trust and have faith in something higher and greater than themselves. If they refuse to bend, their load will become so great it can break their spirit and their will. Truths and principles are not rigid but ideas that can be applied and molded to a situation. When the essence of their truth is understood, they learn that living their beliefs is far more effective than fighting for them. Yes, they should keep their indomitable will strong, but learn to let the power of the universe help them. This way, they won't wear out before they accomplish their dream.

IF EGO TAKES THE LEAD: Without a touch of Spirit, life for the *One* is tough. Somewhere along their path they encounter hard, inflexible opposition to whatever they desire. Others, particularly authority figures, hold them back. Since trust is out of the question, they feel isolated because they can only rely on themselves. They encounter strong, powerful, authority figures who try and force them to surrender to their will. When Ego pretends to be spiritual it acts superior, it gives to others and charities, but has its own advancement in mind, not the needs of others. Without true Spirit the *One* can be ruthless. Success is their only goal, and control is how they plan to get there. Without a conscience, there is little they won't do for this success. Their greed and selfishness is often masked by an incredible magnetism and charm, which gets them past many a closed door and fools the soul who is anxious to believe that they are acting for a higher purpose.

Two/Moon (2, 11, 20, 29) Cancer/Yin/Feminine

PURPOSE: To accept all your emotions—love, self-indulgence, pain, and joy—and then to rise above them by sharing them with another, ending isolation, activating healing, and creating a family that is bonded through feelings.

Two is duality. *Twos* fluctuate with the rhythm of the moon, the ruler of **CANCER.** With their ability to intuit a situation, *Twos* know what's going on above as well as under the table. Don't be fooled by their ultrasensitive nature, their mood swings, or their emotional tirades. They've had your number long before you learned their name. Needing to withdraw in order to protect themselves, they live with fears most of us have never contemplated. Shy, critical, and even unsociable, you only enter their lives through trust. If they like you, all your faults are forgiven; if they don't, you'll be lucky to get a return phone call. *Twos* have no time for superficial relationships, unless those relationships provide a touch of the unusual. You see, they're attracted to the strange and the extreme. It's an outlet for their overwhelming emotions. More positive creative outlets are necessary, or they will always be worrying or complaining about illness, even when there's nothing wrong. Because they tend toward obsessive behavior, their nature offers only two choices: to indulge or deny their strong desires. *Twos* can be self-absorbed or act childishly when they don't get their way. The challenge for *Twos* is to rise above their own needs and reach out to others. Spirit is the key here. When they have it, their feelings of isolation vanish. Women play an important role in the life of all *Twos*. After all, it's the mother who puts aside her own needs to protect her offspring. Hiding behind a veil of mystery, *Twos* are endowed with warmth and charm. They make great companions and committed partners because they are kind, gentle, and loyal.

IF SPIRIT TAKES THE LEAD: When Spirit leads the *Two* energy, intuition, and sensitivity are at an all-time high. In fact, this is a problem. They overreact to everything because they feel things so deeply. Their sensitivity makes them psychic, open to visions and to fears. It can cause them to lose themselves in the emotional life of another person. If that person is filled with pain and suffering, they will be, too. Panic and fear of separateness can also keep them from their path. Their desire to heal others can lead them to a service position, or turn them into a doormat. If they really want to help others, first they need to reclaim their own emotions. Everyone learns best through positive example.

IF EGO TAKES THE LEAD: With Ego at the helm, *Twos* are selfish, isolated, and consumed with feelings of hurt. Their revenge list is long, and they glance at it at least once a day. Either they feel persecuted by someone or they're doing the persecuting. Neither is healthy. They look for ways to be different and then wonder why they don't fit in. Their life is dramatic and filled with crisis. Their world is populated with people who are selfish and can't be trusted. The truth is painful. They must look to themselves to end their pain and isolation. They need faith in something more than themselves to become unstuck from the past and see a new perspective. Once they get off their wounds, come out of their hole and use the insight from their pain to help someone else, they discover that the world can be a wonderful place.

Three/Jupiter (3, 12, 21, 30) Sagittarius/Yang/Masculine

PURPOSE: To allow Spirit the full force of its rebellion against earth and its limits; to be humbled by the experience and to learn that surrender to fate brings grace and is more powerful than defiance.

Positive and expansive, **Threes** vibrate to the planet Jupiter, which rules **SAGITTARIUS.** Naturally adventuresome, they crave freedom. Their curiosity about life and their search for truth draws them to faraway places. Able to step back from almost any situation and take a wise, philosophical perspective, they don't sweat the small stuff. Being too positive has its downside; *Threes* attract people with mood swings or depression and it strains them to keep smiling even when it's not appropriate. Concerned with truth and justice, gifted with wit and humor, *Threes* need to feel a part of the larger picture. They have an aura of importance that attracts attention wherever they go. Upbeat and fun to be with, few people realize that *Threes* don't fit into the everyday mold. They live by their own rules. They're the Godfathers, the David Lettermans, the Marlon Brandos of the universe. The world adapts to their beliefs, not the other way around. This is great, as long as they don't get arrested. Caught between rebellion and a desire to surrender, they're true loners who are tough to pin down. If it's a relationship you want from a *Three,* loyalty and trust come first; the rest will follow. Attracted to the underdog, they love to help someone who's down and out, particularly if that someone shows some spunk. They make great friends, and if you're lucky enough to know one, he's probably been a catalyst in your life. Their wit is their sword, so don't get into a verbal battle. You won't stand a chance. They make great writers, editors, gurus, lawyers, and judges. *Threes* need to allow themselves to explore the world, but shouldn't ignore their personal needs. Otherwise, they might find they have quite a journal, but no one to share it with when their hair turns gray.

IF SPIRIT TAKES THE LEAD: Here, Spirit tries to get the soul to accomplish the impossible. It seeks out insurmountable obstacles and without experience and maturity, the soul will fail and lose faith in itself becoming stuck and feeling defeated. The trick here is for them to either pace themselves or learn to break these insurmountable obstacles into surmountable parts. Truth and justice make them feel righteous and judgmental. Add perseverance and stubbornness to the pot, and they're constantly repeating the same mistakes. They're either running into a brick wall or surrendering too early. When the collapse happens, they can appear a victim or a lost soul. Without an impossible challenge they can neglect their bodies and lose interest in the world. Their favorite place to escape is through seeking adventure in faraway places. Natural vagabonds, they roam from place to place, seeking something that this earth alone cannot provide.

IF EGO TAKES THE LEAD: This is big sugar daddy, the rebel, and the know-it-all. They are witty, unique, and strong. They want to do things their way and they don't care how it affects anyone else. This comes from an inflated sense of power and position. Unable to take orders from anyone, they run into trouble with authority or the law. They are gifted with strong personal magnetism and the power to impart their beliefs into someone else. This makes them great leaders who are capable of convincing others that their way is the only path to take. Often generous, their magnanimous nature is really a lack of self-worth and their way of feeling important and superior to others. Without Spirit, and consciousness, there is little they won't do to achieve their goals. Listening is not their best quality, because they learn from experience and their ability to process all information through their own perceptions.

Four/Uranus (4, 13, 22, 31) Aquarius/Yang/Masculine

PURPOSE: To express your differences and individuality with confidence, knowing you can place yourself among others with strong opinions and respect their truths without compromising your own.

If you know a *Four* today, you may not recognize him tomorrow. *Fours* have the incredible ability to change their lives from black to white and back again. No boundary is too high when you leap over it, and that's what *Fours*, and the planet Uranus, the ruler of **AQUARIUS,** do so easily. Struggle is not a distant stranger. Before the leap of faith, *Fours* are wrought with tension and restraint. With no other choice, they overcome all odds. Able to handle several ideas, projects, or beliefs at one time, *Fours* are quick-minded and capable of assimilating a myriad of different facts. Unique to a fault, they insist on doing everything their way, and their way seldom resembles the accepted norm. Stable and persistent, they get things done, but they're hard to pin down. A *Four's* mission is to break free, so commitments are a challenge. *Fours* need to be around friends or with organizations that represent their own ideals. When the sword of justice rules they can be cold and detached, unlike the warm humanitarian many are seen as. Fairness is important to *Fours*; somewhere in their lives, they've experienced injustice. They struggle to manifest their hopes and dreams, and to help others become strong, independent individuals. When they're sure of themselves, there is no one like them, not in their humor, their style, or ability to effect change. Don't be misled by their sociability. They're stubborn and persistent, particularly when their truth is challenged. Their gift is their diversity, and their ability to act in harmony with the moment without losing sight of their goals. They can separate what they don't like and bond with what they do. This allows them to accept everyone. They are the champions of the outcasts of society and support and fight for those who are viewed as unacceptable to the collective values.

IF SPIRIT TAKES THE LEAD: Too much Spirit here creates a constant fight for equality and justice. As visionaries, they sacrifice the intimate things of life—family, friends, and relationships—for the larger issue. Their minds rule their lives and work so quickly that relationships suffer. They're constantly restless and never in the same place for long. Incredibly stubborn when their principles are at stake, they only listen to the beat of their own drum. The need for structure and inner discipline is important. Without a proper dose of Ego and the practical world, they will continue to chase rainbows seeking change for its own sake and following empty dreams.

IF EGO TAKES THE LEAD: These are rigid, unyielding, loners, who have all the answers and give them to others whether they're interested or not. They are tough, distant, unique, calculating, sometimes even cruel. Capable of genius, they feel superior to everyone and choose not to belong to anything that is accepted or commonplace. Their judgment and choices suffer because they have not yet learned how to surrender their reason to their heart. Compromise is not a possibility—no matter what the cost. The only way that life gets their attention is through crisis, and crisis follows them everywhere. It's the tension they like, they seek it unconsciously hoping to resolve opposing forces through their own energy. The danger is that they will promote self-destruction rather than resolve the problem, because they are attached to conflict and chaos. Once they learn how to transcend their personal needs, life will begin to return some of the things they have tried so greedily to grasp.

Five/Mercury (5, 14, 23) Gemini/Virgo/Yang & Yin/ Masculine & Feminine

PURPOSE: To experiment and play with life and not lose sight of your intentions or your goals; to see the consequences of your choices and desires which begin the transition from earthly pleasures to the more lasting ones of the inner journey of Spirit.

The ruler of **GEMINI** and **VIRGO,** Mercury and *Fives* are the connectors— seekers and explorers of the world. Social, organized, and very busy, they know how to make everyone happy. Collectors of odd pieces of information, gossip, knowledge, and misfits, it's a *Five* you call when you need something no one else has. Their curiosity and ability to gather and explore makes the issue of *intent* very important. If they're not clear on what they are doing or why they are doing it, they can easily get caught in the web of their own intrigue. When this happens, their lives lack direction and they are overwhelmed with *things to do* and never feel as though they have accomplished anything. Natural actors, they play the varied roles of life with ease. Their curiosity keeps them young. *Fives* must learn to tune into their own intuitive nature or their world will always be filled with division and conflict. They need to learn to play and to have a good time. When they do, they're the life of any party, and the worries and responsibilities that usually hold them back take on a different perspective. If the Virgo *Five* is dominant, stubbornness and determination are high. The choice will be to pursue pleasure and desire or live a life of self-denial. Accepting their dark side or all of themselves is a necessity. Control is an issue and so is the need to help others. These are the hard workers of the world, and they can accomplish great things when they don't let the details of their lives keep them from their greater goals. Their minds never stop analyzing, exploring, and inventing, which gives them a penchant for worry and restlessness. Their challenge is to make a choice without exploring every option. This requires faith in themselves and a clear idea of their priorities. Once a path is chosen, one must accept responsibility and move forward leaving behind the safety and security of the "known."

IF SPIRIT TAKES THE LEAD: When Spirit and a *Five* get out of alignment, there is too much to do and not enough time in which to do it. They are versatile to a fault. Gifted with organizational skills, they are driven to make perfect whatever exists around them, including anyone who gets in their way. Idealistic, they don't concentrate enough on their own mission of purification, instead they try and improve the lives of others. This creates stress, anxiety, and worry because nothing is ever perfect, and somebody always refuses to be happy. They may be so idealistic that they attract their opposite—liars or unreliable people. Of course, this can affect their health. So, if Spirit rules their world, they must acknowledge their own path as their primary goal. When they face their fears, and accept all of themselves, then they are on their way to a healthy and happy life.

IF EGO TAKES THE LEAD: Selfishness is a problem here. It's "me first" and whatever they get is never enough. They have incredible appetites for sex, pleasure and work. They can be humorous, clever and manipulative. All those demons they haven't faced have power and can be attractive to a pure heart who has denied the dark side of itself. Their lack of scruples and morals makes them untrustworthy and dangerous. They can work like a maniac and are great at finance. Without conscience, they lie easily and can make the tough decisions— the ones that favor financial rewards over the heart. Without the ability to give, their worlds will become more and more empty and they will live their lives isolated and alone.

Six/Venus (6, 15, 24) Taurus/Libra/Yin & Yang/ Feminine & Masculine

PURPOSE: To develop your truth, your identity, and the moral boundaries of your inner world so that you will not identify solely with your own thoughts and actions and believe that the mask you wear for your protection is the whole truth.

The beautiful face of Venus reflects the number *Six.* Ruler of **TAURUS** and **LIBRA**, a *Six* is romantic, gracious, charming, loving, and excessive. You like them. It doesn't matter if you disagree with their politics or point of view. *Sixes* enter where others cannot tread. When you don't make waves, it's easy to mask your real purpose. It's easy to get things done. They're adaptable and flexible, but unyielding when it comes to truth. Faith and love come easy to these souls, so don't misjudge their strength. Gifted with concentration, they have unique and inventive minds that are always evolving and seeking to unify people, places, and things. They attract whatever they need and seldom have to reach for anything. Natural psychologists, they know what makes others tick. Their challenge is to know who they really are so that the mask they are creating for protection does not become their whole truth. To do this they must develop a value system and be able to set boundaries by saying no. *Sixes* have a special destiny. They are headed for a *fall.* They have to change a perspective and let go of a strong attachment, something that is holding them back from growing. Remember, *Six* rules desire, and desire led to the fall of Adam and Eve. The less attached you are to something, the less of a crisis you will encounter when it is threatened. *Sixes* must learn to balance their desire for financial security with a little faith in themselves and the universe.

IF SPIRIT TAKES THE LEAD: Unconditional love is the problem here. With Spirit strong the only thing that matters is the heart. They yearn for love and a desire to connect with others. This creates a lack of discipline, destroys discrimination, and feeds an obsessive nature. Addiction can be a problem because they have not yet formed a clear identity and a strong moral code. Without these protections and boundaries they will be attracted to others who are strong and well-defined, to relationships that provide the limitations that they themselves should self impose. Separation is an issue, they fear the abandonment of love. It's time to leave the warmth of the mother and become their own person. Their idealism and perfectionistic nature makes self-acceptance difficult, but necessary. Discipline is the key, with it they begin to blossom.

IF EGO TAKES THE LEAD: Ego makes these *Sixes* self-absorbed, seductive, and manipulative. They know how to use love, deceit, and kindness to get their way. They don't have faith or a conscience, so lying is easy and so is using truth to their advantage. Their nature is obsessive, so addictions can be a problem. Ruled by their senses, this makes them impatient, impulsive, lazy, and self-indulgent. Separation from love and their addictions will eventually occur and when it does the soul may find itself in a crisis. If they start learning about themselves, their limitations and their talents and then reach out and help someone else, they will begin to experience a pleasure that is more lasting than all the others they sought and quickly lost.

Seven/Neptune (7, 16, 25) Pisces/Yin/Feminine

PURPOSE: To take the place you have earned in the spiritual world through your dedication to truth and justice. Your personal purpose must surrender to a higher cause, for it is the last thread that binds you to the mundane world.

Like Greta Garbo, a *Seven* needs to be alone to be successful. Companion to Neptune, the ruler of **PISCES,** *Sevens* are often misunderstood. Perfectionists by nature, they strive for what can never be and so divine discontent is part of their nature. So is making quick, decisive judgments in order to eliminate chaos and uncertainty which they hate. This is linked to their need to be in control. Relationships offer them solace and insight into their complicated nature, but they'll settle for nothing less than a soul mate. Not an easy quest, even for a magical number. They believe in love and they long to surrender to something larger and greater than themselves. This makes them idealistic and prone to being deceived. But they have good, analytical qualities, and they process their experiences from within. Being alone is okay; in fact, it's necessary for their growth. Their spiritual, idealistic inclination is both their strength and their weakness. It helps them overcome great odds, but keeps them from being realistic and in-the-now. *Sevens* need to believe in a cause, an idea, or have a spiritual faith in order to feel secure. Driven by a desire to do something to make the world a better place, they easily attract others who are needy and depend on them too much. They must set boundaries and learn how to say ''no,'' otherwise they can become victims. Their mission is to be in the moment, be able to adjust their truth to its demands with confidence and faith in themselves and their destiny. Their special gift is their ability to communicate without words and bond with others who have trouble expressing themselves. They are loners and both a link and a chasm in mathematical equations. *Sevens* should stop worrying about where they are now: with a click of their sequined slippers they can be transported to the clouds and back again. Once they learn to seek their answers from within, they'll know that different choices merely reflect the two sides of the same coin.

IF SPIRIT TAKES THE LEAD: Too much Spirit for *Sevens* spells real trouble. Without Ego and its ability to create separateness, they are very easily hurt and vulnerable to abuse. Self-deception is common when idealism is high and reality is missing. They are subject to destructive religious fervor and other fanatical ideas or pursuits. Being the victim, surrendering to others unworthy of their gift, and not taking responsibility for their life, are all major problems for them. They shouldn't expect someone else to rescue them; instead, they should take charge of their life. This is their responsibility. Their loose grasp of reality requires life to kick them in order to get their attention. The challenge is to come down off the clouds and manifest the love they seek within themselves.

IF EGO TAKES THE LEAD: A strong Ego and the *Seven* creates a master of deception and a dictator, one with little or no conscience. These souls live a double life. They are, for example, the upstanding citizen who builds churches with money earned from the sale of drugs. Control is an issue. They want it at all cost. *Seven* is the number of dreams and fantasies and they use others' dreams and fantasies to get their way. They are a master of illusion and could be a great creator, inventor or magician. They struggle with escape issues such as drugs, alcohol, almost anything addictive. As someone who uses his creative gift to advance in the world regardless of the consequences to others, they need to be careful of the law. Remember, *Seven* is the number of institutions, the kind with bars. It's a shame to waste such great gifts on fleeting rewards. Their success could be everlasting if they used it for the good of others.

Eight/Saturn (8, 17, 26) Capricorn/Yin/Feminine

PURPOSE: To receive the rewards from your journey. Spirit gives you respect and reputation. Ego gives you a position in the world. Both are based on how you have behaved in the pursuit of your desires and goals.

Eight is the only closed number. (It is comprised of two complete circles.) *Eight* has the challenging position of vibrating to Saturn, the ruler of **CAPRI-**

CORN. *Eights* are powerful people, but very self-contained. You just don't reach an *Eight* without his consent. *Eights* are masters of their world, however limited or grand. They lack spontaneity and trust, believing only in what they know and can control. *Eight* is the number of fate and these people know they must accept the hand that life has dealt them. After all, life is nothing more than the consequences of their choices and actions. Grace is possible once they learn to trust their instincts and rely on their heart as the center of their soul. Balance between faith and reality, between intuition and reason, between Ego and Spirit is the challenge of the *Eight*. This is the sign of the process, of taking things one step at a time. The reward is in the work, not the paycheck at the end of the week. So please make sure you do work that you love, then your reward will manifest in both worlds—the spiritual and the physical. You'll get a paycheck and a good reputation for doing your job well. When *Eights* put their minds to it, they are successful at whatever they do. But they crystallize too easily and need someone to help keep them fluid. They tend to base their value systems on the opinions and expectations of others, which makes them seem judgmental and critical. They have a keen eye for what's not working: scrutiny is their gift and their demise. Their challenge is to trust their instincts and believe in themselves, despite the disapproval they are sure to attract. They must act from their heart, and listen to their soul, forget their self-consciousness. If that means jumping into the water they should hold their noses and take the plunge. No one knows how to swim better than they do.

IF SPIRIT TAKES THE LEAD: When Spirit leads, the *Eight* is an idealist. Their goals are high and there is nothing they can't do. That's on a good day. The rest of the time, they battle dark moods and depression. Suddenly, anything is much too much to ask: They're perfectionists and extremely hard on themselves. They're always pushing to do more, work harder, and be better. The end never seems to be in sight. Responsibility is not balanced. They tend to pay too much attention to details, and not enough to others. They need to learn to pace themselves and then they'll live longer. Trust is an issue and so is the need to accept life exactly the way it is. That includes oneself. When they can rely on instinct and love then the transforming power of love will do the work, they won't have to.

IF EGO TAKES THE LEAD: If Ego is leading, the soul won't get far. Ego needs to be in control and that means its world is small, smaller than it has to be. Tough, persistent, domineering, and critical, the *Eight,* ruled by Ego, is not a happy camper. They live lives that are tough, cold, hard, and sometimes, cruel. Spirit is needed here, the ability to let go and soar over obstacles. It's almost impossible to grow when you reject expansion. Their focus is inward, they need to be in control, and so they become isolated. They hate repetition, but when you don't grow, what else is there? The side effect of repetition is ulcers, tension, and high blood pressure. They need to learn to risk themselves and open up. It's amazing how much fun one can have if one lets go and responds to life, living in the moment.

Nine/Mars (9, 18, 27) Aries/Yang/Masculine

PURPOSE: To formulate a point of view that encompasses both your spiritual and worldly desires in a vision, to protect and advance toward that vision by conquering or discarding whatever you encounter on your path.

A *Nine* runs the race with Mars, the ruler of **ARIES**, but it doesn't matter who wins. *Nines* are competing with themselves. *Nines* constantly test themselves. They are assertive and masculine and, yes, very sexy. Their mission is to conquer; but once they do they lose interest. Action is their law, and there is no greater crime than doing nothing. Athletic, adventuresome, constantly on the move, a *Nine* seldom reflects, processes, or waits. They're impulsive, heroic, and self-oriented. Once they have a direction or a vision, they are fearless and unrelenting in its pursuit. They're leaders and innovators, capable of doing almost anything they set their minds to. Eager to make their mark and secure a place in the world, they're ready to fight for what they want. If a *Nine* is coming your way, step aside, unless you're ready to go to war. The more difficult the obstacle, the more enthusiasm they exhibit. Their style is direct and honest; often they appear insensitive. They strive for perfection, but all their answers are gotten from within. Don't bother giving them advice; they need to burn their finger in the fire in order to know it's hot. As they are able to dominate their chosen field with their personal sense and panache, you must never underestimate their power and their need to be the best. Multitalented, they often have trouble deciding on one path or goal. They have a gentle side and, yes, lots of love and compassion. They know how to motivate others and bring out the best in souls with less courage than theirs. On the downside, they tend to overdo everything, they're obsessive, and their bodies take great beatings because they never stop. Without the ability for self-control, they can crash right into obstacles instead of leaping over them. Remember, if you run a red light often enough, sooner or later you're bound to hit a truck. *Nines* should keep their accident insurance current and learn to meditate.

IF SPIRIT TAKES THE LEAD: If Spirit is strong, the *Nine* could be an evangelist, a mystic or a missionary. They know there is a higher power, and they want the rest of the world to know it, too. But that's their problem—they insist on things being their way. They believe they know better, and perhaps they do, but everyone must make his own mistakes. They are generous, loving, and loyal and when they give of themselves, they give all. In fact, they might find themselves lost in someone else's world. The only way to get their identity back is by leaving. Is it possible to put on the brakes? Sure, but they have to want to. They're obsessive, and addiction could be a problem, particularly of the religious kind.

Their body needs care. It's the temple of their soul, and its endurance level is not as high as their Spirit.

IF EGO TAKES THE LEAD: If Ego is strong, so are the issues of power, control, passion, and instant gratification. The *Nine* wants everything, and they want it now. Without a conscience, they could be dictatorial, cruel and domineering. They are definitely selfish and egocentric. They only hang out with others who think they're wonderful, or who are too passive to tell them the truth. They get their way by being a bully, or by using their incredible powers of persuasion. They need to become less concerned with their own needs and reach out to another human being. When this happens, their perspective will change, and so will their life.

THE FORMULA

Now that you know your number and the sun sign that it represents, you are ready to find your personal formula. The following twelve chapters deal with each of the zodiac signs. If you don't already know your sun sign, look for your date following one of the zodiac signs: Aries (March 21–April 20), Taurus (April 21–May 21), Gemini (May 22–June 21), Cancer (June 22–July 22), Leo (July 23–August 23), Virgo (August 24–September 23), Libra (September 24–October 23), Scorpio (October 24–November 22), Sagittarius (November 23–December 21), Capricorn (December 22–January 20), Aquarius (January 21–February 18), Pisces (February 19–March 20). Once you have your sign, combine it with your birthday number. Remember, all numbers are reduced to a single digit between one and nine. For example, if you are an Aries born on March 29, you would add the double digits together until you got one number (**29** = 2 + 9 = 11 = 1 + 1 = **2**). Reduce *all* double digits to a single number. Now you have a sun sign and a number. Each sign has nine aspects. For example, you are no longer just an Aries, but an Aries with one of nine possible expressions, each with its own unique challenges. The Aries/*One* (March 28, April 1, April 10, April 19) needs to learn to stand up to authority and take their own path in order to become successful. The Aries/*Two* (March 29, April 2, April 11, April 20) has quite a different challenge. She must transform her fears and weaknesses into strengths, and then use them to move forward, succeed, and help others heal. Each of the Aries combinations has its own unique challenge, but they all share common Aries traits. They are all concerned with learning how to assert themselves, protect themselves and form a goal and vision to carry them through their journey. Each sign is described, giving details and examples of famous people who have taken that path. Once you have your combination, you're ready to go. Remember fear and limitations are all in your head.

Don't be disappointed if you don't immediately identify with your dynamic. Remember, **opposites are the same.** An Aries can express either the greedy or the compassionate aspect of the sign. However, neither the taker nor the caretaker has learned to integrate his needs with those of others. Examine your dynamics from this point of view. Are you the source of the energy, or do you feel everyone else has the qualities described by your sun sign and number? If it's the latter, then you need to incorporate these qualities. If you don't, you'll continue to be frustrated when encountering them in others. What we deny in ourselves we tend to see in others—it's called projection. **If you are not like your sun sign, then you are like the sign of your birthday number.** Read the sun sign represented by your number and you'll recognize yourself. Then go back and read your actual sun sign. When you can blend the two energies together you're on your way to a better life, one with unlimited choices and possibilities. For example, if your birthday is July 9, and Cancer traits seem to appear in everyone *but* you, then you must look to the nine which translates into Aries. Cancer qualities are concerned with caring, nurturing, sentiment and feelings. Aries gets annoyed when it has to wait, even in regard to emotions. Aries is a creator and initiator, and it's not concerned with healing old wounds—that's the Cancer. If you're the Cancer/*Nine* you need to concern yourself with both energies. You can no longer turn your back on one, and express only the other; not if you want to feel good about yourself and overcome your limitations. The Cancer/*Nine* will have to learn patience, and will have to adjust to emotions, neither wallowing in feelings, nor disregarding them, but finding a healthy expression of emotion based on the situation, the state of mind, and the needs of the moment. Remember, balanced energy attracts balanced energy. If you want better relationships, change yourself. Victims attract abusers, givers attract takers. Learn the value of both and you're on your way.

PART I
THE ESTABLISHMENT OF EGO

*I*n **Aries, Taurus,** and **Gemini** we encounter Spirit and her struggle as she reenters the world, taking on a body and all its limitations. In **Aries** she is strong, but has lost her footing and her timing. She knows what she can do, yet she is unable to act as quickly and skillfully as she remembers. Ego's protection must be had; she needs him as a buffer for her quest to return home. But they no longer work in harmony, and instead of being One, they now have to take turns leading the way. This creates indecision, uncertainty, and a sort of start-stop dynamic in the first three signs of the zodiac. The sooner Spirit realizes she needs to step back and allow Ego to take the lead, things become more harmonious. Ego must establish himself in the world and try to fulfill his earthly goal before Spirit can show her face and choose her own path, one that will eventually unite them both in a common goal. But for now, they must tolerate each other's differences and try to work together. Spirit, with her patience and her impulsiveness, her reacting to the moment on her instincts and changing directions at the last minute because of an inner feeling or voice, is difficult for Ego to fathom. He desires to conquer her, seeing her as an enemy, a competitive force trying to tell him what to do and where to go. Yet at the same time she intrigues him, for she is mysterious and alluring. Unwilling to admit he finds her attractive, he demonstrates his feelings through dominance and power. His actions are harsh, direct, and sometimes crass. Unrefined, he has not learned yet how to be subtle, to get along with others; it's his way or not at all. He rushes ahead, believing he has beaten her, never realizing it's all according to her plan. She knows the time will come to make her move, and so she lets him play, amused by his inflated perception, his feelings of independence and freedom, his belief that he needs no one but himself to continue his journey.

In **Taurus,** Ego gets to rest from the race; sometimes he becomes even lazy. Spirit must develop the inner world of the soul, a place within the soul itself that it can go to retreat from the demands of others. To do this, Spirit must arrange the inner workings of the psyche, putting in order the soul's desires, teaching the power of mystery, the ability to mask one's wishes by not revealing one's intentions to the outside world. Ego becomes bored and causes trouble. He breaks the rules whenever he can. Ego is experimenting, learning just how far Spirit will let him roam from their path. This will be the moral boundary of the soul.

In **Gemini,** Spirit wants to play; she knows that through the act of soul expression, she can invite the divine spark to play, too. She is eager to feel God's presence once more, and so she sets out to explore the environment playfully. Ego eagerly follows her example, for it's up to him to choose which role he will take in life. This will be the means through which he will conquer his environment. He stalls, unable to decide which path to take, who he should be—a beggar or a king, a poet or a politician?

Aries

(March 21–April 20)

For Aries the ram, spring is the season.
Torn between his heart and reason,
He needs a goal, a lofty cause.
Love and truth, these are his law.
Never content with the here and now,
It's perfection he seeks, it's his solemn vow.
They're natural leaders, they are the best,
And what they love is the impossible test.

Ruler: Mars   **Symbol: Ram**
Element: Fire   **Number: Nine**

The soul, strong from its respite in the world of Spirit, is ready once again to break the chains of desire that keep it bound to earth and its pleasures. Gathering all its power, passion, and will, it throws itself into the act of creation. It's time to be born! Aries is spring. It is raw potential, eager to unfold. Innocent and tough, bold and shy, worldly and spiritual, Aries people are nothing less than total contradiction. The reason for this is simple, Ego and Spirit have united. Their nature is now dual and the tension from their opposing forces must be harnessed and directed. As a person struggles for balance he begins to achieve his destiny—a state of self-knowledge, an unfolding of consciousness that leads to self-awareness. This is the ultimate goal.

Aries have spiritual and physical power. They explode onto the scene with a burst of energy. Sexy, smart, and multitalented, their lesson is to travel the extremes of their experiences and ideas and define their limits. Once they know their boundaries they have the heart—it's at the center and that's where they want to be. They love attention and without admiration they fade, doubt rushes in and depression threatens to invade their positive attitude. Gifted with courage, strength and enough intuitive power to forge blindly into the unknown, they prefer to jump into life rather than tread with caution. They have confidence, the kind that can change the world. This is the sign of Thomas Jefferson, Eddie Murphy, Marlon Brando, Warren Beatty, and Bette Davis. They defy tradition, and impose their personal ideas and style on others demanding their perspective become the accepted norm—and it often does. They teach us to push beyond our limits, they show us the power of perseverance, the contagiousness of passion and courage, and the inspirational power of faith. They are leaders, creators, tyrants and saints. Burdened with prophetic visions, they yearn to change *what is* into *what could be.* They struggle with impulsiveness, unquenchable curiosity, and a driving need to be in control. They can rise above problems and see the greater picture, or argue over petty details unimportant to their purpose, but not unnoticeable to their discerning eye. Justice and freedom are what they live for and when they are wronged, they never forget, nor do they let go. Driven by a need to learn, improve and grow, they represent all the greatness of new beginnings and the passion that comes from a spirit who has not yet forgotten that anything is possible.

In Aries, the battle for supremacy between Ego and Spirit is strong. Both feel their full power and neither wants to compromise. The first challenge of the zodiac is the ability to focus and to direct and use your powerful will. That will must be centered in you, in the moment, and anchored by a vision. This precarious balance can only be maintained through the relationship of Ego and Spirit. Both are necessary to complete the journey, so let's begin with an understanding of who they are.

Ego is the master of illusion; it is king of the earth and all its pleasures. It's concerned only with its own needs and the delights of the senses. Spirit represents heaven, and its goal is unity and love. Its desires are directed toward serving others. When Ego and Spirit are out of alignment you have pain; when they work together, you have harmony and strength. If you want to know what it feels like when they are in sync—have a crisis. Like oil and water, when shaken Spirit and Ego will temporarily fuse. The result is a feeling of wholeness, a sense of power and invincibility. Just ask any Scorpio. They live from crisis to crisis. These moments of unity give a person a taste of the feeling of wholeness and its unlimited power. There is a less painful means of achieving this. Just follow the signs from Aries to Pisces and you'll learn how to meet each of life's challenges. Every new choice you make leads to change; change realigns your energy which adjusts your balance and brings you closer to wholeness.

Aries, like all firstborn, are in a hurry. They see the goal, and they're anxious to get started. Conflict is not a deterrent: these souls are attracted to it and to a good fight. Sure, their ultimate goal is peace, but as their opposing sign of Libra will also learn, peace is something earned and rarely valued before the experience of war.

Aries is rebirth and spring, the first blossoms of a flower, the delicate and powerful surge of a new idea. Hope and all possibilities are within reach. Enthusiasm is high, and Spirit is undaunted. Ego has not yet been humbled by failure and fear of the impossible. Memory is of heaven, of limitless freedom and love. This is the child filled with curiosity, exceedingly open and vulnerable, seeking unconditional love and protection. Of course, these are the gifts the Aries also offers. When they are good, the Aries give you their heart without reservation. And when they see anyone in need, they reach out to help. Thomas Jefferson (April 13), one of the founding fathers and president of the United States, raised his sister's children when her husband died. Henry Luce (April 3), publisher of *Time* and *Life* magazines, shared his blankets and quilts with his boarding school roommate. When his mother asked him why the blankets she sent were not on his bed he answered, "This boy hasn't any of his own, and I am so glad to share them with one who needs them."

Life is a continuous circle, and to enter the karmic wheel through birth requires the willingness to battle, the courage to travel into the unknown, and the ability to create a point of view. To take and hold your place in life means you need an opinion of yourself and of your relationship to others, your community, and the world. This opinion is your point of view. The stronger it is, the more powerful your presence is felt. If you're not getting enough attention, you've probably taken an insignificant detail of yourself and mistaken it for your main theme. Being a Harvard graduate; living in London; being president of IBM; having a beautiful pair of violet eyes— these are details, not your purpose. You can change details any time you want, but to do that effectively you've got to have a well-formed point of view. A central force around which all other themes can coalesce.

To fulfill your destiny, you must become a creator. Creating is nothing more than rearranging furniture; you take what you have and present it with a fresh face. Of course, you can make someone else's ideas your own. Henry Luce created *Time* magazine, the weekly periodical with a point of view. The news was old, but the presentation was original. He dressed it up with anecdotes, snappy writing, and pointed opinions. He made serious subjects such as religion, medicine, science, and culture accessible. Luce's approach was original and the world loved it.

We learn to create by first existing in someone else's space. When you were a child, your mother was your entire reality. That is, until she put you in your crib, alone. Then you suffered separation and abandonment. The Aries constantly battles the duality of surrender and standing alone, of joining and separating. By losing themselves in the world of another, by exploring and learning how someone else creates, they acquire knowledge needed to improve their own process of self-creation. To an Aries, the mother is the key to their feelings of unity and abandonment. Often, an Aries was either the apple of his mother's eye, or suffered her emotional absence. Robert Frost (March 26) said of his mother, "She had so much love to spare that she nearly smothered her children with it." Toscanini (March 25) on the other hand, was ignored by his mother. "I cannot remember my mother ever having kissed me. Did she love me? I wonder?'' Henry Luce said of his mother, ''She had persuaded me early that her whole existence would somehow be justified in me.''

Unfortunately, to be so central to another's existence doesn't allow for normal integration into life. Spoiled or wrought with feelings of abandonment, Aries carry this burden with them into all their relationships. Many never learn how to separate, and so miss out on acting the part of creator.

So, you have an opinion. Now, it's time to create a vision. It is the size and strength of your Ego that gives your vision its dimensions. If your Ego has confidence because it has been loved and nurtured, then you will believe in your ability to play with creation and to convince others to believe in you. This ability to dominate your space and influence your friends and acquaintances, gives you the confidence to allow your imagination to soar. When this happens your vision is broad and grand. Without confidence a vision remains small. A healthy Ego is important for other reasons. It provides earthly strength that protects you from the desires and will of others. It does this through its fearlessness in the face of conflict and through creating the illusions of differences and separateness. A strong Ego demands space, and those with less of one quickly step aside. This immediately reduces opposition and clears the path of interference. Separation is also achieved through titles. We are given names such as: policeman, president, and teacher; we feel separate because of differences in strength, wealth, the color of our skin, our nationality and religion. With consciousness you learn to respect the work of Ego without accepting its illusions as ''real.'' Differences are not seen as permanent barriers, only temporary distancing mechanisms.

Spirit provides protection too, it does this by giving you spiritual strengths—things like love, faith, dreams and hope for a better and more perfect tomorrow. It helps you endure and shows you real power, the kind that transforms. Both Ego and Spirit need each other; alone their strength is weakened. Without Spirit, Ego loses its staying power and it strays too easily from its path and its goals. Self-deception is Ego's greatest talent and it truly believes it can take this journey alone. Without Spirit it relies on its ability to inflate, manipulate and imitate. It loves to act, play roles, brag and pretend, but without Spirit these images are empty and when confronted they collapse; only Spirit can provide the essence and the ability to endure and overcome obstacles, for Spirit's roots are anchored in heaven not earth. Without the balancing force of Ego, Spirit becomes obsessive and too perfectionistic. It pushes so hard the body suffers and if it continues to ignore its physical needs, the body will become ill or break down. When faced with reality, it can get lost in its dreams and try to escape through its power to see the world the way it wants it to be. This is illusion. The greater the discrepancy between the practical and the ideal, the more unprotected the person is and the more fear it feels. Unable to cope with conflict and the unknown, the person becomes paralyzed or immobile. Without movement pressure increases and a crisis is inevitable. Thus, Ego and Spirit each provide an important ingredient to help the person find the strength and the courage to move forward into the unknown, confident that it will survive.

Limitations have a purpose. They build or store our energy, creating internal conflict and forcing us to sort out our desires, and our goals. A difficult child, a destructive or absent parent, too much responsibility too early, all these handicaps develop our strength and our power, the kind we will need when a leap of faith is necessary in order to continue on our journey. All great men and women have had strong visions and experienced great opposition. Many have faced what seemed like impossible odds. But with their eyes on their purpose, they found the faith to overcome their limitations.

The way to enlarge your world is by gathering support and eliminating opposition. Aries are great at both. They are connectors and are gifted with the power of persuasion. They meet opposition head-on, and more often than not enjoy the interaction. As their world expands they realize that what they need is a strategy. The tasks before them must be divided into smaller, more manageable parts. Their ability to reduce their mission into surmountable obstacles, challenging enough so that there is enough resistance to keep them striving, is a determining factor in their success or failure.

Aries are visionaries and they know at an early age what they want to do. If the opposite is true of you, don't panic. The problem is not a lack of talent; on the contrary, it's too many talents. You're versatile to a fault. Leonardo da Vinci (April 15) was called the *universal man* because he was a genius in many fields. He was an artist, a writer, a scientist, and a philosopher. It is said of him that "Nobody else was ever interested in quite so many problems at once."

Aries know that knowledge is an advantage and because of their competitive nature, they want to know everything—from the smallest detail to the most complex philosophical perspective. Thomas Jefferson was smitten with this passion. "There was a time of life when I was bold in the pursuit of knowledge, never fearing to follow truth and reason to whatever results they led and bearding every authority which stood in their way." Henry Luce's secretary said of the famous publisher of *Time* and *Life* magazines, "After you had been with Luce for a day you felt as if a suction pump had been applied to your brain and pulled every bit of information out." However, most of the knowledge Aries receive comes from within. They don't trust easily, and so their major source of information is experience, intuition, and the ancients. At the tender age of twenty-two, René Descartes (March 31), the famous sixteenth-century philosopher, set out "to seek no knowledge other than that which could be found either in myself or in the great book of the world." With instinct as their guide, they know that somewhere in their unconscious is all knowledge and all truth.

Subjective truth. Is there anything else? Not for Aries. Aries are masters of manipulation or coercion to their point of view. Henry Luce didn't worry about making enemies; he had little if any trepidation about rearranging the facts to support his perspective. According to his biographer Ralph G. Martin, *"Time,* each week, was a world of good guys and bad guys, absolute and dogmatic. The editors got the facts, then re-arranged them according to the truth they wanted to tell." Luce himself said, "When you put facts together to make stories of them, you endow them with values they did not have before. And that can raise hell with the truth." Truth to an Aries is a very personal thing. It's fashioned around their point of view. "Show me a man who claims he's completely objective, and I'll show you a man with illusions," said Luce.

Creation is nothing more than a juggling act. Evolution is the ability to recreate something more useful from what already exists. To evolve means the new must replace the old; therefore, Aries is also about destruction. Descartes said, "Once in a lifetime we must demolish everything completely and start again right from the foundations."

You've got an opinion, a vision, and you're working at being a creator. Now, it's time to develop some important skills. In order to protect yourself, you've got to know how to fight. The Aries environment will provide plenty of opportunity to practice this basic talent. If you're an Aries without an attitude, it's time to get working. You can't get ahead if you hide from confrontation. You've got to learn to speak out and up. Without a voice, you can easily become a victim, or just get lost along the way. If you're an Aries with too much attitude, eager to show everyone that they can't step on your toes, then self-restraint and good judgment are characteristics you need to develop. Here's where the proper proportion of Spirit is a must. It provides a desire for peace and gives patience to a reactional nature. Without the right amount of Spirit, the battle will resemble an elementary-school playground. Fighting then was simple—you tackled your opponent and by the sheer strength of your will you held him down. Domination and mutilation do work, but there are better ways. The more sophisticated or Spirit-balanced the Aries is, the more strategy will come into play. Aries can use their highly honed intuition as a weapon. It tells them exactly what and where the strengths and weaknesses of an opponent are.

Aries are gifted strategists. This is the sign of conspiracy, getting others to work with you against someone else, and it's the sign of hiding a small, despicable purpose in a greater, more spiritual cause. The ability to present a detail as the whole truth is an Aries specialty. Clarence Darrow (April 18) defended hard-core criminals and won by blaming the crime on society or the environment.

Spirit provides our moral boundaries and creates our inner limits. In order to accomplish your goals, you've got to know ahead of time what you're willing to compromise. Without a proper dose of Spirit one can easily stretch the truth to unrecognizable dimensions. Just because you have mastered the art of persuasion, know how to apply pressure, are able to focus so intensely that resistance magically disappears, doesn't mean that you should employ all those skills. Make sure that the goal is a *just* one. If you're on the receiving end of the Aries laser, open your mouth and speak your mind. A simple statement of objection goes a long way.

War, the military or just plain hostility is usually a part of the Aries history. Aries represent the first battle of life—being born. This basic need for conflict often makes them choose professions in which aggression is required. Darrow compared the courtroom to an ancient battle. ''An old-time lawsuit was like a great tournament . . . the combatants on both sides were always seeking the weakest spots in the enemy's armor, and doing their utmost to unhorse him or draw blood.'' Oleg Cassini's (April 11) parents expected him to have a military career, a commission in the Imperial Guards was secured for him at birth. But the soldier was also evident in his life as a designer. ''I know that I have, throughout my life, prospered only when I thought strategically, believing each day was a battle to be fought and not merely another interlude at the office.'' The desire to battle, to fight for what one wants, is a part of the Aries psyche. They need resistance to achieve. Racial ridicule was the heavy childhood burden of Wayne Newton (April 3). Born the son of two half-American Indians, success lay on the other side of prejudice. The greater the odds the stronger the Aries. Today, Newton is known as the King of Las Vegas.

If you are in love with an Aries, don't make life too easy for your hero, or he will lose interest. Allow him to rescue you from a demanding family, a financial crisis, or a hurtful relationship, and let him see the admiration in your eyes. If you are that Aries, I'm wasting my time telling you not to take on more than you can handle. The only thing that interests you is a challenge.

The acceptance the Aries desires from the world must first come from within. The need to feel worthy, a feeling Aries seldom achieve because of their high standards, is at the root of their need to prove themselves through heroic deeds. But once the soul begins its inner journey and battles the dragons that lurk in the caves of its own existence, it will find that the world, usually filled with opposition, has made a place for it to rest. With wisdom comes the insight that conquering the simple challenges of everyday life is heroic, as is smiling when you feel grief, giving when you have needs, taking responsibility when you long for freedom.

The talent for strategizing gives the Aries skill in theories, hypotheses, and abstract thought. They can also be great artists, inventors, and mathematicians. René Descartes developed general algebra and Leonardo da Vinci told a story in the smile of his Mona Lisa.

The child of the union of Spirit and Ego is Thought and it too is dual in nature, divided by head and heart. These two energies have different goals and thus Thought is fertile ground for conflict. Like most children, Thought has a mind of its own. Most of us favor one side of our intelligence and push the other down into silence and darkness. We're either stumbling over our feelings, overreacting, and yearning for an unrequited love, or we are examples of logical, stoical beings, capable of making hard, cold choices.

Experience is the best teacher, and with it the Aries soon acquires a sense of justice or common sense. St. Teresa of Avila, the great sixteenth-century mystic, believed intelligence or good judgment was *the* requirement for her novices. "An intelligent mind is simple and submissive; it sees its faults and allows itself to be guided. A mind that is deficient and narrow never sees its faults, even when shown. It is always pleased with itself and never learns to do right."

Balancing emotions with reason, seems simple, but it's not. Thomas Jefferson seemed to be both, "the carefully controlled philosopher of the Age of Reason and the tortured Romantic possessed by sudden and powerful emotions." When the balance of heart and mind is not achieved early, the distortion is carried into all one's decisions and choices.

If one follows reason to the extreme, logic has the upper hand, and life is cold, harsh, and without sensitivity. Relationships suffer, and so does Spirit, which provides the ability to overcome limitations and obstacles. When head and heart work together, compromises are made in *just* places, harmony is achieved, and all are content. To be born, to begin the journey of self-awareness, is to embrace the voice of divine discontent which whispers at every victory *and* every defeat, *"You can do better, yes there is more."* The soul's mission is not to be complacent, but to move forward toward consciousness and full enlightenment.

Once good judgment is acquired, good habits follow. Habits are formed by the choices we make. How you direct your thoughts, who you choose to hang out with, what hobbies occupy your time—all these decisions and more help create your environment. Aries must master their passions instead of becoming their slaves. Thomas Jefferson said, "Dispositions of the mind like limbs of the body, acquire strength by exercise ... exercise produces habit ... the exercise being of the moral feelings produces habits of thinking and acting virtuously." Since Aries tend to merge too easily with their environment, it is especially important for them to create a positive environment for growth.

Justice is a primary concern for Aries. Unable to see an innocent person hurt, they will fight for something others see as inconsequential. They know that once a simple truth is overlooked, a slight dismissed, it can grow out of proportion. Where justice is concerned, they don't think of consequences. This is one area where they never hesitate to stand alone. Yes, sooner or later, Aries will have to feel the impact of separateness and take sole responsibility for their existence. Thomas Jefferson wrote about the death of his father: "When I recollect that at fourteen years of age the whole care and direction of myself was thrown on myself entirely without relative or friend qualified to advise or guide me and recollect the various sorts of bad company with which I associated from time to time, I am astonished that I did not turn off with some of them and become as worthless to society as they were." His desire for truth kept him on the right path and made him uniquely himself. Expressing your truth creates a sense of separateness; being different can cause both rejection and acceptance. Bette Davis (April 5) was a different kind of star. At first, she was viewed as sexless and somewhat ugly. But her audience loved her spunk and her sense of drama. She became a legend, not just as a movie star, but as a woman of unique courage and wit.

Moral consciousness is only present if one believes in a higher power. When an Aries has faith, he or she has a gentle, giving heart. Without this faith, the Aries can be cold, ruthless, and unyielding. A friend said of Henry Luce that "he could have been a gangster if he had not been so stirred by God." Energy is another source of trouble. Without Spirit, it comes in short, intense spurts, but dies out quickly. With Spirit, the Aries has staying power and perseverance, but learning to pace themselves is always a challenge. Director William Wyler said of actress Bette Davis, "her gestural style was fussy, mannered, with movement that all too often blurred into one another because she hadn't learned how to pace herself, to let a performance build and gather momentum. So desperate was she to exercise her powers at every instant that she tended to wear out her effects." This lack of timing is due to their memory of perfect synchronicity achieved in the last sign of Pisces. There, instincts were in perfect alignment with the moment. Now, body, intuition and environment must realign themselves and learn to work together.

With or without faith, one thing is certain—Aries are special. They know this at a gut level, and you'd better know it too or they'll work tirelessly to convince you of the fact. Bette Davis told Mae West, "You see, there were reasons we made it. We're just special people." This sense of specialness does not make them contrived; on the contrary, they are natural, instinctive and spontaneous. A friend said of Toscanini, "He was utterly unselfconscious. As simple and direct in movement as the rain—and as driven by his task as the rain is by the wind." This naturalness can also be translated into confidence. "He [Henry Luce] was so sure of himself and what he wanted, so little bothered by doubt, and so impressively energetic." This natural or instinctive way of responding to life, affects everything they do. Thomas Jefferson wrote the Declaration of Independence in practically one draft because it came from his heart.

The opposite of naturalness is the crude and yes, without the refinement of Spirit, an Aries can appear raw, blunt, and uncultured. When they're low or base, get out of their way. They have no conscience and the only person they care about is themselves.

In the sixteenth century, Descartes said, *"Cogito ergo sum"* ("I think, therefore I am"). You exist and you're a thinking entity with both a heart and a mind. It's time to look around and see what's outside. The answer is, God. For most Aries there is no question of a higher power. They know it exists. This sign has no trouble accepting things on faith; as the first sign of the zodiac their relationship with their inner voice is still strong. The pleasures of the world are seldom enough. Vincent van Gogh (March 30) quoted Joseph Renan, a French historian, in a letter to his brother Theo. "To be active in the world is to die in oneself. Those who are to become missionaries of an idea can no longer belong to any other county but that idea. A man is not here below to be happy nor is he here to be simply honest. He must acquire nobility and overcome the vulgarity in which the majority of individuals drag out an existence." Vincent van Gogh was a minister of God before he became a painter. His clothes, food, all his money went to the poor miners in a region of southern Belgium called the Borinage. The miners, a mistrusting and isolated group, accepted him and his offering of salvation, because he surrendered his life and his soul to them with total devotion and love. Most Aries don't have to choose between the life of a gangster or a saint. Rather, they struggle to bridge their desire for worldly pleasures with their need for spiritual fulfillment.

Once God's existence is accepted, the desire to become God-like is powerful. This desire was the cause of Adam and Eve's fall. Just the *presence* of a forbidden fruit, the fruit of the Tree of Knowledge, created separateness, duality and the inevitability of the fall. Desire is responsible for the collapse of innocence, the need for separation and the abandonment of God. And this is the theme of Aries. Like Adam and Eve, they must now discover their true nature. To accomplish this requires the shedding of instinct for consciousness. In Aries, good and evil are not within, but choices made without. Experience makes them real and embodied. This is why Aries only learn by touching the fire. As they experiment with life on both sides of the path, playing, conquering, helping, transforming, and surrendering, they begin to embody truth and form an identity. This identity or truth is an evolving thing and always dual in nature. It's important to have heart and still make the tough decisions; have courage and still be humbled by God; be strong and exhibit gentleness. If you succeed, you're a hero and an Aries.

Aries have magic and it's contagious. We would willingly follow the best of them into hell and back. In return, we strive beyond our own limitations for they bring out the best in others. Their unrelenting faith in themselves and God allows them to share their strength and their courage, helping us all overcome our weaknesses and our losses.

Pain is essential to growth. Pain and suffering provide the depth of one's soul. They give character to a face and enrich the personality. Wisdom is impossible without it, and so is experience. Pain anchors us through memory not to soar so high that we lose sight of earth and not to chase after worldly desires so much that we get lost in acquiring rather than in giving and receiving love. Pain is nothing more than the discrepancy of goals between heaven and earth. The greater the discrepancy, the greater the pain. When you're centered, all is well. According to Evelyn Underhill, pain is nothing more than the disharmony between the Ego and the human Spirit.

The pessimist sees events with little hope of escape. The optimist views pain as the complement of love—a guide on the path of physical evolution. Most Aries are optimists. They use their pain to get to truth and to get themselves going. Discomfort is synonymous with growth. Henry Luce said, "The most astonishing thing about a human being [is] his range of vision, his willingness to suffer grief and frustration for a dream." And a dream is all an Aries needs to walk barefoot across a bed of nails. Robert Frost saw life as a challenge, a means to test ourselves and learn. "If our souls do come to this earth from heaven, then each must choose to come! Heroically and courageously, each must want—and must therefore choose—to be tested or tried by the ordeal of earthly existence." Aries know full consciousness includes misery as well as happiness.

The discrepancy between the world of the senses and the world of Spirit manifests for the Aries as two personalities or the need to live in two worlds. Oleg Cassini lived this double life. He frequented nightclubs with beautiful women on his arm. He seemed the dapper gentleman, a man who didn't need to work. The truth was he worked hard and long for little money, and could barely pay his bills. Thomas Jefferson desired to free the slaves, yet he owned them himself. When a higher view of any issue is taken, both extremes are seen and our view and emotions change. Robert Frost ". . . saw something comical in what he had previously viewed seriously and something serious in what he had formerly laughed at."

Because Aries are not afraid of pain, they are risk takers. Their unconcern for consequences can make them potential heroes—or fools. The hero in the Aries comes alive when justice is an issue. Thomas Jefferson spoke out for all Americans against British rule and risked being convicted of treason. Bette Davis challenged the all-powerful studios that ran her life. In those days it was career suicide to question the studios' power, but then courage is what Aries is all about. Their courage and determination is unequaled. They bring out the best in others and their persistence and drive inspire all those they know.

Aries seldom hear *no* but when they do, it's usually an angry one. They push so hard, sooner or later someone pushes back. Unfortunately, the Aries won't want to hear this unless life has already taken its toll, left him with scars from lost battles. Aries, beware. Stop having to prove yourself; not everything is worthy of your efforts. You get your way by wearing people down. You seldom see the horror on the faces of those to whom you've just told the truth. They think you're rude. You think you're helpful. With this scenario, is there any hope for peace? Not unless you learn to hesitate before you respond.

One more piece of advice. You're not responsible for everyone you care about. If your life is overwhelmed by responsibility, then it's time to stop doing everything and let someone else share the load.

Since Aries is the act of creation their influence is felt in many, many professions. What binds them together is their passion. They put their whole being into whatever they do. Consider van Gogh. This famous painter threw himself recklessly into his creations. A compatriot, Cohen Gosschalk said, "Rarely has an artist fed his art with his blood and his heart as much as he. His art gnawed at him like a fever." The art of Aries is not contrived. It's intuitive, bold, colorful, rich, passionate and personal. Gifted with vision and an eye for detail they can be exceptionally talented. Cassini knew instinctively how women wanted to look. "I had the power to envision women as they wanted to be seen, to help them create fantasies about themselves." He dressed some of the most famous women in the world including Grace Kelly and Jacqueline Kennedy.

The act of creating has a few requirements. Solitude is important; so is spontaneity. Creating involves a vision, an idea and a risk. You've got to have the courage to jump in and make it happen. It requires you to be in two places at one time—in the moment and one step ahead. Aries is all things, and thus the art created by Aries has a sense of unity. The great ones achieve the balance we are all seeking and it is through their creations that we get a glimpse of that balance. Masterpieces are made from equal parts technical skill and passion. Mosewius, a fellow musician, said of J. S. Bach's (March 21) music: "One thing is needful—an inner unity of soul is absolutely indispensable in performing Bach; and every individual chorister must not only have thoroughly mastered the work technically but must preserve his spiritual forces unbroken throughout."

This acute sensitivity and artistic nature doesn't inhibit Aries competitiveness. They're great athletes who go for sports such as boating, car racing and mountain climbing—anything that demands courage and versatility. Jean-Paul Belmondo (April 9), the French actor who emerged in the 1960s, had the typical Aries sexiness and athletic prowess. An ex-welterweight, he performed his own film stunts and owns part of a soccer team.

Let's talk relationships. Aries are passionate and persevering, good qualities in the sexual department. But, as with everything else, Aries do it all. You can expect just about everything from them—betrayal and loyalty, romance and pettiness, intensity and disinterest. They love love, but they tend to look for perfection. If Spirit is too strong, they will fall in love with someone unavailable. If Ego is too strong, they can overwhelm you, taking control of your every thought and action.

Prone to disappointment in love because of their high ideals, Aries need to be in the moment. And when they are, watch out. They are sexy and charismatic; their intensity and primal energy gets your attention immediately. Someone said of Eddie Murphy (April 3), "You can feel him before you see him." Aries sexual appetites are insatiable. Don't flaunt your assets unless you want to be consumed. Once they are focused on you, you won't stand a chance. They can become absorbed in your words, your smile, and your space.

Remember, Aries seek perfection in their mates. Let them know that you think *they* are perfect. The pressure's off you, and they're happy, too. With an Aries, one person usually must surrender. However, love can bridge the gap and give you both a chance at the helm. When Clarence Darrow was asked how he was getting along with his second wife, he answered "Fine, because Ruby and me, we both love Darrow." Oleg Cassini was quite the ladies' man before he married Gene Tierney. To her, he gave his all. Cassini said, "There was a compulsiveness to her behavior; she had to know her lines. And I was willing to indulge her: indeed, this was my great Svengali secret, my great hold on her—total devotion." Cassini was successful as a lover because he had perfected the art of seduction. "The art of the seduction was always far more fascinating than the ultimate result. There were infinite subtleties and challenges in the manner of the chase. Indeed, fifty years later I can remember the strategies and events of my amorous campaigns like a career military man, but I could not care less about the precise results."

It's always the chase, not the trophy that counts for this fire sign. Intuitive and impulsive, Aries make decisions quickly and from their gut, particularly when it comes to love. When Henry Luce met Clare Booth at a party he was smitten, and a married man. When Ms. Booth left the party, Luce followed her to the lobby. Without preamble he said, "I've heard about this happening, but it has just been happening to me. It isn't easy to say it. I've just made the most important discovery. I want to ask you a question, possibly the most important question I shall ever ask you and you will ever answer. How does it feel to be told you are the one woman, the only woman, in a man's life?" Like a smart woman, Booth didn't answer him, but she was impressed. Later, she married him. Everyone likes being important, and Aries know how to make you feel like the center of their world. When they focus on you, it's mesmerizing. Luce had this ability. He was very sensual, tremendously masculine, and at the same time exhibited a certain vulnerability and an ability to care for others. That Aries contradiction—soft and tough, cold and loving—gets them rewards every time.

If your Aries is a female, she's not typical of her species. More assertive than most, she may pursue you. When the flowers and candy are delivered at your door, my advice is find a vase and eat the chocolate. You'll need the strength if she stays in your little black book for longer than twenty-four hours. Yes, Aries are jealous. However, their jealousy arises from the need to protect what's theirs. When it comes to intimacy, the Aries extreme nature gets in the way. Either they're counting their partner's heartbeats and breathing in rhythm, or they're on a plane to Thailand without you. Even something as ordinary as a TV remote can provide the distance the Aries suddenly needs to reclaim his identity.

Compulsiveness and obsessiveness are parts of the Aries nature. Bette Davis had an obsession for neatness and order. She would clean when she was upset, and even when she wasn't, everything had to be in place. At school, Robert Frost was so obsessive that "one serious slip of the pencil would be enough to send him into such a rage of disgust with himself that he would tear the page out of the book, so he could begin again with a perfect sheet." As for Toscanini, "If he failed to reach the standard he had set for himself his reaction was sheer violence, a hurling and breaking and kicking and tearing of music stands scores, furniture, clothes, anything that was near to be hurled or broken, kicked or torn." Often, the Aries crosses the line of reason and into madness. Van Gogh moved back and forth across this line, exhibiting schizophrenic qualities, becoming depressed, and finally losing himself to madness. Madness is an Aries issue; perhaps it's nothing more than passion. When it's directed toward God, one is called a mystic; when toward earthly endeavors, one is considered insane. Even mystics, in their own time, are often labeled mad. St. Teresa of Avila was thought to hear the devil, rather than God's voice.

What is real? What is illusion? Aries will continuously struggle with these questions. Their extreme sensitivity gives the Aries psychic ability. For example, as a child Robert Frost heard voices; later, he became a great poet.

As for careers, the Aries need challenges to keep them interested. They need enough freedom and authority to allow their creative side to emerge, and enough of the unknown to make them want to invent or discover something wonderful. Persistence is not a given; it is there only when heart and soul have surrendered to something. The Aries is attracted to what's never been done. Aries Sandra Day O'Connor (March 26) was the first woman nominated to the Supreme Court. Gloria Steinem (March 25), the courageous feminine activist, paved the way for women in the world of business. Alene Duerk (March 29) made her name by becoming the first female U.S. Navy rear admiral. Irving Lazar (March 28), the notorious literary agent, used the Aries quickness to his advantage. Nicknamed Swifty because of the speed in which he completed a deal, he battled his way to the top of his field. Speaking about his childhood in Brooklyn, Lazar said, "I was born in a jungle, and I'm still in a jungle—a little classier, but it's still a jungle."

Remember, the Aries should choose a job that allows them to initiate and inspire. When the project is ready to be implemented, the Aries has left the scene and moved on, seeking something new and even more challenging. The Aries must recognize his limitations, and make allowances for them. He should hire others who complement his work, and when possible, be his own boss. Aries do not respond to authority; they *are* the authority.

Visionaries with lofty goals, Aries face the challenge of living in the material world while striving for a spiritual ideal. Instinctual, they know things without needing proof; they lead without having a direction, and they know no matter what happens, they will survive. The knowledge they accumulate earns them the right to judge, at least what belongs in their world. Their passion for life is unequaled, and so is their courage in the face of injustice. They can see the moment and enlarge it into a vision; this makes them great leaders and navigators of the unknown. They walk the razor's edge between the spiritual and the worldly life using the tension of their extremes to keep them on course. They are heroes who are shy and fearful; rebels who cry at the sight of a beautiful sunset; and leaders with the curiosity and sensitivity of a child. All life's potential is their inheritance, and yet they feel humbled and small before the majesty and power of God and His creation.

THE ARIES ENVIRONMENT

The Aries environment confronts a person with energy that is aggressive, isolating, and demanding, or warm, nurturing, and intimate. The soul's challenge is to maintain its center regardless of the opinions of others. Events will push and prod, trying to distract the person from his path. Rewards only come when he can stay centered and believe in himself. He must choose a difficult vision with high ideals, in order to harness the strength of Spirit and Ego so that he may move out of the inertia of safety and into the fear of the unknown. To begin any journey takes maximum effort, and a strong will. The Aries' skills are those of any good warrior: common sense, the ability to fight and protect, surrender and retreat. Their environment will test them wherever they are weak and demand that they learn to turn their mistakes into future victories. This is the challenge of the Aries.

Aries/*One* (March 28, April 1, April 10, April 19)
Mars/Sun

PURPOSE: To become independent and strong, expressing your creativity in your own unique way, taking your own path even when it means separation from those you love.

"To conquer fear is the beginning of wisdom''—Bertrand Russell. There's no place for fear in the Aries' world; they risk themselves on a daily basis. These souls have conquered their fear of rejection by overcoming a physical handicap, emotional fear or environmental prejudice. Their belief in themselves is what gets them to the top of their professions and makes them strong leaders. The Aries/*One* must take a stand; this means they will also take some blows. The violence of those blows depends on the Aries/*One's* skills of persuasion, their spiritual and physical strength, and their ability and readiness to fight. The love of freedom is important here, and an Aries/*One* will fight for it above everything else. Confidence is gained through firsthand knowledge of their limitations and strengths, through the experience of victory and defeat, and surviving them. Discipline is a must; if the Aries/*One* didn't acquire it as children they need to find it through a job or their own efforts. They are competitive, and if something isn't difficult or nearly impossible, they're not interested When it comes to love, the Aries/*One* has a big heart. They want children—lots of them. When they give, they give too much; when they're cold, they can be ruthless. Sex and love affairs are important, and others find them sexy. The Aries/*One* knows how to have a good time and loves being the center of attention. However, they can also be shy and private. Few know the real person. Their high principles and sense of justice can get them into trouble; they don't bend even when the price is high. The Aries/*One* often feels alone, and yet they know they are loved.

IF SPIRIT TAKES THE LEAD: When Spirit is strong, so are ideals and for the Aries/*One*, freedom of expression is a primary concern. Trying to be the best that they can puts them in a competitive environment where self-perfection is important. The body suffers; give it some respect. Spirit likes to show what it can do, and what it does best is the impossible. Instead of being compelled to save the world they need to choose which causes to fight and which unjust acts deserve their time and effort. In order to continue their journey, balance must be achieved through remaining centered in their *own* destiny.

IF EGO TAKES THE LEAD: The world of Ego meets problems through force and physical strength, not sensitivity. These souls are self-consumed and obsessive. They're ambitious and competitive and so they go after what they want and usually get it. Charismatic, they have their choice of mates, but commitment is not easy; they love their freedom. Winning, conquering, and proving to themselves that they are better than anyone else are all they care about. Success in the business world is a piece of cake; after all, they have few scruples. In spite of their success and power, life is hard. They're constantly battling to keep their positions. Others attack them for no reason, and they find themselves alone because they trust no one. They need faith and Spirit to get them out of themselves and back into humanity.

DUDLEY MOORE (April 19)

Actor, teacher, musician.

Dudley Moore did not avoid the perils and pain of the Aries/*One* combination. Instead, they were transformed into magnetism. Moore became a reluctant sex symbol, proving to the world that sexy is synonymous with self-acceptance. Just ask model/actress Susan Anton, one of the many beauties to whom Moore has been linked. Given the burden of stunted growth and a club foot, he developed a sense of humor as a child to prevent the cruel harassment of his peers. "I got funny so I wouldn't get beaten up anymore." Despite his misfortunes, Moore was also gifted with talent. A natural musician, music helped him believe in himself. Yet, Moore remained an outsider at Oxford because of his working-class English accent, until he discovered his niche . . . the Oxford theater group. By tapping his creativity, he found freedom of self-expression and came into his own.

ST. TERESA OF AVILA (March 28)

Foundress of the Discalced Carmelites (A.D. 1582), author of *Interior Castle, Way of Perfection, Foundations,* St. Teresa is one of the best-known mystics in the world. Her book, *Interior Castle,* came to her in a vision, and it reveals the seven stages a soul must pass through in order to reach enlightenment. Here, the Aries' desire to map the unknown is brought to new heights. Who else but an Aries would lead the way back to Him? From her writings, the world gets a rare glimpse of the ecstasy and rapture of the mystical experience. St. Teresa was close to both her parents. Her mother died when St. Teresa was fourteen and in her grief, she turned to the Blessed Lady and asked her to be her mother. At fifteen, she was sent to be educated at the convent of Augustinian nuns in Avila, and at twenty, she took her vows and became a nun. God favored her almost immediately with visions and "interior communications." Some thought these communications to be the voice of the Devil and not that of God's, but St. Teresa's sincerity and humbleness eventually brought validation from the Church. "I lost the fear of death, of which I had formerly a great apprehension." St. Teresa tried to live her life as close to her spiritual beliefs as possible. She set an example that has endured through the centuries. By the age of sixty-five, she had established seventeen foundations or homes of contemplation. She was canonized in 1622.

Aries/*Two* (March 29, April 2, April 11, April 20)
Mars/Moon

PURPOSE: *To transform your fears and weaknesses into strengths through understanding them and sharing them with others.*

"Mirror, mirror on the wall, is who I see, you or me?" This is the question every Aries/*Two* asks each morning. They face the challenge of recognizing their own feelings and not confusing them with those of others. Remember, the world is fickle. It loves and rejects according to its needs, not our deeds. There is no way to please it, so the Aries/*Two* must learn to please and nurture *themselves*. To do this, they've got to be able to bond with others without becoming dependent, and to be separate without feeling abandoned or alone. Remember, family is composed not just of those of the same blood, but anyone with whom we choose to share our intimate feelings. When we bond with others we increase our strength.

Like children the Aries/*Two* either can be absorbed in their own feelings or lost in someone else's. Incredibly sensitive, they are easily hurt and hold on to pain. Their protection is retreat or attack. If they choose to attack, they are ruthless. Anger is a great defense mechanism; it's just not a happy one. Because they live so close to their feelings, they're creative, and anything they produce will be unique. Obsessive, they throw themselves into their art, and find it helps them express themselves. Learning to openly communicate emotions is their challenge. Their gifts of intuition and psychic ability distort their expectations— others should know what they want and need. When it doesn't happen, they become disappointed and retreat further within themselves. If they're old enough to complain and be miserable, they're old enough to begin sorting out the avalanche of feelings they've been accumulating since birth. None of these talents will serve them well if they can't step out of themselves. The Aries/*Two* must get rid of self-piety and begin to make those dreams come true. All they need is to see themselves as separate, to learn to nurture themselves, and use their courage to help and protect others. Then, when they look in the mirror, they'll know who's looking back.

IF SPIRIT TAKES THE LEAD: With Spirit out front, the emotional needs of others are all that count. These are the protectors of the defenseless, the providers for the homeless, and the healers of the abused. They probably suffered as a child, and their pain is their link to others. They are charismatic, dramatic, and creative. Intensity is something that attracts them. They must be careful. High ideals can drive them to change their family and the world. Unfortunately, they can easily become the victim of someone else's garbage. The hook is their attraction to danger. They may try to heal a drug addict or an abusive person, and this can make them a victim, not a hero. They need to give their soul to someone who will use it to blossom and not to someone who will pull them down.

IF EGO TAKES THE LEAD: When Ego is strong, emotional needs are inverted and the person becomes self-indulgent, obsessive and consumed with the past. The past occupies the present and prevents anything new from happening. Revenge is strong, as is the pain and hurt they live in. Lost in isolation, they feel detached from the world and try to strike back at any opportunity. They're stuck because

Spirit is what gives them the strength to overcome their problems and move forward. Without confidence, they feel they need to overprotect themselves, which makes them even more isolated and mistrusting. Their obsessive nature could lead to the use of drugs or alcohol or to crazy behavior. These are eccentric souls, with a love for drama. If and when they learn to have faith in something other than themselves they can begin to make a difference in the world, while connecting to their personal power.

HANS CHRISTIAN ANDERSEN (April 2)

Danish author, one of the greatest storytellers of all time.

The creative genius of Hans Christian Andersen was nurtured by doting parents. Raised in a poor town in a poor family, Hans was indulged and protected by all those around him. This insular world of the Aries/*Two* helped him develop his creativity and build an incredible world of fantasy. However, he was not unaware of the suffering and pain of others. His own intense emotional nature needed a positive outlet and he found it in writing children's stories.

In love with the theater, and having the adventuresome spirit and courage of an Aries, Hans set off for Copenhagen at twenty-one. The stories "The Ugly Duckling," "The Snow Queen," and "The Tinderbox" exhibit the healing quality of the Aries/*Two*. Andersen took the creative side of the Aries/*Two* dynamics and combined it with the pure imagination of the Aries child. The results are poems and stories that continue to touch the hearts and minds of everyone.

LIONEL HAMPTON (April 20)

Jazz showman.

The creativity of the Moon found its outlet in the drums and vibraharp which Hampton played with Louis Armstrong and Benny Goodman during the Big Band Era. Experiencing the struggle of Aries, Lionel had to fight the color barrier in entertainment. He made jazz history in 1936 when he joined the Benny Goodman Quartet. A black man had never been accepted in a white band before. Like a true Aries, he wasn't happy until he was his own boss. Four years later, he started his own group. In 1980, President Ronald Reagan saluted Hampton's fifty years in music, calling him one of the most respected musicians in America.

Aries/*Three* (March 21, March 30, April 3, April 12)
Mars/Jupiter

PURPOSE: To take your place as a leader, anxious to enlarge your influence by convincing others that your philosophy is the one to be followed; you need an impossible task to conquer, this will test your beliefs and make them stronger.

"Ilsa, I'm not being noble. The problems of three little people don't amount to a hill of beans in this crazy world. Someday you'll understand that. Here's looking at you kid." Rick, played by Humphrey Bogart, in *Casablanca*. Personal needs don't stand a chance in the presence of a larger cause. Here, the Ego surrenders to Spirit. The earthly desires of the Aries/*Three* are diminished in the face of a greater need. This is Marlon Brando (April 3) giving up his Academy Award to bring attention to the Native American; van Gogh surrendering his life to his religious mission; Thomas Jefferson speaking out for justice and human rights. The Aries/*Three* takes a stand and holds it, no matter how threatening the adversary. The Aries/*Three* must watch out for the lure of the impossible. They're suckers for trying to move the stone no one else can budge. Although they are capable of great things, if they tackle too much too early in life, they may experience failure too often and lose faith in themselves. The Aries/*Three* should not waste their greatness on defying everyone who tries to tell them what to do. They've got to earn their positions. If they can endure early discipline, they'll become souls with the courage to stand up against the world and speak out for their version of the truth. They are leaders who have the power to influence the masses. Remember, though, Ego has to be deflated before Spirit can take the lead, then heaven will humble her, making unity finally possible.

Jupiter, for the *Three*, is the planet of expansion, justice, religion and travel, and it demands we identify with a belief system. This is about choosing a religion, a university to study at, or a country to live in. The Aries/*Threes* need to make these decisions. If they don't, they run the risk of being swallowed up by someone else's beliefs or rules, or of becoming a law unto themselves, like David Letterman (April 12) His larger-than-life persona brought him a larger-than-life deal with CBS. Financially, he is now in a league of his own.

IF SPIRIT TAKES THE LEAD: When Spirit is strong with the Aries/*Three,* the impossible is attempted on a daily basis. If the difficult is chosen too soon, failure will prevent their self-esteem from ever getting off the ground. Loyal to a fault, Aries/*Three* supports their friends and the underdog, even when the price is their own success. They can easily become attracted to false gurus or religions. These are born leaders; but to take their place in the world, they must first have their *own* philosophy based on experience. Don't be afraid to learn from others, but sooner or later you've got to take what you've learned and make it your own.

IF EGO TAKES THE LEAD: Ego and the Aries/*Three* are the best of friends. These souls have presence, and when they walk into a room, everyone knows it. They may appear generous, but they're only buying loyalty. They eat with gusto, have affairs, love luxury. A loner, they surround themselves with people who look up to them, not people to whom they relate. The political arena appeals to them. They have the ability to lead and to influence others, but they are not to be trusted. People are in their life as long as they serve their needs. They are attracted to combat or anything that involves brute strength. They have an inflated sense of themselves, and they like to bully others. However, without Spirit, they don't have staying power and will back down. Their heart and soul are invested in desires, and not more lasting things.

WARREN BEATTY (March 30)

Actor. Film credits include *Bonnie and Clyde, Reds, Dick Tracy,* and *Bugsy.*

A long list of talented lovelies will swear that Warren Beatty is the best . . . lover, that is. He managed to escape commitment until Annette Benning got him to say I do. A talented actor and director, Warren is attracted to the roles of men like himself, men with a larger-than-life persona. That's Jupiter for you; it's always trying to live as a law unto itself. Drawn to politics, Beatty considered running for office. "Anyone who says an artist should stay out of politics is a fool." A loner who hates to give interviews, he exhibits the intensity and intimacy, then distance of the Aries/*Three,* in both his work and personal life. Every movie requires his total attention, followed by periods of seclusion.

VINCENT VAN GOGH (March 30)

Artist, missionary.

Vincent van Gogh lived a life of extremes which led to great pain and suffering. His quest for truth took him away from cities and comfort and led him to become a missionary. He went to the coal mines, where the poorest of the poor struggled to survive. He comforted their souls, he gave them his clothes, he shared with them his small allowance. God and truth were all he sought to keep. Eventually, his passion drove him to create. Van Gogh's paintings were unique, his perspective of the world totally his own. He sold only one painting in his entire life, although he did trade some for supplies and gave them away to pay the rent. Today, his paintings fetch millions at auction houses. His life, short and intense, was lived with his entire heart and soul. His obsessive nature pushed him to cross the thin line between genius and insanity. The last few years of his life were spent in an institution. His letters to his brother Theo gave the world unique insight into the mind of a great man. He was tormented, but always felt humbled before God and His creation. He gave his art "his blood and his heart," and to an Aries/*Three,* there's not really a choice.

Aries/*Four* (March 22, March 31, April 4, April 13,) Mars/Uranus

PURPOSE: To be secure enough with your individuality that you can position yourself between two points of view and not lose sight of your truth; to manifest that truth in a world divided by conflict—a world that offers you both support and open hostility.

"The reasonable man adapts himself to the world: the unreasonable one persists in trying to adapt the world to himself. Therefore all progress depends on the unreasonable man."—George Bernard Shaw. The Aries/*Four* is different, and everyone knows it. In fact, they are catalysts, people who affect the lives of others in a profound way. Their energy is explosive. The Aries/*Four* needs to remember that self-control comes from inner discipline. If they can't confront what's really bothering them, anger and frustration will build and it won't take much to set them off. Their challenge is to keep a clean inner house so they don't explode at the wrong time, at the wrong person, and over the wrong issue. They are attracted to tension, dispute, and the feeling of being pulled apart. The tug of war between two worlds, two religions, two strong people gets them going. The Aries/*Four* needs to learn to live in someone's world, but not to lose sight of their own. Friends are important to them and are from all different walks of life. Eclectic in the way they dress, their love of change often prevents commitments or stability. Living on the earth plane is a challenge. They're inventors, rebels, geniuses, and instigators. They move suddenly and their reaction time is remarkable, but they are also accident-prone. Driven and inspired, others have trouble keeping up with their pace. They are either undercover or demanding maximum attention. Until they learn to accept themselves, identity can be a crisis. Anthony Perkins (April 4) became an actor to escape himself. "There was nothing about me I wanted to be," he once said, "but I felt wonderfully happy about being somebody else."

Uranus rules the individual. It represents how you have uniquely put together your experiences, your beliefs and your feelings. When coupled with Mars, the world either admires the Aries/*Four* uniqueness or turns its back and runs. In the words of Emerson, "Whoso would be a man must be a nonconformist." But if the Aries/*Four* is having trouble fitting in, they need to review what is causing their difficulties. Their style is not gentle or flexible but shocking, and so if what they have to offer is also difficult to digest, they may find themselves alone.

IF SPIRIT TAKES THE LEAD: When Spirit is strong, these unique souls are off fighting for the rights of others. They value freedom above all things, and they'll give their life to an idealistic cause. They make great terrorists, freedom fighters and activists. They are attracted to conflict, and make great negotiators because they're used to being in the center of tension. This is dangerous, for without an earthly Ego, the Aries/*Four* will take the brunt of everyone's anger. They need to focus on their own needs, and realize that not all battles are worthy of being fought. As a child, they either received their sense of self through creativity, or they found themselves an island in the midst of hostility. By diffusing tension, they felt empowered and this became their identity. The results are constant crisis, unless they can learn to receive their identity through new endeavors. They're talented—so they should pick one and go for it.

IF EGO TAKES THE LEAD: Stubborn is an understatement here. These souls don't listen to anyone but themselves. They think the worst of others—they see them as manipulative and unyielding—and yet they seldom realize how their own behavior contributes to their tough life. They're loners, selfish, and obsessive. Because they don't respect the ideas and differences of others, they often find themselves on the outside. They pretend to ignore society but what they want most is to fit in. If only they could learn to compromise, they would find life more accepting. They are driven to get attention, but the world seldom responds, even when they're gifted with genius. This superior knowledge or insight contributes to their separateness and gives them permission to tell everyone else what to do. Locked in their own world, they can become abusive and experience fits of explosive anger.

ANDREW LLOYD WEBBER (March 22)

Composer, creator of *Evita; Phantom of the Opera; Sunset Boulevard.*

Andrew Lloyd Webber's genius was easily recognized by his musical family, his father a composer and director of the London College of Music and his mother a piano teacher. At the age of eight, he was staging shows in his home. By nine, he had published his own composition.

Lloyd Webber went to Oxford University's Magdalen College for a year, then transferred to the Royal Academy of Music. Hooking up with Tim Rice as his lyricist, he wrote the play *Joseph and the Amazing Technicolor Dreamcoat,* first produced in England in 1968. Then came the controversial rock opera, *Jesus Christ Superstar* in 1970, followed by such superb hits as *Evita, Cats,* and *Phantom of the Opera.*

Andrew Lloyd Webber revolutionized the theater with his rock-style opera, choosing subject matters others dared not touch. His unique approach to theater helped create his success.

MARCEL MARCEAU (March 22)

Premier pantomime artist in the world. Trademark role of Bip, the doleful, white-faced clown.

With quick, intelligent movements Marcel Marceau is able to create a story without words. A critic once said of Marcel, "He accomplishes in less than two minutes what most novelists cannot do in a volume."

The son of a kosher butcher, Marcel used the Aries/*Four* energy to its maximum potential. He worked for the French underground in World War II. When the war was over, he studied mime at the Charles Dullins School of Dramatic Art in Paris, then joined the theater group of Jean-Louis Barrault and became famous. That's right, overnight. Things always happen quickly for this combination.

Aries/*Five* (March 23, April 5, April 14) Mars/Mercury

PURPOSE: To play with life as it plays with you, but never losing sight of your intention: to improve your ability to make choices and play varied roles, regardless of the reception the world gives your performance.

"All the world's a stage, and all the men and women merely players: They have their exits and their entrances; and one man in his time plays many parts,"— Shakespeare. Mercury is the master role player, easily bored; it changes masks without looking back. One's parts are endless, major and minor, humorous and tragic. The key for the Aries/*Five* is not to be invested in only one and not to let the fickle world decide which one they should play. *Fives* are challenged to overcome their environment and in Aries, the cheers can turn to jeers for no apparent reason. The world is inconsistent. They must learn to play with it.

Connectors, middlemen, good friends, or busybodies, this combination is never still. If they're not mending a broken teacup, they're fixing your marriage or finding you a job. Unable to escape the battlefield of Mars, war is apparent in their conversations. Arguments and harsh words, clever, witty attacks won't be alien to anyone with this combination. When Mars and Mercury work together, the strength and force add conviction to ideas and make them happen.

Mars is the athlete. Mercury brings dexterity and coordination. Sports with speed or continuous action attract this combination. Aries/*Five* is a social energy; society and parties are usually a part of the schedule. Either the center of attention, or sitting on the sideline, Aires/*Five* people never stay in one place. Prone to worry, their continuously thinking minds create a restless, perfectionist nature.

IF SPIRIT TAKES THE LEAD: When Spirit leads, the desire to be good and fix the problems of others becomes the problem. They're more invested in keeping everyone else on track, than in living their own life. It's a way of avoiding issues, goals and problems, but sooner or later, they'll have to be faced. If they're smart, they'll become selfish and stop asking for advice. They want to please and end up doing what others want them to and not what's good for them. This is the path to ulcers, not enlightenment. Take your life back! Create a goal! Make choices and reconsider your list of friends. It's important to receive as well as to give. *You* decide who stays in your life. Don't be chosen—*choose.*

IF EGO TAKES THE LEAD: Ego is always selfish, and with the *Five* energy, the soul uses gossip and information for power. These are master manipulators, and they use the wishes and desires of others to achieve their goal. They enjoy telling people off, or calling their bluff. They can pester someone to death, or ignore her completely, whatever it takes to get her to react. With little or no conscience, they change their value system as easily as they do their coat. They fake sincerity so masterfully, they sometimes fool themselves. Remember the golden rule—what you do comes back to you, tenfold.

BETTE DAVIS (April 5)

Actress. Eight nominations and winner of two Oscars, one for *Dangerous* in 1935 and *Jezebel* in 1938.

Known for her quick wit, her courage, and her strength, Davis portrayed women ahead of or apart from the mainstream of life. She took on the movie studios when everyone else was too afraid. The press recorded her witty remarks and she became as well known for her spunk and her tongue as for her acting ability. Her mother lived her life through her daughter. In spite of their closeness they had terrible battles. The obsessive side of the Aries/ *Five* manifested in Bette's need to clean continuously. Things had to be in order or she couldn't rest.

Not intrigued by society, she chose to remain a rare participant. She said, "As far as Hollywood was concerned, a debutante was evidently a girl who owned an evening wrap and knew who her father was." Always restless, she once commented, "You'd better be thinking every minute about something. Lots and lots of actors aren't thinking every minute. They're waiting for their cues . . ."

HERBERT VON KARAJAN (April 5)

Conductor and musician, conductor of the Ulm Opera House in Germany at twenty, artistic director of Salzburg Festival.

Herbert Von Karajan had no trouble finding his niche in life; he knew he belonged at the hub of powerful energy, as the conductor. Through him, sounds joined together in harmonious music. However, the restless and confrontational energy of Aries/*Five* makes harmony more difficult to create in one's personal life. Known for his verbal battles, Von Karajan had several famous fights with his contemporaries. He also exhibited the strong physical and competitive side of the Aries/*Five* with his love of speed and sports.

Aries/*Six* (March 24, April 6, April 15) Mars/Venus

PURPOSE: To accept yourself and learn how to control your desires and your impulsive behavior through self-discipline and good discrimination.

"Sexy" is the only way to describe the Aries/*Six*. These people have charisma, with lots to spare. Actor Billy Dee Williams (April 6) personifies the sexy image of the Aries/*Six*. Quoted as saying, "nothing else in the world competes with making love," it's rumored he's even better in bed than his fans assume. Gifted with natural charm, this energy has a tendency toward excess and obsession. They're ruled by desire and a love of beautiful things. What they need is experience, discipline, and a failure or two to make them strong.

Venus adds harmony and easy access to difficult places. The Aries/*Sixes*' ability to bond gets them through doors closed to others. It did for Harold Washington (April 15), the first African American mayor of Chicago. Houdini (March 24), the famous magician, secured his fame with his ability to escape impossible restrictions. It didn't matter if he was hanging upside down in a straitjacket—he got out, quickly.

It's nice to know you can run away, but why waste such magical energy fleeing when you have the power to wrap someone wonderful around your little finger? Remember, choosing is the challenge.

IF SPIRIT TAKES THE LEAD: When Spirit leads, watch out. Love is the priority and if the soul seeks it too passionately, they'll end up with notches on their bedpost and no one in the bed. Lack of discrimination is the problem. This leads to poor self-worth and no self-acceptance. Since their identity is weak they attract strong, overdeveloped egos and then feel overwhelmed, lost, deceived, betrayed or abandoned. Fooled by appearances, they need to beware of the false guru, to see the truth even when it's in sheep's clothing. They shouldn't trust their senses. Time will reveal the truth. While they're waiting, they should not trust too easily, love too quickly, or give too much. Intuition and experience are needed to see what's *in* the package without having to remove the ribbon.

IF EGO TAKES THE LEAD: Addicted to pleasure and beauty, these souls know how to be seductive. Sex and instant gratification, not love, are the quest. With ulterior motives and strong instincts, they know how to use your desires to get what they want. They're smooth operators. People like them. Their lack of identity becomes an asset when they use it to mold themselves to fit someone's desire. Empty and unfulfilled, they seek to alleviate this feeling by the acquisition of things. Obsessive, generous and undisciplined, they have no boundaries, and are headed for a fall. They need to crash in order to let go of some false sense of security. This could mean a loss of money or faith in themselves. This temporary fall is nothing less than a new opportunity—a chance to rebuild on something more sturdy and meaningful. They should not waste their suffering feeling sorry for themselves. It's important to get through the pain and to the other side. There they'll find what they've been seeking all along—a true sense of themselves.

BOB MACKIE (March 24)

Hollywood dress designer, four-time Emmy Award winner, and three-time Academy Award nominee.

The excitement, creative genius, and sensual side of the Aries/*Six* combination finds a way to show off on the fabulous figures of some of the world's most famous women. Bob Mackie has dressed the likes of Carol Burnett, Diana Ross, Barbra Streisand, and Cher. Venus luxury is the theme of his gowns, covered with rhinestones, beads, and ostrich feathers. His gift of knowing and demanding the best has put him at the top of his field.

Bob Mackie got his break as assistant on TV's *Judy Garland Show.* His film credits include *Pennies from Heaven, Lady Sings the Blues, Funny Lady,* and *Max Dugan Returns.* Unfortunately, Bob Mackie's recent notoriety had to do with a debt to the Mafia rather than his talent for creating sexy gowns. He reminds us of the tendency of the Aries/*Six* to lose fortunes as well as make them, emphasizing the necessity for Aries/*Six* to have a strong value system and good discrimination. Discipline and boundaries are necessary for the Aries/*Six* to work at its full potential.

DONALD DOUGLAS, SR. (April 6)

Founder of Douglas Aircraft.

The charisma and adventurous spirit of the Aries/*Six* is not only found in movie stars and dress designers, but in men such as Donald Douglas, Sr. Venus loves to make money, and matched with the courage and ability to take risks inherent in Aries, there was little choice for Donald in 1920 but to head west with only $600 in his pocket. Setting up a biplane business in the back room of a barbershop, his little business grew to support a million-dollar-a-day payroll by 1958. As we know, Venus souls can lose a fortune as well as make it. When the Boeing 707 came on the commercial jet market, Mr. Douglas lost nearly $100 million. Douglas wasn't discouraged. "No great plan is ever carried out without meeting and overcoming endless obstacles that come up to try the skill of man's hand, the quality of his courage, and the endurance of his faith."

Aries/*Seven*(March 25, April 7, April 16) Mars/Neptune

PURPOSE: To integrate your highest spiritual ideals in your daily life through love, and to live them regardless of how the world accepts or rejects your efforts.

"When she was good, she was very, very good. And when she was bad she was horrid." Like the nursery rhyme, the Aries/*Seven* is carried to their highest expression or dropped to depression. Capable of great success or failure, extremes are a part of their life. Howard Cosell, the sports announcer, was one of the few people to support Muhammad Ali's refusal to be inducted into the U.S. Army on grounds of conscientious objection. "What the government did to this man was inhuman. Nobody says a damn word about the professional football players who dodged the draft . . . but Muhammad was different . . . He was black and he was boastful." Thousands of letters poured into ABC, urging Cosell's dismissal.

Cosell's courage and energy made him stick to his beliefs. Besides, he loved a good fight.

The Aries/*Seven* is prone to deception, betrayal or abuse if their idealistic nature has them off the ground. They tend to sugarcoat the things they don't want to hear, so the truth they value so much is often missed. They need to pay attention to life's menial details. It will keep them anchored in reality. Pay the bills on time, argue with the PTA, get the groceries bought. Such tasks might not excite or inspire, but rewards do come.

Love for the Aries/*Seven* is powerful, and surrendering their ego is what it's all about. Where they go wrong is in giving their love to an earthly being who can only misuse the gift. They seek inspiration, but need to remember it does not have to be an unattainable affair or faraway causes. Inspiration can be found in the simple things. They must ground themselves in the moment, for example, by helping someone today. The goal is for them to feel both the earth between their toes and the mist among the clouds.

IF SPIRIT TAKES THE LEAD: Too much Spirit means there could be a victim, someone who puts everyone else's needs before their own because they can't stand up for themselves and say no. They have a strong dose of idealism, and the desire to give love can be so powerful they seek to help others who are beyond help and bring themselves down in the process. Ego is needed to set boundaries and prevent the total surrender of their life to another. If you've chosen an earthly being as your god, you're in trouble. Create your own life. You can contribute to the world and to others, and still be your own person. You have great imagination. Use it to make money, not avoid the truth. Love triumphs when it comes from strength, not from empty, idealistic illusions.

IF EGO TAKES THE LEAD: When the Ego is strong, fanaticism is the result. These souls believe their way is the only way. Religious or righteous, they lack true compassion. Weakness, in themselves or others, is intolerable. Instead of working toward perfection, they criticize everyone and everything they encounter. Their lives are filled with obstacles because they refuse to bend or compromise. Without a spiritual base, they can be a great con artist, able to transform any reality into one that fits their needs. They live a double life; their thoughts and beliefs don't match the person others see. They struggle with loneliness and feelings of not belonging. Love is the answer. It's the only thing that will heal the pain and transform them into the wonderful human being they truly are.

CHARLIE CHAPLIN (April 16)

Silent film star. The Little Tramp.

The ability of taking a piece of oneself and raising it to a height few can ever achieve is a talent of the Aries/*Seven* and the genius of Charlie Chaplin. His portrayal of the character of the Little Tramp made him a legend in his own time. Chaplin began life as a bastard child. His mother died in a poorhouse, and for the next two years he lived in an orphanage. "There were floggings, deprivations, and solitary confinements." Arriving in America at age twenty-one, he began his movie career as a Keystone Cop. By the time he was thirty, he was a millionaire and known as a comic genius. The issue of religion and faith, so important to the Aries/*Seven,* finally caught up with him. "As I get older," Chaplin once said, "I am more and more preoccupied with faith. A long time ago I told the composer Rachmaninoff that I did not believe. 'How can you practice art without religion?' he asked. I replied, 'For me, art is more of a sentiment than a belief.' Rachmaninoff retorted, 'So is religion.' I now know Rachmaninoff was right."

KAREEM ABDUL JABBAR (April 16)

The all-time leading scorer of the National Basketball Association.

Able to reach the heavens just by standing tall, Kareem Abdul Jabbar soared to the top of a very competitive profession. The Aries/*Seven* needs space and time alone, and Abdul Jabbar makes sure he gets it. A known introvert, he has felt the disillusionment of his sport and society. Divine discontent keeps the Aries/*Seven* striving for perfection. His great success made him realize the emptiness of monetary rewards. Abdul Jabbar is committed to Islam. His Islamic name means generous, powerful servant of God.

Aries/*Eight* (March 26, April 8, April 17) Mars/Saturn

PURPOSE: To learn the process of success step by step, mastering the technical while never losing touch with your passion.

"Always do what you're afraid to do."—Emerson. This is the energy of blocks and breakthroughs. If you stay blocked long enough, you'll have a nervous breakdown or a breakthrough. Sandra Day O'Connor became the first woman on the Supreme Court in its 208-year history. Diana Ross (March 26) crossed boundaries of race and age with her music.

The Aries/*Eight* dynamic is about living the spiritual life in alignment with the Ego's needs. Control is an issue for these people, and so is their acute ability to scrutinize a situation and themselves. They strive for perfection and drive themselves and everyone else crazy. This prevents their talents from emerging and drains their self-confidence. Their anger is turned inward, making them frustrated and giving them headaches. They erect impenetrable boundaries or have none at all, and wish that someone would take care of them. Their world can only be as large as they can manage by themselves. They have so much more to offer if they can just access their faith and have a little trust in the right people. They must learn to confront what's really bothering them. Therapy is positive. Aries/*Eight* is a great combination for analysis.

Remember, the world will never be satisfied. It will always demand more. Consider Eliza Doolittle in *My Fair Lady*. Snatched from her simple life, then pushed, prodded, and even threatened into being perfect, once there she was abandoned by her teachers and left in a state of crisis. She didn't fit in anywhere. My advice would have been not to bring Rex Harrison his slippers, but to shove them down his throat. The Aries/*Eights* must be who they are and forget what others expect from them.

IF SPIRIT TAKES THE LEAD: When Spirit and the *Eight* get together, they find endurance, patience, and an ability to postpone needs. Their ideals are lofty, and the desire to be perfect in a world of imperfection is the quest. That's a goal that's sure to lead to trouble. Work is their god, and thus they sabotage their success. They exalt the process, not the end results. Always the perfectionist, they never tolerate mistakes, at least not without self-punishment. They need to please and are constantly striving to meet the expectations of others. When they encounter pressure or resistance, they give in, never realizing just how strong they are. When they become tired of being a doormat, they'll stand up to the opposition. They should take some self-assertiveness training, and they'll be surprised how quickly they gain a voice.

IF EGO TAKES THE LEAD: The *Eight* and Ego add up to control. Tough on themselves, nothing is ever right and everything must be done their way. Even with success they feel stuck, isolated, and lost. They don't have faith in themselves or anyone else. Trust is desperately needed, and so is therapy. They're under much tension and have no place to channel it. They have an enormous need for material security. Depression and an inability to take action are part of the package. If they could just get out of themselves and allow things to unfold, life would take on a new meaning. Age makes matters worse. The older they get, the smaller their world becomes. They need to stop the retraction and fill themselves up with faith and love.

BETTY FORD (April 8)

First Lady of the United States.

The Aries/*Eight* found a public figure to display its strength. Betty Ford, the wife of Gerald Ford, former president of the United States, showed us what dedication and courage was all about. No one experiences the invasiveness of the world like a political wife. Every word and action is scrutinized and splattered across the morning papers. Betty found herself overburdened, and unappreciated. Addicted to alcohol and pills, overwhelmed with responsibility, she finally broke down. What emerged was wisdom and strength, two wonderful qualities that come when both sides of this energy call a truce. Betty became a true leader by announcing her mastectomy to the world, helping other women cope with the trauma of breast cancer. Later, her honesty and courage surfaced in her fight against alcohol and pills. She established the Betty Ford Center to help others recover from addictions.

MICHAEL BENNETT (April 8)

He conceived, directed, choreographed, and coproduced the famous Broadway play, *A Chorus Line*. It won nine Tony Awards and the Pulitzer Prize for Drama, 1976.

Stress, ambition and hard work, the backbone of Aries/*Eight,* found a creative outlet in Michael Bennett. At the age of three he took his first dance lesson. From that moment on, he knew where he belonged. The pinnacle of his career was the unique and inspirational story of the dancer's life, depicted in the Broadway play *A Chorus Line.* The essence of the Aries/*Eight* is depicted in their lifestyle: the constant competition, the short intense gigs, followed by periods of no work. By honoring the loyalty, hard work, and struggle of Saturn as the major theme of his play, Bennett received his greatest success.

Aries/*Nine* (March 27, April 9, April 18) Mars/Mars

PURPOSE: To keep your purpose and sense of self in the face of great opposition and competition.

This sensual, dynamic combination means action for action's sake, conquest for conquest's sake, and the chance to be better and brighter than anyone else. Competitive? Yes. And that's the problem. These people get ahead on perseverance and a pushy style, but sooner or later the bruised egos around them will get even. What we do to others always comes back. Patience is not their best virtue, nor is reflection or an objective point of view. Experience is their only teacher. The Aries/*Nine* needs to slow down and choose battles instead of fighting them all. Getting wounded by inconsequential issues keeps them from using their powerful force to make a difference. Honest to a fault, they seek the truth, astonished that others do not care. They are magnetic and sexy; often, the only way to slow down is to abstain. Their priorities are their own, yet they are surprised when others don't meet their standards. The Aries/*Nine* needs to pause and reflect. They'll find their life easier to balance. To test the self and not self-destruct is a formidable challenge, and one reserved for the final stage of Aries. Consider the quest for the Holy Grail. In *The Last Crusade* Indiana Jones had to step off a cliff onto an invisible bridge in order to find it. Blind faith and a trust in the unknown was required to succeed. For the Aries/*Nine,* the journey is spiritual and the challenges great. If they find what they're seeking, they'll know in the silence of their heart.

IF SPIRIT TAKES THE LEAD: When Spirit leads, the soul believes that nothing is impossible. They have a great need to help others and make a difference in the world. However, they are fanatical. This might be good for the cause they're championing, but not for their body, their family, and the people who work for them. They are unrelentless, and their desire for perfection can do damage. They will push themselves beyond their physical limitations. Although they get the most from others, they carry resentment and seldom experience a moment of victory, only another challenge. Remember, life is not just the seeking of a vision; it's living happily in the now. Unfortunately, the present is not a place the Aries/*Nine* ruled by Spirit is often found. They're off chasing some distant dream while their world slips by them unlived and undiscovered.

IF EGO TAKES THE LEAD: With Ego strong, everything is about being right and being first. They do things on fast forward and have no patience or self-control. Sex and the pleasures of the world keep them chasing, and conquering, but not accomplishing anything worthwhile. Fanatical, obsessive, and unable to turn away from a challenge, they have trouble staying on one path. They believe they are invincible and sometimes they are, but more often than not they pass the finish line and keep on going, right into the wall, not the victory stand. They try to dominate the thoughts and actions of others because they think they know what's best for them. They are insatiable. They never have enough love, money, fame, and power. The rest of us know that having it all is impossible, but convincing an Aries/*Nine* with an attitude—now that *is* impossible.

HUGH HEFNER (April 9)

Owner and chairman of *Playboy* magazine, host of late night TV *Playboy after Dark* and *Playboy Penthouse.*

Sex is one of the objectives of the Aries/*Nine,* and Mr. Hefner certainly reached his objective. Always his own boss, a very important factor for the Aries/*Nine,* he graduated from the University of Illinois in two and a half years. With stubbornness and undaunted spirit, he became a publisher when he was turned down for a five-dollar-a-week raise. He mortgaged his furniture twice, borrowed from friends and relatives, and sold stock in a magazine called *Stag Party,* for about $10,000. When *Stag* magazine objected to the publication name, he called it *Playboy.* Enough copies were sold to finance a second issue, and the rest is history.

Exhibiting a life of excess, his parties at his California mansion are legendary. It took a heart attack to slow Hugh down. Married again in his seventies to a woman half his age, Hugh has found happiness with his new family and two small children.

DENNIS QUAID (April 9)

Actor. Films include *The Right Stuff, The Big Easy, Everybody's All-American,* and *Great Balls of Fire.*

The charismatic sex symbol Dennis Quaid did not always feel so desirable. In fact, in high school he hardly dated and did not play football. His ego had not yet come into its own. Remember, when a sunsign/birth number dynamic demands a lot from us at an early age, often the easiest way to deal with it is to avoid its nature. But in order to find peace and balance we must eventually embrace the energy. And embrace it Quaid did. Needing to be challenged, he took up acting. Before filming *The Right Stuff,* he learned how to fly. For the film *The Big Easy* he spent time with the police. Today, Dennis is a millionaire with twenty-two films to his credit.

SUMMARY

The Aries is the warrior of the zodiac. Born under the sign of the ram, they choose a path of challenges, an obstacle course that develops courage, perseverance and a belief in their ability to overcome great odds. These qualities, along with their powerful instincts, are necessary for survival. Aries represents beginnings. Gifted with vision, courage and a drive to explore the unknown, they're the leaders who inspire the best in us because they demand so much of themselves. They've been tested through experience and both victory and failure are their teachers. Their purpose is the return to Eden, to paradise and love, and they're willing to help us all get there. They know that beneath the battle of opposites lies unity, and if they can see beyond separateness to a place which includes both sides, they will reach it. With their eye on their vision, armed with self-knowledge and powerful instincts, they're ready for the next stage of the journey, which is found in Taurus. There the length, width, and breadth of the inner world will be mapped. It's time to learn about moral priorities.

SELECTED SOURCES

Oleg Cassini *In My Own Fashion: An Autobiography* Simon & Schuster 1987

John Cottingham *The Cambridge Companion to Descartes* Cambridge University Press 1992

Lao-Tzu et al *Tao Lao Tsu Te Ching* Translated by Gia-Fu Feng and Jane English Rand 1982

Barbara Leaming *Bette Davis: A Biography* Simon & Schuster 1992

George R. Marek *Toscanini: A Biography* Atheneum 1975

Ralph G. Martin *Henry and Clare: An Intimate Portrait of the Luces* GP Putnam's Sons 1991

Louis Pierard   *The Tragic Life of Vincent van Gogh*   Translated by Herbert Garland   Houghton Mifflin Co.

Willard Sterne Randall   *Thomas Jefferson: A Life*   Henry Holt & Co. 1993

Albert Schweitzer   *J. S. Bach*   A&C Black Limited 1980

Rachel A. Taylor   *Leonardo the Florentine: A Study in Personality*   Harper & Brothers

Lawrence Thompson and R. H. Winnick   *Robert Frost*   Holt, Rinehart and Winston 1981

Kevin Tierney   *Darrow: A Biography*   Thomas Y. Crowell 1981

CHAPTER THREE

Taurus

(April 21–May 21)

Stubborn it's true, is Taurus the bull,
With a heart warm and tender and yes always full.
Seductive and sexy, he knows how to charm.
Protective and smart, he avoids evil's harm.
Truth and beauty, these are his quest.
Perfection and love keep him from rest.
Creative and smart, his style is unique.
He uses his strength; he transforms what is weak.
Whatever he touches is left not the same.
His courage allows him to gain from his pain.

Ruler: Venus   **Symbol: Bull**
Element: Earth   **Number: Six**

Taurus completes April and brings in May. The gentle sprouts of spring now take root and grow. The earth provides nourishment, and where the resistant earth gives way, providing acceptance, and unconditional love, that is where the Taurus will anchor itself and build a foundation. Aries is division and duality. Taurus offers the gifts that cannot be divided: love, loyalty and truth. Seductive, mysterious, magnetic, and intimate, Taureans get your attention through the power of their presence. They know how to reflect what you lack; in one magnificent moment you feel whole. Rulers of desire, Taureans are adept at the use of resources—theirs and yours. Anywhere, anytime they can create what they need. Instinctive, unique, restless, and rebellious, they have only one authority—their truth. They can be loners, set apart from the masses. As they pass through your life they leave a wake of change, conflict, and a special excitement that makes you want to be near them at any cost. Fighting is not their style. The sign ruled by Venus has learned to use a more powerful weapon than anger—the sword of truth. It has the ability to cut through illusion, denial, guilt, Ego, and the intellect.

The Taurean truth is simple, straightforward and it comes from their center. Once they find this place within themselves, they have access to it in everyone else. Truth without protection—the knowledge of how to use it—is dangerous. Truth enrages those who want to avoid it and frightens those who are not ready to have their mask penetrated. Don't take truth lightly. If you carry it around innocently, you can self-destruct.

Perseverance and stubbornness are necessary to accomplish the Taureans' tasks and as a fixed sign, these qualities are part of their nature. They are loyal and devoted to all those they love. This innate capacity to retain, particularly facts and figures, makes them appear brilliant and gives them an edge in the business or creative world. They store whatever they need and recall it when necessary. It's Venus that's the connector, and the ability to merge with the object of desire gives the Taurean an intense focus and obsessive nature. Andre Agassi (April 29) uses this focus on the tennis court. Taureans have magnetic powers. If a Taurean sets his sight on you, my advice is to surrender. They have the ability to overwhelm.

Taurus is texture. It's the tempo, rhythm, and pitch of your being; it's your style. Taurus is the slant you give a collar, the tilt of your head, the attitude of your stance. It's Fred Astaire (May 10) moving effortlessly across the dance floor in a series of ballroom turns. It's the audience knowing that no one will ever be able to do it exactly that way again. He has created something original and unique. These souls are magic. This is where the poetry of our being is imposed on others. Magnetism is created when one accepts one's total self. Don't dismiss the sadness in your eyes; it can be a source of power rather than a source of shame when you own it. Ignore it and it weakens the whole.

Taurus is protection. It provides resistance to penetration. It is feminine. If Taureans are inept in this area, their life can represent a party of uninvited guests who eat their food, steal their ashtrays, and leave them with a mess to clean up. The good news is they can change. Before you can protect anything you've got to own it. This means you need to accept yourself— the good, the bad, and the ugly. There's no other way to security.

In Aries, you found the center or heart of something by exploring its extremes and dividing it in half. This determined the horizontal perimeters of your world. Now you need to determine the height and the depth of your personality. The formula is simple. Take your greatest victory as your ceiling; your worst defeat becomes the place where your foundation will be built. Once that's in place, you've got a frame which you will fill with joy and sorrow. From your center will come the creative force of your being, your truth and your instincts. It is from this place that everything else evolves.

Be careful not to build your frame too large, or the space between you and the dream will be open to invasion. Your identity should represent your truth, not exactly, but symbolically, so that those who are at your level of expression can find their way in, and those you want to avoid will be kept out. We grow and change with every experience, and so our mask or identity should also evolve. However, once it's created, few of us bother to bring it up-to-date until we're forced to change through crisis.

Our early experiences have the most profound effect on our personality. When success is tasted in youth, it is easy to reach for the sky when you set out into the world to make your fortune. If all you've known is defeat, then you'll be stuck in the darkness of pain and unable to move forward. The challenge here is to be able to draw from others as well as oneself. If all you've known is applause, you won't know how to nurture yourself when the show is over. And if criticism was your daily diet, then you probably ignore support from others. The dimensions of our identity and whether or not we have used both our pain and our joy, determine the strength and protection we will be able to call on in times of trouble.

Ego must alter its natural, aggressive nature in Taurus in order to succeed. It's time to try a little Spirit or yin. Here unity, or the desire to be whole, is what one feels and what Ego uses toward its own end. Ego becomes a seducer. It hones in on what you yearn for, then feeds your desires until you become addicted. Ego's new office is inside, and so without much effort it can head you off at the pass. This is generosity with an ulterior motive, this is giving with an eye to gain. Ego inflates, and because Taurus rules our height, the ceiling of our existence, the Ego dominates by using feelings of superiority. If Ego is damaged and Spirit is not strong, the soul will feel inferior, defeated and lack self-worth. The need to please will dominate, and there will be fear of moving forward. Pauline Kael describes all this when she talks about Orson Welles's (May 6) *Citizen Kane.* "... it is about size and the doomed quest for significance. The little boy versus the big man, getting more and feeling less; getting bigger and seeming smaller, projecting the image bigger and bigger, so the center seems further and further from the surface."

Taurus shows us our weaknesses and then we have the choice to use them as strengths or let others use them to control us. In Taurus, we experience a lack, but in truth all that is missing is someone to reflect back what we believe is missing. This is love, a person who makes us feel whole by seeing in us what we felt didn't exist. If your mother or father only loved parts of you, rejecting pieces of you according to their needs, then what you didn't get is what you will want. All you have to do is find someone who can see it in you. When you recognize what you were seeking in their eyes, it's yours. Spirit heals through union. It is never diminished by another's greatness, but learns from those higher and better, allowing their spirit to lift its own. When Spirit sees weakness or fear, she supports, connects, and heals with love.

Taurus is a crossroads, a place where a reversal of fortune is possible. Experience gives us knowledge, knowledge gives us choices. With awareness or consciousness we can change defeat into victory or use Ego to turn victory into defeat. Sometimes, God decides to show us who's boss. Machiavelli (May 3) the author of *The Prince,* was an influential man. He lost his position as chancellor because of a change in government. He never recuperated from this loss. Orson Welles never quite regained fame or recaptured opportunities after William Randolph Hearst (April 29) had him blackballed at the studios. Timing is Taurus. It's part of our instinctual nature. When it's on, everything we do is perfect. It's about the rain falling just in time to save the crops; your house selling just before it's taken over by the bank; and it's the subway arriving as you put the coin in the turnstile. This is the hand of God. When He chooses, and for His reasons alone, our lives change. No matter how well prepared, protected, or deserving we are, life is transformed. Never get too cocky or secure. Instinct keeps you one step ahead of the Fall. When you plug into this remarkable energy, life reveals a touch of magic. Just don't believe that *you're* the magic. God giveth and taketh away. So stay humble and you'll be fine.

Love is what an Aries seeks and love is what a Taurus must accept. Aries feel they are special just because they're alive; Taureans must own their specialness through the acceptance of their differences and their idiosyncrasies. The mother is the key here. She is the source of nourishment for both body and Spirit. Her milk carries all the nutrients a child needs to grow big and strong and her unconditional love is what feeds the Spirit and allows courage and moral strength to blossom. With love comes self-acceptance and the desire to reach out and take risks. Without this mother, the soul remains dependent and needy, always hoping it will receive the love it was missing early in life. Thus the mother, or women in general, play an important role for a Taurus. Often, she is a strong, supportive female or the dominant creative force of the family. This woman provides the Taurean soul an opportunity to be overindulged and nurtured before setting out into the world to find its own self-expression. Freud said, ''A man who has been the indisputable favorite of his mother keeps for life the feeling of a conqueror, that confidence of success that often induces real success.''

Courage, a Taurus gift, can also be traced to the security of a mother's love. When we feel accepted we can take risks. However, too much love and overindulgence produce the fear of the loss of love and fosters dependence. Orson Welles said, ''Whenever (my mother) left me, the moment the door had closed, I would burst into tears, afraid that I would never see her again.'' Taurus is motivation and if emotional independence is not achieved, the child will strive to fulfill his parents' unfulfilled desires instead of his own.

Love develops good instincts; it links the inner and the outer world through an instant impulse. Strong instincts give us courage and confidence, and keep us from making mistakes. This is the ability to walk into an unfamiliar situation and know what to do. Without love, instincts shrivel up and retreat; what takes their place are impatience and Ego.

Taureans seek emotional expression, which reaches its greatest height in the opposing sign of Scorpio. Emotional impact is more important than technique. Barbra Streisand (April 24) first sang in a talent contest at a New

York restaurant. She had never had a voice lesson, yet she stirred her listeners with her emotional power. She won the contest and got her first singing job. This emotional sensitivity makes Taureans attuned to the voice of social change, and change is what they seek. Horace Mann (May 4) tried to change human nature through moral indoctrination. He struggled toward an ideal society and was involved in every major reform movement of his time. Theodor Herzl (May 2) picked up the yearnings of the scattered Jewish people and united them in establishing a homeland. Even Orson Welles had dreams of changing the world of theater. "I wouldn't be happy if I couldn't convince myself that I will alter at least the cultural course of history in the theatre."

Taureans have special antennae that connect them to all emotions. They gather and unite the invisible threads of feelings created by desire. As they are linked together, a bridge is built for others to cross. To create is to change; to create is to progress; to progress is to evolve. You'll find Venus energy behind any great transition. Taureans draw whatever they need from their environment, rearrange it, then return it to the world with something of themselves added.

Taurus is transition and evolution. When President Roosevelt died, Harry Truman (May 8) became president of The United States. It was up to him to end the war and heal a nation. He carried the nation from the battlefront to the home front, guiding us with his simplicity, honesty and truth. Jack Paar (May 1) transformed the entertainment show into what is now known as *The Tonight Show*. Alone, he created a new TV genre. Martha Graham (May 11) dancer and choreographer, developed her innovative style through experimentation, another Taurus trait. She alone changed *the root* control of dance, giving the world a new system of balance and rhythm.

More often than not, change does not come through revolution and rebellion but occurs step by step, with patience and discipline and perseverance. Discipline is the Taureans' key to success. Without it, they self-destruct. They need resistance from the outside world, the pressure to force them inward and make them struggle to understand. They've got to organize the inner chaos that leads to creation, nothing will get off the ground without limits and boundaries. Often, those who have it tough early on build the kind of self-discipline necessary to achieve success and resist temptation. Brahms (May 7) said of his youth, "I would not in any account have missed this period of hardship in my life, for I am convinced that it did me good and was necessary to my development."

The discrepancy between inner truth and the outer world, between content and packaging creates a gap, a Taurean issue. If your identity or mask doesn't reflect your truth, you're attracting something other than what you really need. It can be experienced in something as simple as deciding your vocation. Karl Marx (May 5) said, "If we have chosen a position for which we have no talents, we shall be unable to fill it worthily and shall soon recognize with shame our incompetence.'' The gap can also manifest as class differences, dividing the rich and the poor, then a Taurus like Karl Marx will try to bridge the chasm. It is also experienced as propaganda and advertising. Taureans are wizards at misrepresentation or reproducing exact replicas.

Of course, knowing or accepting our whole truth is not so easy. We are all contradiction. Orson Welles said, ''Everything about me is a contradiction, and so is everything about everybody else. We are made out of oppositions; we live between two poles. There's a philistine and an aesthete in all of us, and a murderer and a saint. You don't reconcile the poles. You just recognize them.'' All you've got to do is accept both sides. However, most of us mistake a detail of ourselves for our life purpose. If you believe your profession or relationship is your whole purpose and identity, you're in trouble. Devote some of your time to the rest of your self. A good mask or identity contains shades of light and dark, the beautiful and the ugly. It alludes to everything and acknowledges nothing. It's mysterious and revealing at the same time. To create such a masterpiece requires you to use subtleties, nuances, and texture—no more extremes. You've got to blend your mistakes and your victories, your pain and your joy into something multidimensional. Then it's up to you to choose when and how something comes to light or disappears into the shadows. You become the master of your truth, hiding or revealing whatever is necessary to achieve your goal. To learn this skill requires self-acceptance.

Identity is developed in Taurus. That means, one's sexuality is also determined here. Sexual roles can be confusing early in life, particularly if you earn love and acceptance for playing a role other than the one with which you were born. The sorting-out process is confusing, even for those who seem certain of who they are or what they want to be. Don't be afraid if you've questioned your own expression. It's part of the process of self-discovery. Orson Welles struggled with his homosexual desires because he so desperately needed to be wanted. ''From my earliest years, I was the Lillie Langtry of the older homosexual set. Everybody wanted me.'' Get your emotional needs sorted out. Then you can be comfortable with any choice, because you've made it.

Taureans are natural and unique. Their challenge is to accept what makes them different and see themselves as special. One easily recognizes Barbra Streisand's profile, Bing Crosby's (May 3) voice, Cher's (May 20) style of dress. Being unique means you value your specialness, and if you're courageous enough to accept your weakness or your dark side, then you'll find a strength that can be an example to us all. Stevie Wonder (May 13), a man who never let his handicap interfere with his talent, exhibits this kind of self-acceptance. Being blind never stopped him from enjoying life. He played ball, roamed the neighborhood like other children, and even got in trouble with girls—another Taurus talent. Wonder said, ''I finally told [my mother] that I was happy being blind and I thought it was a gift from God.'' With over a dozen Grammys under his belt and a career that spans three decades, Wonder displays the Taurean talent of holding on and evolving.

Protection is the next step. It means discrimination and the ability to judge. Judgment eliminates possibilities, narrows our options, and prevents us from having to experience unnecessary events and people. It is important for survival. The ability to recognize seeds of trouble and to avoid bad habits is excellent protection. This skill is derived from imagination—the ability to envision what could be. Only when authority, the law, or instinct has been undermined does imagination soar. Brahms the composer said. ''One must draw inspiration not from without, but from within.''

Venus, the planet known for her beauty and love, has another side—the bad and the ugly. In order to deflect, reject, and keep others at a distance you've got to be unpleasant—yes, even hurt someone's feelings, if necessary. Let's say someone asked to stay with you for two days, and two weeks later they're still eating your food and using your phone. Ugly is the only thing that works. Being nice is what got you into the situation. Your radar has been sending signals that you can't say no. If you can't speak your truth and set some boundaries, you're in trouble.

Fear of rejection and abandonment are real, but without the ability to express your own truth, you become a victim of the morality and value system of others. If you didn't learn how to stand up and fight in Aries, Taurus lessons will be impossible to develop. To protect your truth, you've got to confront, but once you *can,* you seldom have to. You need to know how to use both virtue and vice. Machiavelli said, ''A man striving in every way to be good will meet his ruin among the great number who are not good.'' He goes on to say that ''. . . some habits which appear virtuous, if adopted would signify ruin, and others that seem vices lead to security and the well-being of the prince.'' Taureans will always have to face decisions that require a balance between good and evil, lofty causes and earthly needs. Both are necessary for survival. The choice will be made by what you believe to be your purpose.

Loyalty is another one of those Taurean gifts that can't be divided. To be loyal means to choose, even when you don't want to. Being in the middle is not the Taurean position. Machiavelli said, ''A prince is also esteemed when he shows himself a true friend or a true enemy, that is . . . he takes his stand with one side or the other.''

Versatility is a talent that depends on where and how Taureans plant their roots. If they're rooted in worldly things, then the world will see Taureans as rigid and unyielding. If however, they are anchored in Spirit, their roots are strong and flexible. John Houseman commented on how Welles directed *Citizen Kane.* ''It was clearly going to be an extraordinary piece of work. Once again I was astounded at his instinctive mastery, the sureness with which he moved into a new medium and shaped it to his own personal and original use.''

Moral conscience is developed in Taurus and it's done through disobedience. Adam and Eve set the example when they disobeyed God's authority and ate forbidden fruit. A child disobeys his parents, testing life and its choices for the pure pleasure of it. We all must learn through disobedience, and moral consciousness is the result. It provides protection by limiting our behavior and keeping it within the confines of our purpose. To build this ethical infrastructure one must be adept at organizing experiences, feelings and motivation. Freud is a Taurus and he is considered the Father of Psychoanalysis. Surrounded by inner chaos, Taureans seek law and order, but while they're working out the plan, they like to cause a little chaos, too. If you're a problem causer, you can become a problem solver. It's good to be able to do both. For moral consciousness to kick in we need pain and suffering. Once we are humbled, we see God's greatness, and suddenly, we value what we have lost. Taurus or *Sixes* often only learn the value of a person or a thing through its loss. Good and evil are moral choices in Taurus. The ability to weigh a decision and choose well is important.

Taureans can be rebels, because personal truth often conflicts with authority or the collective majority. Their mothers deserve a medal. Martha Graham once told her mother, ''I wish to go to this man whom I love with all my heart and I want time and I want privacy and I am going to a hotel with him.'' Taurean mothers learn early how to ask for divine guidance. Golda Meir's (May 3) mother must have held her breath every time her daughter left the house to sneak off to Zionist meetings in Russia.

Seduction, mystery and magnetism are all Taurean gifts. How do the rest of us acquire this power? It's all about what you choose to hide. What you hide, not what you show, gives you power. The hidden becomes a magnet. If you hold back some of your talents, strengths, and intellect, and reveal them only when it's appropriate or necessary, then you've got a magnetism that will get attention. Some lucky Taureans—and this is the sign of luck— get the arrangement right by chance. They can be weak and appear strong, impotent and appear sexy. Consider Valentino (May 6) the silent film star who made women all across the country swoon. Married twice, he never consummated his first marriage and probably not his second. In fact, women didn't interest him as much as a plate of pasta. Valentino's funeral caused a riot. Filled with grief at the loss of their ideal, women broke through the police line and hurled themselves at his coffin.

An earth sign, Taurus gathers knowledge and wisdom through practical and sensual means. Nothing less than a direct experience will do, and Taurus only knows how to resist or surrender. Ruled by Venus, they are attracted to beautiful people, either in appearance or because they live close to their truth. Even Karl Marx was taken in by beauty. He married the most beautiful girl in his town. Adoration is another thing they love in a relationship. They want to be special. The real pull for a Taurus is surrender. They have a great need to merge emotionally with someone and have the other take care of all their needs. Dangerous, if they don't know how to come back and be their own person. Passion is a given, and so is jealousy. Remember, ownership is a Taurean specialty. They love pleasure; they long to be touched, excited, and aroused. They seek the kind of stimulation that tingles their whole being; the danger is when they seek it indiscriminately. The gentle, loving Taurean needs a spiritual mate, as well as an instinctual one. They will never ask for things they don't think are practical, yet it is these loving, caring sentiments they desire the most. Taureans are very connected to their physical bodies. They like things to feel, sound, taste, and smell good. Yes, Taureans are experts on pleasure because in order to give it, you must first know how it feels.

All Taureans should read the story of Midas, the king who got his wish and wished he hadn't. Everything he touched turned to gold and when he touched the daughter he loved so dearly, she also turned to gold and he suddenly realized the value of love. Taureans wage the battle between possessions and love, between worldly values and spiritual wholeness. When they have good taste, no one has better. And there is nothing worse than a Taurean with bad taste; all they do is acquire.

Growth doesn't happen without pain. Pain is protection; it lets us know when we're hurt, physically or emotionally. It has another purpose. It's a link or a bond, a way to unite with someone else. In fact, it is often easier to resonate with someone's sorrow than with his joy. Pain heightens awareness; it creates the hills and valleys of the psyche that develop motivation. It gives us character, depth, and understanding. We cannot move through Taurus without experiencing pain. Two malefic stars are keepers of the exit gate of Taurus. To leave, one must pass Algol and the Pleiades, the Weeping Sisters. Pain comes with any separation, even if it is natural and positive. Each new step on our journey requires that we leave something behind and embrace something before us. The philosopher Hegel, a Virgo, another earth sign, said, "The life of the Spirit is not the life that shrinks from death and keeps itself untouched by devastation, but rather the life that endures it and maintains itself in it. It wins truth only when, in utter dismemberment, it finds itself. . . . Spirit is this power only by looking the negative in the face and tarrying with it."

The challenge for Taureans is not discovering truth—they have the ability to ferret it out no matter how well hidden—but rather whether to seek it in something other than the beautiful. Beauty is their oxygen. It's the only thing they can't live without. Whether buying or selling it, building or creating it, marrying or divorcing it, they kneel in its presence. Sometimes they get cheated because they've only seen the pretty paper and not the gift. In

Emerson's words, "Though we travel the world to find the beautiful we must carry it with us or we find it not."

Venus, the planet of beauty and love, is the most underrated energy of the zodiac. One has only to consult history to see that monarchies were toppled, articulate men turned into babbling idiots, honest men into thieves—and all for the love of a beautiful woman. Women sell their souls for beautiful possessions and a gorgeous model can command thousands of dollars an hour. Beauty is impossible to avoid; it attracts our eye no matter how we feel about its value. Our quest for beauty is not based entirely on aesthetics. On a deeper level, beauty means survival. A symmetrical wingspan, a well-balanced antler, a perfect physical body attracts a mate. It's nature's way of signaling who is better capable of proliferating the species. Defects mean a lack of ingredients necessary for survival. Beauty also has the power to transform. Behind its mask is a spiritual face. Hegel said, "Beauty is merely the spiritual making itself known sensually." Love and beauty unite us with the object adored. They stir our souls and free the creative force. Venus's incredible power of concentration adds to Taurus's spiritual nature. Whenever our focus is intense and unrelenting, we easily pass through limitations, boundaries, and feelings of separateness, to be united with the object of our desire. Artists experience bonding with truth and beauty. Evelyn Underhill says the purpose of art "was not to reproduce the illusions of ordinary men but to catch and translate for us something of that 'secret plan,' that reality which only the artistic consciousness is able to perceive."

Taureans appear honest; there is a naturalness to whatever they do. Jimmy Stewart (May 20) made his fame by portraying characters who struggled to do the right thing. Frank Capra, (May 18) the director said about Stewart, "I sensed the rock-ribbed honesty of a Gary Cooper (May 7) plus the breeding and intelligence of an Ivy Leaguer." Social and easily liked, Taureans instinctually know how to get along with people. Whether at a black-tie event or sitting around a bonfire, they adapt who they are to the moment.

Taurus rules the voice. Their mesmerizing voices are impossible to ignore. Orson Welles had a voice that was called "a gift from God." Barbra Streisand's voice is legendary.

Most Taureans need little encouragement to work and make money. They attract jobs that have the greatest potential for the riches they desire. Money managers by nature, they have little fear of high numbers and know exactly how to hold on to money and make it grow. Professionally, Taureans are masters of advertisement and propaganda. They can create a package to fit any product. Constantly trying to fit content to image, they also make great architects and decorators. They do well in any field where connecting with people is important. Concerned more with emotional integrity than technique, they have the ability to stir feelings and lead others through the power of their personality. Spontaneous in the face of opportunity, they move quickly for a chance to achieve. Employers adore their persevering and reliable Taurean workers, who know it's only through commitment that something gets done. Musicians, singers, artists, and owner of galleries, Taureans combine their creative nature with a head for finance.

Taureans are asked to strengthen themselves through struggle. Talent that endures takes time to ripen. For Taurus, the second challenge begins when the talent is ripe. Then the test is adaptation. Can you blend, mold, or present your talent or belief without compromising its truth? Taureans sometimes must forego allegiance to a party, team, or family in order to be true to their talents.

The Taurean challenge is an enviable one: to see beyond surface beauty to the truth, and to have the wisdom and faith to transfer the truth to new experiences. Adding your special uniqueness to the lesson making it your own. Life for a Taurus is a process, that is meant to teach detachment; the gift that comes from the release of desire. Only one who has had everything, knows how meaningless possessions are without the driving force of life itself . . . love.

THE TAURUS ENVIRONMENT

The Taurus environment is either loving and indulgent or hard and disciplined. It caters to the emotions, and it supports the uniqueness of a soul. You're different, and that difference is what gives you your style. Taurus adds mystery, charm, magnetism, and intimacy to any combination. It demands the truth and adds richness and texture to whatever it encounters. When it's mature and disciplined, it provides moral boundaries, loyalty, and love. When it's raw and uncontrolled, it can be obsessive, self-destructive and rebellious. Attracted to beauty, it seeks perfection and demands change. Its burden is its restlessness, which comes from its constant struggle to rearrange chaos into order, to evolve and grow, to leave whatever it encounters eternally changed.

Taurus/*One* (April 28, May 1, May 10, May 19) Venus/Sun

PURPOSE: *To learn how to present your truth and protect it, using your ability to mask and hide without inhibiting your self-expression.*

"The people who get on in this world are the people who get up and look for the circumstances they want, and if they cannot find them, make them." The words of George Bernard Shaw provide the wisdom needed for the Taurus/*One* dynamic. These are seductive human beings who know how to present themselves to the world in order to get ahead and achieve. They're masters at creating images and their social skills are exceptional. Attached to truth and freedom, they don't deal well with authority. However, when Venus energy is strong, their ambition is masked behind their charm. Financial success will never be enough. If a Taurus/*One* is the CEO, with an expense account equal to the national debt and still unhappy, the answer is simple. The *world* told him this would make him happy. If he can connect with his inner voice, he can still turn things around. He might want to drive to work instead of taking the limo, or bring the needlepoint pillow he's been stitching to a high-powered lunch. One person's courage to be honest brings out the same in others. Best of all, the Taurus/*One* will be happy.

IF SPIRIT TAKES THE LEAD: With Spirit strong, principles are high, and the obsession for truth fills their life with battles. They refuse to present themselves with any kind of protection. However, truth without a mask puts the owner in danger. They need to learn the value of nuances and the skills of protection. Their mission is not to prove to the world they can see through its lies; rather, it's to learn how to play the game so they can impose their truth and receive acceptance for their ideas. Stop fighting and join the parade. Truth doesn't have to be forgotten; it just shouldn't be worn on a sleeve.

IF EGO TAKES THE LEAD: With Ego leading, the Taurus/*One* loves to party. Obsessive, manipulative, and a great liar, they are not who they seem. They have a shadow side and few souls enter their secret world. They are image makers, perfectionists, and lovers. They avoid commitment; they're attached to freedom. Gifted with charm, competitive to a fault, they're both mentally and physically strong. If, however, the Taurus side is in charge, they could be reclusive, lazy, and indulgent. They may go through life without moral boundaries, always trying to get their way no matter the consequences.

FRED ASTAIRE (May 10)

Dancer, actor, singer. His classic films include *Easter Parade, The Band Wagon, Daddy Long Legs, Funny Face,* and *Silk Stockings.*

Venus finds the perfect partner in Fred Astaire. The fluid style and good taste so innate in Taurus is obvious. Astaire changed the nature of dance in films, doing it with the class and exquisite taste that became his trademark. Another Taurean talent is bringing the essence of something to the surface. Astaire's ability to extract the perfect emotional meaning of each song he interpreted separated him from the mainstream. He nurtured his gifts with discipline, rehearsing a routine over and over again until it was perfect. The world rewarded Astaire's efforts, his distinctive voice, his flawless movements. He became a legend, not just because he was a great dancer, but because he presented his talents with superb and unequaled style.

JAMES A. BAKER III (April 28)

Chief of Staff and Secretary of the Treasury for President Ronald Reagan, Secretary of State for President George Bush.

Here we see the incredible organizational skills of Taurus used in a powerful and effective way. Referred to as "the best manager who's ever run the White House," Baker never confused his own views with his position. "My job is not to go into the Oval Office and advocate a view because I happen to believe it strongly. My job is to let the President know what I think is best politically."

As a young lawyer, Baker was a conservative Democrat. After the death of his wife, he was convinced by his country-club buddy, George Bush, to help him in his bid for the Senate. The experience transformed Baker into a pure Republican. Venus allows one to change parties, titles or position; its allegiance is to personal truth, not the package or the title. Mr. Baker developed his own style, demonstrating the ability to unify by presenting facts in a way that brought divergent sides together. Baker used his power to sway the public's opinion to the president's position.

Taurus/*Two* (April 29, May 2, May 11, May 20)
Venus/Moon

PURPOSE: To accept your uniqueness and sensitive emotional nature through your ability to use both pain and joy as strengths instead of weaknesses.

"Morality is not properly the doctrine of how we may make ourselves happy, but how we make ourselves worthy of happiness."—Immanuel Kant

Unable to separate feelings and issues, the Taurus/*Twos* can be great unifiers, creative geniuses and healers, or overwhelmed with emotions and feelings. Venus indulges the Moon's needs and idiosyncrasies, creating an excessive nature. In many cases it creates a unique soul with a heart of gold, a person who feels the suffering of others and extends a hand to help. But extremes are all too prevalent here. It's possible to become attached to anything, including sacrifice, pain, and suffering. Too much of anything, even understanding, kindness, and unconditional love, leads to trouble. Life has to have consequences. The Taurus/*Two* has to learn to slam the door, yell back, and if necessary, hit below the belt. Otherwise, they can end up wallowing in suffering, acting spoiled, or using drugs, alcohol, or sex to escape taking responsibility and living a life of discipline. When the Taurus/*Two* chooses his obsession, he can bring himself fame, fortune, or a great sense of personal satisfaction, either by creating something unique or helping others.

When this energy is blocked, it stirs up trouble, making the Taurus/*Two* vulnerable to poor mental or physical health. Boundaries are difficult for them and often dictated by pain. Self-understanding is important, so that the thoughts and feelings of others are not seen as their own. They must learn how to protect their differences and emotions, while at the same time not hiding or denying them. It is only when we embrace our weaknesses that we transform them into assets. Their task is to weave a mask that reveals and protects at the same time. The Taurus/*Two* must work on himself before he tries to influence others and he'll find that the Venus/*Two* energy can be imaginative, creative, sensitive, and rewarding.

IF SPIRIT TAKES THE LEAD: If Spirit is the leader, then sacrifice is the name of the game. They live for love, are drawn to the pain of others, and spend a lifetime trying to heal everyone but themselves. Obsessive, unique, and a loner, the emphasis is on others, inhibiting the development of their own identity. They need to remember, they've got to have an Ego before they can surrender it. It's important to take back their life, and when they know who they are, they can give it to anyone.

IF EGO TAKES THE LEAD: With Ego strong, so is protection. Intimacy could be a problem. A strong sensitive nature is hidden behind a facade that pretends that everything is all right. They don't react to life; they block experiences and deny the powerful feelings they hold inside. Frightened of their desire to feel and need, they look to possessions for fulfillment. A loner, they are attracted to different and unique people. Their need to express themselves is worked out through their interaction with them. Stop watching and start participating. Inside is a crazy, wonderful person.

SALVADOR DALI (May 11)

Surrealist Artist.

"I do not take drugs—I am drugs." This comment is a wonderful example of the addictive feelings of a Taurus/*Two*. Dali claimed that his waxed moustache was an antenna for the muses. A genius? Perhaps. Eccentric? Definitely. His trademarks include images such as lobster telephones, soft watches, and rain-filled taxicabs.

Dali was born after the death of an older infant brother. The issue of identity was a crisis for Dali. All his life he competed for the adulation his parents gave to the memory of their departed son, whose picture hung above their bed. Emotional and often ill, Dali rebelled against his authoritarian father. Surrounded by women—his overprotective mother, his unmarried aunt, his nurse Lucia, his sister and the maids in the kitchen—he used his eccentricity as a way of enraging his father and diverting attention from his own highly sensitive nature. Gifted with Venus's power of concentration, his artistic talent was evident early in life. With the timing and luck of a Taurus, his first teacher was an excellent artist who imparted the classical draftsman's skills needed to develop Dali's natural ability.

Dali married Gala, a clairvoyant and complicated woman ten years his senior. Gala was obsessed with releasing the full force of Dali's genius. The moon's need for a close, intense relationship encouraged Dali to surrender to her and allow her to take over the practical side of his life so he could devote himself to his artistic endeavors.

ZUBIN MEHTA (April 29)

Music director of the New York Philharmonic.

Born in Bombay, India, Zubin Mehta taught himself the violin from a record. At age seven, he was teaching piano and the violin. By sixteen, he was conducting full orchestras in Bombay. As a child, he suffered from spinal meningitis but the lucky timing of a Taurus was with him. The drug, sulfa, had just been made available. Although it cured him, Mehta was sent to a sanitarium for a year where he experienced loneliness and abandonment. His sense of isolation was reversed when his father, a talented musician who started the first symphony orchestra in Bombay, was given a grant to study the violin in New York for four years. This left Zubin alone with his mother, a Taurean dream.

It was in Sienna, Italy, that Mehta received his first opportunity as a conductor. An indisposed colleague couldn't conduct Tchaikovsky's Fifth Symphony scheduled for the following night. The professor asked if anyone else was familiar with it. Zubin raised his hand, although he had never studied it. "You must be ready to take a chance when it is presented to you," he said. "And when you get those chances, you had better do well or you may not get any others." Mehta used his Taurean courage to take a chance, and trust the power of Venus to concentrate and memorize. By the following evening he knew every note of the score. "I made half my career by jumping in at the last moment. I sometimes think my success was due almost entirely to the misfortunes of my elderly colleagues."

Taurus/*Three* (April 21, April 30, May 3, May 12, May 21) Venus/Jupiter

PURPOSE: To believe in yourself and take your place as a leader never losing touch with your sense of humbleness, which comes with the acceptance of fate.

"There is no great genius without some touch of madness."—Edgard Varèse. The Taurus/*Three* person has his own laws and God help anyone who interferes. When talented, no one can touch them. Burt Bacharach (May 12) is in a musical league all his own, as is singer James Brown (May 3). Excessiveness can be exhibited, since Jupiter tends to enlarge, expand, or support whatever it encounters. The Taurus/*Three* dynamic asks people to own their own importance, that is, to know their beliefs and not to depend on the opinions of others. They can be attuned to social change, and if truth and justice are their strengths, they might find themselves at the helm of a revolution. Determining their own boundaries is paramount to their growth. Otherwise, they may feel overwhelmed and victimized. However, if boundaries are overdeveloped, the Taurus/*Three* may find that their beliefs are in conflict with others or the law. The Taurus/*Threes* call the shots; however, once the ball is in motion, it is out of their hands. If they have chosen wisely, the results will bring home runs. If not, their friends will be writing to them in care of the Bureau of Prisons.

IF SPIRIT TAKES THE LEAD: Spirit loves *Threes* and Jupiter. However, too much Spirit makes truth and justice too powerful a priority. These souls fight and never surrender. They have charm and a positive attitude, but they also have a relentless will, impossible goals, and awesome accomplishments. They want to lead the world toward social change. They are rebels who need help with their personal lives, if they even have one. Unique, loyal, and supportive, they live by a moral code that makes a saint look bad. Intimacy is an issue and so is their need to make the world accept and respect the differences of all people.

IF EGO TAKES THE LEAD: Ego loves separation and with the *Three,* it guarantees a loner. These souls have authority issues, in fact, they must be in charge. Resilient and strong, they invented the word stubborn. If the Taurus side has a greater pull, then they may surrender their power, lose themselves in someone else's beliefs, and follow their rules. When they're not in charge, they lose their sense of values, and decision making is almost impossible. However, if they choose the path of self-empowerment, they make strong leaders, even if they lack a sense of compassion and sensitivity. They are righteous. They're convinced they know better, and before long, people believe them. It's hard to oppose someone who puts their entire being into whatever they do.

GOLDA MEIR (May 3)

Prime Minister of Israel.

Golda Meir is one of the greatest women of this century. She easily exhibits the strength and courage, the ability to hold to personal conviction so indicative of the Taurus/*Three.* Born in Russia in 1898, Golda immigrated to America with her family when she was three. Even as a young girl in Milwaukee, Meir fought constantly with her mother as well as her teachers. At fifteen, she left home and went to live with her sister in Denver.

Beautiful and magnetic in her youth, her strength of conviction, combined with her compassion and sensitivity, opened doors closed to others. David Ben-Gurion once called her "the only man in my cabinet." She yearned to see Palestine returned to the Jews, and for this she was willing to fight her entire life. Meir raised the money needed for Israel's survival. She traveled continuously and spoke around the world. Meir never used notes. She spoke from the heart and from her personal experiences. Present at Israel's Declaration of Independence, Meir went on to become her country's first woman prime minister. Before she died, she witnessed the signing of the peace treaty between Egypt and Israel.

GEORGE CARLIN (May 12)

Comedian.

Humor is the medium George Carlin chooses to channel the Taurus/*Three* energy. The desire for truth and justice is brought to the ridiculous in order to make its point. Choosing the idiosyncracies of language to speak out against convention and political double talk, George Carlin makes his audiences laugh their way to new awareness. *The Tonight Show* brought him national attention, but TV was too restricting for his imagination. After all, Jupiter refuses to be told what to do. Personal freedom is all that matters. This attitude, combined with Venus's quest for truth, can create the rebel with a cause, someone who refuses to be labeled. In the early seventies, Carlin risked his career by drastically changing his appearance. The tuxedo went, he grew his hair long, and directed his routines to a younger, more politically conscious audience. His topics were drugs, government, and censorship. Taurus/*Three* can bring conflict with the law. Carlin's routine entitled "Seven Words You Can Never Use on Television," got him arrested on charges of public profanity. However, his popularity remained intact.

Taurus/*Four* (April 22, May 4, May 13) Venus/Uranus

PURPOSE: To use your constant need for change and tension for a positive goal that will allow you to experience your personal truth and be a positive catalyst for others in their lives.

"You are unique, and if that is not fulfilled, then something has been lost," said Martha Graham, a true Taurus. With Taurus/*Four* the individual prevails. The challenge is for them to remain their own person while being part of a relationship.

A born catalyst, the Taurus/*Four* has the power to effect change through ideas, experiences, and sometimes just by their presence. They may be shunned because they're provocative, but they'll never be accused of being boring. This dynamic is restless and in a state of constant flux. Few people can keep up with their ability to transform the moment, arriving at a new place and perspective while others are still trying to understand something the Taurus/*Four* discarded ages ago. They are often misunderstood. But with maturity they begin to respect their ability to effect change. Hopefully, they use this ability in a positive way and not just to create trouble. These people reach a point in life when they don't care what others think. Their uniqueness brings them success. They bring excitement wherever they go. Their ability to handle many different things simultaneously astounds even their biggest fans. However, if they are indiscriminate and ruled by their need for excitement, they could find themselves wondering who is next to them in the morning. Too much togetherness makes them nervous. They need space to grow. Uranus tends to embrace ideas and causes rather than the personal or the intimate.

IF SPIRIT TAKES THE LEAD: If Spirit leads with the *Four,* truth and human rights are a priority. They can be a cause fighter, a rebel, or a good friend. They stand up for the truth no matter the consequences. However, there is a need for caution. They could dedicate their life to fighting every injustice or act of discrimination they encounter. Their adrenaline will be high, but they'll be alone on cold winter nights. Intimacy is a problem; boredom sets in, then they want to flee. They are dedicated to changing the world, but they need to work on their personal lives and learn how to serve their practical needs.

IF EGO TAKES THE LEAD: Ego here is strong, rigid, and unrelenting. These souls know what's right and wrong, it's their way or no way. Refusing to listen to anyone but themselves, they learn through crashing into the wall or facing the dire consequences of their actions. Discipline is important, the more the better. They look to themselves for all answers, or they give away all their power. Seldom centered or balanced, they fluctuate between being stubborn and abusive, and meek and martyrlike. Without faith or a belief in themselves, life is nothing but trouble.

AUDREY HEPBURN (May 4)

Actress, United Nations representative for children. Films include *Roman Holiday, Sabrina, Funny Face, Nun's Story, Breakfast at Tiffany's, My Fair Lady.*

Born in Belgium, the daughter of a Dutch baroness, Audrey Hepburn yearned to be a ballerina, but was too tall. Lacking self-confidence, it took time for her to believe in her own uniqueness. "When I was a little girl," she recalled, "my nose wasn't pretty and I was terribly thin. I was sickly too, and quite miserable about my prospects." Venus had given her the comforts of life, but it would be the rebel quality of Uranus that would help her find her own identity. During World War II, she became a courier for the Dutch Resistance in Holland.

Her career in films came after the war. By then, she had developed her own style. She easily achieved the position of one of the highest-paid actresses in film. Exhibiting the natural classic taste of Venus, she was nominated to the world's Best Dressed List several times.

The combination of Taurus/*Four* has the ability to cross boundaries where others struggle to pass. Audrey called several countries her home, including the United States and Italy. Socially conscious, she reached out to help starving children as a representative of the United Nations.

MOSHE DAYAN (May 4)

Defense Minister of Israel in 1967 during the historic Six-Day War and the Yom Kippur War.

Born in Palestine, he was raised on a kibbutz, which meant the simple luxuries of life were missing. What did exist were strong discipline, values, and hard work. Living in the ancient homeland of the Jews brought Dayan close to his roots and gave birth to a love of archaeology. The explosive quality of Uranus, its need for change and evolution, found the perfect setting in the volatile situation of the Jewish homeland. Dayan joined the Haganah, the Jewish underground dedicated to protecting their communities under the British rule. There he was taught the use of firearms and began military training. A natural leader, with an incredible eye for sizing up a situation and making quick, important decisions, he moved easily up the ladder of success. Drawing on Venus's ability to see the value and use of divergent things, he wrote a manual called *Fieldcraft,* expressing his ideas on the importance of using the natural terrain as part of military action.

Dayan's early childhood was not without creativity and love. His mother was a writer who contributed many articles to the local newspapers. His childhood friendships with Arabs forced him to deal with the issues of identity and to develop his own uniqueness. The need to survive, so much a part of a Taurean's consciousness, forced him to know his priorities and values.

With the capture of Jerusalem, the Taurean desire for unity and truth were expressed in his statement to the press. ''We have returned to the holiest of our sites, and will never again be separated from it. We have come not to conquer the holy places of others, nor to diminish by the slightest measure their religious rights, but to ensure the unity of the city and to live in it with others in harmony.''

Taurus/*Five* (April 23, May 5, May 14) Venus/Mercury

PURPOSE: To understand your truth, be aware of your intentions and the consequences of your actions so that choices and decisions don't lead you astray.

''Truth can only be experienced. It cannot be described and it cannot be explained.''—*A Course in Miracles.* That won't keep a Taurus/*Five* from trying. People born with this energy are multitalented and agile. They are capable of being forerunners of the future, creating or expressing themselves in a timeless way. The ability to understand the psychology of someone is provided by Venus.

Mercury secures the surface, seeking to link together missing pieces of a puzzle. Together, we have an inventor of incredible magnitude. New ideas come to them without struggle. In fact, new ideas can prevent them from dealing with the moment. They are obsessive, and the lesson of letting go is a challenge. However, whatever they do is done with wit, for Mercury is the prankster and practical joker. With an emphasis on youth, the simple and the ordinary, all Mercury souls have the ability to reach the masses or the common man. Halston took a basic cashmere cardigan and made it high fashion. Karl Marx produced a doctrine that exalted the masses. The Taurus/*Five* could put a peanut butter and jelly sandwich on the cover of *Gourmet* and it would become the rage. Their reflexes are as quick as their wit, their curiosity out of control, and their appointment book filled for the coming six months. Being busy keeps them running in circles. They need to save some time for rest and contemplation, things necessary for their growth.

IF SPIRIT TAKES THE LEAD: Spirit and the number *Five* creates stubbornness. Their intentions can be fanatical. The need to be true to a purpose, to be looked upon as good and special, may be their primary motivation. If their purpose is a lofty one, they could dedicate their life to a helping the poor or those who are denied personal dignity. Their need to create change and unify diversity could make them speak out publicly for what they believe. Perfectionistic, they never rest, and worry consumes them. They need to feel in control, but life seldom obliges them.

IF EGO TAKES THE LEAD: They need to be special, to appear more wonderful than anyone else. A master at manipulation, they have few moral boundaries, and thus anything is possible. They are talented communicators. Gifted with charm and seductive powers, they always get their way. They're versatile, and always on the go. Exceptional creators, inventors, and con artists, they know how to fulfill the desires of others which in turn gets them what they want.

VLADIMIR NABOKOV (April 23)

Poet, writer, teacher.

"A creation of perfect beauty, symmetry, strangeness, originality, and moral truth." Mary McCarthy on *Pale Fire*. If that's not a perfect description of a Taurus with the writing skills of the *Five*, I don't know what is. Taurus, always seeking truth, and the *Five*, always seeking reality, find a stage in Nabokov's novels and poetry.

Born in St. Petersburg, Russia, Nabokov grew up in a rich, cultured, and liberal family. He published his first book of poems at seventeen and at twenty, the family was forced into exile because of the Russian Revolution. Nabokov came to the United States and studied at Cambridge, Massachusetts. In 1925 he married Vera Stonim and moved to Berlin, where he continued to write poems and novels in Russian. He supported his wife and son by giving tennis and French lessons. His first English novel was *Maskinka.* Exhibiting the restless nature of the *Five*, Vladimir moved again, this time back to the United States. There, he taught at Wellesley and continued to write in English. His first big success was *Lolita.* The Taurus theme of seduction and the issue of youth provided by the *Five,* combines the dark side of both energies in a compelling story. The novel made him enough money to move to Switzerland. The *Five* is a trickster; it enjoys games of the mind and intrigue. Nabokov's novels are filled with twists and turns. "We speak," he once said, "of one thing being like another thing, when what we are really craving to do is to describe something that is like nothing on earth."

HALSTON (April 23)

The dress designer of the seventies.

"You're only as good as the people you dress," and dress them he did, from Lauren Bacall, and Liza Minnelli, to Candice Bergen and Jacqueline Onassis. Halston demonstrated the androgynous quality and fluid lines of the Taurus/*Five* in the tailored and simple lines of his clothes. He took the common and made it elegant and stylish. Patrick McCarthy, in *WWD,* said "Whether it was a cashmere sweater set, Ultrasuede shirt dresses, bottomless jackets, tie-dye caftans, or simple cardigans tied loosely around the shoulders, Halston's clothes were distinguished by their utter lack of contrivance."

Exhibiting the social side and versatility of Mercury with the beauty of Venus, Halston extended his talent to perfume and cosmetics. The containers of those products were works of art themselves. Surrounded by celebrities, his private lunches at his Sixty-eighth Street boutique, were coveted invitations.

Taurus/*Six* (April 24, May 6, May 15) Venus/Venus

PURPOSE: To strive for self-perfection through love, not judgment, channeling your obsessive nature into positive outlets.

"Self-respect is the fruit of discipline; the sense of dignity grows with the ability to saying no to oneself."—Abraham J. Heschel. Definitely a lesson worthy of attention here. Excess is rampant in the Taurus/*Six*. They are talented and creative and quest for truth. Perfection and genius are two curses of this combination. However, some decide it's too much work to be a perfectionist; they watch the world go by. This is a waste of their talents. What these people need is inner discipline, a strong sense of values, and the ability to say no to what they *think* they want.

Shirley MacLaine (April 24) used the Taurus/*Six* energy to her advantage, reclaiming her power and finding her spiritual center. Determining limits and goals is what Taurus/*Six* is all about. Without these internal disciplines, they can still achieve success, but might have a hard time holding on to it. Divine discontent is the constant companion of the Taurus/*Six*. It makes the Taurus/*Six* question himself, an important talent for any Venus person.

IF SPIRIT TAKES THE LEAD: Spirit finds Venus or the *Six* an easy playmate—too easy. With Spirit strong, perfection is the quest, and nothing is ever right. These souls either quit because they can't live up to their own impossible measures, or they strive constantly to improve and understand themselves, their motivations, and those of others. They're creative, desire unity and wholeness, and will do almost anything for love. They have an unquenchable thirst and passion for life. Their desire for truth keeps the soul always seeking and filled with divine discontent.

IF EGO TAKES THE LEAD: Ego and the *Six* have a seductive nature. These souls get what they want, when they want it. A love of luxury and physical possession, and a need for beauty are their obsessions. Desires rule, and so passion, love, fame, and fortune are all high on their list. They have an addictive nature. They can be a tyrant or a victim, depending on their mood, which changes constantly. Depression is a possibility, and so is the inability to take action. What helps is discipline and a strong spiritual cord.

BARBRA STREISAND (April 24)

Actress, director, singer, producer.

Whether before the camera or behind it, entertaining at President Clinton's inauguration or recording a new album, Barbra Streisand knows what she wants and doesn't settle for less. Demanding of herself, she uses the divine discontent of the Taurus/*Six* dynamic to continually push herself to new heights of creativity.

Life was not always easy. Streisand's father died when she was fifteen months old. "Emotionally my mother left me at the same time—she was in her own trauma . . . I didn't have any toys to play with, all I had was a hot-water bottle with a little sweater on it. That was my doll. . . . Growing up I used to wonder—what did I have to do to get attention? When I started to sing I got attention."

Streisand's mother told her daughter she'd never be a singer because she wasn't pretty enough and her voice was too weak. The lack of encouragement helped Streisand develop exactly what she needed, determination and a strong belief in herself.

The distinct quality of Taurus/*Six* or Venus/Venus is evident not only in Streisand's voice, packed with emotional power, but in her appearance, which she smartly refused to alter. Her manager begged her to change her name, fix her nose and sing more conventional songs. But her Taurus strength told her to be true to herself. Again, her instincts were right. Her uniqueness is a major part of her success.

SIGMUND FREUD (May 6)

The father of Psychoanalysis.

The deep inner workings of the subconscious mind finally got mapped and labeled. It had to be the work of a Taurus/*Six* person. The father of Psychoanalysis, Freud was born in Freiberg, Austria, and received his degree in medicine at the University of Vienna. Words like "id" and "superego" gave new meaning to why we are driven to behave the way we do. Freud described the pleasure principle—that pleasure is relief from painful tension, rather than positive enjoyment. Intensely close to his mother and overwhelmed by emotions, Freud needed to understand his feelings, and so he chose the path of reason and truth. He developed the process of psychoanalysis, creating a means for us to unravel our pain and find our center.

Taurus/*Seven* (April 25, May 7, May 16) Venus/Neptune

PURPOSE: To use the power of love to transform your life and the lives of others, without feeling a loss of control and power, or without judging or living in a faraway dream leaving your truth unprotected.

"If you can dream—and not make dreams your master . . ."—Kipling. Neptune has the power to create illusions and dreams. It can transport us to the heavens and keep us chasing clouds forever. Imagination is king with Taurus/*Seven* and those who have this dynamic rule the creative world. They are capable of accessing information privy only to the gods. Most Taurus/*Sevens* don't have a clue to their potential. Their incredible sensitivity and intuition keeps them on the defensive, and prevents them from using their energy to make their dreams become a reality.

Neptune is impossible to contain or control, so balance is difficult to achieve. What the Taurus/*Seven* needs is a process, something channeled through him. The choice can either be inspiration, creativity, visions, and spiritual quests; or, on the negative side, escapism (lying, drugs, or alcohol abuse), illusion, or deception. These people tend to see things in black-and-white. It's their need to clarify the chaos they feel. Meditation or prayer is powerful with this energy, and a spiritual mission is not uncommon. Evita Perón (May 7) or the Lady of Hope, as the Argentineans called their first lady, was considered a saint by the working classes. Given to excessive behavior, she loved luxury and her wardrobe included shoes sewn with precious jewels. However, her quest for power never overshadowed her ability to reach the hearts of the common man.

Taurus/*Sevens* must remember that the gifts of Neptune and the *Seven* are not tangible, and must not be claimed as their own. They are the instrument or channel through which the energy happens. They must learn to let go, and when they do, the universe has an opportunity to send a steady stream of blessings through them.

IF SPIRIT TAKES THE LEAD: Spirit is illusionary here. It believes that love has the power to heal all. And perhaps it does in the hands of a saint, but chances are they're saving some undeserving soul who is only depleting their energy. The danger here is lack of protection. They live in their dreams and hope for a perfect tomorrow. Their absence from the present allows anyone to take advantage of them and places great strain on their body. It's time to get back in the now and start dreaming dreams that they can grasp.

IF EGO TAKES THE LEAD: When Ego is strong with the number *Seven,* we have obsession and a will of steel. When they make up their mind, nothing gets in their way. They are perfectionists who can drive everyone around them crazy. A double life appeals to them. They show the world one side, but their truth is another. Good at deception they lack a sense of truth and consequences; they need to be careful with the law. A part of them feels as if they can do anything; another feels lost and alone. They've never felt connected. They hide their differences and yet are attracted to others who display their uniqueness.

EDWIN H. LAND (May 7)

Inventer of the instant-photo Polaroid camera.

Edwin H. Land didn't have a dream to manifest, he just wanted to please his daughter, who wanted to see the picture her daddy just took . . . immediately. What would the world do without the Polaroid camera?

Holding some 525 U.S. patents, Land once said, "I am addicted to at least one good experiment a day." His work in light polarization is pioneering. Some of his early inventions include polarizers that reduced the glare on headlights and nonglare Polaroid sunglasses. Neptune gives us visions and visionaries. Edwin H. Land is certainly one of them.

LIBERACE (May 16)

Pianist and showman.

Whether running the keys of his piano with exaggerated flair, or astounding Las Vegas audiences with the shimmering spectacle of his costumes and set, Liberace had no equal. Imagination reached new heights with this talented pianist who brought the concert piano out of the confines of concert halls and into the hearts of the masses. That's Venus evolving, once again. Liberace became the world's highest paid pianist, earning more than $2 million for each twenty-six week season. Unusually gifted, he played by ear at four, and by seventeen he was on scholarship. Though his popularity never waned, Liberace's personal life was rocky. Obsessiveness was evident in everything he did, from his diamond rings to his relationships. Sued for breach of contract by his male lover, he eventually died of AIDS.

Taurus/*Eight* (April 26, May 8, May 17) Venus/Saturn

PURPOSE: To risk yourself; to learn your truth and keep your goals and your moral boundaries from becoming too rigid.

"Good ideas and innovations must be driven into existence by courageous patience."—Admiral Hyman Rickover. Here the feelings of Venus must take a form and Saturn provides the container and the process. If they reflect each other's needs, they work well together; if they don't, the misrepresentation will be the cause of trouble. The Taurus/*Eight* is asked to be aware of duality. They must begin by asking, "Do I present myself the way I really am?" The package attracts. If it's misleading, then so will be the rewards.

To balance the Taurus/*Eight* energy requires continuous adjustment and no group is harder on themselves than these people. Driven to improve themselves, the Taurus/*Eights* never relax. Few of us change habits and appearances to reflect our physical or spiritual growth. We gain weight but refuse to buy clothes in the next size. My advice to all Taurus/*Eight* souls is to change. They need to shake up their world, alter their hemlines, wear the new shirt. They'll be surprised at how great it feels to acknowledge those urges so easily dismissed. The Taurus/*Eight* must learn to encourage their growth.

IF SPIRIT TAKES THE LEAD: With Spirit strong the soul is a perfectionist and a saint. They limit their ability to grow by their need to take on all responsibility. These souls believe in an ideal. They are incredibly talented but often don't succeed because they are their own worst enemy. They view themselves as supermen or superwomen and every mistake is blown out of proportion, self-worth is nonexistent. They try to please others and stay in control. Stress is common, and a nervous breakdown is likely unless a little rest and balance enter the picture.

IF EGO TAKES THE LEAD: With Ego at the helm, the soul is judgmental, critical, and never happy. Nothing is right, nor will it ever be. They are dictators who wants recognition and do whatever they can to get it. They're soft and insecure inside, and feel they must appear tough and unrelenting on the outside. They make enemies easily because they are often misunderstood. Others see them as uncompassionate; they don't give themselves a break, so why should they give a break to anyone else? They don't have a clear inner identity; they present a stiff and unbending facade to the world. Intimacy is a problem; they don't trust easily. They're afraid to take a leap of faith, but this is the only thing that will help them get on the road to healing.

I.M. PEI (April 26)

Architect of The John F. Kennedy Library in Boston; The East Building of the National Gallery of Art in Washington, D.C.

Born in Canton, China, the son of a prominent banker and economist, I. M. Pei has been successful in integrating the energies of East and West, of function and form, of Venus and Saturn, of Taurus and the number *Eight*. Believing his destiny is to discover the "middle way" between extremes, he designs buildings that balance rigid geometry and deep psychological needs. He is a link between modernism and tradition.

SUGAR RAY LEONARD (May 17)

Welterweight boxing champion.

Compelled by the Taurus/*Eight* energy to be truly represented, Sugar Ray Leonard demanded to be known for more than just his lightning fist and merciless combination punching. "I don't consider myself a fighter," said Sugar Ray. "I'm a personality."

When in harmony, the Taurus/*Eight* energy creates good coordination. Sugar Ray was definitely gifted in this department, winning thirty-three fights in a row. He lost only to Roberto Duran in 1980. Later, in a rematch in New Orleans, he beat him in eight rounds. Saturn, unfortunately, makes us pay for every gain. Sugar Ray was forced to retire from boxing when his retina detached eight months after a fight with Thomas Hearns. But he quit while still on top, having earned thirty-five million dollars. Balancing this energy is not easy. The rigidity of Saturn or the number *Eight* can lead to blows. Sugar Ray chose his form of punishment and made money doing it, a choice that proves he is also more than just a "personality."

Taurus/*Nine* (April 27, May 9, May 18) Venus/Mars

PURPOSE: To use the power of your magnetism to attract and repel whatever you desire; to learn to say no to unhealthy desires without feeling deprived, using your power to attract with good discrimination.

"Two souls with but a single thought, Two hearts that beat as one."—Maria Lovell. The perfect partners, Venus and Mars go together like Romeo and Juliet. They fit, they complement and they create an energy and magnetism few can ignore. People born with this energy have the power to topple countries, unite opposing forces, and get a date for Saturday night. They're the stuff legends are made of. But what they choose is the challenge. Romeo may have found the love of his life, but what good is love without a life? They have powerful desires and setting limits is not their specialty.

It is vital in this dynamic for the Mars energy to have a positive place for expression. The Taurus/*Nine* needs to be able to stand up for his rights and demand respect. Highly magnetic, Taurus/*Nine* is powerful, charismatic, beautiful, and charming. These people must own their power and their sexuality. It's a gift from the gods, and they don't like their gifts ignored. The Taurus/*Nine* needs to assert himself or herself in any situation. So go for the gold, ask out the girl you've been ogling in the library, and take a step closer to your dream. You have a winning combination, but you can't win until you play the game.

IF SPIRIT TAKES THE LEAD: These souls are willing to fight and die for what they believe. Obsessive, they know how to give their all. They merge with their truth and follow it wherever it leads. They are possessed with great charm, beauty, and style. They often present themselves as an ideal, and spend their life trying to fulfill their own idealistic goals. The quest is important here, not the attainment. They desire peace and harmony, but they must learn that to have them requires that they know how to fight. They long for the perfect mate, but their relationships are usually idealistic and personally unfulfilling.

IF EGO TAKES THE LEAD: When Ego rushes ahead, it's strong and seductive. These are the lovers who use love for personal gain or the experience of pleasure. Charismatic, charming, and impatient, they do whatever is required to accomplish their goals. No moral boundaries here. Impatient, demanding and controlling, they need to be first and best. Nothing is ever enough because they want it all. Competitive, ambitious and ruthless, they get ahead in the business world. Unafraid of consequences, comfortable with lying, life is about getting their needs met, and with their charm and persistence, they usually succeed.

MARGOT FONTEYN (May 18)

Ballerina.

''In history there will be a Pavlova, a Karsavina, a Spessivtzeva—and there will be a Fonteyn,'' said George Balanchine in honoring Fonteyn with the position of being the first non-Russian of her era to dominate ballet. Fonteyn made British ballet a world-class power and only at age forty-nine began to reduce her schedule and think of retirement. But, Rudolf Nureyev changed all that. The fluid, emotional and classic style of Venus met the powerful physical force of Mars, when Margot Fonteyn and Rudolf Nureyev met in London and danced *Giselle*. Twenty-seven curtain calls later, their names were linked forever in the hearts and minds of ballet aficionados. Together, they created something greater than their individual talents. Taurus/*Nine* seeks the perfect mate. When found, it's yin and yang at its finest. Although Fonteyn was his senior, it was Nureyev who cared desperately about technique. Fonteyn, like a true Taurus, was more interested in the emotional aspects of the performance.

Fonteyn's childhood was spent traveling with her engineer father and coffee-heiress mother. During five years in China, her mother managed to find a Russian to teach her daughter dance. On her return to England, Fonteyn was accepted at the Sadler's Wells Ballet school. Soon after her 1934 debut as a snowflake in *The Nutcracker,* she began to take on important roles. Fonteyn's legendary association with Frederick Ashton began at this time. In the years to come, he would create ballets especially for her. James Monahan expressed the unique quality all Taureans bring to the things they love. "She has been loved, not primarily for her virtuosity but for some genuine, poignant essence of personality which is all her own."

Sorrow came to Fonteyn's life when her diplomat husband was shot down on the streets of Panama and paralyzed. The violent side of Mars emerged and was experienced through her husband. Devoted to him, Fonteyn kept him alive with love and understanding.

CORETTA SCOTT KING (April 27)

Married to Dr. Martin Luther King, Jr., civil rights leader.

Dignity and style, two important qualities of Venus, are synonymous with Scott King's name. The daughter of a prosperous storekeeper from Marion, Alabama, Coretta was studying voice in Boston, Massachusetts, when she was introduced to Martin Luther King. Venus's ability to express the tides of social change were certainly activated in this union. Proposing to her on their first date, King, with Coretta at his side, would become the driving force behind the civil rights movement of the 1960s. Taurus/*Nine* needs the perfect partner. Spiritually, the couple might have fit like a glove, but Mrs. King's life was not easy. Her courage was tested constantly by bombs, shootings, and angry threats as the couple fought to bring equal rights to African-Americans in the South. King was dedicated to passive, nonviolent resistance, a position his wife upheld even after his assassination. "She has maintained a calmness," her husband said, "that has kept me going . . . and has a unique willingness to sacrifice herself for (the movement's) continuation." Scott King was the calm needed to balance the force and power of Martin Luther King.

SUMMARY

As the soul enters Taurus, the second stage of its journey, it must learn the process of discrimination and organization. The lessons and knowledge acquired in Aries during its search for truth in external things, must now be sorted and absorbed internally through a system of values. Our ability to understand our needs, to see beyond the lure of a pretty package and recognize the true sustenance of life, is the key to survival in Taurus. The body can live on bread and water, but the soul cannot live without truth, beauty, and love. When love is received and returned, a process begins that develops self-acceptance and courage. Discipline is necessary. With it, the soul is able to reach out and take the risks necessary to acquire the skills that assure survival.

Ruler of our desires, Taurus demands we understand the importance of what we hold close to our heart. Desires are magnetic; they attract whatever they need to fulfill their destiny, which is to unite with the object of their love. The Spirit longs for reunion with God. The body seeks God in earthly things. Thus it is the seeds of our yearnings, planted in the earth sign of Taurus, that brings us both happiness and pain. So do not take lightly the feelings you choose to covet, for they are the roots of what you will later sprout and the fruit you will later bear.

When you have forged your identity with the skill both to present and hide your truth, you are ready for the next stage of the journey, where the soul has a chance, in the forever active and curious sign of Gemini, to test, play with, and explore its choices and desires.

SELECTED SOURCES

Simon Callow   *Orson Welles: The Road To Xanadu*   Viking 1996
Niccolo Machiavelli   *The Prince*   Appleton Century Crofts 1947
Saul K. Padover   *Karl Marx: An Intimate Biography*   McGraw-Hill 1978
Irving Shulman   *Valentino*   Trident Press 1967
Evelyn Underhill   *Mysticism*   E.P. Dutton 1967
————*A Course in Miracles*   Foundation for Inner Peace 1992

Gemini

(May 22–June 21)

Quick, alert and never still,
Gemini has a very strong will.
Needing to ask, to search, to see.
It's driven by its foe, curiosity.
At parties with pranks, they're at their best.
They'll make you laugh, they'll never rest.
Choice keeps them going, they're on the run.
So put on your tennies and have some fun.

Ruler: Mercury   **Symbol: Twins**
Element: Air   **Number: Five**

The soul has entered the world through opposition in Aries, developed roots through inner struggle in Taurus, and now in Gemini, it's ready to explore. Freedom is the quest, but finding it is not a simple matter. Life has turned itself upside down, and what you see is not what you get. Ego, the ruler of the mundane world, and Spirit, representative of heaven, have decided to have some fun in teaching you the next lesson. Good and evil now have the same face, it's up to you to recognize them in spite of the costume they're wearing or the role they're playing. This is Clint Eastwood, (May 31) the tough guy who rescues the damsel in distress; this is Brigham Young, (June 1) the spiritual leader of the Latter-Day Saints, saintly and violent, lustful and a man of God. Tall and lean, Geminis represent a new shoot, a surge of growth, a thin and delicate creature, with the inner strength and courage to risk themselves in the unknown. Often gangly and uncomfortable with their bodies, they appear both awkward and natural, immature and wise. They are paradoxes and contradictions. Their personalities exclude and invite; they are majestic and simple, warm and cold. This is the phase of the journey where to survive you must be willing to change directions at any given moment. After all, life is a risk and and unless you're prepared to alter your course, you could meet your demise. In Gemini, there is no clear path to good and evil; survival depends on your ability to use both energies for your own end. Morality is purely personal, determined by the needs of the moment.

Gemini is the game of life. This is about winning and losing and experiencing both with equal detachment. Everything happens to illuminate your consciousness, to help you understand yourself and your journey.

Geminis may feel caught between their allegiance to their destiny and their desires. The world of your immediate needs is the world of the infant. Your world must expand to include more than just you; just *you* can only go so far. The need to change comes from the pain caused by *not* changing, and your desire to escape it. As you left Taurus, you had to pass over those two malefic stars, Pleiades, and Algol. They're there to make you uncomfortable, and to help you separate. Now, you're ready for anything. You hear a voice from within. This voice pulls you out of yourself and toward your destiny. Following that voice is risky; you step into the unknown and leave certainty behind. You want to go, and you want to stay. This doubling back creates consciousness, awareness of self. As you move away from isolation, you enter the process of Being. You need distance from yourself—objectivity—in order to understand who you are. To get distance, you must take action.

Consciousness is intention. It's the ethereal bridge that links you to where you're going. If you have strong intention, you'll encounter less resistance. Casting out your intention is knowing how to project yourself to where you want to be. It means using your imagination. See yourself there, then come back to you and move toward your intention through action.

We all have a small self and a large self. The small self desires only to nourish its own needs, to see through its own vision. This creates a world filled only with one's personal perceptions and experiences. To get to your large self, you need to view life through someone else's eyes. This is called projection. You put yourself in someone else's shoes, and for a short time you see his visions and learn through his choices. Then you can return to your world and use the knowledge for your own ends. That's all there is to transcendence.

Once you have experienced life through someone else's eyes you have entered your larger or universal self and are ready to recognize the fact that you are connected to the universe. In *Song of Myself,* Walt Whitman (May 31) wrote: "And I know that the spirit of God is the brother of my own/ And that all men ever born are also my brothers, and the women my sisters and lovers." Emerson called the larger self the oversoul, by which he meant a supreme intelligence or universal mind. Each of us is a part of the oversoul. By building a relationship with this higher mind, man can transcend everyday experiences. This is the goal of Gemini, to move away from isolation and the inner world of the infant and instinct out into consciousness and the world of others.

The ability to act creates the first conscious feeling—resistance. What propels the Gemini beyond the opposition is its desire for a direct experience or the desire to be in the moment. Being is terrifying because it implies the death of the moment and the birth of the next. Becoming is not a place, but a process.

The decision to reach out is an instinctual one. At some level the soul knows that to remain static is dangerous. Illumination or consciousness must occur. To alleviate the fear of a direct experience and to keep the moment at a distance the Gemini has developed several defense mechanisms: abstract thought, imagination and emotion. By placing an experience at a distance, you gain understanding gradually. Distance should be used as a means by which to move cautiously closer to the moment or experience not to maintain isolation. Abstract thought raises you above the now, objectifying the experience. You view the experience as an object, something outside of yourself, and thus you can analyze it and render it harmless.

In Gemini, knowledge is not always trusted. Ideas become objectified, thoughts become facts, and facts become laws. Once something is objectified you can play with it and make it your own. Geminis can transcend the object by embodying it, altering its expression, and returning it to the world as something uniquely theirs. It's creation and it's transcendence and it's what Gemini is all about.

Imagination takes you away from the now and into the future. It's better than the moment; you can imagine life to be whatever you want it to be. Geminis often get involved in relationships that are not in the here and now, either physically or emotionally. They prefer to dream about the person and create them in their own image. Emotions are another form of protection; they take us into the past and out of the now. They add drama, spice, and texture to a story but they're not the story. Emotions make us long for what is lost, not appreciate what we have. They support imagination.

Gemini is also about maintaining two points of view, yours and someone else's. If you can't hold two opposing views within yourself, you will judge others. Everything is seen as a threat to your perspective. Instead of learning from differences, you will try to avoid or deny them, obliterate and remove them. When you feel strong, the desire and needs of others, their opinions and their actions, do not affect you; when you feel weak and unsure of who you are, you feel easily threatened. Fear makes us recoil; confidence makes us reach out. Fear is a major obstacle for the Gemini; it emerges with thoughts of limitation. Choice becomes the demon the Gemini cannot face. For those who can't choose androgyny—or the middle way is an option. This is a real identity crisis; the soul is unable to choose its sex, male or female, and so it becomes bi-sexual.

The avoidance of identity throws the soul into depression. Without a clear sense of the self, Geminis may feel as if they are living in a house without a foundation. The desire is to disappear. They imagine themselves shadows rather than full human beings. Life seems cold and lonely. The desire to break free of their isolation is overwhelming. Without any connections to the outside world, thoughts of death abound. Life itself becomes undesirable.

The good news is that it's only a temporary moment every mutable sign must go through just before the leap of consciousness, before one crosses the chasm of self to others. Something is ending and something is about to begin. Despair is great motivation. Use your misery as a springboard to your higher self. The way out of isolation is through others. By projecting oneself into the world of another, the soul experiences life from a new perspective. This is how you transcend your boundaries. What needs to die is your outmoded, infantile perceptions of the world. Who you project yourself into is determined by what qualities you have owned in yourself and what qualities you feel you lack. What you believe to be missing is what you will seek.

Choice and freedom do not conflict. Freedom is found not by the avoidance of commitments, but through the acceptance of limitations and responsibility. We limit ourselves through choice, but that limitation provides the necessary boundaries within which to create. Taking responsibility gives us the strength to meet our resistance and move forward toward our goal.

Many Geminis get pulled into the challenge to unravel, expose, or unfold whatever is hidden and secretive, and if they don't have a strong sense of direction, an inner voice that reminds them of their goal, they will become lost.

Details can either hold you back or help you move forward. If you're still in your small self, details can strangle you or provide an anchor, something to keep you from being pulled into the void. "We're afraid of being sucked into life. We need the constrictions of extraneous activity—only then can we devote our time to meaningfulness."—Kafka. However, if you have reached your larger self, everything you do contributes to the building of your foundation. In Gemini the whole is understood through the sum of its parts. Geminis seek to put details into their larger context. Ralph Waldo Emerson said, "The main part of life is made up of small incidents and petty occurrences. The test of virtue is how a man lives in these daily experiences."

Limitations can help the soul reconnect with itself. When the inner world is sought, the outside world becomes a hindrance. Sounds, smells, and activity are a distraction. The soul turns within and seeks the spark of creation from silence. God is silent, and to be close to Him, so must you be. Liberation is found in the night, in the unconscious and in solitude.

The quest to reach a pure state is Gemini. For Gemini the past, present and future are one. They seek a fluidity in life. This is synchronicity. What makes it happen is being in the moment. The more committed you are to the now, the stronger your past and your future emerge. Choose an identity and you highlight the things that enhance that identity, refuse to choose and everything remains in a fog. Your commitment to the moment defines your power in that moment. However, that means you must be responsible for that moment and whatever it entails. A moment is duality in action. It's the state of Becoming. When you choose to remain uncertain and undefined, your past may be cloudy and your future stuck in fantasy. Marilyn Monroe searched for an identity and found one in the women she created for the world to love, but it only represented a piece of herself. Her identity crisis was reflected in the confusion of her past—she was abandoned by both parents and never knew her father. Geminis not anchored in the moment don't trust the past or the future.

Truth for a Gemini is not simple to find. The challenge is to recognize it even when it's surrounded by lies, hidden, or out of place. Instinct and experience are what they need to rely on.

How God is experienced depends on our consciousness. In Gemini, God is either humanized to the point of being petty, wicked, and small, someone a Gemini can make a deal with—if you give me this then I'll do that—or he is an unfathomable being that calls us to hear his voice and follow him into the unknown. It is "the play" of God that must be experienced in Gemini. This is the game of life and God is the master player. The world is nothing more than your creation; perception has determined the world you see. Your challenge is to conquer your environment, not be victimized by it. When you play, you act spontaneously, taking risks, responding to life rather than trying to control it. Whenever you play you call on God and Spirit to join you in your creation. This invites luck or grace into your life.

Dissatisfaction is a result of not being in the moment. If you live in your imagination, then nothing in the now is ever enough. The dinner is never cooked to perfection and the world could be a better place. The Gemini can be unavailable, noncommittal, remote, mysterious, or uncertain. They seek things in the distance because that's where they live. If you want to be with a Gemini, pack your bags. They never stay in one place too long.

Gemini rules siblings and the immediate environment. You learn how to play with your sisters and brothers. Each day you choose a different role. Soon you've been them all: the mother, the father, the sheriff and the bad guy. Siblings are important to a Gemini. They usually have many and their position in the hierarchy is their first encounter with fate. If they're the first child they have all the choices of which role they will choose in life. If they're the last child, then the role of good student, athlete, and rocket scientist may be taken and the only way they can get attention is by becoming the rebel. Of course they can compete for positions already taken, but most children follow the path of least resistance. The catch is to choose a healthy role and not one that attracts negativity or punishment. Remember, sooner or later you'll have to play more than one role. The message is not to get stuck in one way of responding to life or you'll find yourself in a crisis that demands you change. Pat Boone lost his popularity when his wholesome values were in conflict with the times. He refused to gyrate with Elvis and the Beatles, or kiss Shirley Jones on screen.

A Gemini's environment needs to be mastered or it will master them. Often, they have tough beginnings. Of course, this is to get them out of their childhood and on their way. Play is often denied the Gemini child. Remember, we seek what is missing in our lives. Judy Garland had a demanding youth. She was performing at the age of two. Once she was discovered, she represented the innocence and yearnings of youth, the very experiences she never had. Brooke Shields (May 31), was another Gemini child star performing sexy scenes long before most children knew what the word meant. And Josephine Baker (June 3), the black entertainer who took Paris by a storm, gave up her youth to escape a bad environment, marrying at the age of thirteen. Ralph Waldo Emerson's father died when he was young and his mother supported the six children. On very cold days, Emerson shared his winter jacket with his older brothers, meaning he could go to school only on alternate days. Leslie Hope, known to the world as Bob Hope (May 29), had six brothers, an alcoholic father who didn't always provide for the family, and an overworked mother. Hope overcame his environment and created a classy image for himself. Remember, you have the power to choose your role and change it. Bob Dylan (May 24) is a master at changing his identity. Born Robert Zimmermann, he has changed his name and his style on a regular basis. Define your existence and remember that risk is part of the package.

Gemini is the sign of the common man, of the everyday things of life, and when you're with a Gemini, those simple things become special. They have the ability to represent or reach the masses. At one time Pat Boone's (June 1) image personified mainstream America. Walt Whitman dressed like common workingmen and exalted them in his poetry. Geminis or *Fives* are drawn to the most basic elements of life: the smell of the earth; the sounds of a market.

Spirit and ego have quite a challenge in Gemini; they have to be able to play each other. Spirit gets to disguise itself as the bad guy and Ego appears as godly. With Ego strong, selfishness and ambition are strong. Geminis want to be recognized and chosen for what they have to offer. This is the beginning of envy, jealousy, and the desire to use everything for their own end. Siblings are usually first on the list of people envied. Remember the story of Cain and Abel, the first siblings. God favored Abel's sacrifice over Cain's and that made Cain so angry he killed Abel.

Justice is an issue, and it, too, is a paradox. To punish or take vengeance hurts the person who punishes and can prevent his happiness. The need for justice must be recognized, but in actuality, it is impossible. God solved the problem by marking Cain on the forehead, protecting him from others, but making him live with the knowledge of what he had done. Thus jealousy and violence are held in the heart. Good is in evil, evil is in good. They are interwoven paths that lead to the same place. Sin or desire must be conquered. God says to Cain, "... sin is lurking at the door; its desire is for you, but you must master it."

In Gemini, Spirit delves into the unconscious and helps the soul bring to light what has been hidden. This is how we learn to make a bad situation good, or how to turn something around to our advantage. Ego may cause an injustice, but the results can be understanding and healing. You've got to enter the wound to extricate the bullet. Spirit may send you help through an outcast, someone you or the world sees as worthless. If you turn your back, you're the one who loses. Ego, meanwhile, is having fun deceiving through playing the role of martyr, dealing out forgiveness when rage is what the soul feels. It will speak the right words, perform the right actions, and use your innocence to get whatever it desires. This is Brigham Young sanctifying the massacre of the gentiles, because the Mormons themselves had been persecuted. Good and evil are found in one face. Ego's mission is to hold the fragmented pieces of identity together by the sheer power of its will. Ego feels empowered by Spirit's apparent absence, free to commit acts without moral consciousness or fear of consequences. Mercury, Gemini's ruler, is often accused of immorality. It plays the middle road all the way.

Gemini is the sign of the scapegoat. From Abel's grave came rebirth and God's sacrifice of his son Jesus Christ for our salvation. But sacrifice or martyrdom can be negative if it happens because everyone is avoiding responsibility. Every group needs a person in which to deposit the negative energy of the group. If your identity is not strong, this could be you. Geminis are often the victims of others who want them to be responsible for their mistakes. When the position of sacrifice is made voluntarily, it can benefit everyone. But when it is imposed against your wishes, then you'll find yourself angry, hurt, and withdrawn from the world. Taking more responsibility than is necessary or taking none at all is a Gemini conflict that constantly needs renegotiating. If you have a strong identity, you won't be chosen as the scapegoat. Only those with cloudy intentions will be picked for the sacrifice. This is survival of the fittest.

Geminis are very dexterous. They are good dancers and athletes. They're natural jugglers, whether it's apples and oranges or dates in their little black book. They easily can change something simple into a web of complication. If your mate is a Gemini, change your concept of togetherness. You and me includes at least ten other people. A Gemini's heart can expand to include a miniuniverse. Find your spot and don't leave it, even for a second, or when you return you'll have to ask someone to leave.

Choices are a Gemini's enemy. For a Gemini, all consequences of any action must be considered. If I wake her up, she'll use the shower first. If I don't, then I'll have to make the coffee. If they're superstitious, it gets worse. Getting out of bed on the left side is bad luck. The bed itself should be placed in an east–west direction like the movement of the sun across the sky. The person sleeping should not be touched by moonlight. Just how detailed and complex is the Gemini's life? It doesn't matter that all these options were considered in a blink of the eye. Their mind is a computer, but even a computer can get overloaded and shut down.

Geminis occupy a pivotal point in the cycle of becoming. Gemini rules perception and perception determines everything else. According to *A Course in Miracles,* "Perception is a mirror, not a fact. And what I look on is my state of mind, reflected outward." Perception is a choice made from learned behavior. We all have trouble separating information from assumption. Transference happens to the best of us. So what to do? Begin by identifying your perceptions, the ones that always get you in trouble, and know that it's all right to choose a different point of view. Differences are what makes life interesting.

The dilemma of Gemini is avoiding entanglement in the web of their own making. If they lie, they're good at it and so they continue until they get caught. They're comfortable with intrigue, strings attached and IOUs. They're good at bartering, selling, and maneuvering anything and anybody. They make great strategists and good leaders because they can handle many different kinds of people and projects at one time. Geminis have a special understanding of and connection with the common man and so we find many great political leaders born under the Gemini sun, for example, Presidents, George Bush (June 12) and John F. Kennedy (May 29).

Geminis love the mysterious, the distant, and the hard to reach. They need to go inside something or someone to understand what makes them tick. If your mate is a Gemini, he'll want to know ever last detail about you. Jealousy is also a Gemini emotion. They want to possess not just the body but every glance, every gaze, every thought. They desire intimacy. They want to eliminate the gap between themselves and the other. This kind of intimacy usually is not accomplished by proximity. Geminis struggle at the same time to be close and to keep their distance. If you're dating a Gemini, remember, get close slowly, or once you become real you may become history. As far as qualities are concerned, the Gemini will probably seek someone who is stable and well defined, someone who slows them down and makes them finish their process of self-discovery.

Geminis will probably have many relationships before they settle down, but when they do, they can be loyal. Remember, commitment is not easy, but their longing for security helps them take the plunge. The good news is they carry their curiosity and love of experimentation into the bedroom. They've probably tried all sixty-four positions of the Kama Sutra, the classic Indian love treatise, and perhaps even invented a few of their own. When

Geminis know you're serious and trustworthy, their resistance dissolves. However, do not get jealous when your chameleon's eyes never stop roaming around a room, or glancing at the next table at a restaurant. They are addicted to looking. Give your Gemini some free rein, but don't add extensions to the leash. They need to know just how far you'll allow them to go. Once their boundaries are established they'll be content. They need change and excitement, but in the confines of security.

As far as career is concerned, Geminis do well with anything that requires imagination and communication. They love to travel, but since the profession of vagabond is not too practical when you're over thirty, it's a good idea to think about a more reliable career. Long hours and commitment can have their rewards. Broadcasting, writing, sales, teaching, law or advertising are professions at which Geminis excel. They're good with paperwork and figures. Be an accountant, become the secretary a boss can't live without. Just don't forget you need diversity and a place to use your mental agility. Your problem is sticking with one thing, so pick a profession that offers variety.

The Gemini artist can reproduce exact details or turn away from appearances and create abstract art which can lead the viewer toward a dream state that invokes the unconscious. Here, art desires a breakthrough, something that will free the viewer from his or her limited perceptions.

The Gemini environment presents constant choice. Choice creates the need to judge, to reject, and assures a certain number of mistakes. If you're not discouraged by disappointments, but use them as building blocks, you're on the road to success. "If I had to live my life again, I'd make the same mistakes, only sooner."—Tallulah Bankhead. Anthony Robbins has based a whole philosophy on this perception. "There is no real success without rejection. The more rejection you get, the better you've learned, the closer you are to your outcome." One thing is for sure, Geminis who are in touch with their larger self have a positive view of life and tomorrow.

Gemini is the first phase of the journey where knowledge outside oneself is acquired. The moral decisions made in Taurus must now adjust to those of others and your environment. When you can keep your truth and present that truth with different faces, you have learned a needed lesson in survival. Gemini's are driven to explore, discover and experience life, in order to gather information that will facilitate their choices. However, having to choose fills the Gemini with fear: freedom may be compromised, or a better choice may be lost once a decision is made. Remember, it is not the choice, but what you do with it, that matters. The lesson is to turn whatever hand fate plays you into your advantage. When you can take a difficult beginning and make yourself a winner, you've learned your lesson. As you gain experience and risk yourself you learn that you are not alone but a part of a larger picture and connected to everything and everyone you have or ever will encounter.

THE GEMINI ENVIRONMENT

🌙 😊 😊 🌙

The Gemini environment demands you know how to use whatever is on your path for your own end. If you don't, it will use you. The variety of alluring objects is endless. What you need to know is how to choose only things that will help you reach your goals. A strong identity is vital to not being manipulated. If you're still in the clouds about who you are or where you're going, solve this dilemma as quickly as possible. Without definition, you'll only get more confused. Your mission is the ability to be versatile, to change your face and your role to fit the moment. If you can't, the confusion of life will keep you chasing your tail. The Gemini environment needs to be mastered or it will make you seem like a victim of chance.

Gemini/*One* (May 28, June 1, June 10, June 19)
Mercury/Sun

PURPOSE: To use intrigue and camouflage as a means to accomplish your goals, instinctually knowing when to make a stand and state your truth.

"Self-expression must pass into communication for its fulfillment."—Pearl S. Buck. The *One's* desire for freedom and self-expression finds itself challenged in Gemini. These are souls willing to fight for the oppressed, eager to change the world into a place where everyone has the freedom of choice to be who they so desire. The challenge here is flexibility, and their tendency to become attached to truth and not see that freedom also exists in restrictions and responsibility. The Gemini/*One* is challenged to understand the potential and limitations of the masks he chooses to wear.

Gifted with writing and oratory skills, they have high principles and a tendency to be stubborn. They need to remember there is more than one way to pursue the truth and that when they meet an obstacle, it's up to them to transcend it. They have the power and the magic. Able to live for someone else, to give their life for a cause, Gemini/*Ones* need to remember they are here for their *own* journey. They can't let their own paths become secondary to someone else's. They should exchange ideas and explore other worlds, but bring it all back and make it their own.

IF SPIRIT TAKES THE LEAD: With Spirit strong, so is the desire for freedom from all limitations. These souls are eager to sacrifice themselves to help others achieve liberation—whether it's from an oppressive government or a controlling boyfriend. Courageous to a fault, they risk themselves for the slightest injustice.

Their unbending nature causes them many unnecessary hardships. The world will use their need to be right and their desire for truth against them. They can be the scapegoat of a group. They take on too much responsibility or none at all. When they learn to hide or disguise the truth and let unimportant slights pass, they'll find life can also be fun.

IF EGO TAKES THE LEAD: With Ego inflated, deception is at an all-time high. These souls know how to appear as anything but themselves. They can mold their personalities to be what you want, and they'll say what anyone wants to hear. They deceive themselves until life demands they be present, then fear takes over and they're gone. Good at taking advantage of any situation, they know how to use their talents, their fame and their abilities for their own end. The need for attention is strong, but so is the fear of discovery. They are charming and mysterious, passive and aggressive. They can recoil when close to being exposed. Their greatest fear is that someone will discover that underneath everything they do is a frightened, helpless person.

F. LEE BAILEY (June 10)

Defense attorney.

His clients have included Albert DeSalvo (the Boston Strangler); Charles Schmidt, Jr. (the Pied Piper of Tucson); Dr. Sam Sheppard; Captain Ernest Medina (of the My Lai Massacre); and Patty Hearst. He also was part of the Dream Team defending O.J. Simpson.

The reason and intellect of the planet Mercury prevails in Bailey. Choosing to fight for the underdog, he finds his identity in saving those whom the world has already judged. This is a prime example of good and evil intermixed. The daring of this sign found its outlet when Bailey flew as a jet fighter pilot in the marines. His intellect was evident when he scored one of the highest academic averages at Boston University's Law School. Drawn to the pen, like most Geminis, he has written sixteen books, has had his own television show, and has been a regular legal expert for *Good Morning America.* And yes, this Gemini was married more than once . . . four times, last count.

JUDY GARLAND (June 10)

Singer, actress, legend.

Born Frances Gumm, Judy's was not a planned birth. In fact, her mother tried to abort her several times. Once she was born, she became the apple of her father's eye. Competitive, like a true *One,* she wanted to be on stage. When she was only two, she raised a fuss until she got her chance. On New Year's Day she sang ''Jingle Bells'' at her father's theater. She brought down the house and had to be carried offstage because she wouldn't stop. Never called anything but Baby before she was a teen, Judy struggled with finding an identity separate from her incredible voice. Her voice had the power to express emotions well beyond her years. Judy's life was a typical Gemini roller coaster. She fluctuated between success on film, drug abuse, and failed marriages. The chaos of a Gemini's environment eventually killed her at the age of forty-seven. Her most famous movie was *The Wizard Of Oz,* a classic that will keep her a child in the public's memory forever. Her theme song, ''Somewhere over the Rainbow,'' was from this film and it symbolized her own quest for something beyond the life and environment she herself had failed to overcome.

Gemini/*Two* (May 29, June 2, June 11, June 20) Mercury/Moon

PURPOSE: To use the feelings and imagination of others to open you up to your own creativity without avoiding the direct experience and the truth.

''Whenever I have to choose between two evils, I always like to try the one I haven't tried before.''—Mae West. Now doesn't she make it sound like fun? The two evils for the Gemini/*Two* are mind and emotion. They both try to keep the person from a direct experience and from the truth. When mind and emotion work together, logic directs the creative spirit to action, and doesn't allow it to wallow in self-absorption. But when mind and emotion oppose each other, one pulls the other out of its chair. The Moon is intuitive, emotional and eccentric. Mercury is cool and mental, with the common touch. Gene Wilder (June 11) exhibits the eccentricity of the Moon in his characters. Teamed with Mel Brooks in *The Producers* and *Blazing Saddles,* insanity reached new levels of mass appeal. Bill Walsh, the 49ers field boss, said of quarterback Joe Montana (June 11), ''He is one of the coolest competitors, one of the greatest instinctive players this game has ever seen and I think he's just getting started.'' Instinct is the gift that will serve the Gemini/*Two* in everything they do.

Mercury/Moon people can have distinctive physical features like Bob Hope's nose, Stacy Keach's (June 2) harelip, and Gene Wilder's bug eyes. Denying emotions can create physical or mental problems for the Gemini *Two.* J.F.K. was a sickly child. He had asthma, a bad back, and a roster of childhood diseases. His personal feelings were considered only after he fulfilled his father's political ambitions. As a result, intimacy was a problem that plagued John Kennedy throughout his life. Loners by nature, they fear having the love they so desperately desire.

IF SPIRIT TAKES THE LEAD: With Spirit soaring, these humanitarians are at their best. The needs of others come first, healing, sharing, and nurturing are given spontaneously. Caught in their own past pain, they use it to connect with the wounds of others. This habit keeps them out of the moment and shields them from having to take responsibility for themselves. They need to come back to the direct experience and help others from a position of strength, not because they can't say no. They make great leaders in the face of danger. They protect others instead of themselves. Without an emphasis on Ego, they can easily lose their way because they can't turn their back on someone else's pain.

IF EGO TAKES THE LEAD: Ego and the Moon are not compatible. When they get together, fear takes over, and the soul recoils from life through isolation, flights of imagination or absorption in the past. Avoidance and denial are the name of the game. They will only feel safe and protected when they acknowledge their place and needs. Leave the nest of infancy and embrace their higher self. Share their feelings with someone else.

JACQUES COUSTEAU (June 11)

Underwater explorer, writer, and TV personality.

"I don't think it's good to categorize human beings, but if you have to categorize me, I think I am an explorer. I want to see what is underneath." Excitement and an adventuresome spirit finds a willing soul in Jacques Cousteau.

Born in St. Andre de Cubzac in France, he later entered the French Naval Academy. Exhibiting the courage and daring of this sign, he worked for the French Resistance during World War II. He earned the Legion d'Honneur and the Croix de Guerre. Cousteau is responsible for many inventions such as the Aqua-Lung, frogman breathing apparatus, minisubs, Bathygraf Cinecamera, and the Deepsea Camera Sled. The first underwater research colonies were developed by him and he has produced more than fifty films. His nurturing and protective side finds an outlet in his work for Planet Earth and the Cousteau Society.

MARVIN HAMLISCH (June 2)

Pulitzer Prize-winning composer and pianist. Record-breaking winner of three Academy Awards in one evening. (Two for *The Way We Were,* One for *The Sting.*)

The youngest student ever to be admitted to Juilliard, Marvin Hamlisch has won Academy Awards, the Pulitzer Prize, and nine Tonys. The Moon, often indulgent, finds its ultimate expression in a Jewish mother, like Mrs. Hamlisch. No demand was too outrageous. If Marvin wanted an ice-cream sundae at 1:00 A.M., he got it. Creativity is also a product of the Moon. Early in life, it was Mercury and the power of observation that dominated. Marvin copied everything he heard on the radio and later, show tunes. "I had no style of my own. Whatever I heard, I imitated." Marvin learned from others, then made the work his own. That's what being a Gemini is all about. Eventually, Marvin found his signature sound. His film scores include *Ordinary People, Sophie's Choice,* and *A Chorus Line.*

Gemini/*Three* (May 30, June 3, June 12, June 21)
Mercury/Jupiter

PURPOSE: To learn from the belief systems of others and from them to construct your own truth and sense of justice; to become a leader through your ability to apply your wisdom and knowledge to any situation.

"A soul occupied with great ideas best performs small duties."—Harriet Martineau (June 12). To handle the big things in life we must first be able to take care of the everyday challenges. Jupiter or *Threes* have the philosophical approach and the wisdom from experience to get ahead. Mercury is the masses and when you combine it with Jupiter, you've got a leader of people. These souls know how to take advantage of anything that comes their way. Josephine Baker, the black entertainer who took Paris by storm, used what made her different to make her a success. Foreign places bring good luck to *Threes*. They love to travel and expose themselves to new places and ideas. George Bush, the forty-first president of the United States, was better at foreign affairs than domestic issues. A Gemini/*Three* who is still living at home hasn't come into his own.

IF SPIRIT TAKES THE LEAD: Spirit soars with the number *Three*. It feels so strong it bangs its head on heaven and comes crashing back to earth. These souls are the boss, and they want to transcend and overcome everything they encounter. Attracted to impossible feats, they fill their lives with too many tasks and too much responsibility. Nothing gets done. They need a dose of humility and a respect for weakness in order for true spiritual work to unfold. They should honor daily life and use their leadership qualities to organize their own world before they tackle everyone else's. This way, they won't lose sight of truth, and spend their lives fighting for freedom and some distant cause.

IF EGO TAKES THE LEAD: With Ego and the *Three* strong, nothing less than ruling the world will suffice. These souls have mystery, magic and presence. People notice them and they listen. They make great politicians, diplomats, and businessmen. The danger is their fear. They are lonely, and run from commitments and intimacy. They seek power, not love.

JEAN-PAUL SARTRE (June 21)

Existentialist philosopher.

Sartre expressed ideas on virtually every subject and used his prestige to defend the rights of the ultraleftist group. For a while, he was revered for protesting the Gaullist regime and America's involvement in Vietnam. The issues of justice and Jupiter found a willing advocate in Sartre. "The task of the intellectual is not to decide where there are battles but to join them wherever and whenever the people wage them. Commitment is an act, not a word." His philosophy mirrors the Gemini theme. "Each lives in his own world, each creates his own situation. Frequently, this existential choice is buried in a lower level of consciousness. But to become truly alive, one must become aware of oneself as an 'I'—that is, a true existential subject, who must bear alone the responsibility for his own situation.''

TONY CURTIS (June 3)

Actor.

From poor beginnings, not uncommon with Mercury/Jupiter energy, Bernie Schwartz found himself a new name and became a popular matinee idol. His good looks opened the doors in Hollywood, but then took him on a journey for which he was not prepared. The persona of Jupiter kept demanding he live up to a larger-than-life image. He couldn't, and drug addiction followed. However, Curtis did manage to forestall his demise, creating himself as he went along. Curtis epitomizes the incredible versatility of the Gemini/*Three.* As an actor, he worked in comedy and drama. One of his most popular roles was in *The Great Impostor,* a true story of a man capable of becoming expert in any profession he chose, a perfect part for the Mercury/Jupiter man. Unfortunately, Curtis's personal life exhibited the same restlessness inevitable with Gemini/*Threes.* Known for his womanizing, he has been married several times.

Gemini/*Four* (May 22, May 31, June 4, June 13) Mercury/Uranus

PURPOSE: To be individualized enough to share your hopes and dreams with others, without compromising your own; to be able to set boundaries so that your humanitarian energy is not used against you, but helps you establish truth and justice in the world.

"One of the most important results you can bring into this world, is the you that you really want to be."—Robert Fritz. It doesn't matter what everyone else is doing, the Gemini/*Four* does it her way, even if it means walking alone. The individual prevails. The Gemini/*Four* takes her vacation in San Salvador during the revolution. She moves to the city when everyone she knows is leaving. She wears her thrift shop find to an exclusive dinner party.

A loner, the Gemini *Four* gives others their space and rarely gives advice. However, everyone is always trying to tell her what to do. Differences are always threatening to others, so the Gemini/*Four* should try to be more discreet and she'll have less trouble.

The opposite might be the case. If the Gemini/*Four's* space has been invaded without her permission, her mission is to use her repressed will to assert.

Gifted with a keen intelligence and fast mind, the Gemini/*Four* can easily finish most people's sentences or stories long before they do. Her genius, talent, and impatence encourages her to take on too much. She is restless by nature, and constantly assaulted with ideas and changes. Things in life happen to her suddenly, and without preparation. She never ends up where she started out. Her life is one leap of faith after another. It's part of her charm and the excitement of being a Gemini/*Four*.

IF SPIRIT TAKES THE LEAD: With Spirit ready to go, these souls are eager for a leap of consciousness. Breakthroughs are common and occur one after the other. But living on such an edge means they have no time to contemplate and enjoy. They're stuck in the process of transcendence and hooked on the feeling of freedom that follows each crisis or revelation. They can be judgmental and take on too much responsibility, being of the opinion that things won't get done unless they do things themselves.

IF EGO TAKES THE LEAD: Ego takes the *Four* and chooses isolation. These shield themselves from participating in the mainstream of life. They prefer to observe and judge, rather than embrace a direct experience. Their observational skills are excellent and they can gather information and facts with incredible ease. Selfish, egotistical and always one step ahead of everyone else, they tend to avoid commitments, responsibility, and intimacy. The key here is to loosen up and learn how to play.

NORMAN VINCENT PEALE (June 4)

Preacher, writer, editor, religious innovator.

Pastor of New York City's Marble Collegiate Reformed Church and author of twenty-five books, the catalytic force of Uranus finds the perfect soul in Norman Vincent Peale. His 1952 best-seller, *The Power of Positive Thinking,* made a significant impact. Peale's message urges the combining of positive belief with affirmative prayer, and explains the technique of imaging and purposeful action. Peale's ideas changed people's lives, and that's what Uranus is all about. He alone sparked a postwar revival of religion. In this dynamic it's not only possible to make a difference, it's your mission.

CLINT EASTWOOD (May 31)

Actor.

"Make my day." Eastwood's most famous line says it all. The characters Eastwood plays on the screen don't step aside for anyone. On the contrary, they look conflict in the eye and relish the challenge. Incredibly successful, Eastwood remains a loner. "Maybe being an introvert gives me, by sheer accident, a certain screen presence, a mystique. People have to come and find out what's inside me. If I threw it all out for them to see, they might not be interested."

Gemini/*Five* (May 23, June 5, June 14) Mercury/Mercury

PURPOSE: To face yourself and your resistance to moving forward and becoming; to be gifted with incredible versatility and a sense of humanity; to have the courage to risk yourself so that you can expand your consciousness and realize your large self.

"There is no pleasure in having nothing to do; the fun is having lots to do and not doing it."—May Wilson Little. For the Mercury/Mercury person, having a lot to do will always be a dilemma. Activity and an inner restlessness pushes them to accomplish much, and gives them ulcers or makes them badly confused. They have two choices: change or self-destruct. Some choose a nervous breakdown as a self-imposed vacation, but if they've done this too many times, it ceases to be satisfying. The Gemini/*Fives* need to risk themselves. Think of a first date. If they don't have the courage to expose their true self in the beginning they doomed to play games for the rest of the relationship, which is often no more than one night.

The Mercury/Mercury combination keeps Gemini/*Fives* in a rut; they face their own issues and limitations in others. They need to take a chance and meet people eye to eye.

The next time the date calls, tell him you prefer casual, don't laugh at his jokes unless they're funny, and eat your hamburger without guilt. If he likes you for the right reasons, he'll be in your life.

IF SPIRIT TAKES THE LEAD: The Gemini/*Five* is obsessive when Spirit is strong. These souls allow others to use them, never knowing how to say no without feeling guilty and selfish. Without a strong sense of identity, it is easy to get lost in someone else's life. They feel responsible for everyone, and find it difficult to make a choice because they feel they're letting someone down. A perfectionist, they are their own worst enemy; details drive them crazy and they have to do it all. Choose one direction and one identity and you'll find your life moves forward with amazing ease.

IF EGO TAKES THE LEAD: With Ego strong the choice is paralysis or an obsession with doing and gathering information. Fear can be strong, and the soul can become a cripple, unable to make a choice. This is an identity crisis. They condemn themselves and stay in a small, protected world where they feel some sort of control. If they're action-oriented, they will use their imagination to escape the now. These are the analytical geniuses; they can choose any subject and discuss, dissect and relate it to a larger picture. Relationships can be problematic, because intimacy is an issue. They don't want it.

BOY GEORGE (June 14)

Musician, singer.

Androgyny is certainly the middle road, or the inability to make a choice. An admitted bisexual, Boy George, born George Alan O'Dowd, came from working-class roots to become the lead singer of the *Culture Club*. The group's sound combined Jamaican reggae with American soul and British new wave. Known on the London club scene for his costumes and makeup, Boy George brought the many faces of Gemini to a new level of creativity, yet always struggled with feeling stuck. "I never thought I'd get it together to even be able to sign a check." He experienced drug addiction and other personal problems.

BILL MOYERS (June 5)

Journalist, writer.

Bill Moyers, like many Geminis, had several professions. At fifteen, he was a cub reporter. Under President Kennedy he became deputy director of the Peace Corps. He was President Johnson's press secretary, and publisher of *Newsday*. In 1971, Moyers became executive editor and correspondent at CBS and on public television. Today, he is one of the most respected journalists in the industry. His series *A Walk through the Twentieth Century,* was named the outstanding information series of the year in 1987 by the National Academy of Television Arts and Sciences. Moyers's latest book and public television series, *Healing and the Mind,* presented new ideas to the public from a very objective point of view, a Gemini specialty.

Gemini/*Six* (May 24, June 6, June 15) Mercury/Venus

PURPOSE: To be able to maintain your truth and still play many roles, enjoying life and experiencing freedom because your moral boundaries are well-defined.

"The man who listens to reason is last. Reason enslaves all whose minds are not strong enough to master her."—George Bernard Shaw. This combination has the power to master the mind with ease. Venus gives them a strong spiritual cord, a toughness or ability to concentrate, an innate wisdom that helps them get to the meaning of things. Those with Mercury/Venus energy may feel a strong calling to serve the people, and will have the ability to inspire them. Sukarno (June 6), the man who led Indonesia to independence, spent a lifetime trying to unify diverse peoples under a single nation, language, and culture. "I am a man of the people. I must see them, listen to them, rub against them. I'm happiest when I'm among them. They are the bread of life for me. I feed off the masses."

The Gemini/*Six* must remember to listen to his own calling. When the Gemini/*Six* does what he loves, his feelings, inspiration, and healing powers emerge.

IF SPIRIT TAKES THE LEAD: With Spirit in the lead, so is inspiration and the ability to get at and reveal the truth. These souls desire love and intimacy and give it too freely to those who take advantage of their good nature. They need to learn to mask their truth, set boundaries and say no. They can be poet, politician, or writer; they have an ability to communicate from the heart.

IF EGO TAKES THE LEAD: With Ego strong, so are protection and manipulation. These are excellent sales people; they know how to transform whatever they're selling into something the customer wants. Only someone who can recognize the truth can really use it to their advantage, and this is their gift. Unclear about their identity, they can change their mask, their name, and their jobs as often as the seasons. Creative, gifted with good imagination, they avoid their personal lives because they're afraid of losing their freedom. If they start taking responsibility in their career and personal life, they will find that the truth they have been avoiding will bring them everything they've desired.

MARIO CUOMO (June 15)

Governor of New York, writer, speaker.

"I had no youth, it was just school and the store—always the store. I remember a thousand days being alone in my own quiet world while all the neighborhood's activity was going on steps away or the other side of the door ... Alone, but not really lonely." The inner world of Venus is only developed when desire is denied and we're forced to go within for answers. Cuomo's simple beginnings set strong boundaries he has carried with him throughout his life. Fortunate to have a good education, his brilliant mind and athletic ability helped him win a scholarship and become a lawyer. Then, he went on to make a name in politics. Cuomo is a spiritual man. His belief in something greater than himself makes him an inspirational speaker and writer.

BJORN BORG (June 6)

Tennis pro. Five-year winning streak at Wimbledon.

Bjorn Borg abdicated his throne at the peak of his profession. Just like Greta Garbo, he wanted to be alone. The hectic life on the tennis circuit kept him from experiencing his inner self. After taking several months off in 1982 he said, "During my break, I had plenty of time to discover how nice life was without tennis, and that there were other things in life." Known as the Iceman, Borg exhibited the concentration of Venus. His coach said, "I recognized his mental toughness at an early age." By fourteen, he was the best junior player in the world. By age seventeen, he was beating the top-ranked players.

Gemini/*Seven* (May 25, June 7, June 16)
Mercury/Neptune

PURPOSE: To bring your dream into the moment and recognize your power to create and transform your life and those of others.

"Spirituality is a kind of virgin wisdom, a knowing that comes prior to experience."—Marilyn Ferguson. Gemini/*Fives* are psychic. Mercury/Neptune persons are high on imagination, but they pay a price. The names of things and places elude them like invisible ink. When thoughts dissolve, the Gemini/*Seven* has been transported, either to the angels or the snake pit. No middle ground here. As with all Neptune combinations, Spirit and faith are paramount. This combination moves quickly. In a blink of an eye their ideas have changed and so have their circumstance and awareness. Exterior security does not exist, that's why their instincts are so important.

Gemini/*Sevens* must choose between dreaming about life or living it, not an easy task for this combination. The stars seem to pull them into their embrace and hold them high above the pettiness of life. However, from that height they have perspective, not experience, and experience is what being a Gemini is all about. The danger of pursuing dreams is that the dream becomes reality, and Gemini/*Sevens* are left with the need to create something new to pine for. If they have taken on the perfectionist side of this combination, they might find they want it all or nothing. Some succeed, but most are left with nothing. Life is a mixed bag, so use your Gemini daring and try a bit of everything. It can only make you a better person.

IF SPIRIT TAKES THE LEAD: Spirit and the number *Seven* are soul mates—and that's the problem. Here perfectionism, sacrifice, and responsibility are all taken to the nth degree. Strong-willed and judgmental, they demand that every little detail of life be lived perfectly. Religion and God are powerful forces as well as the need to be a martyr. Their need to help others and sacrifice themselves is distorted. They need to develop a strong identity, set boundaries, and learn to protect themselves from being used by others.

IF EGO TAKES THE LEAD: Ego becomes very manipulative when it hooks up with the *Seven*. This is the double life, the false facade. These are master salesmen or religious fanatics who use Spirit for power instead of truth. Strong-willed, judgmental, and perfectionistic, they have an obsessive nature and a great imagination. They're mysterious beings, who know how to create mystery in their lives and their endeavors. Afraid of the unknown, control is an issue, they want it all the time. What they need is faith and the courage to take a risk.

ROBERT LUDLUM (May 25)

Novelist.

After twenty years as an actor and producer, Robert Ludlum tried his hand at writing, the Gemini profession. Only a true Gemini would attempt this. A string of best-sellers followed, starting with *The Scarlatti Inheritance,* which featured intricate plots, exotic locations and an ending in which the hero had the last laugh, all Gemini qualities. Even as a youth, Ludlum was eager for adventure, and set off at the age of sixteen to pursue an acting career. He won a role on Broadway, then served two years in the U.S. Marines. After getting his degree in theater at Wesleyan University, he began playing the favorite Gemini professions, "homicidal maniacs and lawyers." Later, he moved on to producing, and established the first major, year-round theater in a suburban shopping center. Don't forget, Gemini appeals to the masses. Other Ludlum novels: *The Rhinemann Exchange, The Matarese Circle, The Bourne Supremacy,* and *The Icarus Agenda.*

RALPH WALDO EMERSON (May 25)

Writer, poet, minister.

Emerson was born into a religious family. The faith of the number *Seven* had an immediate impact on this soul. His father, a minister, died when Emerson was eight years old, and his mother, a woman of great faith and strength, kept the family together. From the beginning, Emerson struggled not just for his own identity, which was easily lost among five brothers and a sister, but also to survive. Without a father to support them, every member of the family had to work for the bare necessities. This is not an uncommon experience for a Gemini. Shy and introverted, Emerson lacked the self-confidence to reach out and make friends. Instead, he turned his attention inward toward self-discovery and honed his naturally analytical nature. A perfectionist, he sought his entire life to live up to the high standards of his strong moral code. He believed that "God has wrought man in a perfect mold, quickened him with exquisite senses and lastly inspired him with intelligence," an intelligence that he could use for good or evil. Emerson believed it was up to each of us to use these gifts appropriately. Emerson suffered from feelings of despair and of spiritual exhilaration. His purity of purpose, which is Gemini's challenge to act with good intent, was something he strove to perfect all his life.

Gemini/*Eight* (May 26, June 8, June 17) Mercury/Saturn

PURPOSE: To accept responsibility for wherever you are in life and to use your mistakes and experience to learn about yourself, constantly adjusting your position and knowing that you are here to transcend whatever limitations you encounter.

"Think wrongly, if you must but in all cases think for yourself—unknown

The Gemini/*Eight* must not let criticism and the fear of being judged keep them from expressing themselves. They must ignore the opinions of others. If Mercury dominates Gemini/*Eights*, they will try to escape commitments and responsibility. Too tough on themselves, they block their ability to trust their instincts. When Saturn and Mercury cooperate, Gemini/*Eights* are perseverant and hardworking, are sure-footed, and mature.

Saturn has an inclination toward depression. Dorothea Lange, (May 26) a Mercury/Saturn person, photographed the Great Depression, documenting the effects of poverty and despair. This was a positive way to work out her negative feelings. The ability to use your instincts and respond to life with faith in yourself and a better tomorrow is the challenge. The Gemini/*Eight* must build a life that makes her feel secure. Security is only a belief in oneself, and that's the real lesson here.

IF SPIRIT TAKES THE LEAD: With Spirit in the lead, a tough life is assured. These souls do everything the hard way, even when they don't have to. Judgment is an issue, and so is responsibility. Somewhere in their life they're taking on too much or none at all. Often, they avoid their own problems and deal with everyone else's. If you avoid the practical aspects of life, you'll find that your foundation never gets set and your roots never have a chance to grow. Pick a path and stay on it. You have the ability to be steadfast and strong. Use your strength for yourself first, then it'll be easier to see who deserves your endless support and faith.

IF EGO TAKES THE LEAD: If Ego takes the lead, security, money, and the practical things of life are very important. These souls want control, don't trust, and are afraid of taking risks. Very clever and capable of sizing up a situation, they run into trouble when a little faith is required. Afraid of letting others in, they tend to do everything themselves. Serious to a fault, they have forgotten how to play and have fun. Stress comes from their unrelenting dialogue with themselves, all of it negative and demanding. They need love. It will provide the security they've been looking for in things.

JOAN RIVERS (June 8)

Comedienne, TV personality.

"Oh grow up!" That's what Joan Rivers tells her audience, and that's what Gemini/*Eight* is all about. Saturn is age and Mercury is youth, and together, they spell maturity. Joan loves to say, "Can we talk? Look, I'm a very sensitive person, I only go after the ones who are big enough to take it." The Gemini humor and love of gossip finds a fitting profession here as talk-show hostess and stand-up comedienne. But as with every combination with Saturn, nothing comes easily. Joan defied her parents and starved as a Greenwich Village comic. When she appeared on the *Jack Paar Show,* he hated her act. The week before she made it onto the *Johnny Carson Show,* her agent advised her to quit. Here's a soul who knows how to take rejection and turn it into success.

FRANK LLOYD WRIGHT (June 8)

America's greatest architect.

Wright revolutionized American architecture. In his late twenties, he scaled houses down to human size, enlarging the windows to let in light, eliminating basements, expanding rooms. He invented furniture for these homes, building massive tables of irregular shapes, incorporated as a part of the house. In his mid-thirties, he designed a building in steel and concrete with innovations like glass doors and steel furniture. His Imperial Hotel survived a Japanese earthquake. Saturn creates struggle with authority and Frank Lloyd Wright continually fought the conservative majority his new style of architecture threatened. He was a hard worker who made his way to the top, not by luck, but by daily effort. Saturn is a taskmaster, and in Gemini, Saturn was used here to explore new ideas which have changed the face and interior of buildings in America.

Gemini/*Nine* (May 27, June 9, June 18) Mercury/Mars

PURPOSE: To use all aspects of life as a means to get you where you need to go; to end passivity and to take responsibility for wherever you are, balancing your needs with your desire to help others and live in a perfect world.

"All anger is nothing more than an attempt to make someone feel guilty." — Guilt is universal but it shows up in the anger of Mars, here coupled with Mercury the communicator. Humor, wit, a sharp tongue, verbal attacks Gemini/*Nines* have it all. But it's nothing more than a defense, to make everyone keep their distance. Their Ego is struggling for some sort of recognition, and no one is paying attention, at least not to what really counts. If they deal with the real issues, their voice and actions will lose their edge.

Mars loves a challenge and with Mercury, it gets it nonstop. The key here is for them to avoid giving or receiving verbal abuse. The Gemini/*Nine* needs to learn to ask for what he needs so he doesn't bully others for what he's not getting. A well-developed ego is the balancing point of the energy. The *I* must get recognition, or it will be swallowed by the whale. Gemini/*Nines* must let the world know they are alive and resourceful. Conformity calls to them; they can acquiesce or listen to the beat of their own drum.

IF SPIRIT TAKES THE LEAD: Spirit and the number *Nine* are very idealistic together. They don't know how to give less than everything. Eager to do it all, they have trouble choosing. Their perfectionistic nature often makes them let go of it all, because they can't do it all the way they want. They need to learn to love themselves and not try so hard to be the best. Many steps lead one to the top. They need to take them one at a time. When they learn to pace themselves, make a choice, and follow it, the world becomes a pleasant place.

IF EGO TAKES THE LEAD: Ego and the number *Nine* are pals—they like to be best and first. Gemini provides too many choices and their inability to let go makes them run first here then there, never accomplishing anything. They need to learn how to focus. Their strong opinions create opposition, yet they're good at using the ideas and resources of others to get their own needs met. Take responsibility; when they do, they will find that life begins to fall in place.

PAUL McCARTNEY (June 18)

An original member of the Beatles, composer, singer.

McCartney is one of the richest men in the world, not bad for the son of a cotton salesman. Born in Liverpool, he was a good student and almost went on to university. McCartney had to make the big choice—go into teacher's training or meet a date with fate in Hamburg, Germany. He went to Hamburg, and there the Beatles were discovered by Brian Epstein. The rest is history. Known as the "cute one," McCartney married Linda Eastman and has remained with her for years. That's because he sowed his Gemini oats before he settled down. *Time* magazine said, "The Beatles' cunning collages pieced together scraps of tension between the generations, the loneliness of the dislocated 60's and the bitter sweets of young love in any age."

ISADORA DUNCAN (May 27)

Dancer.

Isadora Duncan was a genius as a dancer, directing the Ego force of Mars to bring her revolutionary concept of dance to the public. Her personal life was scandalous. The instability of Mercury and the childishness and intensity of Mars made her flaunt her obsessive affairs. She walked barefoot and dressed in gauzy tunics like those worn in ancient Greece, in an era when thick and cumbersome clothes were *de rigueur.* She insulted her audiences, then demanded they give her support for her projects. She died suddenly and tragically when her scarf was caught in the wheel of her car and choked her to death.

SUMMARY

Gemini is the phase of the journey where the world is an adventure. Life is exciting; it fascinates and stirs the curiosity. As the soul experiences new things, it begins to see how everything is connected, that life is a continuous flow. Differences are nothing more than costumes of the gods. And so, although Gemini is caught in the process of discovery, of trying to connect the missing links of change invisible to the eye, it intuitively knows that one heart lives in all things. It loves to disarm the liar, the do-gooder or the thief. It is like coyote in the Indian Medicine Cards, who always finds humor in the problems it has created. Gemini is invested in stirring the pot. It loves to light a match then step back and watch the fireworks. As it moves from isolation to oneness with all, it amuses, inspires, and makes the simple things of life come alive. The soul's path now leads to the fourth phase of the cycle, where it will settle down and begin to build a home in Cancer.

SELECTED SOURCES

Earl Blackwell   *Celebrity Register, 1990 (50th Anniversary Edition)*   Gale Research 1990

Alan Bowness   *Gauguin*   Phaidon Press Ltd. 1994

Pietro Citati   *Kafka*   Translated from the Italian by Raymond Rosenthal Alfred A. Knopf 1990

Paul Gauguin   *The Writings of a Savage*   Edited by Daniel Guerin   DaCapo Press 1996

Arthur Gelb, A.M. Rosenthal and Marvin Siegel, eds.   *New York Times Great Lives of the Twentieth Century*   Times Books 1990

Bill Moyers   *Genesis: A LivingConversation*   Doubleday 1996

Catherine Reef   *Walt Whitman*   Clarion 1995

Jean-Paul Sartre   *Truth and Existence*   University of Chicago Press 1992

John Beilenson   *Sukarno World Leaders Past and Present*   Mda 1990

Robert S. McElvaine   *Mario Cuomo: A Biography*   Scribner 1988

———*A Course in Miracles*   Foundation for Inner Peace 1992

PART II

THE EMERGENCE OF SPIRIT

*I*n **Cancer, Leo,** and **Virgo,** Spirit makes her move and shows her face. It's time to take the lead, to remind the soul that there is a spiritual path that must be followed. She displays her strength and her resilience for all the world to see. The impossible becomes easy once she chooses to demonstrate her powers. In **Cancer,** Spirit is courageous, resilient, and willful. She reaches out to help those who are in need. She puts herself at risk, taking on those who seem much bigger and stronger than she is, showing them the power of patience, the importance of timing, and what can be accomplished when one refuses to settle for anything less than the best. Ego gets its first encounter with defeat. He does not have the will or the vision to persevere. He has underestimated Spirit's powers, and he tries to imitate her actions for his own end. He preys on the weakness and the strength of others, and he learns to imitate Spirit in order to fool those who seek her presence. In **Leo,** he achieves his goal and reaches the top of his profession, gaining attention and approval from the world. Spirit achieves her goal in Leo, because God has heard her request, and he visits the soul leaving it with a feeling that life has meaning and there is more to reality than what one can see. In **Virgo,** Ego continues his pursuit of power; he conquers those that rejected him and reaches beyond even his dreams. The top, however, is a lonely place, and instead of contentment he feels more isolated and alone. Spirit, in Virgo, allows her need to serve to be taken to extremes. She reaches out to help those that society has rejected, those who are lost, abandoned, and alone. It doesn't matter if they're strangers; she knows we are all connected. Both Ego and Spirit express their differences to their maximum within the framework of reality. Ego gains fame and fortune; Spirit gives her life to those who have less, who need help in order to survive.

Cancer

(June 22-July 22)

Cancers are a mysterious lot.
They seem so moody and yet they're not.
Like the moon, they'll change their face,
But inside they keep an even pace.
Sensitive and caring, they're also tough.
Yes, they're a jewel, but in the rough.
So get out your chisel and make a date.
The crab is waiting for his soul mate.

Ruler: Moon   **Symbol: Crab**
Element: Water   **Number: Two**

The soul, having mastered its environment in Gemini, once again turns inward. In Cancer, the sounds of the street no longer invite it to explore. The attraction is to inactivity and silence, to the darkness of the unconscious, to the power of the unknown. Confronting worldly authority is no longer a fear; the Cancer easily fights society, bosses, parents, friends, and bureaucracy. Their present opponent is much more formidable; it's the watery power of the collective psyche. This primordial chaos includes everything. Here you will rediscover and integrate your fears and phobias, your erotic emotions—everything you thought was unacceptable, useless, and unworthy. This is the home of Spirit, and from the Cancer's womb Spirit will burst forth, uniting the hidden world of unconscious motivation with the conscious world of choice. In the fourth house of the zodiac, unity reigns, and nothing is turned away; even distortions and abnormalities have their place in the world of Spirit. No one is beyond God's love and forgiveness; nothing is too base to be ignored. In Cancer, you learn to bring your ancient wounds into the light to be healed and reowned. What is hidden has power. It attracts and controls without your consent. Once your wounds are in the light you can begin the process of understanding. With understanding comes the ability to objectify the wounds and the power to use them to heal or manipulate others.

When Ego is dominant, Cancers can turn a disadvantage into an advantage. If they're ill, you'll be running their errands; if they lack social graces, you'll be making their calls. Marcel Proust (July 10) was an expert at representing himself as helpless. His ill health was "a method of blackmail . . . a means of procuring all the indulgence he found necessary."—Richard H. Baker.

Denial is dangerous. Own your weaknesses and then unity provides protection. Ignore your eccentricities and they become distorted; their weight becomes a burden that keeps your spirit from breaking free. Cancers struggle with illness, for what we do not love withers and dies. Disease is nothing more than an unloved part of yourself manifested on the physical plane. Because of this, your mind has the power to heal. Mary Baker Eddy, (July 16) founder of the Church of Christ, Scientist, preached the power of the mind over the body. "Disease is only a belief of the mortal mind." Healing power belongs to every Cancer and the number *Two,* if they choose to share their pain instead of remaining isolated. This union of spirits invites God to enter the process and produce healing in the body.

Once Spirit is free in Cancer; the full power of its nature is revealed. Language connects the unspoken with the conscious world. Without the ability to express your feelings, you become their victim. Verbalize your feelings and you cast light on depression, acquire patience and strength, and end isolation. Confidence is the reward of self-expression. It is the key to reconnecting with faith. Once the soul believes in the power of unity and healing, it is restored. Without Spirit, confidence is temporary and dependent on others; with Spirit, confidence fills you with endless hope and love.

In Gemini, the soul was urged to move out of its selfish perceptions and embrace its universal self, the one that knows it is connected to all things. If this did not occur, then the phase of Cancer will be difficult. The self becomes imprisoned in itself and indifferent to others. Spirit provides warmth, compassion, and understanding; when it's missing, reality appears distorted. Emotional needs become "black holes," and nothing in the material world is enough to make the soul feel secure. The dark feelings of the Cancer find relief in humor and in an interest in society and all its frivolities. Cancers are either the king and queens of superfluous behavior or courageous navigators of truth and the unknown.

As the soul turns away from the world and focuses on its inner nature, it learns to accept its whole being. Once weaknesses are embraced with love, compassion for others emerges and intimacy becomes a possibility. Cancers either keep you outside the castle gates or let you into their hearts. Cancers who seek to experience God know that He is found within, and that prayer is the language which links the human with the divine. God has changed His image once again. No longer the vengeful God who cast Adam and Eve out of the Garden, He is now a loving deity, filled with forgiveness and a desire to help His children heal. Helen Keller (June 27) learned about this loving God from her dear friend, Bishop Brooks. "There is one universal religion, Helen—the religion of love. Love your heavenly Father with your whole heart and soul, love every child of God as much as ever you can, and remember that the possibilities of good are greater than the possibilities of evil; and you have the key to Heaven.''

Any birth is painful, and the birth of Spirit brings psychological torment. The weight of nothingness from which all creation is born helps Spirit burst forth and break the psychological barriers of fear, depression, and a sense of isolation. For Helen Keller, the birth of Spirit came with the arrival of Mrs. Sullivan, her teacher. ''Gradually I got used to the silence and darkness that surrounded me and forgot that it had ever been different, until she came— my teacher—who was to set my spirit free.'' What set Keller free was language. The ability to identify what you see without with what you feel within creates unity.

Spirit brings patience, unity, and endurance. Spirit knows that in the end, God, goodness, and beauty will prevail. Cancer exhibits a deep hope for a better tomorrow. Cancers with Spirit are superhuman souls with the power to unify. The scapegoat of Gemini has transformed into a collective symbol of hope and courage. This is John Glenn (July 18), the first American to orbit the earth in space. This is Nelson Mandela (July 18) sacrificing his own freedom for the freedom of all mankind. This is Hellen Keller, deaf and blind from childhood, who goes to college in an age when most women cannot meet that challenge. This is P. T. Barnum, (July 5) who rejected puritanical inhibitions by bringing pure enjoyment to the world. On the other extreme is frivolousness Imelda Marcos, wife of the president of the Philippines, owner of more than a thousand pairs of shoes, unconcerned that her people go barefoot from poverty.

Cancers are spiritual beings who know without a doubt that the world is made up of more than what the eye can see, the ears can hear, or the hand can touch. ''Human reason is inaccurate; and the scope of the senses is inadequate to grasp the world of truth, and teach the eternal.''—Mary Baker Eddy. These spiritual beings are tender and sensitive, malicious and calculating, emotional and creative, dependent and leaders. They fill our souls with joy, they share our troubles as if they were their own. They are easily slighted, fight with vengeance, and struggle with depression. To understand them is impossible; to love them is inevitable, for they are unique and gifted with the power of intimacy. Love is their ruler and because they give it generously, you can be pulled into their world. If you choose to stay, you must accept the whole package, the good and the bad, their weaknesses and their strengths.

To the navigators of the invisible world, the universe gives superb instinct, a strong inner voice, and a thin skin. Oversensitive, they become irritable without an obvious cause. Aware of nuances and subtleties, they act according to the needs of the moment, and what they perceive is a world of motivation, thoughts and hidden agendas. Psychic and intuitive, they know the truth, even though they can't back it up with facts. Don't be fooled by their sensitivity; they're made of steel inside. Like nature they can appear gentle and be dangerous. Once they decide what they want, nothing stands in their way because their desire is embraced by their heart. In Cancer, the heart is enlarged through sharing, praying, and preparing for a visit from God. These experiences become the source of nourishment for Leo, the sign that rules the heart. The environment needed for the heart to grow is solitude and silence. The great mystic Teresa of Avila, tells us that the soul needs the nourishment of solitude and prayer in order to begin to separate from worldly desires; "the senses and all external things seem gradually to loose their hold on him, while the soul, on the other hand, regains its lost control." If you're a Cancer, you need peace and quiet and time to reconnect with your inner self. When you do, your world blossoms.

Passive resistance or defiance is the way Cancers deal with opposition. If they're doing the attacking, they will wear you down with their persistence. Compromise is not in their vocabulary; instead, they endure longer and withstand more. If you're trying to change the world, these qualities can be an asset. But take these qualities and place them in a personal relationship and what you've got is trouble. If you want to go to dinner with friends and your Cancer mate refuses, chances are you'll have to go alone.

Since Spirit cannot be divided, Cancer represents unity and the sacred silence within. The circle is negotiated through psychological divisions such as memory and the past, fantasy and the future, the conscious and the unconscious. The past, however, is Cancer's primary concern. It desires to go back and heal the unresolved. Memory is a complex thing; it is a mixture of fact and fantasy, and it allows you to remember selectively what you wish. Many Cancers long for the past and what they believe were happier times; some stay stuck in a wound, one they lick and expose, instead of allowing to heal.

The danger of going back is becoming stuck. The resistance is a continuation of the Gemini challenge to grow up. Everyone finds it difficult to leave the nourishment and safety of the past and step into the unknown. The desire to stay an infant, wrapped in the needs and desires of oneself, is powerful, particularly when one doesn't feel as if those needs were ever met. To fulfill them ourselves requires that we *leave* that space and grow. With expansion, we learn to give ourselves nourishment and not expect it from others. It's independence, and it's Leo, the next sign.

The dilemma of Cancer is still the Gemini issue, the avoidance of the present. Marcel Proust said, "Only the past, which we invest with charm in the act of remembering it, is ever truly satisfying." The disillusionment of the present is a constant source of pain for this water sign. To counter the pull of the past, the Cancer is given a powerful imagination. If the soul knows how to swing between its memories and its fantasies, it can keep itself out of the present, but not without some loss of truth. It's a small price to pay to relieve the threat of death that lurks around being in the moment. After all, the moment ends and another begins; the moment is evolution, not static. It's a tough place to be, and only the Scorpio enjoys the challenge.

To the left of Cancer is memory, to the right is fantasy, above is consciousness, below is the unconscious. At the center is Spirit. That's the place the Cancer seeks for nourishment. Once the source is found, the soul is connected to the invisible world, the one that reveals truth, harmony, and order, the one that heals. The ethereal world is governed by changeless laws, ones that shelter all who obey them; it is not affected by praise, pageantry, or ritual. It is ruled by God's law.

Nourishment is a primary concern for Cancers. If you don't believe in Spirit and have a desire to help others, food can be an issue, one that can translate into weight problems or psychological food-related illnesses like anorexia. Food is the body's nourishment. However, without spiritual nourishment, the soul will try to fill that void with food. Insecurity drives the Cancer to eat more and more to alleviate the emptiness only satisfied by love.

Cancers need to own their idiosyncrasies. If you're a Cancer, you probably love the freaky, the erotic, the exaggerated, the outcast. Through your ability to accept the weirdness of others you learn to accept the distorted parts of yourself. Laughter is a Cancer talent which requires distance from the issue. Humor is an indication of maturity and objectivity. P. T. Barnum built his fortune on the "eroticism of others." "His goal was to awaken a sleeping sense of wonder, to help open the eyes of his fellow citizens to the amazing diversity of the human and natural world. To accomplish this, he lifted up the rare, the strange, the beautiful, the awesome."

When you are good at mixing fact and fantasy, you become a showman, someone who invokes the unreal and promises a glimpse of the unknown. Of course, without moral boundaries, this can lead to deception, and Cancers know how to spin a tale. Barnum believed that the public actually enjoyed being deceived, as long as they were being amused. The truth is that what we doubt we are drawn to.

Art, in Cancer, is a mixture of truth and imagination. This is no longer just the limited perception of the physical world; Spirit has added unconscious feelings. With the psyche a part of the projection, the image is distorted. Art is a manifestation of Spirit, in Cancer, form and images are not yet clear. The art of Cancer invokes wonder and demands that you use your own inner voice to lead you to the understanding of the object.

The game of life played in Gemini is brought to a new level in Cancer. Cancers play with truth. They love to mix up the facts and add ridiculous lies. They're attracted to the mysterious and the unknown. Spirit rules the processes of life, things that can't be easily defined, things that must be experienced in order to be understood. Love, thinking, God—these are some of the issues of Cancer. Rational thought, the reflective and analytical process is there to balance Cancers' strong emotional natures that make them prone to powerful mood swings. Language is the link between the known and the unknown. Words represent more than an object; they represent an experience. Words are miniworlds, small archetypes that when linked together create a full and powerful story. This story allows the conscious and unconscious to flow in harmony and move the soul out of lethargy and chaos into action and creativity. Helen Keller was in a prison of silence until she was able to attach her feelings (the unconscious) to an object in the outer world (consciousness). This happened when she linked the feeling of water to the word water. "The beautiful truth burst upon my mind—I felt that there were invisible lines stretched between my spirit and the spirit of others." This sense of connectedness is what creates compassion. Before Helen had made her association she had smashed a china doll to the floor without remorse. As soon as her spirit was freed, and her worlds connected, she ran upstairs and tried to put the shattered pieces of the doll together. Compassion had emerged. Language also helps us create intimacy through the process of sharing our affections. It is only through the sharing of ourselves that we learn to love and experience intimacy.

The Cancer relationship is an intimate one. Nothing short of sharing the innermost most parts of your world will do. Even when it feels like the perfect union, one that doesn't require words, it is important to speak. Bring to consciousness your feelings and share them with your mate. It will bring you closer. When you can't express your feelings, you could believe that living alone is wonderful, but the truth is that you need nourishment and love to survive. The lesson is not to lose yourself in someone else, except for short periods of time.

Let your partner know you need space, and choose one with emotional courage. They should have the ability to break through your resistance, and still be able to accept your desire to protect them. Your acute sensitivity needs a tough—and out going—partner. Nine out of ten times the woman who will catch your eye will be the one dancing and wearing the red shoes.

Now, sex is another story. For a shy person, you certainly don't exhibit fear in this department. In fact, you're attracted to it early. Maybe that's because sex has a hidden and forbidden nature. It's also about coming together. Whichever way you look at it, you're a sensitive, caring partner. Don't be surprised if you're attracted to the kinky stuff, too. Remember, Cancer is the sign of the unusual.

Cancers are natural psychologists. They know what makes others tick. P. T. Barnum was "coming closer and closer to knowing the ins and outs of human nature, what caught people's fancy, what tweaked their curiosity." Proust "forged a new kind of novel, a work in which the new psychological knowledge was for the first time applied to fiction, in which the subconscious plays as large a part as overt experience in which the very flow of time is captured and, for a moment, held in check."

For Cancers time is relative. Spirit lives in the moment. You can enter the moment through meditation or turning inward. The inner space is beyond limitations; time feels suspended. This is the experience of devotion and prayer. This is the process of connecting to everything and everybody.

Cancers are sponges; they absorb rather than embrace. They find it difficult to separate distinguish, differentiate. Who am I? Who are you? These questions aren't easy in the sign of the crab.

Cancers must sort out the feelings they have accumulated from all their experiences. To do this they need a safe place to retreat to. Cancer rules the home and the nurturing principle. Cancers struggle to balance their need to be with others and their desire to be alone. The Moon is complete within itself, but cannot be seen without the Sun, whose light she reflects. Moon people feel the need to experience themselves through someone else. Like peanut butter and jelly, some things are just better together. When your Cancer mate wants to be alone, don't get upset. As soon as you leave the room, he'll wish he had asked you to stay. Remember not to stay away longer than ten minutes; if you do, he'll feel like you've abandoned him. As children, Cancers often fear abandonment by their mothers. They are learning how to emotionally separate and so any absence of the mother is acutely felt.

Their inner torment and their desire for intimacy makes Cancers either great companions or dependent bundles of need. Gifted with the ability to feel the pain and the needs of others, they can show great compassion. Compassion is a way for Cancers to come out of themselves. It's the only way they can put an end to their feelings of isolation and loneliness. There is joy is self-forgetfulness. A word of caution: The Cancer's ability to become one with another is great when tenderness is desired or there is an emotional crisis, but it can crowd the other person if it's continued for too long. Another source of trouble is the Cancers' habit of expecting others to know their needs without their having to tell them. They have to put their feelings into words; it's how they connect and relieve their sense of isolation.

When a Cancer has confidence, he or she has the ability to open up to the world. These are the great observers of nature and people. In fact, Cancers have a talent for imitating the actions and styles of anyone they find amusing. They make great actors and comediennes. Of course, if carried to an extreme, it becomes voyeurism, something separate but intimate, a Cancer's dream. Gilda Radner (June 28), comedienne, said, ''Before I became a celebrity, I used to follow people—watch them, listen to conversations. So many of my characters came from that voyeurism.''

Cancer is the womb that gives life form. As a child, you didn't have a choice where you lived, as an adult, you're old enough to impact your environment. Don't roll around in memories or waves of longing. You've got to overcome *yourself* as an opponent before you take on the world. Everyone has a dream that needs to be released. Put yourself at risk, so you can experience your Spirit and feel yourself soar. The only thing that can stop you is fear.

Sylvester Stallone (July 6), a Cancer, created the character of Rocky, a fighter with Spirit greater than his talent. Rocky is a winner, not because he wins the big fight but because he overcame impossible odds. Rocky had a girlfriend to support him, and most of you will have help from some courageous woman, probably your mother. Some of you, however will feel totally abandoned by your mother and have to do it alone. Unfair? Not at all. It will make you strong. Remember, life is only as hard as you are stubborn.

We're all attached to perceptions; in order to move forward, we must let go of them. If you see yourself as a savior, then in Cancer you will have to save yourself; if you need to be needed, then your list of dependents will increase until you scream *no more!* Cancer is obsessive. Whatever you choose, you'll get triple the dose until you learn how to put it in perspective. The only safe choice is to reach for something greater than yourself. Make a sense of responsibility to others and a desire to help others succeed with the help of your strength and your will a priority. Balance your image of the mother, the woman who comforts in times of need and who sacrifices herself for others. This does not mean you take in everyone who crosses your path. You must learn to give with respect to yourself. Remember, to give help doesn't mean you have to identify with the abandoned—the stray dog down the street or or your adopted girlfriend. True giving helps both parties. While waiting for his big break, James Cagney (July 17) was struggling to put food on the table. When Artie, a friend from the old neighborhood, learned of Cagney's problem, he gave Cagney half his paycheck. He continued to do so for almost a year until Cagney and his wife were on their feet. Cagney never forgot his friend's generosity. Artie remained one of his closest friends for life. Saint-Exupery (June 29), the French author of *The Little Prince,* called such a gift an *exchange.* ''Sitting in the flickering light of the candles on this kerchief of sand, on this village square, we waited in the night. . . . We told stories, we joked, we sang songs. In the air there was that slight fever that reigns over a gaily prepared feast. Yet we were infinitely poor. Wind, sand and stars. The austerity of Trappists. But on this badly lighted cloth, a handful of men, who possessed nothing in the world but their memories, were sharing invisible riches.''

The gifts of the heart are the ones that never leave us. We are only truly alone if we see ourselves as separate. If we learn to share our history, our yearnings, and our feelings, if we value camaraderie and helping others as much as self-advancement, if we can see through the multitude of colors, costumes, and cultures that disguise the soul and relate to every human being with dignity and respect, then there is no way isolation will creep into our lives and make us feel unworthy or alone. To give of ourselves regardless of our circumstances and limitations, defining our choices and gifts by our

Spirit and not by our pocket books, is the true key to Cancer's strength and courage. Here in Cancer, life provides chances for Spirit to soar above physical reality and triumph. Many Cancers have contact with the handicapped. What better way to observe Spirit triumph over physical limitations?

Though few Cancers ever have the safe, secure home they long for, the ones who do have it have a head start. Van Cliburn (July 12), the concert pianist, had an ideal Cancer childhood. His mother, Rildin Bee, was a talented pianist and his teacher. "There was nothing I ever wanted for, nothing that I ever needed, nothing I ever wished for that I didn't have." Cliburn's parents were not rich, but they fulfilled their son's emotional and creative needs and allowed his natural talent to blossom. Cliburn's confidence helped him give a near-perfect performance in Russia during the cold war. He won the USSR's most prestigious music award and became an overnight international sensation. Cliburn was a natural pianist rather than an intellectually sophisticated one. Van Cliburn did not play with the traditional approach and the Moon's ability to lose itself in something triumphed. "He had almost a soul mate-like connection with the Soviet audience. When he played the Third Concerto by Rachmaninoff, it was not conductor and soloist. They had the same approach, they were both in one music. It was something unbelievable."

Strongly influenced by their surroundings, Cancers pick up other people's garbage—anxiety, anger, confusion—and good stuff, too, if it's around. It's one reason they need a safe place as a refuge. They rarely use their Psychic Power beyond their immediate instincts; their fear of their own power keeps it in check. Cancerian children need to understand that not everyone feels what they do. They know Aunt Mary is angry, that Cousin Ted is lying, and that Mommy can't wait for everyone to leave. But when they state the truth, they're often punished. It's a tough message to untangle. Their comic side serves them well here. Unable to tell the truth directly, they find an acceptable path, through humor. It's how they face themselves and others—it's how they heal their wounds. However, because it's a form of protection, the Cancer humor has a sting. It's a positive defense mechanism, a way Cancers explore their feelings. Ask any good comic why they learned their skill. It was usually to deflect the attacks of others or to get the attention they were missing. Some of our best comedians are Cancers—Bill Cosby (July 12), Phylis Diller (July 17), Robin Williams, (July 21) and Milton Berle (July 12).

Wisdom is their savior, for objectivity is impossible. As water sign, feelings are too deep to gain distance. But they *know* the truth behind your words, they sense your sincerity. Loners by nature, obsessive and eccentric when given the chance, Cancers struggle with inner discipline. They tend to overdo. They'll order triple cheese on their pizza and then wonder why they can't taste the tomato sauce. If it's love, they're lost in the person and no one else exists. Without good internal boundaries, things easily get out of control. Moon people can be attracted to gambling, drugs, alcohol, food, love and sex. Food is particularly important for it's the prime source by which we are nurtured. Richard Simmons (July 12) is a healer. He once weighed several hundred pounds, and now he helps others lose weight because he can easily touch the pain of those who are paralyzed by it. If you're living with or married to a Cancer, keep the cupboards stocked. It makes them feel loved.

Cancers struggle with mood swings, and their obsessive behavior demands they learn emotional control. Constantly battling frustration, they seek stability in their environment. It's why they like antiques, tradition, and the past. It give them a feeling of connectedness, and belonging. They are prone to collecting and easily fall into habits. They'd rather repeat an experience any day than try something new. They can easily get stuck in a rut. A mate can help here. Often Cancers are attracted to partners who bring the change they themselves are afraid to initiate.

All Cancers deal with fear. It's the neck brace that keeps them rigid. They also all struggle to contain emotional tension, beginning in childhood. Geraldo Rivera (July 4) had a Jewish mother and a Catholic father. Two totally different worlds coexisted under one roof. As a talk-show host, Rivera tries to make sense of the behavior of angry, volatile people. The tension of conflicting emotions is the stuff that breeds creation.

Creativity comes from chaos and the unknown. However, the danger comes when children are put in a position to take care of the needs of adults. As they grow up they will try to recreate their feelings of powerlessness or of being overwhelmed by someone else's needs. Because of this early distortion, the Cancer soul will choose men or women they can never heal or satisfy. They might also choose a partner without needs, which will create the same feeling of emptiness. Remember, "When the student is ready, the teacher will appear." Make yourself open to heal, and the universe will help you.

The mother, is the symbol of this sign. If you're lucky enough to have one, she will be larger than life. She may be physically weak, but her spirit is indomitable. She rises to any crisis and she does it with dignity and fairness. Usually to balance this formidable woman, the Cancer's father is emotionally contained, missing, a dreamer, passive, or even abusive. Supermodel Jerry Hall (July 2), the mother of Mick Jagger's children, had a father who beat her. Her mother kept the family together despite her husband's violent nature. Milton Berle's mother was married to a man who seldom kept a job longer than a few weeks. Evicted from their apartment, the children, with their father, watched their few possessions on the street corner while the mother went hunting for a place to live. Several hours later she returned, with an apartment and a wagon to haul their possessions. She was a resourceful woman who hired herself out as a department-store detective when things really got rough. It was her yearning to be onstage that brought her son Milton to show business. Cancer children often are influenced by the yearnings of the mother. Unfortunately, this mother lived her life through her son, even after he married.

James Cagney's mother was a petite women; her children loved and feared her. When his brother, Harry, was beaten up unfairly by a neighbor, Mrs. Cagney took care of it. "My mother at the time possessed two handy items: a thick, six-foot-long horsewhip and a blazing temper. When she heard of the injustice done to Harry, she put on her little jacket, ran downstairs to the watchman, and whipped him up and down the street. He howled his head off, but he never bothered Harry again." These tough, loving women teach the Cancer soul the courage and strength to survive, a major gift of the sign of the crab.

Of course, the Cancer child could find himself unprotected and abandoned, sometimes even an orphan. Barbara Stanwyck's mother died when her daughter was little, and her father immediately disappeared. Her older sister tried to raise her, but she was a child herself, and had to put Barbara (July 16) in foster care. Because there was no one to protect and nourish her, Stanwyck's vulnerable side became hidden. Cancers like her, those afraid of being hurt, refuse to show emotions no matter the situation.

The truly creative Cancer has no choice but to rebel. Creativity is free and spontaneous; by its nature it defies authority, tradition, and rules. Lady Diana Spencer (July 1) broke with tradition when she refused to be separated from her newborn son and brought him on an official trip in spite of protests from the palace. She also broke with tradition by embracing causes unpopular with the royal family. If the rebel is your mate, he wants to experience the surge of power that comes when the spirit is awakened. Unfortunately, this can mean developing bad or dangerous habits. Milton Berle gambled. Saint-Exupéry flew mail into hostile Arab territory. Nelson Rockefeller, (July 8) a man worth over two-hundred million dollars, became governor of New York. Cancers should choose a healthy safe way of experiencing freedom, and don't let your desire for risk and danger get you into trouble.

Don't ever underestimate Cancer opponents. They have incredible staying power, and it gets them ahead in the world. However it also overwhelms and overburdens them, as they can wallow in negative feelings. Anyway, watch that friendly smile; a Cancer can charm you right off the barstool and into his bedroom. Under the covers they may not be acrobats like Geminis, but they have deep passion and know what you want before you ask for it. Remember, your Cancer mates can't ask for themselves, so you'll have to read their signals. Be alert and remember they have two personas, Mr. Tough and Mr. Nice Guy.

Mr. Tough usually appears when Cancers feel the need to protect themselves. If someone gets too close, they can turn into vicious attackers. Their intuitive side is like radar. They know where to strike to stop you dead in your tracks. However, when their need to protect is put to good use, they can adopt an abandoned child, Pearl S. Buck (June 26) had nine; Barbara Stanwyck, an orphan herself, adopted one. Tom Cruise (July 3) a Cancer and his wife, Nicole Kidman, adopted two children, and Norman Cousins (June 24), the laughter doctor, adopted a "Hiroshima Maiden."

Cancers are shy, but once out in public, they are often the center of attention or the life of a party. It's getting them there that's the challenge. They have to go through their list of resistance and fears. Ignore them. They'll get upset if someone pays attention to their hypochondria; it makes them wonder if there's *really* something to worry about. Next time your Cancer says *no* to an invitation, tell him it's a fund-raiser for abused children. Emotions rule a Moon child. Cancers want a foot massage or a glass of warm milk. They need you to care. Then they'll follow wherever you lead them.

Cancers have the best job in the world. They're the mothers who listen to problems, knowing its not as important to solve them as it is to be there for someone you love. In any job you choose, you'll eventually call the shots. You're the foundation of the zodiac and it's a position you feel comfortable in. Things revolve around you, your cooperation or your lack of it. Being in the limelight is not as important to you as having the power to choose who takes the bow.

Anything concerning the home brings out the best in a Cancer. Jobs related to that environment, such as chefs, caterers, and decorators, are appropriate. Great with clients, they often know what people want before they ask for it. Tradition attracts them, and so antique dealers and family businesses often find Cancers at the helm. Their talents are diversified. Fantasy, imitation, and imagination are strong; acting, directing, or performing comes easily. Because they have a strong sense of justice, politics is also a possibility. A little idealistic, they need to learn to work with what is. It's not the profession as much as the security and the mood a career provides that attracts the Moon child.

Cancers are wholesome people. *Cosmo* said of Tom Cruise that he "projects a potent wholesomeness . . . an optimistic air of knowing how to survive." Phyllis George (June 25), Miss America of 1971, has that wholesome appeal; she also was involved in the Special Olympics.

Cancers also can be attracted to the dark, hidden and dirty side of life. Anything unaccepted—pornography, eroticism, the disgusting—there's a need to not exclude anything. If these are your interests, don't deny them. Integrate them in some positive way. Explore them intellectually, produce a documentary, help those who are lost in the negative. When these things are not kept secret, they have no power over you.

Cancers divide the world between family and nonfamily. Family here means anyone who shares their feelings and their love. Spirit rules Cancer and so it is important to recognize the dignity in all and see that we are all connected by a common thread. This will end feelings of isolation and the need to judge others. Expand your world and don't focus on differences. Then peace, love and harmony will be yours.

THE CANCER ENVIRONMENT

The Cancer environment is twofold: it either indulges your weaknesses, allowing you to stay isolated and infantile; or it empowers your Spirit and gives you the courage to take risks. When you connect to Spirit and learn to share your feelings with others, you gain strength, and confidence. Nothing seems impossible when hope, patience, and fortitude are your allies. The danger of the Cancer environment is that it will nurture pain instead of growth and use the closeness of the sign to keep the soul feeling stuck. Use Cancer energy to stay helpless or become invincible—the choice is yours.

Cancer/*One* (June 28, July 1, July 10, July 19) Moon/Sun

PURPOSE: To use both strength and weakness to manifest your creative talents, turning adversity into advantage by your ability to use all sides of yourself spontaneously and without fear; to share your strength and fears with others, helping them to grow.

In this dynamic, Sun and Moon should have equal billing; unfortunately, balance is not easily maintained. For the Cancer, the needs of others are probably overwhelming. There is a magic word that can make everyone disappear if said with conviction. It's "No." The Moon and Sun will be in harmony when yes and no have equal opportunity. The Sun/Moon dynamics must know its limits. The Cancer environment is very indulgent, whatever Cancer offers, the world will take and ask for more. Their competitive spirit also makes it hard for them to say no. Leslie Caron, a wonderful actress and dancer had to leave Hollywood in order to stop the excessive demands placed on her. "Most miserable period in my life, I hate musicals. I had toe shoes on from eight thirty in the morning until six every night. I was constantly in agony ... I had bruises and sprains that couldn't heal. When I walked out of Hollywood, after years of unhappiness, Fred Astaire and Gene Kelly both told me. 'Leslie, you're so smart to quit while you can still walk.' " The Cancer should practice setting limits and their reward will be space enough in which to express themselves.

IF SPIRIT TAKES THE LEAD: With Spirit in the lead, these souls know how to use their weaknesses and strengths, and how to hide their strengths to make themselves appear vulnerable. They are versatile and can adjust to any misfortune. The danger is their desire to be perfect, and always appear in the right, even when they're wrong. They have a will of steel and a strong sense of defiance that can topple the most powerful opponent. Their need for justice and truth, to prove themselves right, and to overcome impossible odds, can cause them to sacrifice the people they love. This is the battle between their career and personal life; their personal needs and their responsibility to others; their need to nurture and the need to be nurtured. If they can give themselves a chance to reflect and heal, integration will happen on its own.

IF EGO TAKES THE LEAD: With Ego strong, a double life is possible. Helpless, infantile, and selfish, they can appear strong, in control and charming. They hide their feelings, but when they're alone, they wallow in them. Life becomes abusive, because it doesn't reflect their reality. It's all fantasy; they need to use their courage and strength to nourish themselves. Their lack of Spirit makes them feel lost, abandoned and alone. They can be vicious if someone comes too close, or can give too much of themselves to the wrong person. Instincts are distorted because their emotional needs are not met and so their ability to make good decisions is weak. They need to come out of themselves and help others.

DIANA SPENCER—FORMER PRINCESS OF WALES (July 1)

Former Princess of Wales, mother of the future king of England.

Diana is a perfect example of the Moon/Sun dynamic. Her prince was none other than the future king of England, but a fairy-tale romance turned sour when the princess took the limelight. Diana did her job so well, exhibiting the warmth and caring side of Cancer, and the competitive spirit and ability to shine of the *One,* that she soon surpassed her husband's popularity. When Charles retreated, the public became her partner. The danger is that a "loving public" has no limits to its demands. Boundaries are needed, as is the ability to contain the disappointment of others. Issues of abandonment are strong for Diana. Her mother died when she was young, and Charles certainly revived Diana's abandonment feelings when he rekindled his affair with his former girlfriend, Camillá Parker Bowles.

The Cancer theme of tradition is nowhere more predominant than with the royal family. However, there is a rebel in Diana, and the desire to be who she is in spite of outside limitations. The mother of two handsome sons, Diana broke with tradition when she refused to leave her newborn at home while she left on an official trip. Her courage and dedication to unpopular royal charities such as the fight against AIDS has endeared her to the world. She exhibits the warmth, caring, and healing qualities of this dynamic, coupled with the loneliness and inner struggle often evident in a Cancer.

SAUL BELLOW (July 10)

Nobel Prize for literature in 1976, author of *Henderson the Rain King, Herzog, Mr. Samler's Planet*

Mr. Bellow's writing reveals the gloomy side of this dynamic. His ideas are profound but represent the depressing truths of life. However, the Sun also has a say, and so he portrays the truth with humor and hope. Bellow expresses the Cancer's quest for pure feelings: "Every writer draws on an innate sense of what being is. Ultimately, his judgement depends on it." Environment has a powerful influence on a Cancer. "We have no mind control yet, but we do have received opinion. It comes from universities, journalism, television, psychiatry . . . The whole thing is a crowd phenomenon and very American." Like a true Cancer, Bellow draws on his ability to observe and imitate; many of his characters are drawn from real life.

Cancer/*Two* (June 29, July 2, July 11, July 20)
Moon/Moon

PURPOSE: To conquer your fears, direct your obsessions toward healthy goals, and to use your strength to help others in need.

"The difference between genius and stupidity is that genius has its limits." Extremes and the abnormal intrigue the Cancer/*Two*. The truth is the Cancer/*Two* is creative, smart, and different. But they wouldn't have it any other way. Extremes can cause problems. The need to indulge their desires as well as those of others, can lead to empty bank accounts, excess weight, too much sex—you name it. Their moods shift faster than their luck at the blackjack table. Depression could be a problem, if they don't anchor themselves through work, faith, or self-awareness. Gifted with intuition, they can disarm a fake facade with one brutal well-aimed remark and have a crowd or audience eating out of their hands. That's their challenge. They either give too much or bolt the door so that not even a wayward ant could find space to crawl under the door. If they block their fluctuating nature, they see everyone else in their life as inconsistent. It may help to read *The Little Prince,* the author is a Moon/*Two* person. "It is only with the heart that one can see rightly; what is essential is invisible to the eye." Consistency of the heart is the key to the Moon/Moon dynamics. Nothing else matters to them. The Cancer world is constantly in a state of flux, but their heart yearns to be tamed by someone they can trust. Moon/Moon people seek a soul mate and yet they're afraid of being abandoned. Keep *The Little Prince* by your bed to remind yourself that what is given with the heart is never lost.

IF SPIRIT TAKES THE LEAD: Too much Spirit makes these souls sensitive, reactive, and eccentric. Compassion is so strong they may need to remove themselves from others in order to live their own life. The simplest things can make them cry or raise their wrath. More than anything else, they desire to feel united with love. This yearning to be a part of someone else can make them lose their sense of self. Instead of being empowered by unity, they will feel helplessly under the thumb of whomever they love. They have no boundaries. Their heart is too big and their desire to trust and help too great. They are often deceived and taken advantage of. Distance seems to be an easy choice, although it won't solve the problem. They need to discern to whom to give their heart, and never forget to return to themselves and make the experience their own. Without faith in a higher power, they project their ideal onto a person, and disaster is only a matter of time.

IF EGO TAKES THE LEAD: If Ego is strong, so is fear and the sense of isolation. These are the children who don't want to grow up. Instead of using their weakness and wounds to heal, they return to the pain and keep it alive. They feel stuck; they fear getting too close and never getting their needs met. These souls are masters at recognizing and using the weaknesses of others, of keeping others helpless like themselves. If they can't grow, no one else will. If you're strong, you're avoided, so why be strong: But don't think by any means that they are weak. It takes strength to remain a child and fight the forces of growth. They have a dangerous will. If someone tries to pull them along, they'll bite their hand.

TOM HANKS (July 2)

Actor.

One of Tom Hanks's greatest successes was *Big*. His adult child was incredibly believable—and probably easy for a Moon/Moon person. *Sleepless In Seattle* allowed him to portray the caring father and the lonely man. *Philadelphia* tackles the suffering and healing of Cancer. And only a Cancer could make *Forrest Gump* a hit at the box office.

A natural comedian, Hanks began acting in high school. Then, he studied drama at California State University. He was a good classical actor and interned with the Great Lakes Shakespeare Festival in Cleveland. He made his professional debut in *The Taming of the Shrew*. He moved to New York, where he continued working on stage. Finally, he landed a part in the television sitcom, *Bosom Buddies*. From there it was on to the movies.

THURGOOD MARSHALL (July 2)

The first African American on the Supreme Court.

"The most important Black man of this century—a man who rose higher than any Black person before him and who has had more effect on Black lives than any other person, Black or White," said *Ebony* contributor Juan Williams. For twenty years, Marshall used the Constitution to force state and federal courts to protect the rights of African-Americans. His most successful achievement came when his legal team challenged public school segregation in *Brown vs. Board of Education.* The long-standing "separate but equal" doctrine of racial segregation in public schools was overturned.

Head of his class at Howard Law School, Marshall returned to his hometown to practice law. He was invited to join the legal staff of the NAACP, and soon was heading the organization's assault on state segregation laws.

The tough side of Cancer emerged when as a child, his father taught him to fight. Dignity and fairness are also Cancer issues. With any double dynamics, we meet ourselves. Marshall saw his own pain and unfulfilled needs in everyone around him. Instead of complaining, he used the toughness and persistence of the Moon to make changes.

Cancer/*Three* (June 30, July 3, July 12) Moon/Jupiter

PURPOSE: To integrate your feelings of independence, leadership, and freedom with your sensitivity, and your need to be nourished and loved, and not see it as a weakness but as a unifying strength.

In a league of their own. That's the only way I can describe this combination. Either no one can touch them or they've been tossed around unmercifully. It's how they developed their own rules, their incredible resourcefulness and the confidence to do what others won't even consider. Jupiter people always live as a law unto themselves. A love of travel, and foreign customs may prevail. The Cancer/*Three* has an ability to be more objective than other Moon combinations; their philosophical side helps them step back from their feelings. Their instincts are strong, and they have the gift of the common touch. They sense the pulse of the public.

Cancer/*Threes* must own their own importance, and when they do, their potential will take them right to the top. The danger is that once there, they will begin to believe they're invincible. That's when they're ready for a Humpty Dumpty fall, usually caused by someone they consider their inferior. The Cancer/*Threes* will find themselves either shivering alone in the cold, or the center of the party. When they believe in themselves, the red carpet is rolled out and their next challenge is not to get caught up in their self-importance.

IF SPIRIT TAKES THE LEAD: When Spirit is powerful, so is the rebel. These souls are revolutionaries. They may be shy, but they're tough and they don't give up. Human dignity is important to them, as is justice. They spend their lives overthrowing unfair authority, or they learn to work for truth within the limits of the law. Compassionate and a leader, they tend to take too much responsibility for everyone else. When they pay too much attention to their problems and their pain it keeps them from growing.

IF EGO TAKES THE LEAD: With Ego ahead of Spirit, independence and the desire for freedom are strong. The Cancer/*Three* works it out in one of two extreme ways: either they refuse to take their power and align themselves with someone strong and independent who feeds their weaknesses, keeping them dependent and obligated to them, or they are too independent and they feed the weaknesses of others, using them to do whatever they need done.

MIKE TYSON (June 30)

Heavyweight boxing champion.

From a painfully shy boy in the ghettos of Brooklyn, to the youngest heavyweight boxing champion, and a convicted felon, Mike Tyson portrays many of the difficult characteristics of the Moon/Jupiter combination. Tyson never knew his father. His mother, a gentle woman, became an alcoholic. Always trying to get his mother's attention, Tyson felt emotionally abandoned. She died before he became famous. "My mother didn't believe in violence. She detested it. I was very shy, almost effeminate shy," he admits. The neighborhood kids used to beat him up and steal his belongings. Finally, he fought back. Almost overnight he changed from a shy victim to an aggressive victimizer. That's Cancer, tender and tough at the same time. Jupiter took over (it loves to live by its own rules), and he broke the law: pick-pocketing, mugging, purse snatching, and robbing stores. Sent to a reformatory in New York, he assaulted another inmate and was transferred to Elmwood Cottage, for out-of-control prisoners. Fate had it that Bobby Steward, a light heavyweight champion was a staff member. Steward became Tyson's first trainer. Tyson's shy/aggressive nature made him unpredictable in the ring. He lost his bid for the Olympics and had to work his way to fame fight by fight. His former wife, actress Robin Givens, suffered abuse and claimed that Tyson was a manic depressive.

BILL COSBY (July 12)

Actor, comedian, author.

Getting ahead was not easy for Bill Cosby until he tapped the humor and childishness of this dynamic and took a chance in showbiz. Cosby remembers trying to get a summer job while in college. "I got some of the worst excuses for not hiring me. I got so tired of riding buses and spending money to hear some guy say, 'Well—', Finally I just called and said over the phone, 'Do you hire Negroes?' No." Later, appearing at the Gaslight in Greenwich Village, New York, he was singled out by a *New York Times* reporter and his career was launched. His television hit, *The Cosby Show,* exhibited the humor prevalent of this combination, and used the Cancer theme of home and family as its format. Known for his ability to understand kids, Cosby developed a cartoon series called *Fat Albert & The Cosby Kids* and an album entitled *Cosby and the Kids.*

Cancer/*Four* (June 22, July 4, July 13, July 22) Moon/Uranus

PURPOSE: To use your ability to communicate with many different and opposing people to bring about unity without becoming attached to drama and crises.

"Only dead fish swim with the stream."—Unknown. The Cancer/*Four* was swimming against the current in the womb. The wise ones have learned to avoid the rocks and debris; the stubborn souls are still getting banged about. Cancer/*Fours* are comfortable with tension and whizzes at negotiations. They can bring anybody together. Jack Kemp (July 13), former secretary for Housing and Urban Development, is known for his negotiating skills. Ann Landers (July 4) has used her integrity, wit, and wisdom to become one of the most widely read columnists in America. "Whoso would be a man must be a nonconformist."—Emerson. Cancer/*Fours* do not like things dull or easy; they make great sacrifices just to keep their differences. Extremes demand caution, for they don't lead to peace. Peace is not what they seek. The meeting point of two opposing forces is where they are comfortable. Their choice is the road less traveled. They know how to turn things to their advantage because they're versatile—and versatility is power.

IF SPIRIT TAKES THE LEAD: When Spirit is strong, the need to help others is powerful. These souls go out on a limb and break the rules to make sure human dignity and justice prevail. They are activists in a constant state of tension and evolution. When several things are happening at one time, they love it. They wade through the emotional context, make sense of it, and use it for a positive end. When they're too spiritual, they are used by others who seek them as their savior. They need to value peace and allow it into their life.

IF EGO TAKES THE LEAD: With Ego giving orders, what gets done is a lot of everything. These souls can be so talented, others can't keep up; nor do they want to try. They like chaos, confusion, and emotional stress. They create it or use it for their advantage. Because tension, hostility and powerful, emotional scenes attract them, their personal life is a mess. Either they are unfaithful, or they choose dependent people whom they can control. They can be cold or compassionate.

GERALDO RIVERA (July 4)

Journalist, reporter, talk-show host.

"I'm not smarter, or better than Phil, Oprah, Johnny, or David, but I am different . . . These mid-life eyes have witnessed the full range of the human experience: from exhilaration and triumph to the pits of misery and despair.'' His own words sum up the vast emotional variety of this dynamic. He's unique and likes to burn the candle at both ends while holding it in the middle. His TV talk show is at the top of the ratings and features sensational subjects and exciting people. He made his mark with his shocking reports on the Willowbrook State School for the Mentally Retarded, and established himself as a passionate reporter. Obtaining a key to the facility, he took a camera crew to film the patients, without authorization. As a result, Governor Rockefeller reinstated $20 million that had been cut from Willowbrook's budget. "I make no pretense of objectivity. But I'm not in the business of making people cry. I'm in the business of change." Uranus at its best.

HARRISON FORD (July 13)

Actor.

Success did not come overnight for Harrison Ford. He made a living as "carpenter to the stars" while trying to break into films. Caught between two opposing beliefs since birth—his mother is a Russian Jew, his father an Irish Catholic—Harrison struggled for his own identity. As a teenager it was too much for him to handle and he flunked out of college three days before graduation. Signed by Columbia Pictures, "I did a year and a half and got kicked out on my ass for being too difficult." He finally got his chance to show his talent in *America Graffiti*. But it was *Star Wars* that gave him his big break. Exhibiting the resistance of Moon/Uranus to be labeled, he said "The natural state for an actor is that of observer, where you can learn something. Instead, I'm a focus of attention."

Cancer/*Five* (June 23, July 5, July 14) Moon/Mercury

PURPOSE: To share your sensitivity, your keen perceptions, your unique insights with others, so that you may experience new ideas and solutions to your problems while at the same time expanding your sense of self.

"Work spares us from three evils: boredom, vice and need."—Voltaire. Cancer/*Fives* can always fit one more thing into their schedule. Workaholic and restless, everything must be in motion. They are as busy as a bee—the killer kind, and what they kill is you. Limits are a must. They plan to slow down, but most things stay in their head. Mercury makes them analyze everything to an extreme; still, nobody gets things done like Cancer/*Fives*.

Slowing down is a necessity and when they see the results of their sharing, they'll never doubt the power of unity. "It's not so much how busy you are, but why you are busy. The bee is praised; the mosquito is swatted."—Marie O'Connor.

IF SPIRIT TAKES THE LEAD: With Spirit leading the way, the need to share and help others is the problem. There's no time for self; sharing is used as a means of avoiding their issues. They need to set aside time for being with themself. Without silence and solitude, growth and understanding is not possible.

IF EGO TAKES THE LEAD: Ego responds to Moon/*Five* power by becoming quite versatile. It is a master of everything and nothing. These souls are always busy. Capable of professions and relationships of all kinds, they have trouble making choices. Afraid of abandonment they need to cling. The tendency is to allow the world to choose them. That's dangerous because they will only get their needs met by chance. They avoid pain and the moment by choosing people who are unavailable and creating a life filled with crisis. This assures they'll never have the silence needed to reflect. They should slow down and allow their feelings to emerge. The results will be a happy home life.

INGMAR BERGMAN (July 14)

Swedish filmmaker.

Major films include *The Seventh Seal, The Magician, Wild Strawberries, Through a Glass Darkly, Persona, The Silence, Cries and Whispers,* and *Fanny and Alexander.*

Known as one of the foremost creative forces in world cinema, Bergman uses the pain and joy of this combination in his films—"mankind's search for love in a universe where God remains inexplicably silent." That's the seeker or number *Five* who still thinks he's going to find the answers in something outside himself. One critic said, "His films are Munch paintings come to life, offering the highest happiness and the deepest misery. Offering all that being alive can bring." Using the extreme sensitivity of the Moon, it has been said he has a mesmeric ability to bring out the hidden resources of his actors.

The son of a clergyman, Bergman was raised with strict punishments and beatings. He dropped out of school to become an errand boy at the Royal Opera House. There he began to learn his craft. He tried his hand at scriptwriting, but it wasn't until his 1956 *Smiles of a Summer Night* that he received acclaim as author and director. One critic said, "he has made forty-three films in forty years; he had six wives and nine children; he has lived in exile, been sick unto death, fearful unto loathing, as well as having had the strength and charm to find life rich and entertaining."

POLLY BERGEN (July 14)

Singer, actress, lecturer, businesswoman.

"I'm not good at being idle, I suppose it comes from an early work ethic background where work is what you did." The daughter of a construction engineer, Bergen attended forty-five schools in twenty-eight states by the time she was eighteen. Determined to be a singer, she was discovered singing hillbilly tunes in a Hollywood café. In 1965 her turtle oil cosmetics became a great success. Eight years later she sold the company to Fabergé, where she served as director for three years. One of the first women appointed to the board of the Singer Company, she is always on the move. At one time she owned three dress shops while promoting the ERA and maintaining a busy lecture and acting career.

Cancer/*Six* (June 24, July 6, July 15) Moon/Venus

PURPOSE: To use love and faith to resist the endless pressure to conform and fulfill the world's needs; to develop a strong identity through owning your weaknesses and vulnerability, unafraid of what the world will think.

"Falling in love is not an extension of one's limits or boundaries, it is a partial and temporary collapse of them."—M. Scott Peck. Moon/Venus have no boundaries. Cancer/*Sixes* need love. If their emotional needs are not met, it could lead to excessive sexual or escapist behavior. Unconditional love has negative side effects. Overprotecting people doesn't teach them how to cope with life, and it opens the protector up for abuse. If their need to give is uncontrollable, they should channel that powerful force into a creative endeavor. Write a book, design a dress for the senior prom, or redecorate the bedroom—the Cancer/*Six* has style, flair and excellent taste.

The other extreme is also possible. These persons may have too many boundaries. They can be cold, controlling, afraid to use their soft side because it usually uses them. The heart and soul of the Cancer/*Six* is in everything they do.

IF SPIRIT TAKES THE LEAD: With Spirit ahead, the soul is strong, resilient, and tough. They're compassionate, too. They are perfectionists who will strive to improve the life of others with or without their consent. Their need to please may make them too moldable, allowing others to be insensitive because they can feel and understand their pain. Too responsible, they can avoid their own issues through losing themselves in another. Their apparent selfless nature hides a strong and tenacious will.

IF EGO TAKES THE LEAD: If Ego is strong, the soul can be either lost and needy, seeking love and never finding the sense of wholeness they know they need; or they can be cold, ignoring their emotions and those of others. Compassionate or icy, they are capable of being both—sometimes together. They have great charm and make a wonderful showman. Gifted with the ability to imitate, they can transform into what someone else wants, hiding their truth from themselves and the world. They are lucky; opportunities come their way, but without Spirit nothing is ever enough. They live for luxury. Love is what they're seeking, but wealth and possessions are what they believe they desire.

NORMAN COUSINS (June 24)

Editor of *Saturday Review,* author, medical guru promoting laughter therapy.

Faced with a rare collagen disease and given a slim chance for survival, Cousins "laughed himself back to health." Here's a man who knows how to use the humor of Cancer for a healing purpose. *Anatomy of an Illness,* in which he shared his personal experience, became a best-seller. Cousins believes that long-term depression and negative emotions can impair the immune system and that positive emotions help recovery by producing physical and biochemical changes. As a child, Cousins was a victim of tuberculosis. "I learned the philosophy of coping with disease." That's Spirit overcoming limitations.

SYLVESTER STALLONE (July 6)

Actor, writer, producer.

"The champion represents the ultimate warrior—the nearest thing to being immortal while mortal," says Stallone. The survival qualities and strength of this dynamic eventually became the theme behind Stallone's movies and success. Told by his teachers he was retarded, Stallone decided to develop his physical talents. Venus is beautiful and no one will deny that Stallone has a beautiful body. His early attempts at acting were not successful until after seeing Muhammad Ali fight, he was inspired to write *Rocky.* Ali was in the ring with an unknown named Chuck Wepner, who managed to go the whole fifteen rounds before being knocked out.

Success is never easy for a Venus soul to maintain. They tend to overdose and lose what is most important to them because they haven't learned inner boundaries. Once a star, Stallone separated from his wife and two children. But he has a soft side, too. He is chairman for the New York March of Dimes.

Cancer/*Seven* (June 25, July 7, July 16) Moon/Neptune

PURPOSE: To use faith to rise above your mood swings and dark thoughts that threaten your confidence, directing your spirit toward creativity and projects that help others.

"I have a feeling inside of me that without playing—producing my own sound—I'm lost, I need to do it."—Pinchas Zukerman. In the Cancer/*Seven,* pureness of spirit prevails. Music and faith in God are wonderful media for this energy. Loners, creative geniuses and sometimes victims, they often struggle with poor physical health. The body is often weak when the Spirit is strong; sometimes a weak body forces them to strengthen their Spirit. Neptune represents strong idealism and a desire to escape the harsh realities of life. When combined with the Moon, obsessiveness is the only way. Moon/Neptune people need a strong Spirit and a good relationship with their Ego in order to survive. "When we talk to God, we're praying. When God talks to us, we're schizophrenic."— Lily Tomlin. They're either spiritual or crazy; often, they are psychic. Grounding themselves in the simple tasks of life is key to keeping the spiritual world from disturbing their everyday life.

Many Moon/Neptune people are orphans. Being alone gives them a unique opportunity to find themselves. Pure, clean and unadulterated, they are eager to emerge and leave their mark on the world. They have the power to heal; this requires a brief journey into the soul of someone else. The danger is that they won't return.

IF SPIRIT TAKES THE LEAD: When spirit is strong with the Cancer/*Seven* then love, faith, and self-sacrifice are powerful forces. These souls are being asked to stand alone. Help from the outside world will not come until they take full responsibility for their lives. The support they give to others must first be given to themselves, then the world opens its arms and the love they desire becomes a reality. Once they learn to set boundaries and say no, their fear of surrender is conquered and life becomes less isolating.

IF EGO TAKES THE LEAD: With ego in the lead, the Cancer/*Seven* becomes manipulative, impulsive, and judgmental. Their will is strong; they want things perfect, and they don't care who they hurt, or eliminate in the process. Strong leaders, control is a constant issue—they seek it in order to calm the chaos they struggle with inside. Without faith this combination will never feel satisfied, be consumed with restlessness, and a desire to dominate whatever or whomever they engage.

RINGO STARR (July 7)

The Beatles' drummer.

Ringo was born the only child of a barmaid and a house painter. Very sickly as a child, he spent many years in bed or under treatment. He had peritonitis and a mass of broken pelvic bones. For one year he had pleurisy. It was music, Neptune's favorite form of expression, that helped Ringo find acceptance and develop a strong belief in himself. Fate took over when he replaced Pete Best as drummer for the Beatles. Then Neptune took him to the top of the mountain of fame.

BARBARA STANWYCK (July 16)

Actress.

"I had to cope with loneliness at a very early age." Orphaned at four, Stanwyck was raised by her sister, Mildred, and later in foster homes. She worked as a night club dancer and landed a part in Ziegfeld's *Follies*. Tough, like most Cancers, she never used a double. Struggling for security and acceptance because she was abandoned as a child, she learned to hide her sensitive side to keep from getting hurt. Stanwyck's popularity as a young and beautiful leading lady did not diminish with age. She won an Emmy for Best Actress in a Dramatic Special for her part in the miniseries, *The Thorn Birds*. She said, "I'm not a yesterday's woman. I'm a tomorrow's woman."

Cancer/*Eight* (June 26, July 8, July 17) Moon/Saturn

PURPOSE: To know that life is a process, that patience and inner questioning brings growth and rewards; to let go of control and use your courage to share your talents; to use your position to help others.

"Happiness is not a goal, it is a by-product."—Eleanor Roosevelt. For Saturn, the process is more important than the result. Hard work is usually required, and those who do it without cutting corners reap its rewards, which can be great and lasting. If your emotions rule and refuse to be bound by training and experience, then the creative spirit is undisciplined and talent remains unproductive. Not the case with Cynthia Gregory. This prima ballerina was known for her impeccable technique as well as for the power and spirit of her interpretation. Anna Moffo (June 27) combined her fabulous beauty with an exquisite voice. If Saturn dominates, the exterior and form are important; when the Moon takes the lead, inner feelings and emotions prevail. The trick is to get them to work together—and work is the key word here. "The only thing that separates successful people from the ones who aren't is the willingness to work very, very hard."—Helen Gurley Brown. The Moon adds a touch of obsessiveness and a perfectionism is possible. Other side effects can be a critical or judgmental attitude. When the Moon and Saturn work together there is a feeling of wholeness and satisfaction. That's because what you put into a project or relationship is in proportion to its demands.

IF SPIRIT TAKES THE LEAD: If Spirit is strong, responsibility is distorted. They believe that, if they don't do the job themselves, it won't get done right. They're perfectionists. The results are stress, an overloaded schedule and a lack of respect from others. If they don't pay attention to their needs, why should anyone else? They need to let go and have faith that things will work out the way they're supposed to. Their job is to value the process of self-discovery.

IF EGO TAKES THE LEAD: If Ego is strong, we've got a dictator. Control and isolation are issues. These souls are hard to reach; they don't trust. They're perfectionists, but instead of striving to perfect themselves they turn a critical eye on the world. They judge rather than love; they hoard rather than share. They need to open up to the universe and have a little faith.

DONALD SUTHERLAND (July 17)

Actor.

A self-proclaimed workaholic, he is known to value the creative process more than the completed film. The desire of Saturn to do the work for its own sake is definitely apparent in Donald. "I work so much because I like to . . . I'm very happy being an actor." Always trying to reach the essence of a character, he finds something of himself in all the roles he plays. "I see myself playing roles where you can say, 'That's perfect for him'—not as a character actor, but as an actor performing a character which is close to one's self." One of his most perfect roles was the surgeon Hawkeye Pierce in the film version of *MASH.*

RAFFI (July 8)

Singer, composer.

"My music respects its audience. By understanding that children are whole people with important feelings and concerns, we give them the best chance of becoming healthy, loving adults." The creative side of the Moon is expressed through music and children, the favorite people of Cancer. Saturn brings respect and dignity. Raffi was born in Cairo, Egypt; his family then moved to Canada. He discovered his talent with children when his mother-in-law asked him to play his guitar and sing at her Toronto nursery school. Records, books, concerts, videos, and songbooks followed. Raffi is a pioneer in producing exceptional music for children.

Cancer/*Nine* (June 27, July 9, July 18) Moon/Mars

PURPOSE: To use your power and your ego to break through the resistance and fears of others so that you can intimately share your world with them, always respecting their space and never forgetting your own goals and path.

"Egotist: a person . . . more interested in himself than in me."—Ambrose Bierce. In Cancer/*Nine,* Ego is all pervasive, especially if the Moon succeeds and nurtures Mars's sense of entitlement. If Mars dominates, then the individual will be strong enough to stand up against the needs of others and do his own thing. The Cancer/*Nines'* challenge here is to keep their sensitivity and concern for others, without letting it overwhelm their sense of self. They must not try to control someone else's direction or lose themselves in theirs. They have healer energy if they can keep their sensitivity. Gifted with great magnetism, power, and sexual energy, opposition attracts them. Early in life they need to learn to protect themselves, and then not become bullies in return. Excess is all too possible with the Mars/*Nine,* but the only way they'll learn is by hitting a few walls. You're powerful, and sometimes you may forget just how forceful your energy can be.

IF SPIRIT TAKES THE LEAD: With Spirit ahead, the passion and desire to change the world is too strong. These souls don't listen, they act. They believe they're right, and once they've made up their mind, nothing stands in their way. They don't respect others' boundaries. These are idealists and dreamers and think they know what's best for everyone. Yes, they're obsessive and seldom listen to themselves. They need to use their great compassion with patience.

IF EGO TAKES THE LEAD: If Ego is strong, they know it all. Whatever the problem, they've got the solution. These are manipulators, they use the weaknesses and fears of others for their own end. They impact their environment with charisma and a definite point of view. They know where they're going and how to get there. If the Cancer sign is dominant, they might be a follower of the person I just described. Self-control is their problem. They're ruled by their powerful emotions. If they feel rejected, they might strike out and hurt others. They want to be first, and they need to be needed above everything else.

ROSS PEROT (June 27)

Billionaire businessman, presidential candidate.

Now here's a man who leaves his mark. He surprised everyone when he first ran for president. For many Americans he made good sense and the direct, honest style of Mars gained him a remarkable following. An action-oriented man, he sprang two of his employees out of an Iranian prison by bribing the warden with $1.5 million. He is known for his charitable pursuits and his love of family. He said, ''The saddest thing that could happen to me is to raise weak children as a result of my financial success.'' He was the first businessman to receive the Winston Churchill Award. He also received the Jefferson Award for Public Service by a Private Citizen, and the Raoul Wallenberg Award for embodying the spirit, and courage of the Swedish diplomat who saved thousands of Hungarian Jews from the Nazis in World War II.

BARBARA CARTLAND (July 9)

Romance writer.

''By her 80th birthday she had finished her 300th book, writing an average of 24 books per year.'' That's Mars for you—always on the go and paired with the Moon, it can be excessive. Cartland keeps her heroines true to the virtuousness of Cancer. About her books she said, "They're about pure love. Romeo and Juliet love, the love of the troubadours, the love of Browning and Botticelli. The love of a decent woman."

Her son, Ian McCorquodale, who is also her business manager, says of his mother, "I hold only one thing against her. Mother simply can't relax. She's never learned how." Exhibiting the fighting spirit of Mars, Cartland says, "Part of my philosophy of life is never to admit that you've been beaten or done down. Quite early on I learned that the best way to survive is to pretend that anything unpleasant simply hasn't happened." That's also a touch of denial. The Moon can be overprotective, not just with others, but also with itself.

SUMMARY

Cancer is the mother who loves her child with all his faults and idiosyncrasies, indulging his desires one moment, and in the next, turning her back so he can learn to survive. The consequences of unconditional love and abandonment are the prevailing issues for Cancer. Alone or merged into someone else, Cancer demands we transcend isolation through feelings that bind us to others. Cancers are good friends and healers. Healing is merely the ability to share pain or pleasure, the unconscious connectedness that exists between us all. This profound understanding gives Cancers a strength seldom obvious in their appearance; they are often seen as vulnerable and afraid. Once their protective instincts are awakened they bring forth their ability to fight. They are able to endure pain and pleasure beyond the capacity of others. Their acute sensitivity and intuition makes them creative, psychic, and often excessive. They need to learn to be supportive without being indulgent, to provide without making others dependent, and to ask but not expect perfection. Once they learn these lessons they will be ready to encounter the fruits of their desires, the freedom, love, and creativity which blossoms in the next sign, Leo.

SELECTED SOURCES

Richard H. Barker *Marcel Proust: A Biography* Criterion Books 1958

Ronald Harwood *Mandela* New American Library 1987

Montieth M. Illingworth *Mike Tyson: Money, Myth and Betrayal* Birch Lane 1991

Helen Keller *The Story of My Life* Introduction by Lou Ann Walker Signet 1993

Philip B. Kunhardt, Jr., Phillip B. Kunhardt III, Peter W. Kunhardt *P.T. Barnum: America's Greatest Showman—An Illustrated Biography* Knopf 1995

Gilda Radner *It's Always Something* Avon 1990

Antoine De Saint-Exupery *The Little Prince* Harcourt Brace Jovanovich 1943

Maxwell A. Smith *Knight of the Air. The Life and Works of Antoine de Saint-Exupery* Pageant Press 1956

Teresa of Avila *Interior Castle* Translated and edited by E. Allison Peers-Doubleday 1990

James Cagney *Cagney* Doubleday 1976

Leo

(July 23–August 23)

Leo the lion is king, that's for sure.
Fearless, and strong, he's honest and pure.
Commanding attention wherever he goes
His strength and his courage everyone knows.
Eager and willing, he'll take the lead.
Generous and giving, he's known by his deeds.
Leos are lovers, they're fun and they're smart.
They're the best for one reason, they're ruled by the heart.

Ruler: Sun   **Symbol: Lion**
Element: Fire   **Number: One**

The soul, having freed its spirit in Cancer, begins to sense its greatness. Earthly limits are no longer an obstacle; they become the resistance needed to hone talents, ideas, and imagination. The greater the challenge, the more focused and pointed the Leo becomes. Once they discover their destiny, nothing stands in their way. All their attention, their energy, and their creativity go toward becoming the best they can be. Magic Johnson (August 14) said, "As soon as I realized I had a God-given talent to play the game [basketball], I was determined to take it as far as I could." Whatever becomes the central focus of your life is given power and grows. This is the Leo's secret weapon. They know how to make themselves the center of your world; they can take whatever they desire from it and make it central to their existence.

Limits don't exist in Leo, even when it comes to knowledge. They journey beyond tradition and into the realm of the imagination. Imagination is a key to breaking boundaries; it takes them out of the moment and allows them to explore endless possibilities. Of course, if it is not backed by hard work and commitment, imagination can be used to escape the moment and its responsibility, two important ingredients for success.

Leo represents strength and courage and their challenge is to use their power wisely. Ego will want to shine at the expense of others, to be the best no matter what the cost. Spirit works toward unity and the betterment of the whole. It uses strength to add harmony and empower others. Leo is not about showing off; it's about reaching the top and using your strength to help others. By lending your confidence and your courage to someone who needs it, you cross the border of self and journey into the realm of others, where true power lies. Percy Bysshe Shelley (August 4) the nineteenth-century British poet and aristocrat, showed this ability at an early age. Handsome and sought after, Shelley was supposed to choose a young lady of "rank and fashion" to lead a dance. However, sitting next to society's finest was a girl who everyone knew had been seduced. Ignoring protocol and gossip, Shelley offered her the dance. Magic Johnson chose to play at Michigan State rather than The University of Michigan; its weaker team needed his strengths. This is the way you as an individual can make a difference. The Leo hero doesn't fight dragons to protect others; he fights to teach others how to avoid problems through knowledge and understanding.

Mysterious, bold, strong, and compassionate, Leos sparkle with the light of Spirit. They command attention wherever they go. This is John Huston, (August 5) the director, who could draw the best from the greatest actors; this is Madame Blavatsky (August 12) the internationally known psychic with a presence that both intrigued and frightened the elite of her time; this is the comical perspective of a Lucille Ball (August 6); and this is the spiritual essence of a poet like Shelley, capable of lifting our souls with his words. These are beings rich with passion, gifted with imagination, and the desire to be the very best. When their hearts are big, they include anyone in need; when they're narrow, they are the most selfish of the selfish.

Leos strive to undermine dogma and tradition that prevent the spirit from free expression. They speak directly and inspirationally from the heart. Menachem Begin (August 16) had the Leo gift of oratory. "His speeches were electrifying. He was learning to use the spoken word as a sharp and effective political weapon." One of the reasons Leos do so well with words is their love of books. They can be obsessed with reading and learning. They are good writers and lecturers. Madame Blavatsky was an ardent reader. "She could not be prevailed to give up her books, which she would devour night and day as long as the impulse lasted." The love of books is a love of knowledge, the anchor for imagination. The more knowledge one has, the more freedom one feels to explore. With the desire to create by using knowledge and imagination, Leo is the beginning of the scientific mind. Lucille Ball loved inventing gadgets. "Along with the director Edward Sedgwick and Buster Keaton, she built a nut-cracker the size of an auto engine . . . Her favorite invention was a device known as a venetian-blind raiser. The contraption would respond to the press of a button when it was desired to raise a blind. As the blind went up, there was a small explosion and a record player ground out 'Hail to the Chief,' followed by a large picture of Louis B. Mayer, which popped up from the contrivance . . ."

Gifted with a radiance, Leos remind us of the Sun and its magnetic power. Madame Blavatsky had "prominent azure eyes, which seemed to observe her surroundings with an intensity that was hypnotic to many and frightening to some.'' Intensity is the key. Leos approach life with a serious nature, which seldom interferes with their ability to have fun. It is precisely their seriousness which demands spontaneity.

Leo is the mastery of our passions, the emergence of Spirit into consciousness and its own power. With passions under control, you can ignite others to accomplish your goals. If passion rules, it overrides reason; it may inspire, but it won't produce any events of consequence, except by chance. Passion without the patience of Spirit is undirected and unproductive. It doesn't even care if it hurts itself, because it's primal and without consciousness. Passion that has been tamed, has the power to unite a world. Menachem Begin used passion with great restraint at a pivotal time in history. His underground group, IZL, was dedicated to driving the British out of the Israeli homeland and to the establishment of a Jewish state. When the British captured and tortured his men Begin, refused to retaliate. He would not allow brother to fight brother.

Leo is the light and the shadow. Its heroes come from the shadow, and with them, something new and wonderful comes to light. This is good that leads to evil, and evil that leads to good. Magic Johnson was burdened with the terrible knowledge of being HIV positive. From a darkness which could have kept him separated from others, he emerged a leader, someone who used his own negative for the good of others by making the public aware of the danger of HIV. Menachem Begin was another hero/villain; he used his courage for both the destruction and building of a nation. Shelley was an aristocrat, but he gave his time and talent to many a cry for freedom. In his pamphlets ''Address to the Irish People,'' were proposals for bettering the condition of humankind. He was for Catholic emancipation and the tolerance of all religions.

Leos must learn to live in both the dark and the light and maintain their faith throughout. This journey in and out of the spotlight tests their commitment to their goal. Spirit is never about immediate gratification; it's about long-term consequences. It makes the tough choice, the one that may deny the moment, but promises an end result.

Besides rising from the shadow, Leo also represents foreshadowing, the indication of something to come. The best foreshadowing of the future is our children. Leo rules offspring and love children. Rose Kennedy (July 22) had nine children. Jacqueline Kennedy Onassis (July 28) protected John and Caroline like a mother lion. Children are our legacy. Jacqueline Kennedy Onassis was expected to give President Kennedy a son, someone to carry on the Kennedy mystique and success. Leos are often the firstborn; this is the position that inherits the crown. A Leo can symbolize this position. Connie Chung is the youngest of a family of girls. She says, ''I often feel like my father's son. I believe I've carried on the family name in a different way.''

In Leo, the past and the future are linked through the child. Leos are often close to grandparents because both the grandparent and the grandchild are essential links in the continuation of the family. John Huston recalled, "My grandmother was, in many ways, more a mother to me than my mother."

Another expression of foreshadowing is the emergence of the protégé. Leos often find themselves under the shadow of someone great, waiting to emerge into the light of their own independence. The teacher or mentor or parent is usually a strong, charismatic personality who overwhelms the Leo's life; often they want to mold the Leo into their own likeness. The primary challenge of the Leo is to take the best from others and create something better and unique from the encounter. To do this means that sooner or later the protégé needs to become independent, and the emergence of his own individuality will conflict with that of the teacher figure. It takes great maturity on both sides for this transition to happen without hurt feelings.

Balanchine was dancer Suzanne Farrell's ballet teacher. In order to get married and live her own life, Farrell (August 16) was forced to break her ties with him. Carl Gustav Jung (July 26) eventually had to sever his relationship with Sigmund Freud in order to express his own views. The separation caused him a nervous breakdown. Joey Buttafucco overwhelmed Amy Fisher's life. Fisher (August 21) learned all the wrong things from her teacher, though he did make her famous. The need to separate from the family, the teacher, the safety of what is known, and journey into the unknown is what Leo is all about. Madonna (August 16) says, "I felt guilty because I felt like I was traveling through people. But I think that's true of most ambitious, driven people. You take what you can, then move on. If the people can't move with you—whether it's a physical or emotional move—I feel sad about that. That's part of the tragedy of love."

Like the Sun, whose presence is the central figure of the zodiac, a Leo needs to be at the pivotal point of any experience. Leos are drawn to the place of responsibility, the center of a collective energy that is either devoid of leadership or ruled empirically by a powerful soul. Sooner or later Leos must become the center of their own universe. John Huston was "the center of almost all the lives he came in contact with, specially among family . . . Wherever John lived for any length of time, they always turned up." Fidel Castro (August 13) rebelled against his strong, authoritarian father long before he led the overthrow of the Cuban government.

Rebelling means taking full responsibility for your actions, feelings, successes, and failures. If you don't, you are doomed to live in the shadow of others. This stage of the journey requires confrontation and separation, two challenges that require courage and strength.

Leos have a powerful presence and personality, through which they win approval. They present to the world what it wants to see and hide the rest. However, identifying with the mask too closely demands a sacrifice of the "real" self as the only way to keep the image intact. Jacqueline Kennedy became a prisoner of her image; to keep the Spirit alive the real Jackie withdrew from the spotlight. When this happens, you are only living a small part of your potential. The mask needs constant adjustments to be effective on a regular basis. Keep exposing new sides of yourself and presenting new talents so that they can be made stronger. It takes a strong person to change his position in order to achieve a goal. Menachem Begin seized the opportunity to make peace with Egypt, an old and bitter enemy. "Towards the end of 1977 he emerged as a statesman capable of changing his views in keeping with circumstances. This reflected a radical shift in his known positions."

Leos approach the world by dividing unity—the conscious and unconscious—in half. Consciousness contains both the revealed and the hidden depending on what you choose to show to achieve your purpose. Unconsciousness is split into that which is deeply hidden and repressed, and that which soars so high into the unknown you feel powerless to direct it. This can manifest as the desire to be perfect, or as overwhelming imagination. The Leo has a double personality, both a charismatic, sparkling side, and a serious side, hidden side. Leo is a public person and a private one. They make great politicians and actors. Who else can manipulate their personality with such skill? George Bernard Shaw (July 26), the witty genius playwright of the late nineteenth and early twentieth century, was known for his audacious manner, but he was really shy and much of his character was orchestrated, rather than true. According to his biographer, Archibald Henderson, he began in his early life "to act a part in public and to hide his real personality behind it." Zoe Sallis, John Huston's lover, said of the famous director, "Nobody touched on what a humane human he was. It was always what a great filmmaker and how talented he was and that bravado thing . . . I hated it. That's the only side John ever showed anybody but I saw the other side. He was just a sweet guy, just adorable."

This duality of public and private, of showman and hermit, represents a powerful tug of war that keeps the Leo off-center. Maturity will teach the Leo that image and reputation are important, but not the sustaining part of life, and that learning to accept all of oneself with equal understanding is imperative to peace and happiness. The more demanding the public life, the more vigilant a Leo becomes with his privacy. No one ever really knew Andy Warhol (August 6). Under the cover of darkness, Malcolm Forbes (August 19) would don a black leather jacket and ride his Harley-Davidson through New York's Greenwich Village.

The father is the central figure for most Leos. Madonna was the apple of her father's eye. Jackie O loved her debonair "Dapper Dan." Bernard Baruch (August 19), the most famous stockbroker of all times said, "My father was the most important guy I ever met." The father's name is what makes the legacy. However, if the father is missing, either physically or because of escapes such as alcohol, drugs or emotional absenteeism then the Leo will seek out another powerful personality to imitate or become the central force himself. Bill Clinton's father died before he was two and his mother subsequently married an alcoholic. Clinton (August 19) took the position of authority in order to protect his mother and brother against his stepfather's abuse.

In Cancer, Spirit was born. It burst forth with great power and created compassion while it fought for unity. In Leo, Spirit strives to become conscious; its desire is to be objectified. The igniting of Spirit is letting God's presence into our soul. Leo has the honored position of hosting a visit from above. Of course, this requires preparation. The body and Spirit must be purified for His arrival. Leos are driven to hold on to their principles regardless of the consequences, because they seek that perfection they believe is required for His presence. Leo is the vessel through which God's creative energy flows. Tolstoy said, "Purify your soul of all stain and he will come and enter you. That is all He is waiting for. He flows into you like water to the extent that you make room for Him." Teresa of Avila said, "God implants Himself in the interior of that soul in such a way that, when it returns to itself, it cannot possibly doubt that God has been in it and it has been in God; so firmly does this truth remain within it that, although for years God may never grant it that favor again, it can neither forget it nor doubt that it has received it. . . . This certainty of the soul is very material."

Before Spirit is awakened, it is in a slumbering state; the being is unconscious and removed from understanding. The soul detaches itself as much as it can from the body awaiting the gift. While the soul waits for Spirit it may appear foolish; its actions are a series of events strung together without consciousness, purpose, or meaning. These are the teenage years, when the soul turns away from those who have provided safety and security and waits for the moment when it will feel its own uniqueness. The future represents the unknown, and the divine spark that will pull the soul onward has not yet ignited. The soul waits for confidence based on faith. Once it happens, the soul transforms its fears and attitudes into a more expansive perspective. Souls that have found their faith appear gifted to the world. According to his biographer, Peter G. Bourne, "Fidel Alejandro Castro Rey is one of those rare individuals history occasionally contrives who rise beyond any reasonable expectation of what their background might suggest and stand so far above their contemporaries to defy any simple explanation of their success."

Through their imagination and their ability to gain great distance from their bodies, the Leo soul has a special connection with the world of Spirit. Attracted to the mysterious and the unknown, Leos are drawn to the past and to the future. Many Leos have experiences with the ethereal world. One of the most famous psychics of all times, Madame Blavatsky, was seeing and talking to spirits at a very early age. When Spirit is strong, Leos can have psychic ability or just great instincts. Many Leos don't have to talk at all in order to communicate what they desire. They have impeccable timing, too. Leos are aware that what is not said often makes a stronger statement than the spoken word. The right questions are more important than answers. This is the quest. When you try your very best, the universe always sends you someone with a raft to carry you across to the other side. The Leos' challenge is to accept the help and use it, not to compare themselves to others and what they have accomplished, just to do their job and be open for a greater and larger perception.

God, at least what others believe Him to be, is never enough for Leos. They want to redefine Him in their own image; they want a personal connection. Their rejection of accepted beliefs can make them atheists or, if they are religious, their faith will be rooted in ancient practices and traditions. Shelley was thrown out of Oxford University for publishing an article called, "The Necessity of Atheism." When Magic Johnson's mother became a Seventh-Day Adventist, she threw the whole family into chaos. The Adventists are Christians who observe the Old Testament Sabbath and the same dietary laws as Orthodox Jews. Suddenly, Magic wasn't allowed to play on Saturdays. However, a compromise for unity was made. The children chose their own religion, and everyone went to church on Saturday and Sunday. That's Spirit doing its best work. Cecil B. DeMille (August 12), the famous movie director, was a spiritual man. He wanted the world to know the story of Christ. His Christ was strong and complex—he could fast for forty days; he had compassion for sinners; he had anger and scorn for hypocrites. DeMille's movie, *King of Kings,* created great controversy and changed lives. DeMille received letters about the effects of his movie years after it was released. *A* Pasteur wrote to him about a visit he had from a Gestapo officer who had seen his movie and became ridden with guilt about participating in the brutal beating of a religious man. He was seeking understanding. The Pasteur said "Perhaps God let you kill that good man to bring you to the feet of the cross where you can help others." The officer became an active part of the Czech underground and assisted in the escape of hundreds of Jews. Evil had brought about Good. In Leo, evil and good are not easily separated. Their cycles spiral into each other and the soul can no longer separate them with certainty. Faith is more important than ever because the exterior world is now a complex composite of good and evil. Like Cain, who is marked on the forehead by God for murdering his brother Abel, Leos must deal with both persecution and protection. Melville's (August 1) Captain Ahab is marked with a scar on his face, and has his leg amputated. Magic Johnson is marked by the HIV virus. Madame Blavatsky had a deformed son who died young. She said, "The past, like the brand of the curse on Cain, has pursued me all my life and pressures me even here, in America, where I came to be far from it and from the people who knew me in my youth." Blavatsky's youthful reputation was tainted by her experiences with "free love." "I have only one refuge left in the world, and that is the respect of the spiritualists of America, who despise nothing so much as 'free love.'" When Menachem Begin witnessed his IZL men being turned over to the British by his own people, he wrote a proclamation that appeared on the walls of Palestine entitled, WE SHALL REPAY YOU, CAIN. In it, he attacked the British for turning brother against brother.

Leos may find themselves in strong competition with a sibling. Their desire to be singled out will make them either the favorite or the ignored. Leo is the house of pride, Cain's downfall. Pride is one of the seven sins, and Ego's favorite expression.

Many Leos experience the cruelty of others. Shelley endured great cruelty at boarding school; Lucille Ball was actually tied outside like a dog when her stepmother couldn't handle her. Magic Johnson had to win over the white kids at his high school; and Arnold Schwarzenegger (July 30) had a cruel father who pitted brother against brother for his attention and approval. Cruelty is the easiest way to end innocence.

Leos are masters at using the strength of others to make themselves better, stronger, and more knowledgeable. A challenge is inviting, and the harder it is, the more they're interested. When you're dedicated to self-improvement, you know the only way to learn is to compete against someone better. Responsible and spiritual, Leos want new ideas. DeMille said, "What I want, what I need, from the people who work with me is not that they be echoes, but experts, I want their ideas, not mine repeated. If we differ, I want them to defend their ideas against mine."

To stay number one, Leos develop a talent for using the resources available. They're able to use people and opportunities to get where they're going. This does not have to be negative. However Napoleon (August 15), whose personal magnetism was legendary, expressed the negative side of this energy. "I only care for people who are useful to me—and so long as they are useful."

Leos make great actors. Acting demands we step aside from ourselves and use bits and pieces of our experiences, impressions, and personal character to bring a role to life. Leos do this naturally. Napoleon was fascinated with acting. In fact, he studied with the famous actor Talma, about how to play his part as emperor.

One of Leos' greatest gifts—and what gets them into the most trouble— is their high principles. They don't budge when they believe they're right. When Madame Blavatsky was sixteen, her parents threatened to force her to go to a ball. "I deliberately plunged my foot and leg into a kettle of boiling water and held it there till it nearly boiled raw." Talking about fighting to create a Jewish State, Menachem Begin said, ". . . We must go to the very end. If we don't succeed, if we are all killed, we will have made our contribution to Jewish history." Shelley was at odds with his father, who threatened to cut off his allowance. He was willing to compromise up to a point of self-esteem.

He could not betray himself even if it meant poverty. "I repeat . . . that I am willing to concede anything that is reasonable, anything that does not involve a compromise of that self-esteem without which life would be a burden and disgrace." When Spirit is strong, worldly rewards are not temptations. Leos know that to obey God's laws means eternal reward. With Spirit powerful, long-term consequences and the betterment of the whole are considered.

Every fixed sign faces the challenge of determining the truths it will use as an anchor in life. The truths of Taurus have become principles in Leo. These principles rule your life. If you have chosen to honor your inner Spirit and your personal truth, you will need the Leo courage to stand up for what you believe. If your choice of anchor is the opinions of others and worldly possessions, you will be forced to change your face and your values often in order to maintain the attention and the acceptance of those around you. You'll be a great liar or just plain unreliable. It's the easy road initially, but it's the painful path long-term. Without strong principles to anchor your identity, you cannot expand and grow. Roy Cohn (July 23), the famous criminal defense lawyer, was a master at changing morals and disguising truths. Though he himself was gay and dying of AIDS, he fought against homosexuality. Principles need to be adjusted and molded if the long-term goal is to be achieved. Desperate to pay his rent, Andy Warhol turned down an offer for a painting because he believed it was worth more. The Leos' burden is great when they try to keep to the straight and narrow in a world of crooked paths. If you're a Leo, hold your truths in your heart. Knowing when and how to stand for truth and principles, choosing when you can make a real difference instead of just creating opposition and problems, is the path of wisdom.

Ego and Spirit continue their battle in Leo. When Ego is strong, so is the will. You can be financially successful, but your desire to stand out among others will be your downfall. Ego wants to fight anyone and anything that declares itself more powerful. Melville creates such an unbending soul in *Moby Dick*. Captain Ahab is a man of passion who doesn't think of consequences. He says, "I'd strike the sun if it insulted me." This kind of defiance can be fascinating. In Leo, both the good and the bad are charming, and the distinction between right and wrong becomes more complex and difficult. Ego and Spirit have taken on each other's qualities; you've got to recognize them not by their faces or their actions but by your instinct. Leo requires the soul to gather its strength and move ahead in the world, while at the same time helping others in need. When a part of the circle is weak, then all will suffer, but when strength is used to help the weak, then humanity benefits. Without a spiritual understanding, Ego becomes inflexible and wants things its own way. Captain Ahab is like Satan. ". . . [he]is determined to have his way even if it damns him. He refuses to recognize the existence of a higher law than his own will and although the spiritual pride is destructive and dehumanizing, it also shows strength, determination, and imagination, all of which are attractive qualities.''

Tolstoy said of art and creativity, ''Art is one of the manifestations of man's spiritual life.'' Art, in Leo, often displays the divine and is not limited to one genre. Herman Melville changed the shape of the novel when he wrote *Moby Dick.* Critics didn't know how to label his creation. Was it a romance, a scientific treatise, or fiction? Art, with Spirit, has the ability to transform lives. Gifted with incredible imagination, the Leo artist often produces something new. Consider Lucille Ball and the sitcom; Melville and the novel; Madonna and the self-transforming artist. These are men and women of transition. Through their imagination and courage we are transported to a new and better place.

Leos represent the creative process. Whether it's giving birth to a child or to an artistic endeavor, there is a moment when the form receives the gift of life. For a child, it's when Spirit enters its being. For an artistic creation it is when your presence gives it Spirit. Your children and your other works of art can be greater than you are. Of course, your dark side, what you fear and hide, might be expressed in your child or artistic endeavor. Remember, to create is to risk oneself.

Leos are attracted to games of chance. At the age of thirty-three, Bernard Baruch gave up a successful partnership in a Wall Street brokerage firm in order to speculate with his own money. He did very well, but not without a few losses, the kind that ''would make an ordinary married man go out and shoot himself.'' Don King (August 20), promoter for Mike Tyson and Muhammad Ali, is known for his gambling habits, from running numbers as a teen to organizing million-dollar promotions. Leos have a knack for rising from the shadow; they can do it many times in their lives. President Bill Clinton has done it so many times, a biography of him is called *The Comeback Kid.* Most geniuses do their greatest work when they find themselves in trouble or pain. Misery is the fastest way to our creative core.

Discipline is necessary for a Leo to succeed. Without it, inner development cannot happen. For anything new to emerge, resistance must be encountered. If internal discipline is not available, the universe will provide it through obstacles and opposition. With crisis and a little tension, the Leo gets moving and becomes clear on who he is and where he's going. Unlike Aries, who seek their battles with others, Leos compete with themselves. Leo always strives to be the best he can, even if no one is watching. Leos are their own best friends and enemies, pushing themselves beyond their limits in everything they do. Madonna is always on time for work and expects everyone else to be. Castro's childhood was tough but undisciplined; all that changed when his parents sent him to a Jesuit school. Jacqueline Kennedy developed strong personal discipline in spite of her parents' divorce and the ensuing chaos.

Leos are willing to pay the price for success, and they know that positioning is half the battle. They go right to the center of action and they stay there until they get their chance to show their stuff. When Madonna arrived in New York City, she told the cab driver, "Take me to the center of everything." He dropped her at Times Square. If the new woman in the office is a Leo, step back and watch what happens. In a matter of weeks, it's her desk everyone leans on, it's her they'll come to for information on what to do, where to go, and whom to see. If she's clever and sees opportunity where others don't, she doesn't even have to leave her chair. It's instinctual and so is their ability to enjoy life, liberty, and the pursuit of happiness.

Never intimidated by mistakes, Leos use them as stepping-stones to success. Arnold Schwarzenegger said, "Good things don't happen by coincidence ... Every dream carries with it certain risks, especially the risk of failure ... If you try ten times, you have a better chance of making it on the eleventh try than if you didn't try at all."

If to be the best is their motivation, then pride is their Achilles' heel. Give them a compliment, and they'll puff up right before your eyes. But don't try to manipulate them with empty praises. They're smart, and that's as close as you will ever get to them again.

When a Leo walks into a room, he or she commands attention. If he doesn't, something is wrong. That Leo needs to focus on the challenge of owning his own power. What Leos have to do is find their area of expertise and declare it to the world. It's important they toot their own horn; it's what they are meant to do.

Ruled by the heart, Leos are not afraid to follow it wherever it leads them and more often than not it's into the arms of a lover. There is nothing a Leo enjoys more than making love. Their instincts are primal. The mission to procreate keeps their libido high and their hormones raging. They're the best because they're able to risk themselves. They've got the secret formula— put everything you've got into the moment and you can't lose. Born with more than their share of persistence and endurance, they'll overcome your doubts with their constant pressure and fun-loving ways. They have a way of cajoling even the most stubborn personalities, and they'll disarm you with the ease in which they plunge courageously into the realm of the heart. However, if it's the Leo who has turned his or her back, save yourself a lot of wasted effort and heartache. Persistence turns to resistance. No one will change *their* minds.

Love is the key to a Leo's heart but freedom and independence are what they seek. Don't be surprised if they're difficult to rein in. You'll have to be patient, and past the test of loyalty to get a Leo to say, "I do." Don't share their spotlight. It makes them depressed and sad if they're upstaged. Being adored gets them interested faster than anything else; they want to be the light in your life and they look for that confirmation in your eyes. Because strength is such an issue, they'll choose someone above or below them. Leos need someone like their opposing sign Aquarius, someone secure enough to set their boundaries and do their own thing in spite of the Leo's demands. It's a catch-22. If you give a Leo everything he asks for, he'll have no respect for you. Hold your own and give only love generously. He can never get enough of that. But if you're not sure of your own position and needs, their strength will overwhelm you.

Leos have relabeled impulsiveness, calling it spontaneity and bursts of spirit. They decide on the spot what they want to do, and they do it. For example, Leo women are not advocates of women's rights; they *expect* freedom and equality and have never paid any attention to what little girls should or shouldn't do. Tomboys growing up, they don't let raised eyebrows or tradition interfere with participation. Amelia Earhart (July 24) played in bloomers instead of a skirt; she slid belly down like a boy on her sled. Madonna was a jock long before she became famous for dancing and singing. Suzanne Farrell could climb a tree better than most of the boys on her block in Cincinnati, Ohio.

For a Leo, humility is not a gift, but a challenge. They want recognition for their deeds, but often patience is required for their reward. Others know the Leo is looking for praise and so it's often not given, just because Leos desire it so badly. Like the Sun that warms everything around it, Leos are great supporters and friends. But whatever you do don't ask for their advice and then not take it. It's disrespectful, and respect is something they demand.

A natural Leo gift is the talent for entertaining. Jacqueline Kennedy's private dinner parties at the White House were legendary. She replaced the long formal tables with round ones; she used colored cloths and low flower arrangements that created a more intimate and glamorous ambiance. The best artists in the country were invited to perform. Malcolm Forbes transformed the notion of ''party.'' His birthday extravaganza in Morocco cost two million dollars. There were six hundred drummers, acrobats, and belly dancers; three hundred turbaned Berber horsemen fired muskets; and twenty women showered guests with rose petals. Forbes chartered a Concorde, a 747, and a DC8 to bring his eight hundred guests to Tangier.

Strength and its pursuit is a strong motivating force for Leos. Because of this they dominate the world of physical fitness. Arnold Schwarzenegger changed the world of weight lifting. Wilt Chamberlain (August 21) said, ''I am proud that I was one of the first, if not the very first, to use strong weight-lifting programs along with my basketball training. Weight lifting was frowned upon when I was a player. I was told never to mix the two.''

The arts are speckled with Leos. Some of our finest stars are born under the sign of the Lion: Dustin Hoffman (August 8), Robert De Niro (August 18) and Melanie Griffith (August 9) among them. Gamblers, at heart, they love speculation, and gravitate to positions as stockbrokers, promoters, or real estate investors. They make great entertainment directors, professional party givers and ambassadors. Their love of things that shine and their creativity gives them an edge as jewelers, especially if they work with gold. Being in charge is important, if not necessary, for they don't take orders well.

Leo is the sign of the Sun, the central authoritarian figure. Though powerful, the Sun does not exist for itself. In Leo, the soul has arrived at a crossroad and must make a choice, to follow the path of those he loves, or to take his own path, the one that will lead him to his personal destiny. The ability to choose what's right for ourselves against opposition and the emotional bonds that hold us, is the challenge. The need to separate is often translated into a desire to travel far from home. Leos have an adventuresome spirit. However, the call to home is always in the heart.

By taking the lead, the Leo gains self-esteem and often the recognition of others. However, his prominent position makes him vulnerable and open to criticism. His spiritual side desires perfection but it desires it to help others who are not as strong. Leos know they have the power to inspire through their deeds. For Leos winning is as natural as breathing.

Blessed with magnetism and a dynamic personality, their path is not easy because the force of their personality creates as much opposition as it does acceptance. And although doors are often opened by their sheer charisma, once on the other side, they must work to stay on top. This is no news for the Lion, who lives to hear his roar at the end of a victory well earned.

THE LEO ENVIRONMENT

The Leo environment is competitive or adoring. Spoiled or treated with downright cruelty, the Lion experiences life on both sides of the coin. The challenge is to keep your faith no matter how much the world adores or rejects you. Life is a place to hone your strengths for the journey. If you don't have discipline, the environment will provide it in many unpleasant ways. You must take responsibility for yourself and your own existence. Develop versatility. The environment will place immovable walls before you, forcing you to alter your position or change your attitude in order to complete your goal. Don't be so stubborn. Know your truths and learn how many wonderful faces they can have without changing their meaning. You can be yourself and still please the world.

Leo/*One* (July 28, August 1, August 10, August 19)
Sun/Sun

PURPOSE: To take your own path, accepting responsibility as you seek to find your own unique voice, to use the power and competition of others to hone your strength.

"When you know what you want and you want it badly enough, you will find the ways to get it."—Jim Rohn. The strength of the Leo/*One* has been fortified by the strong personalities around them. They compete with the best and manage to shine. Coco Chanel (August 19) revolutionized women's fashions. Her Leo need for freedom gave her the courage to discard corsets, shorten skirts, bob hair, and make comfort a part of elegance. Modern bathing suits, costume jewelry, and the little black dress were all her creations. Chanel was raised in an orphanage and worked her way up the ladder through a favorite Leo pastime— love affairs. The duke of Westminster; the Russian Grand Duke Dimitri, Stravinsky, and Picasso were a few of her lovers.

"The block of granite which was an obstacle in the pathway of the weak, became a stepping-stone in the pathway of the strong."—Thomas Carlyle. Sun/ *One* people climb right over obstacles. They must own their competitive nature; otherwise, they can get knocked around. Life wants them to be independent, and to take responsibility for themselves, but it also wants them to have a good time. Leo/*Ones* must realize that they tend to measure their worth against the best and the brightest, but their true challenge is only to be the best they can be. The rewards of Leo are for the effort, not the easy victories. Leo/*Ones* like to be alone and others disappoint them, particularly when they haven't learned to put the team before their own success. They have an excess of imagination and idealism, making them either hopelessly romantic or cold and aloof. Leos can have the best of both worlds, if they know how to be responsible and how to have a good time.

IF SPIRIT TAKES THE LEAD: When Spirit is strong the soul is idealistic and sensitive to the cruelty in the world. Their tender nature must learn to trust, but not blindly; to risk with wisdom; to strive for perfection while recognizing what has already been accomplished. Their need to fight for justice and freedom makes them righteous. Their impulse to overthrow rigid authority makes them rebels. Their desire to help others through sharing their knowledge and strength makes them healers. Burdened with an excessive amount of imagination and emotion, Leos need balance in discipline and strong values. Within every Leo is the call to greatness. For them to achieve this goal they need to take responsibility for themselves, and be independent. The desire to separate can make them rovers who avoid personal growth through the constant exposure to new people, places, and adventures. The mystical fascinates them.

IF EGO TAKES THE LEAD: If Ego leads the way, their will and need for power are strong. These souls want to get ahead in the world at all cost. You have an excess of charm. They know how to use others for their own ends—both in business and their love life. They can be cruel, hard, and uncompassionate or ruled by powerful emotions. They are reactive and unconcerned with consequences. Their problems come from their inability to be flexible and work with others and their desire to be the greatest. The world is not against them—they just keep meeting themselves.

JACQUELINE KENNEDY ONASSIS (July 28)

First lady of the United States, editor.

The competitive and strong independence of the Sun/Sun dynamics was never so evident than in one of its most famous representatives, Jacqueline Kennedy Onassis. For her light to be seen, it had to shine among the brightest—a charismatic husband, world leaders, and a critical press. She showed great courage through the assassination, death, and funeral of her first husband, John F. Kennedy, and, later, in her struggle with cancer. Her devotion to her children gained the respect of the most stern critics. She told a reporter, "My major effort must be devoted to my children. If Caroline and John turn out badly, nothing I could do in the public eye would have any meaning." The lusty environment of a Leo certainly was provided by the men in her life. Her father, John Bouvier and her husbands, John Kennedy and Aristotle Onassis, were notorious ladies' men. Stealing the spotlight early, Jackie was the Queen Deb of the Year when she came out in 1947. When her parents divorced, she lived with her mother and became a photographer for the *Washington Times-Herald* in 1952. Her wedding to Kennedy in Newport, was the wedding of the year. As first lady, the Leo love of elegance helped her redecorate the White House with donations from all over the country. She set fashion trends and her style was copied and envied by everyone.

WILLIAM JEFFERSON CLINTON (August 19)

Forty-first president of the United States.

Bill Clinton entered the world two months after his father's death. While his mother struggled to support the family, he lived with his grandparents, who were strict Southern Baptists. At four, his mother married Roger Clinton and young Bill's life became chaotic and often violent. His escape was school and achievement. His high school friend Carolyn Staley says of him, "He had to be the class leader. He had to be the best in the band. He had to be the best in his class, in grades. And he wanted to be in the top in anything that put him at the forefront of any course." His stepfather's alcoholism eventually forced young Bill into the role of a man. Unable to watch his mother and brother being abused, he became their protector. The turning point in his life was his meeting with John F. Kennedy as a delegate to Boys Nation. From that moment, he wanted to go into politics. The road to his success was cluttered with failure, but his competitive spirit helped him move on, a little wiser and stronger. He lost a race for the U.S. Congress, won the position of attorney general at age twenty-nine, then became Arkansas's youngest governor at thirty-two. He was defeated in 1980, then returned and triumphed in the next election. In January 1993 he became the forty-first president of the United States, defeating the Republican incumbent, George Bush. In 1996, he was elected to a second term.

Leo/*Two* (July 29, August 2, August 11, August 20) Sun/Moon

PURPOSE: To use your imagination, sensitivity, and wounds as strengths; to not be lured by the spotlight or discouraged by rejection; to determine your own creative and independent style which you generously share with others, giving them the courage to expose their weaknesses and use them as strengths.

"Challenging the established rules is necessary to awaken our creativity." — Dr. Roger Von Oech. The uniqueness of the Moon gets support from the relentless will of the Sun. Leo/*Twos* are hot stuff and they know it. More flexible than other Leos, they are also persistent, creative, and competitive. Leo/*Twos* are hard to reach emotionally. They're loners who know how to use their strengths and weaknesses as means to an end. Struggling between childish insecurities and mature and courageous actions, their goal is to be responsible for themselves and to have the faith to take risks. Their charisma is powerful, and others will be attracted to them. Since the Moon represents the family, and Leo is our desire to succeed, there could be a conflict between having a family and pursuing a career. The Leo/*Twos'* instincts are highly tuned and if they listen to them, they'll know when to ask for a raise and when it's time to retire. When Leo and the *Two* work together, everything's just right. However, more often than not these two very powerful forces make life either too competitive and demanding, or too isolated and self-absorbed.

The *Two* is able to heal through the experience and understanding of pain. The Leo/*Twos* can use their feelings of rejection and desire for recognition in a way that will bring peace . . . they can share.

IF SPIRIT TAKES THE LEAD: Spirit is happy in Leo. There are no limits to how high it wants to soar. That's a problem. Their aim is too high and their imagination too powerful. Their Ego needs grounding. They must take responsibility, acquire knowledge and seek discipline. When they use their courage to share rather than hide, they gain a talent for turning disadvantages into advantages. Resilient and defiant, it's hard to keep them down. They battle between being alone and being in the spotlight, the desire to reflect, and the drive to move forward. The challenge is to build a bridge that connects their inner needs with the demands of the world. If they retreat too far into themselves, the world will pound on their door. If they take the spotlight without learning to be a team player, that will be their demise.

IF EGO TAKES THE LEAD: With Ego strong, self-centeredness is at an all-time high. These souls need to be spoiled and indulged. They either feel stuck and oversensitive or indifferent and anxious to risk themselves. They take rejection personally. Always measuring themselves against others, they haven't learned that it's the effort not the result that counts. Able to turn a situation around and use it to their own end, their handicaps often become their advantage, that is until they get to the top. If they haven't learned to be humble, they might fall.

CONNIE CHUNG (August 20)

Journalist, news anchor with Dan Rather, hostess of *Eye to Eye.*

Highly ambitious, Chung always had her sights set higher than most. When asked if she would like to have a nightly network anchor slot, she replied, "My dreams are much more ambitious than that. I figure on being the first woman to land on Jupiter."

Being the youngest of ten children probably had something to do with her survival skills. Exposed to politics by her father, a Chinese diplomat under Chiang Kai-Shek, she started her career as a copy clerk for a Washington, D.C., television station and was quickly promoted to newswriter and on-air reporter. Hired by CBS as a news correspondent, her first break came following presidential campaign of candidate George McGovern. Chung was known for her relentless and tenacious nature. With Watergate, she gained national recognition. With middle age before her Chung faces her greatest challenge—to have a child.

DON KING (August 20)

Promoter.

"I must go where the wild goose goes," said Don King and go he has, with his crazy hair, big rings and unforgettable personality. The Moon or *Two* is unique and when combined with Leo, a rare and unusual soul emerges. The problem here is principles, they are dictated by what will get them ahead. However, Don is creative, and when resilience is your nature, serving time in prison doesn't keep you from success. Two years out of jail, he was a self-made millionaire. His genius was promotion and when he met Cassius Clay at one of his supper clubs, he got a chance to prove it. King is the man behind the Ali-Foreman *Rumble in the Jungle,* and the Ali-Frazier *Thrilla in Manila.* The gambling spirit of the Leo began early in life. As a freshman at Kent State, King took his elder brother's numbers route and by his early twenties, became one of the chief numbers operators in Cleveland.

Leo/*Three* (July 30, August 3, August 12, August 21)
Sun/Jupiter

PURPOSE: To gain confidence and independence through the formation of a unique and powerful belief system that insulates you from the distracting opinions of others, that allows you to separate from the safety of your past and take the necessary risks to continue on that path and to face the dangers of the unknown; to help others find their confidence and formulate a belief system of their own.

''I don't get no respect.''—Rodney Dangerfield. This is powerful energy and those born under its influence can have a persona larger than life. They're expansive, generous, and kingly when balanced, but if self-worth is missing, they can be bullies, or consider themselves above the law. Either the world's against them or the world is rolling out the red carpet. Either way, Leo/*Threes* must develop a sense of justice and learn how their personal beliefs can work harmoniously with those of others. The Leo/*Three* has a strong desire for adventure and travel. *Threes* need to conquer impossible obstacles and overcome great odds. The key is for them not to use adventure to avoid facing themselves or to overwhelm their life with challenges they cannot achieve in this lifetime. They must use their incredible spirit and power to help others believe in themselves. Effort is rewarded, as is patience and persistence. They are difficult to get close to even though they know how to have a good time. If they can climb mountains, they can learn to share their feelings over a cup of cappuccino. The key to peace is the Leo/*Threes*' believing in themselves. When they have confidence, watch out world. When they don't, the world invades their space and abuse is a possibility.

IF SPIRIT TAKES THE LEAD: If Spirit is strong, there is a desire to tackle large and impossible feats. These souls believe they can do anything; in fact, they often can. However, mistakes are part of the learning process. With Spirit strong, they need to accept their weaknesses; they need to support others without taking all the responsibility for their lives. They avoid intimacy by being too responsible for others. They live through someone else's world; they're the caretaker. They need to know the world won't fall apart if they don't do everything. Faith is needed; once they have it they can let go and let others learn from their own mistakes.

IF EGO TAKES THE LEAD: If Ego is strong, power and control are real issues. These souls believe they are the law, and they strive to be better than everyone. They need to learn to use their power to support not demean others. Abuse is possible because sensitivity is lacking. They are cruel and hard and demanding. Of course, since they are Leo, they are all these things and charming, too. They surround themselves with people who allow them to do whatever they want;

their perception of their own strengths and abilities are distorted. This eventually leads to their fall.

ARNOLD SCHWARZENEGGER (July 30)

Body builder, actor.

"Strength does not come from winning, your struggles develop your strengths. When you go through hardships and decide not to surrender, that is strength . . . You must want to be the greatest." Arnold Schwarzenegger had the vision and the competitive spirit to change the body-building world— he won Mr. Olympia an unprecedented seven times—and conquered Hollywood. Schwarzenegger was raised on competition. His father, an Austrian police chief, was a strict disciplinarian and an abusive alcoholic who pitted him and his older brother Meinhard against each other. The Jupiter or *Three* side of this dynamic, which challenges the law, was evident early. Ravenous for attention, Schwarzenegger was a bully. He beat up a milkman, terrorized young girls, and exploited his father's position as police chief. His father never punished him for his violence toward others, but whipped him for putting his elbows on the dinner table. However, Arnold managed to get himself on a positive path by his pursuit of strength and his love of competition. The *Three* or Jupiter often succeeds in foreign countries more easily than in his own. Arnold went to Hollywood. His movie career followed, as well as his marriage to Maria Shriver, the daughter of Eunice Kennedy and Sargent Shriver.

AMY ELIZABETH FISHER (August 21)

Attempted murderer. Lethal Lolita.

Amy Fisher is the perfect example of the need for this dynamic to have a sense of self-worth. Without it they are too easily attracted to someone who will overwhelm their life. Fisher made allegations of childhood abuse against her parents. Leo's predisposition for love affairs added to her trouble. Meeting Joey Buttafucco changed her life. He became the center of her world. She shot his wife, whom she believed an obstacle to her being with Buttafucco. Mary Jo Buttafucco didn't die; she lives with a bullet lodged in her brain. Amy is behind bars, and has received incredible notoriety and attention, a Leo's dream come true. A television movie was produced and a book about her life was on the best-sellers list.

Leo/*Four* (July 31, August 4, August 13, August 22) Sun/Uranus

PURPOSE: To use your versatility, and your catalytic nature to separate from security and manifest your dreams in the world; to change the lives of all you

*meet; to change the world through your ideas, actions, and unique ability to
destroy and rebuild within the system.*

"Men can starve from a lack of self-realization as much as they can from a
lack of bread."—Richard Wright, *Native Son*. The Sun/*Four* dynamic brings
the power to shatter opposition through the incredible ability to use whatever is
available. Life seems like a series of uncontrollable events. Leo/*Fours* love
dodging debris. They are attracted to tension and chaos; if it's not available, they
know how to create it. They are catalysts and the center of other people's lives.
Either through their quiet courage or their outspoken individualism, they give
others strength and insight. Struggle and discipline have toughened the Leo/*Four*.
In fact, this dynamic is so strong, it can be dangerous if it's handled improperly.
Without sensitivity and a desire to contribute something to mankind, Leo/*Fours*
can be hard, cruel, and cold, believing they have all the answers to their lives
and yours. Their ingenious approach to life makes them inventors; they create
what they need as they go along. Leo/*Fours* must not forget that boundaries help
accomplish goals. They must embrace discipline and when faced with impossible
odds, they should tackle the little stuff first. They'll be stronger when a few
obstacles are out of the way. The roller coaster of life will always be there; Leo/
Fours should know that the ups and downs teach them just how good they are
when the adrenaline's flowing.

IF SPIRIT TAKES THE LEAD: Spirit and the number *Four* work together for
change. The *Four* wants to break free of any limitations that restrict its freedom,
and at the same time it desires to unify those who oppose each other. *Four* is
the negotiator. The danger here is that they will forget their own path by trying
to make peace, or dedicate their life to the challenges provided by someone else.
They should never forget they're here for their journey. If Spirit is too strong,
they will use their will to bend others, regardless of the consequences. In the
name of justice and freedom they could commit horrendous acts. Spirit needs to
have faith that good will prevail, that when the time is right, everything will
unfold. To know the truth is only a small part of the process; learning how to
live in a world that often rejects or punishes those who pursue truth is a challenge.
These souls must develop the fine line between self and others and have an inner
sense of responsibility.

IF EGO TAKES THE LEAD: Ego loves working with this combination—it's
always right. Here the Ego is strong, righteousness and stands alone. The problem
is they are bright and hard to prove wrong. But the issue is not whether they are
right or wrong, it's whether they are open to the views and experiences of others.
They need to learn the meaning of compromise and how to work within the
system for harmony and the betterment of the whole. Their isolation keeps them
locked in their own world.

ROSE KENNEDY (July 22)

From birth, Rose Kennedy was surrounded by strong individuals. Her father, a policeman and mayor of Boston, was seldom home. Her mother, a religious woman, ran a tight disciplined ship. It was no surprise that Rose was attracted to a man as overwhelming and unavailable as her father—Joseph P. Kennedy. Exhibiting the Leo love of children, Rose had nine. "I had made up my mind to raise my children as perfectly as possible. What greater aspiration and challenge are there for a mother than the hope of raising a great son or daughter?" Courage, strength and determination were evident throughout her life. The sudden unexpected power of Uranus brought tragedy when four of her children met violent deaths; one daughter was born mentally retarded; and her husband, in his later years, suffered a crippling stroke. In her autobiography, Rose said, "I hope (my family) will realize where they came from and how they happen to be where they are. They came—on the Kennedy-Fitzgerald side—from ancestors who were quite poor and disadvantaged through no fault of their own but who had the imagination, the resolve, the intelligence, and the energy to seek a newer, better world for themselves and their families."

ALFRED HITCHCOCK (August 13)

Director, producer/ King of the Thriller.

Hitchcock's name is synonymous with fear and the thriller. Hitchcock was educated in a Jesuit seminary, studied blacksmithing, lathe turning, screw cutting and draftsmanship. There was little early indication that he would become a symbol of shock and horror. The irony is that Hitchcock considered himself a coward. Perhaps it was his way to deal with the Leo's need for courage—to scare everyone else. The Leo/*Four* energy is inventive. Besides the creativity of his story lines, Hitchcock developed new avenues in special effects. In *The Birds,* the birds were mechanical, an innovation in its time. Hitchcock's comments on the dual nature of the English reflect the Leo/*Four* energy. "Our preoccupation with crime, especially murder, is concerned with the Englishman's aura of outward respectability. But underneath that immaculate exterior—that's quite another story. Heaven knows what pent-up emotions are panting to escape."

Leo/*Five* (July 23, August 5, August 14, August 23) Sun/Mercury

PURPOSE: To end innocence and selfishness by distancing yourself from those who indulge you, by taking responsibility, and by sharing your perceptions and ideas, gaining new insight while contributing to the growth and knowledge of others.

"Our life is what our thoughts make it."—Marcus Aurelius, *Meditations*. The mind is prominent in the Leo/*Five* dynamics. It highlights the issue of intent and how much truth or deception one feels they need in order to accomplish their goal. Mercury or the *Five* tends to become confused through the accumulation of information and nonstop activity. They need to gain some distance from themselves and share their points of view of others. When they are focused, they have the power to get right to the issue. They are intelligent; their minds are beacons of light, highlighting what they choose to acknowledge. When faced with an obstacle, Mercury never surrenders. It just changes the face of things by rearranging the facts—great energy for a lawyer, inventor, diplomat, or other communicator. Leo/*Fives* can become too busy to reflect and can hold such strong opinions there is no room for growth. Books and ancient studies intrigue them. The Leo in them wants attention, but as any good diplomat knows, often what is *not* said speaks louder than what is. Whatever their ideas, they will be challenged.

IF SPIRIT TAKES THE LEAD: When Spirit is strong these souls take too much responsibility and try to solve everyone's problems but their own. This prevents reflection and personal growth. It does allow them to experience new ideas and share with others, but unless they can use that information for their own personal gain, it is useless. They should not forget that they need to learn how to let things pass them by, and to work on intimacy and the sharing of things close to their heart.

IF EGO TAKES THE LEAD: Ego is content when it dances with the *Five*; values and morality are forgotten. These souls know how to use whatever comes across their path for their own end. What they haven't learned is sharing. They are dangerous because they are fabulous liars, who easily believe their own lies. So flexible and creative is this energy that they can forget who they are. They are always too willing to change their beliefs to get what they want. They know how to get a job done, but they can't be trusted when their own interest is at stake. They are unscrupulous and have the genius and versatility to do some real damage.

ROY COHN (July 23)

Attorney.

Sun/Mercury always creates strong opinions, and everyone had one about Roy Cohn. His friends saw him as an intelligent, loyal man who knew how to throw a good party. His enemies saw the evil genius who supported J. Edgar Hoover, the Mafia, Cardinal Spellman, Richard Nixon, and crooked labor unions. During the communist threat, he was Joe McCarthy's brains and the man who sent Ethel and Julius Rosenberg to their deaths. His father, a liberal Democratic judge, had a profound influence on his life. He was an honorable man, whose career did not prosper. Success was the most important thing to Cohn. He dismissed his own feelings for public approval. He died of AIDS while campaigning against gay rights. He amassed a fortune in his lifetime but died broke. He once said, "For me, I didn't count it as winning if the world didn't know about it." In that way Roy Cohn was all Leo.

JOHN HUSTON (August 5)

Actor, director, producer.

John Huston learned the power of the word from both his parents. His mother was a journalist, and his father, Walter Huston, a very successful actor who listed U.S. presidents as his friends. The Sun and the *Five* are responsible for the endless activity, travel, and people that comprised Huston's life. The product of divorced parents, Huston later followed the womanizing ways of his father and the adventuresome spirit of both his parents. His father traveled from show to show; his mother worked for several newspapers across the country. John went with her and so did his schoolbooks. It was the beginning of his nomadic life. His lust for adventure came to a sudden halt at the early age of ten when he was diagnosed with an enlarged heart and chronic nephritis, a disease of the kidneys known as Bright's disease. It changed his life. He was not allowed to exercise or play. Without a doubt, this repression helped mold Huston's later daredevil personality. A legend in his own time, Huston had incredible magnetism, a lust for living, and a personal force that made him the center of wherever or whoever he was with. His films are considered classics. *The Maltese Falcon, The Treasure of the Sierra Madre, Key Largo, The African Queen,* and *Prizzi's Honor* are just a few. The wit, the practical joker, the communicator, all qualities of the *Five,* are empowered in Leo. Tony, his son said, "Dad had the finest analytical mind I'd ever run into. He was able to unravel something down to its basics."

Leo/*Six* (July 24, August 6, August 15) Sun/Venus

PURPOSE: To create your identity and sense of self from what you believe, to protect your truth with your mask; to fight for truth and justice by choosing the way of the rebel who attacks its opposition, or the way of the charmer, who seduces others to accept their truth without a fight.

"The pursuit of specialness is always at the cost of peace."—*A Course in Miracles.* Here magnetism and charm get an added dose, enough to make the Leo/*Six* dangerous to whoever falls under their spell. This combination struggles to present the perfect picture. But while exterior beauty fades, interior beauty shines brighter the older and wiser we become. Without Spirit, magnetism can be used to succeed at the expense of anyone who dares get in the way. Napoleon's biographer, Frank Richardson, says, "But the true secret of his charm was the trouble which he took to bring it to bear on those whom he meant to enslave.

He could be compellingly, irresistibly charming, and many of those who fell under his spell, when he chose to play the charmer, tried to analyze and explain his almost hypnotic power to bewitch those whose allegiance or affection he wanted to win. It was in fact studied play-acting, and no man has ever been more thorough in this as in everything that he did.'' On the other hand, Bella Abzug (July 24) showed the rebel side of the Sun/*Six*. She is a nonconformist and a powerful advocate of women's rights. Another aspect of this combination is the ability to see value in what others have ignored. Lucille Ball helped her Cuban husband to become a star.

The Leo/*Six* struggles with the desire for intimacy and the fear of commitment. Discipline and the ability to set boundaries are needed or they'll either give their power away or isolate themselves. Leo/*Sixes* have got to know what's right for them and then fight for it. That means accepting the truth of others, also. ''How can a fact be fearful unless it disagrees with what you hold more dear than truth.''—*A Course In Miracles*. When Leo/*Sixes*' energy is balanced, they are unconcerned with approval and tradition. Julia Child (August 15) was never embarrassed if she dropped a veal chop on the floor. She'd pick it up, dust it off, and toss it into the pot, right in front of the camera. To balance this dynamics, the Leo/*Six* must make a peaceful union between the Sun's need for a prestigious image and Venus's disregard for anything that limits truth.

IF SPIRIT TAKES THE LEAD: Spirit and the number *Six* know how to soar. These are perfectionists and rebels; they fight for justice and take a stand against inequality. When they're centered, they break through barriers with ease; when they're radical, they cause enough uproar to bring attention to the subject. Spirit helps more than it should; the danger is dedicating their entire life to changing the world, or choosing a profession that offers only difficulties.

IF EGO TAKES THE LEAD: If Ego is strong, beauty and perfection are priorities. The heck with truth, these are chameleons, with the gift of charm and magnetism. These souls are so attuned to the needs of others who believe they have their best interests at heart. What they're really doing is indulging your desires, making sure you remain insecure enough to depend on them. They make great salesmen and lovers.

ANDY WARHOL (August 6)

Prince of Pop, painter, filmmaker, publisher, partygoer.

Andy Warhol took the lowly objects of soup cans, Coca-Cola bottles and other artifacts of American consumer culture, and made them into aesthetic objects revolutionizing the arts. The identity crisis of Leo and Venus becomes catastrophic in this combination. Venus seeks personal truth; Leo hides it for success. Warhol constantly reinvented himself, exaggerating and lying about his childhood. The truth was that his father, a religious man, was a coal miner who died when Andy was thirteen. His brothers were abusive bullies. He had no friends and seldom any fun. His acute sensitivity and intelligence were evident. Here the need for inner development was aided by his unusual presence. Albino-looking and continually ill as a child, he found his appearance something that kept others away. His isolation gave him an ability to see through exteriors and develop his inner spiritual nature. His mother was the center of his world and continued to live with him even after he became famous. A trendsetter and homosexual, Andy never truly fit in; he took what others rejected and made it fashionable. Using his *Six* energy, he knew how to position himself so that others needed him in their life.

AMELIA EARHART (July 24)

Aviator, designer, women's rights activist.

Earhart was and is the best-known female aviator in the world. She was the first person to fly solo from Honolulu to Oakland, and the first to make a nonstop, solo flight from Mexico City to Newark. Earhart lived with her grandparents for several years because her father was an alcoholic. In spite of his problem, Amelia loved him. When he couldn't afford her flying lessons, she got a job at a telephone company to pay for them. She also worked as a nurse's aide, file clerk, truck driver, photographer, teacher, and social worker before she crossed the Atlantic in 1928. That flight made her famous as a women's rights advocate and a crusader for commercial air travel. "I know what I want to do and I expect to do it, married or single!" An intensely private person, Earhart was forced to conquer her fear of the public when she became famous. She became a good public speaker and fund-raiser, and was cofounder of one of the first commercial airlines, The Boston and Maine Airways. Earhart also designed the first lightweight luggage and clothing for her airlines. Her last flight, an attempt to circle the world, caused her death. She lost her way on a flight from Lae, New Guinea to Howland Island and died somewhere in the Pacific. Her early death was a true tragedy.

Leo/*Seven* (July 25, August 7, August 16) Sun/Neptune

PURPOSE: To overcome your outward sensitivity and innocence through accessing your inner faith and strength; to impact the world with your own unique talents and expressions, healing others through the power and beauty of your creations.

"All that we see or seem is but a dream within a dream."—Edgar Allan Poe. Dreams are what the Leo/*Seven* is made of. Capable of reaching great heights, they must be careful not to get abused along the way. The Sun highlights Neptune's need to get lost in something greater than the self. Leo/*Sevens* have a strong desire to help others. Neptune is not energy that can be contained; it's felt, it's understood, but it's never held in the hand. *Sevens* always struggle with dissatisfaction because their feet are never on secure ground. Leo/*Sevens* are a channel for something greater than themselves—but they have to be careful it's not drugs or alcoholism. Obsessiveness, perfectionism, and a strong idealism dominates this dynamic and makes the everyday a difficult place to be. The Leo/*Seven* must try to acknowledge the importance of the simple things in life, and learn to accept himself. Everything is perfect when seen from the right perspective. Leo/*Sevens* must use the strength of the Sun to direct themselves to a place where they can experience the ecstasy of something great and the safety of being who they are. Kathy Lee Gifford (August 16) represents the perfect mother and wife. I'm sure the burden of presenting such an image is as stressful as rewarding. The problem with identifying with any ideal is that a sense of self is lost. In a personal relationship, Leo/*Sevens* can put the loved one on a pedestal, or be up there themselves. Both people should be on the ground to avoid a crisis.

IF SPIRIT TAKES THE LEAD: When Spirit and the *Seven* get together, there's trouble; they both have extreme natures. Their desire to live up to an ideal, to fight for a cause, to be good and perfect, makes reality and the present moment a difficult place to be. The danger is that they will lose sight of who they really are. They can project their idealism onto someone else and see them as a perfect being; of course, this leads to disaster. The only real power any of us has is in the present. Start working in the now. Don't be too innocent and naive, and know that love is very powerful when it is not invested in results.

IF EGO TAKES THE LEAD: Ego loves the *Seven* because it gets to play behind the scenes. These souls live a double life. They present a good face to the world, camouflaging what they are really up to. Able to shift their values and change actions to achieve goals, they'd make a great double agent if they'd only be interested in the cause.

The reward would have to be either fame or money. Often victims of their own greed, they believe their own lies.

SUZANNE FARRELL (August 16)

Prima ballerina.

Like most Leo children, Farrell struggled early in life. Her father was a salesman and never home. Finally, her mother divorced and Farrell never saw her father again. Farrell was a tomboy, and competitive as a child. Once she found toe shoes, she focused on one goal—to dance. With hardly any money, Farrell's mother took her daughter to New York so Suzanne could audition for the great George Balanchine's corps de ballet. Her talent and her dedication singled her out and soon she became Balanchine's protégée. His genius was choreography and Farrell was his collaborator in some of the most inventive and dazzling ballets of this century. Balanchine's marriage to another woman and Farrell's high principles kept their relationship on a teacher/student level, but through dance they expressed their deep love for each other. Suzanne verbalizes the difficulty all Neptune or *Sevens* have with keeping a relationship in reality and the moment "and so it is not surprising that our attachment existed in a time and place that was not always here and now as most people define 'reality.' And yet two people were never more in the moment, the present moment, than he and I. In fact, the importance of the moment was perhaps his most vital lesson, and he could not have had a more willing disciple than myself."

MADONNA (August 16)

Singer, actress.

The last of five children, and the only girl, Madonna Louise Veronica Ciccone was born at her grandmother's house in which the family was living at the time. Madonna's life changed drastically at age six when her mother died. She put all her energy into becoming the apple of her father's eye. "I was my father's favorite. I knew how to wrap him around my finger." The family was religious and her father a disciplinarian. "If my father hadn't been strict, I wouldn't be who I am today," Madonna says. "I think that his strictness taught me a certain amount of discipline that has helped me in my life and my career and also made me work harder for things, whether for acceptance or the privilege to do things." Because of her excellent grade point average in high school, Madonna won a four-year scholarship in the Dance Department at the University of Michigan. Before starting, she signed up for a six-week summer dance course at Duke University and was given an audition for a scholarship to study in New York with two top choreographers, the late Alvin Ailey and Pearl Lang. At the age of seventeen, and with thirty-five dollars to her name, Madonna arrived in New York. "It was the bravest thing I've ever done." The rest of her career is history.

Leo/*Eight* (July 26, August 8, August 17) Sun/Saturn

PURPOSE: To strive for balance by achieving success in the world without having to sacrifice faith and love; to use your position and your talent to help others find that balance and to transcend all limitations through the surrender and alignment of your will with His.

"The trouble with most of us is that we would rather be ruined by praise than saved by criticism."—Dr. Norman Vincent Peale. Leo/*Eight*s receive a lot of criticism, most of it from themselves. Saturn creates boundaries and limits. The spirit of the Sun, unable to go forward, turns within, bringing self-analysis with resulting tension and anxiety. Leo/*Eight*s should remember they don't have to struggle quite so hard to grow. They need to accept their fate and use their faith to transcend it. Without faith, they can become lost in tension, trying to turn themselves into the perfect being through the discovery of everything that is wrong. The Leo/*Eight* should pick a profession that provides a positive place to express anxiety. They might become a rock star like Mick Jagger (July 26) or an award-winning ice skater like Dorothy Hamill (July 26). The Leo side of them needs to have a good time; so they must take themselves less seriously. Early in life Leo/*Eights* probably felt ugly or unwanted. Their environment put great demands on acting appropriately and so shyness, self-deprecation, and judgment grew. But Leo/*Eights* have power, and a talent for understanding what makes them and others tick.

IF SPIRIT TAKES THE LEAD: If Spirit is strong, these souls are able to accomplish the impossible. Limitations are never acknowledged; the greater the struggle, the more they are drawn to the situation. They can get so caught up in the process and never get any results. Responsibility is assumed all too easily, and the hardships of life are tackled as if they were meant to be. Their life is filled with stress and tension; the desire to do better makes them their own worst enemy.

IF EGO TAKES THE LEAD: If Ego is strong, so are control issues. These souls seek security at all cost. They want to know what everyone is doing; they want to tell everyone how to do it; they want assurances of the outcome. This is impossible, which makes them more insecure. Critical and judgmental, they are difficult to live with because nothing is ever the way it should be. Success in business is likely; they do everything themselves. However, their success is limited because they don't delegate responsibility. The peace they seek so desperately is there, buried under layers of uncertainty.

CARL GUSTAV JUNG (July 26)

Psychiatrist, writer.

Jung was raised in a hostile home environment. Contrary to his Leo energy, he hated competition and didn't want to stand out. For him it meant getting abused. Jung's father was a pastor. Science attracted Jung at an early age, but his faith caused him great inner conflict. In medical school he found his niche. "Here at last was the place where collision of nature and spirit became reality." His choosing psychiatry, a field not understood or accepted by his colleagues, kept him outside the norm. "My concentration and self-imposed confinement alienated me from my colleagues." Jung's association with Freud was one of the high points of his life. He spoke of it as "that of father and son." But, as with all teacher/student relationships, there comes a time when the student must take his own direction. Jung struggled with this, and when he finally broke with Freud, he suffered a breakdown. However, he emerged a new man, one who used his insight and sensitivity to advance the field of psychotherapy.

DUSTIN HOFFMAN (August 8)

Academy Award-winning actor.

As a child, Dustin was pint-sized, wore braces, and had a bad case of acne. That's enough to make any kid feel self-conscious and unattractive. His first goal was to become a concert pianist, but he changed his mind and pursued acting, graduating from the Pasadena Playhouse. With the courage of a Leo, he packed his bags and left for New York, where he slept on Gene Hackman's kitchen floor. Mike Nichols saw him in a film, and flew him to California to test for *The Graduate*. The rest is history. His views on his friendship with Warren Beatty express the value the Leo/*Eight* places on truth and criticism. "To me a real friend is someone I know who really loves me but is hard on me because he wants me to be and to do my very best." Exhibiting the affection all Leos have for children, he is the father of six.

Leo/*Nine* (July 27, August 9, August 18) Sun/Mars

PURPOSE: To separate from the secure and risk yourself in the unknown; to use your strong personal perspective to give others the courage to follow their own passion and their own ideas.

"The greatest pleasure in life is doing what people say you cannot do."— Walter Bagehot. And no one knows this better than the Leo/*Nine*. They do the impossible all the time. However, this does take its toll. This combination requires that in spite of the strong individuals around them, they do what they know is right for them. Freedom for the Leo/*Nine* must come from inner strength and not from exercising force outside. When they are sure of themselves and committed to a goal, opposition dissolves. When they hesitate, others sense their insecurity and opposition grows. Becoming their own person is not easy, but when it's achieved, no one questions their authority.

IF SPIRIT TAKES THE LEAD: When Spirit is ahead, the *Nine* gets out of control. This is passion, desire, and vision harnessed under a dream. When they believe in themselves, nothing is impossible. The danger comes when they fight too hard, and don't use their incredible sense of timing to gain goals. They can trust others and give away too much power and control. They need to take responsibility for the choices they make.

IF EGO TAKES THE LEAD: If Ego moves ahead with the *Nine,* we find stubbornness, selfishness, and just plain trouble. They are passionate, emotional, and reactive. They tend to be abusive and unconcerned with boundaries set by others. Discipline is a must, as well as the need to listen to others. They may get ahead in the business world, but they'll suffer even there if they don't give a little something to others along the way.

ROBERT REDFORD (August 18)

Actor, director, founder of the Sundance Institute.

"I had so many restraints on me as a kid, being told, 'Don't do this, don't do that.' I'd just go out and do it to show it ain't so." Robert Redford's words are what this energy is all about. Sun/*Nine* people often need to learn self-confidence and self-worth. At some point, the Ego usually meets great opposition. For Redford, opposition came from his father. A mail carrier and later an accountant, he was a rigid disciplinarian who tried to discourage high-blown ambitions in his children. *New York* magazine's Neal Gabler observed, "In character after character, Redford explored the idea that we are all trapped as he is, that we can never quite bring into phase who we are with what we represent to others." Uncomfortable with the Leo desire for attention, Redford shies away from the role of matinee idol. He enjoys unprecedented control over his work and a unique amount of privacy for a movie star of his magnitude.

WHITNEY HOUSTON (August 9)

Singer, actress.

Houston grew up in East Orange, New Jersey, and sang on Sundays at the New Hope Baptist Church. Her mother is the daughter of Cissy Houston of the Sweet Inspirations (she sang behind Aretha Franklin and Elvis Presley) and her cousin is Dionne Warwick. Houston grew up hanging out with Gladys Knight and Roberta Flack. *Nines* have the power to leave their mark on whatever they do. Her first album sold more than eighteen million copies.

Houston's first movie was *The Bodyguard,* with Kevin Costner. The theme song, "I Will Always Love You," sold twenty-six million copies in the U.S. alone. Married to Bobby Brown, she has a beautiful daughter. Speaking of her daughter's birth, Houston says, "I could never do anything that could top that . . . this is the ultimate."

SUMMARY

Like a benign king, Leos rule wherever life places them. Responsibility is often assumed too eagerly and if one must stay a king, intimacy becomes a sacrifice. To unite with someone requires surrender of their specialness, at least for moments in time. What all Leos should remind themselves is that with surrender comes a more powerful kind of specialness. While climbing to the mountaintop, Leos must remember to return the gifts offered them along their journey. They should never feel shame at wanting to shine, but should never forget their actions have consequences. It is only from the greatest height that we can see the chain of events and people that have brought us to where we are. If the chain is severed through arrogance, then the isolation a Leo fears will come to pass. The king must always remind himself he is nothing without his kingdom, and that he represents a unifying figure, one capable of bringing others together by the sheer power of his will and magnetism. It is important for the Leo to remember that the rewards of a journey are the experiences, friendships, and understanding acquired along the way. Having achieved the peak of personal success, the king realizes that true happiness and power lie in the inner journey and the conquest of oneself. In the next sign of Virgo, he will face the demons and desires of his inner world.

SELECTED SOURCES

Charles F. Allen and Jonathan Portis   *Comeback Kid: The Life and Career of Bill Clinton*   Birch Lane 1992

Earl Blackwell   *Celebrity Register, 1990 (50th Anniversary Edition)*   Gale Research 1990

Edmund Blunden   *Shelley: A Life Story*   Oxford University Press 1976

Vincent Brome   *Jung: Man and Myth*   MacMillan 1981

Peter G. Bourne   *Fidel: A Biography of Fidel Castro*   Dodd Mead 1986

Wilt Chamberlain   *Wilt Chamberlain: A View from Above*   Villard Books 1991

Cecil B. DeMille   *Autobiography*   Prentice Hall 1959

Lawrence Grobel   *The Hustons*   Avon 1990

Eitan Haber   *Menachem Begin: The Legend and the Man*   Delacorte 1978

Archibald Henderson   *Bernard Shaw: Playboy and Prophet*   D. Appleton 1932

Charles Higham   *Lucy: The Real Life of Lucille Ball*   St. Martin's 1987

Earvin "Magic" Johnson with William Novak   *Magic Johnson: My Life*   Random House 1995

Rose Fitzgerald Kennedy   *Times To Remember*   World Pub. 1996

Norman King   *Madonna: The Book*   William Morrow & Company 1991

Wendy Leigh   *Arnold: An Unauthorized Biography*   Congdon and Weed 1990

Marion Meade   *Madame Blavatsky: The Woman Behind the Myth*   Putnam 1980

Herman Melville   *Moby Dick*   Alfred A. Knopf 1988

Doris L. Rich   *Amelia Earhart*   Smithsonian 1996

Frank Richardson   *Napoleon, Bisexual Emperor*   Kimber 1973

Teresa of Avila   *Interior Castle*   Translated and edited by E. Allison Peers   Doubleday 1990

Virgo

(August 24–September 23)

Virgo is the sign of sharing.
They lead the way when it comes to caring.
The Ego here must step aside,
That's right, there is no place to hide.
The lesson is we're all connected,
So don't feel hurt and never rejected.
All thoughts and actions return to you,
So pay attention to what you do.
Nothing is simple when Spirit leads.
In Virgo you harvest your planted seeds.

Ruler: Mercury   **Symbol: Virgin**
Element: Earth   **Number: Five**

Virgo is the sign of responsibility and its task is pivotal. Virgo must gather the scattered interests of the self and point them toward one goal. Virgo is the harvest and what you reap is what you have sowed. If you have pursued only earthly pleasures, then your reward could be fame and fortune. Don't get too excited. In Virgo, dissatisfaction is designed to increase with the size of your bank account—*if* you haven't learned how to share your wealth with others. If, however, you have heeded Spirit's voice and turned within to know yourself and if you have had the courage to experience life through the needs and eyes of another, then peace and happiness can be yours, along with worldly success.

Spirit's power is unlimited; there is nothing it fears or cannot conquer. To use it well requires a strong will, one that can override any opposition, ignore temptation, and draw the best and the most from all available resources. If you have the Virgo will, you know you can get whatever you want. The key is to use your will wisely, not just to accomplish some earthly task. Virgo's spiritual goal is union with God. Aware of this quest, the soul strives to be perfect. Purification becomes the challenge and the Virgo can become obsessed with health food, diet and exercise. The anticipation of a holy union keeps it striving to remain innocent and pure. Good health is a priority. Contrary to present beliefs it's your attitude toward food and the balance you have achieved between your spiritual and physical needs that determines whether illness or disease will be an issue.

Virgo represents the young adult; the freedom of youth, the ability to experiment and learn without consequences, is over. Responsibility must be accepted and then expanded to include those who can't help themselves. This is the sign of service and Virgos must learn to put aside their needs for another. Strength becomes dedicated service that teaches humility, ends isolation, and gives you the precious gift of self-worth. When you can get away from yourself and contribute to someone else's existence, you gain self-esteem. Then you set in motion a domino effect that brings confidence, expands into new awareness, new opportunities, an ability to take risks, and finally, success. As you climb the ladder that takes you out of yourself and into the world, you become aware of brotherhood and community.

The act of giving activates receiving and now you have the secret to abundance. Don't expect your gifts to come FedEx or wrapped by Tiffany. The universe prefers to camouflage its offerings to test your discrimination, your intuitiveness, and your ability to recognize truth, beauty and love. If you're judgmental, you may miss your reward. Virgo is the sign of random acts of goodness. The lesson is that giving and receiving can be freeing if you divest yourself of expectations and accept what the universe offers you in return.

Don't confuse the inability to say no with an act of love. If your self-esteem is so poor that you can't refuse the demands of others, instead of giving love, you'll be giving fear, and this serves no one. Another danger point is self-judgment; it can bring on hypochondria. You acted nastily to your best friend. You couldn't bear for her to own the same beautiful black dress that took you days to find. This imperfect thought fills you with self-loathing. Suddenly, that lump you got from banging into the corner of the kitchen table is nothing less than a malignant growth!

Virgo is the sign of Joseph Kennedy (September 16), Lyndon Johnson (August 27), Margaret Sanger (September 14), and Mother Teresa (August 27), men and women of destiny who felt or heard a calling. God sent Mother Teresa into the streets of India to nurture the wretched and the dying. Joseph Kennedy felt the call of destiny. His ruthless methods brought him fame and fortune but never peace. Virgo produces both saints and sinners, though most are a bit of both. Mercury, your ruler, is partly to blame. Its morality is based on universal laws, not human determinants. Because of this, the soul often feels outside the rules and regulations of society. If Virgos lack a spiritual thread, a sense of morality, then they don't have a conscience and are free to manipulate situations for their own ends. Of course, the Virgo can have a large conscience, too. Mother Teresa dedicated her entire life to helping others.

All mutable signs (Gemini, Virgo, Sagittarius, Pisces) bring the soul to a crisis because a powerful shift in consciousness must occur. In Virgo, the crisis is one of realities. What is real? What is illusion? The world of the senses clashes with the world of Spirit. Virgo has two phases: division and unity. In the first phase, life seems to be a choice between you and others, between selfishness or selflessness. Neither choice makes you happy. The path of Ego glitters with fleeting promises of pleasure, fame and fortune. Power is achieved through your ability to punish or reward with gifts: you give and you take away.

Success without a touch of Spirit has its flaws. Without Spirit's love and support, self-loathing, isolation, and loneliness invade. When you choose the path of Ego, nothing makes you happy. Life becomes an endless cycle of acquiring and desiring, of never achieving contentment. This is Goethe's Faust: "I have seized every appetite by the hair, what did not satisfy me, I abandoned; what slipped through my grasp, I let go. I have merely craved and achieved and then desired again and thus I have rushed through my life like a strong storm . . . Demons, I know, are hard to banish, their spirit bonds are strict and will not break."

Virgos have a great capacity to enjoy the senses to their utmost. However, some turn their back on desire. If Spirit rules empirically, life becomes a place of sin and evil. The passions and pleasures around you must be denied, unworthiness must be punished, and purification must be achieved through suffering. Ironically, the results are the same as those of Ego: self-loathing, isolation, and loneliness. Occasionally, these two energies switch appearances. Ego tries to achieve its desires on Spirit's path. These are the false martyrs who use sacrifice or victimization to achieve fame and fortune. If Spirit takes a stroll down Ego's path, we've got the sinner who becomes enlightened, the criminal who does a good deed. Here, in the Sixth house, Spirit and Ego get stretched to their limits, one rising to rule the world, the other kneeling to serve it. When they do battle in one man, totality is achieved, and a universal soul emerges, multitalented but focused on one goal—self-awareness that leads to God.

The division of Virgo is an illusion. You don't have to choose between yourself and someone else. When you can see God in all things, you bring magic to everything you do. In Cancer, you were asked to own your weaknesses and your wounds; in Leo, you learned to use your strength. Now, you must become whole. It's time to forgive those who have shunned you; thus, you forgive your own superiority. It's time to serve those you have judged as unworthy; this heals the parts of yourself you have hated or disowned. Remember, nothing is beyond God's love, and your challenge is to become whole through total self-acceptance. The center of your soul is your destination; it dwells like a castle surrounded by a moat of solitude and quiet, of renunciation and surrender. To cross the bridge and enter your inner space you must be ready to receive love.

You have always wanted to be the one special person to achieve this impossible goal: to be loved so deeply that the outer world doesn't exist, that all worldly possessions and values are really unimportant. But true love in Virgo can be too idealistic. That deep yearning, you feel can never be filled by earthy pleasures. "Real" love is spiritual unity, and to have this you must be willing to enter the darkness of your soul and face your demons.

We all have our Pandora's box. Excess occurs when the lessons of the previous signs have been ignored. A strong point of view, moral limits, strong intentions, loving yourself for your strengths and your weaknesses—these help keep your cravings under control. When desires rule, it doesn't matter what we have; it's never enough. Joseph Kennedy built his fortune to approximately $400 million dollars. It wasn't enough. He wanted fame and power, too. He chose politics as the arena in which to accomplish this goal. Consider Scarlett O'Hara, heroine of *Gone With the Wind,* the green-eyed beauty who pursued her passion without a thought to consequence. Driven by her love for Ashley Wilkes, she used people and cast them aside when they no longer served her purpose. When Ashley was finally hers, it took Scarlett a record-breaking bat of an eyelash to realize she wasn't interested after all. One of her most famous lines is, "I'll think about it tomorrow." Now that's denial, Virgo style. For her to see the connection between her actions and their results requires that she take responsibility. Self-acceptance demands responsibility. You must look yourself squarely in the mirror and love it all because it's you. Once you've done that you're ready to hear your own inner voice. That inner voice is His voice, and that's what you surrender to.

The quality of listening and the ability to be quiet, are strengths that must be mastered in order to voyage into your sacred space. You enter stripped of all protection, masks, and attitudes. You venture into the darkness of your discarded feelings of shame, unworthiness, and nothingness. You face them, own them, and love them, empowering yourself through healing and becoming whole.

The struggle with demons places the Virgo on the edge of madness. Beyond the demons is peace. The danger of confronting your unworthiness is getting stuck in nothingness. When this happens, all you see is what you don't have. There's no escaping this place. Nothingness must be faced and from the confrontation you'll know that something more exists. This is the beginning of faith. Faith is a process. It happens slowly; in fact, you may not even know that God was present until He leaves and you realize your life has changed.

If you have this faith, invest it well by sharing it with others. If you are still wallowing in nothingness, it's time to reevaluate your life. Use your pain and suffering to gain insight into yourself. Are you living a selfish existence? This creates isolation and keeps you from self-worth and growth. Faith cannot be commanded forth; no act of goodness comes with a guarantee you'll be rewarded. This would not be faith. To gain faith you must seek it without expectations. If you yearn for God to be present within you, if you attempt to live your life as close to His laws as possible, then God may grant you a visit and change your life forever.

Once Spirit has united with Spirit, it never forgets the feeling. At some deep level you strive to recreate the feeling of being understood without words; you desire it with a partner, a soul mate. Spirit now seeks unity with another, and if you are not a strong and whole person, you could easily get lost in someone else's life. The need to be whole is a prerequisite to surrendering. Virgos without an identity are either doomed to isolation or to losing themselves in the emotions of another and forgetting their own paths.

Before faith comes the fear that He doesn't exist. Suffering is another way Virgos attempt to purify themselves and to make themselves worthy of God. They see their sins and their failings and are overwhelmed with the need to punish and purify themselves. Suffering provides both and so does sacrifice. In Virgo, you must give something of yourself to others. If you refuse to do it voluntarily, the sacrifice will be involuntary. Whether you let go or the universe demands it of you, a lesson will be learned: you can't own or control anything of true importance. Suffering and sacrifice forces the soul inward. Acute pain helps the soul separate from the body. The separation of Spirit from the soul is accomplished.

There are talents that result from Spirit's ability to leave the soul and unite with another. One of them is the gift of imitation. By projecting its Spirit into another, the soul has access to that other's deepest feelings. With this kind of information, a person can reproduce anything and make it appear authentic. Peter Sellers (September 8), the actor, was a master at this. "I suppose I had a basic need to be bigger and grander than I was. I think I always felt more confident playing somebody else." In fact, Sellers felt as though he had no identity. Michael Jackson (August 29) could watch someone dance and imitate him in a matter of minutes. Mark Schorel said of D. H. Lawrence (September 11), the writer: "He seeks to analyze the instinctual and irrational psychological forces that surge beneath the surface, that determine the complex motivation and behavior of men and women . . . he will be concerned first of all not with the ego that interest the traditional novelist, but with the primal forces, that are prior to character."

Judgment easily slips into the Virgo path. Afraid of the truth and reluctant to take responsibility, they can try to justify their lives instead of learning how to improve things. Put away right and wrong comments and surrender to something higher and better. When you do, not only is your faith restored but you receive the gift of synchronicity—each moment seems magically linked to another. When you need help, it spontaneously appears. Without seeing the link that connects you to your wish, your need, and your destiny, you know it exists. You are supported and encased in the invisible power of faith. With faith, life unfolds. Without faith, life is a burden.

Fate is also linked to the unconscious. What you're not aware of appears to *happen* to you. It's out of your control. However, when something is made conscious, you have choices. Suddenly life is not a hit-or-miss accident. The unconscious is the keeper of your secrets. Every little thing you have hidden from others, and even yourself, is stored in this chaos, and its power is tremendous. When you go too far in one direction, it creates an event that forces you to lean the other way. It can stop you from getting what you *think* you want. Everyone's experienced self-sabotage, the stupid things you do that prevent you from having something you think you want. Let's say you're a housewife who decides to go back to work. You apply for a job. Your unconscious knows the truth, that you're not ready to make this compromise. To get the job requires you give a speech. You don't prepare for the speech, or you leave it at home. You have prevented yourself from getting the job.

The unconscious is a tough teacher; it has relentless patience. It will wait for an appropriate time to awaken a new perception. When you're in place and can't avoid the issue, it spits out your lesson. Each time you refuse to learn the stakes are raised and the crisis becomes more dramatic. Remember, if someone pushes your button, it's *your* button. Look at the issue, see it in yourself. Only with the courage to go inside can you reach your greatest potential. Oliver Stone (September 15) is a talented director because he gets inside. "Somebody really has to worm their way into your psyche and push your buttons and disturb you in order to make you start looking at the world in a different way. That's what Oliver does, and he's very gifted at it." Virgo is War And Peace, and the author of that famous novel was a Virgo—Tolstoy. He knew that the peace one seeks is only found by doing the battle, and that battle is always with yourself.

Virgos often experience a pivotal moment in their lives when a new perception is awakened. Stone says about the divorce of his parents when he was fifteen, "I had a sense that everything had been stripped away. That there was a mask on everything, and underneath there was a harder truth, a deeper and more negative truth." For Mother Teresa, it came in a calling from God, "I was going to Darjeeling to make my retreat; it was on that train that I heard the call to give up all and follow Him into the slums—to serve Him in the poorest of the poor." When Tolstoy was a boy of eight, his family took him to Moscow with a dozen coaches and thirty servants. He discovered for the first time that the world did not end at the boundaries of the family estate. Some years later, Tolstoy (September 9) wrote: "Has it ever happened to you, reader, at a certain period of your life to notice all of a sudden that your way of looking at things has changed utterly, as if every object you had ever seen suddenly appeared from a new angle you had no knowledge of? . . . " Sometimes, a Virgo's life is changed by the kindness of a stranger. For Jessie Owens (September 12), the Olympic gold medalist, it was his junior-high-school track coach. Owens wasn't the strongest or the healthiest kid around, but the coach singled him out and became a second father to Owens.

With a life torpedoed by unexpected events, chaos and confusion necessarily play their part. As a Virgo, you either fear chaos and do whatever you possibly can to avoid its encounter, or you use it to your advantage because you know your way around. That means when things get too calm, you create chaos. If, on the other hand, uncertainty makes you shake in your boots and indecision is a fate worse than death, then what you need is faith in yourself. Otherwise, you will judge things too quickly in a useless attempt to end confusion. Your goal is impossible.

In Virgo, we learn that every act is connected to a chain of events that ties the soul into a karmic web. Nothing is by chance, and every action has a reaction. The good you do today comes back to you tomorrow. J.C. Penney (September 16) made a fortune using the Virgo principles. " . . . I owe so much to my business associates that I am often at a loss to distinguish what it is I owe to myself."

The need to link small events and details to a central focus makes the Virgo a great manipulator. They never forget a favor, either done for them or owed to them. Don't ask a Virgo for a favor unless you plan to return it; they'll remind you of it until the scales of justice are balanced. They know about karma, they just haven't learned to let the universe do the adjusting. Lyndon Johnson was a master at calling in favors. Huey Long (August 30), former Governor of Louisiana, appointed a staff of men who owed him for one thing or another.

This emphasis on little things stems from the Virgo's spiritual desire to remain pure. They know that evil can arise from a small digression. Virgos are both physically and spiritually vigilant. In Leo, God was recreated in one's own image. In Virgo, one tries to recreate a whole religion, one that will establish the Kingdom of God on earth right now. Virgos find themselves at odds with dogma and the church. Tolstoy was excommunicated and contemplated starting his own religion. Impatience for God translates into a soul of action. Mother Teresa didn't wait for funds to start teaching the children of India. She gathered them under a tree and used a stick to draw in the dirt.

The common man and the king have equal standing in Virgo. Sometimes, they switch places. After Tolstoy had his religious conversion he gave up his title of count. He didn't relinquish his estate, but he did dress in the peasant garb, became a strict vegetarian, and undertook a daily regimen of work and exercise.

Virgos are psychic, intuitive, and creative. When they tap their wellspring, they find an endless supply of energy and creativity. This sign produces many a genius and men and woman of a prolific nature. Goethe (August 28) wrote poetry like others keep a journal, Darryl Zanuck (September 5) could turn out a screenplay over the weekend. Lyndon Johnson had more energy than five people and did the work of ten. However, the Virgo's intelligence is not based on logic; it's subjective and instinctual. Peter Evans said of Peter Sellers: "He is a man you cannot anticipate with intelligence because there is no intelligent pattern, no apparent reason, no visible cause." In Virgo, it's not enough just to be smart; you've got to absorb an experience. Mother Teresa said, "To know the problem of poverty intellectually is not to understand it. It is not by reading, talking, walking in the slums that we come to understand it and to discover what it has of bad and good. We have to dive into it, live it, share it." Oliver Stone immersed himself in the film industry and said, "To be noticed in the industry takes a lot. To do that you almost invariably have to become part of the system, allow it to absorb you and work within its dictates for success."

Virgos who are not invested in hiding from the world approach it almost fearlessly. They see life as a game, a challenge, a chance to test themselves against others. They make great politicians and leaders, for they're skilled at bringing opposing forces together to work toward a common goal. On the eve of an election Huey Long, former governor of Louisiana, said, "This is the sport of kings. A contestant in a great arena, a game of high stakes."

Animals, and pets in particular, play an important role in the Virgo's life. They love animals and often have several pets. The American Indians believe that animals provide a spiritual link to God. It is certainly a profound experience to know the unconditional love and surrender of a pet that places his life in your hands.

Art provides a bridge in Virgo. It's the physical manifestation of Spirit's ability to project its feelings into another. Good art unites others through shared feelings and this is what Virgo is about. Art can pass on a point of view, not just an isolated emotion. However, art is selective; the artist chooses what is important to relate. This is legacy. It's one way society teaches and informs those who are to follow. "A real work of art destroys in the consciousness of the recipient the separation between himself and the artist, and not that alone, but also between himself and all whose minds receive this work of art."—Tolstoy.

The Virgo challenge is to learn how to do nothing and accomplish everything. When you turn over your responsibility and let Him guide you, the way will be shown and the work will be done. Outwardly, nothing is happening, but inwardly, everything is being done. Of course, it's possible to get stuck on either side of this dynamic. Someone at the London embassy said of Joseph Kennedy: "Joe Kennedy either wanted to buy it, or sell it. He couldn't see that nonaction might be the proper course in a situation." Passivity is the other option. Virgos can languor in bed, believing they're dying of some dreaded disease when the truth is there's just something they don't want to face. Because they are perfectionists, procrastination may be a form of self-defense. If they start a project, they know they will be consumed by it. When they're action-oriented, it's difficult for them to delegate. They want it done right, which means they do it all. Lyndon Johnson never trusted anybody to do anything; he did it all, down to the last detail. The Virgos' task is self-simplification—they've got to work at eliminating and improving the things they keep.

Love in Virgo is a problem if equality is the quest. You're not interested in someone who fits into your life. You want to cross boundaries, serve or feel superior. You connect through Spirit. Ingrid Bergman (August 29) gave up her daughter, her husband, and her dignity to marry the man she had fallen in love with, Roberto Rossellini. Reporters from all over the world surrounded their villa in Italy. The U.S. Senate even condemned her publicly.

Love in Virgo can be spiritual and idealistic, without physical satisfaction. D.H. Lawrence said, "When I was a very young man, I was enraged when with a woman, if I was reminded of her sexual actuality. I only wanted to be aware of her personality, her mind and her spirit. The other had to be fiercely shut out." With Lawrence there was also an issue of homosexuality. Michael Jackson's sexuality has been in question. His Jehovah's Witness upbringing sanctioned sex only within marriage. This was in stark contrast to his father's actions; he brought women into the family's hotel suite and slept with them in the room next to the children's. Michael idolized his mother and found himself emotionally conflicted.

If the union is not spiritual, then the Virgo could choose a tough, critical mate. Virgos are attracted to partners who make them tow the line. Their need for perfection makes them choose relationships that keep them on their toes. Of course, this does not make for peace and happiness, at least not from the point of view of others.

If you're the Virgo you can be either loyal or a playboy, you either avoid sex or become its slave. Remember, this is the sign of extremes. You're definitely sexy, and you know it. The confusing part for you is choosing between a siren or a saint. You love them both. When you're with someone pure of heart, you long for a little passion without guilt. You need self-control, not a controlling relationship. Don't get discouraged if marriage is not your priority. You hate to limit your possibilities. Love, when it comes, is no less complicated. Good and evil, logic and reason have nothing to say when it comes to the Virgo heart. Greta Garbo (September 18) didn't care that her father was a drunk and he couldn't support her. She loved him even though her mother and sister did not share her feelings. Love in Virgo, fits no category; like God, it has no rules. This is the sign of great prejudice and great universal love. If Ego leads, differences are emphasized: color, money, and social position become important. If Spirit has its way, none of these things matter.

The issue of the mother for a Virgo is usually complex. Larger than life or victims of life, Virgo mothers either overnurture or are lost in their own world of desires. The mother is seen not only as giving unconditional love, as in Taurus, but also as the demon who possesses their child's soul. Trying to separate from that relationship is a great struggle for a Virgo. D.H. Lawrence said about his relationship with his mother, "We knew each other by instinct. We have been like one, so sensitive to each other we never needed words. It has been rather terrible, and has made me in some respects abnormal." When Peter Sellers's mother was dying, he stayed away. It was said that "Every day Peter Sellers wasn't at his mother's bedside was a day of triumph for them both." Oliver Stone had a tormented relationship with his mother. "She was wild, and sexual, a free sprit and she introduced him to the seedy side of life."

Ruled by Mercury, Virgos know how to organize almost anything better and faster than anyone else. They have an eye for separating the good from the bad and truth from illusion. They are great mathematicians because they divide the journey both physically and spiritually; they can match objects with essence. Able to break things down into parts or see the whole from the pieces, they can put puzzles together and invent, simply through their ability to rearrange whatever is available.

Virgos have the minds of mechanics and the hearts of race car drivers. When they're behind, they just increase the speed. Besides organizing your office, they can fix the coffee machine, take apart the clock, and still do the work of three other people. They are incredible problem solvers. William Fulbright said, "When Lyndon Johnson was majority leader he was master at managing the Senate and at reconciling people with diametrically opposed views. Nobody could match him." Ray O'Connell, a lawyer who worked with Joseph Kennedy, said his mind functioned with "machinelike efficiency . . . If you tell Joe Kennedy a problem, he'll listen quietly and separate the wheat from the chaff while you talk. He quickly divides the problem into its components and sees to the heart of the problem. Almost before you're finished speaking he has the answer to a problem you've struggled with for months."

Burdened with the spiritual task of seeking human perfection, Virgos must turn their back on things that tempt the senses. Their journey is to detach and simplify, to resist the pull to acquire. This in no way stops Virgos from having their talent recognized. Remember, it's only the attachment to worldly possessions that needs to be overcome, not the possessions themselves. Virgos know that work and discipline are the key to achieving spiritual fulfillment. At the tender age of seven Sister Pascalina (August 25), the nun behind the rapid rise of Monsignor Pacelli to the position of Pope Pius XII, was eager to work. She startled her parents when she asked to be allowed to help out in the fields. "It will be such fun for me!" The grueling work didn't deter her enthusiasm; she kept up with her older brothers and taught them a thing or two. Virgos need little sleep; their restless nature keeps them burning the midnight oil. They can outlast, outdo and overdo with an ease that leaves others in awe.

Letting go is a difficult thing for Virgos. They want control and develop many ways of fooling themselves into thinking they are calling the shots. High on the list is denial and repression. Here, desires are beaten down. If this is your choice, you rarely expose yourself to excess or luxury. Others may see you as cheap, strange and thrifty. Try not to get too annoyed at those who enjoy their lives. This self-inflicted martyrdom will not make you happy unless your sacrifices have a purpose other than honing your incredible will and proving to yourself you're stronger than your desires. Without surrendering to His will, without rising above your needs, life is just a battle for control.

Workaholism is another popular choice for the Virgo. If this is your area of expertise, you're probably very successful. You seldom sleep more than two or three hours a night; you love obstacles and impossible tasks; money is rarely your motivation. Rather, you are obsessed with a need to prove yourself and do a perfect job. You're a boss's dream and an employee's nightmare—that is, if you're the boss. Success, however, usually means financial rewards and now you haven't avoided temptation at all. You just made those demons hungrier. However, work can be used to express our fears and desires, and to negate our demons. Peter Sellers used his film characters to channel his negative emotions.

Writing is a Virgo talent and many great writers are born under this sign. D. H. Lawrence channeled his repressed sexuality in his writing. *The Rainbow* and *Lady Chatterley's Lover* brought Victorian sexuality into the mainstream. The suppression of his work made Lawrence poor. "Poverty," he wrote, "isn't any such awful thing, if you don't care about keeping up appearances." His Virgo energy made it easy for him to reduce his standard of living and cut his spending back to provide only the barest necessities.

Poverty appears alongside the word Virgo too often to dismiss it as chance. Poverty or denuding would be unnecessary if man did not place false values on things the moment he has them in his hands. Nothing should stand in the way of your journey. Tolstoy believed that the poor held the secret of the meaning of life and death and so he mingled with them, hoping to discover the great answer. However, what Tolstoy discovered was that the answer to God could only be found in himself. "If I exist, there must be some cause for it, and a cause of causes. And that first cause of all is what men have called 'God'." He knew his mission was the painful act of giving birth to himself. From his struggle to accept himself would come a new perception, a new man. Virgos must embrace their imperfections. Because they struggle to do this, they believe that it is a struggle for others to love them, too. They crave approval and love; they need to be liked no matter how powerful they have become.

Another way Virgos attempt to keep their desires under control is to be unhappy but safe. You choose a partner you care about, but not enough so that he or she inflames your passions. It's comfortable, but not exciting. One part of you longs to have your body tingle, but another part knows and fears what will happen if the demons get their way. Once they've been excited they take over and you always obey. If you lack self-discipline, you'll seek it in a partner. The greater your compassion and indulgence, the greater your partner's coldness and toughness. If you're dating the hit man for the Mafia, your self-control is probably nonexistent.

Yet another choice is being alone or with someone who is totally unavailable. Impotence, psychological abuse, fear—all these factors can keep your bed cold and empty, but you can still enjoy the longing and the fantasy. The final choice is that you face your fears, desires, and dark side. This is only for those with real courage. Oliver Stone's biographer says, "He'd conquered loneliness at Hill, vanquished fear in Vietnam, overcome rejection in New York, defeated failure in Hollywood, and purged himself of cocaine in Paris. The only way he knew to overcome something was by facing it." The courage and ability to look what they fear straight in the eye is a Virgo talent. Margaret Sanger realized early the need to face her fears. "To gain fortitude, I began to make myself do whatever I feared the most." Single-mindedness is a Virgo given. J.C. Penney said, "Many men have worked hard and conscientiously and yet have failed to achieve business success because they lacked enthusiasm, vision, and singleness of purpose. Unorganized work performed without thought always fixed on a definite goal, is like rolling a stone up a mountain of sand."

The ability to call on all ones resources to get a job done, is one of the great gifts of Virgo. They become stronger in a crisis, using their incredible will to unite others behind their goal. J.C. Penney describes this process in relationship to his career: "There appears to come a crisis in every career—as in the development of every invention—when the successful resolution of the problem depends upon the capacity for bringing every atom of energy to focus upon the undertaking in hand. One then seems to become a conductor for those greater forces always waiting for creative release in the universe . . ." This is Virgo at its best, harnessing every atom of its being in order to bring something new into the world. From this struggle a new you will be born.

Spirit never settles for anything less than perfection. For Tolstoy, the desire for perfection was as much a curse as a gift. "My true belief then was my faith in perfectionism. Moral perfectionism was soon replaced by perfectionism in general . . . [a] desire to make myself better in the eyes of other men." Sister Pascalina was Pope Pius XI's housekeeper. She ran his house with such perfection that it became impossible to keep a household staff. As mistress of the household, she "anticipated his needs, relieving him of all routine details. As chief cook, she personally prepared every one of his meals with never a day off. As housekeeper, she took painstaking care of his clothes, making absolutely certain that his holy vestments were always immaculate ... His papers were always kept in perfect order by her, and never did he have to complain that she had allowed any one of his many fountain pens to run dry." This desire for perfection can carry over into a dislike for the imperfections of the body. Tolstoy said of his body, "I was modest, but my modesty was increased by the conviction that I was a monster."

Because the battle of the senses is fought in Virgo, they are some of the sexiest people in the world. Consider Sophia Loren (September 20), Ingrid Bergman (August 29), Lauren Bacall (September 16), Raquel Welch (September 5) and Sean Connery (August 25), Richard Gere (August 31), Jimmy Connors (September 2) and Rossano Brazzi (September 18). The paradox of Virgo manifests as the child-woman or the little-boy man. Virgos keep their youthful appearance in spite of the fact that responsibility was placed on them early in life. When only a child, Sean Connery worked full-time delivering milk. Mel Torme (September 13) was singing and earning money at the age of three. According to Spike Melligan, "Peter [Sellers] can look more helpless than any man alive. . . . He is a man-child."

Torn between being too generous and avoiding gift giving, their dual nature is often confusing to others. One minute they're giving you anything in their world, the next they're charging you for using the bathroom. This struggle to give and to hold on to is often experienced in the same moment. As they hand you a gift, they're explaining why they can't give it to you right now.

The Ego is not king in Virgo; in fact, it has little value. To compensate for its lack of power, it feels the need to puff itself up and expand, to make itself feel important. When this happens the personality is extended and one's identity can encompass not just oneself but a job or an object. If you're president of a company, you become that company; when you're out of that job, you've lost your identity and your sense of self-importance. Men who buy fast, expensive cars usually have a need to boost their ego. When they're driving that Ferrari, they're somebody. If, however, you've extended your identity through your values and selfless service, instead of being susceptible to a fall, you'll feel strengthened and more secure.

If the Ego withdraws because it can't get attention, it may become isolated. The world has ignored its potential, so it hides from opportunity and feels unrecognized and misunderstood. It doesn't really believe it is inferior, but it prefers to pout rather than risk rejection again. This makes an oversensitive soul, easily hurt by criticism.

The last but not least dangerous way of avoiding our truth is to give the responsibility of it to someone else. This way you can blame *them* if anything goes wrong. This can be done with a guru, a boss, lover, husband, wife or friend. For Greta Garbo, Mauritz Stiller was the recipient of herself. Her Virgo love of criticism must have made him immediately attractive. He told her, "You are fat, you don't know how to walk. You don't know how to talk. You don't even know how to smile. What is more, you don't know how to behave among people, nor do you know how to think . . . Every hour of every day you will have to obey me. If you do so I promise you I will make you great." She turned herself over to him. "I was the creation of Stiller and my future depended upon him." She became famous, but she lost her true identity. Sister Pascalina first gave her life to God, then to Monsignor Pacelli, who later became the Pope. This is a Virgo dream, to become the servant of the most recognized spiritual leader in the world. However, when he died, her life lost its meaning.

Community awareness is important for a Virgo. J.C. Penney had a knack for understanding a community and knowing its needs, then setting up his stores to serve those needs. His was one of the first franchise stores in the world. "I was there to serve the community and their necessity made our law . . . " For D.H. Lawrence, Rananem was an idealistic community that would form the nucleus of a new society. "I want to gather together about twenty souls and sail away from this world of war and squalor and found a little colony where there shall be no money but a sort of communism as far as necessaries of life go, and some real decency." Mother Teresa held community a priority. "We are all members of one another."

Virgos are vagabonds at heart. They need to travel and explore. Margaret Sanger traveled the world, speaking on birth control. Oliver Stone creates his films in faraway lands. Even Mother Teresa found herself traveling as her Missionaries of Charity expanded world wide. CBS News correspondent Charles Kuralt (September 10) is author of a book entitled, *A Life On The Road.* It opens with the following words: "There is no contentment on the road, and little enough fulfillment . . . I know what I have missed. . . . And still I wander, seeking compensation in unforeseen encounters and unexpected sights, in sunsets, storms and passing fancies."

When a Virgo has charm and magnetism, she's hard to ignore. The sheer power of her presence can overwhelm her opponent. They are able to switch among the many facets of their personality. Virgos have either an innate natural style and sense of manners or they are crude and abhor the false pretenses of society. When naturalness leads, it seems to manifest in their walk or stride. Sean Connery has it and so does Sophia Loren. Jessie Owens revolutionized the existing style of running. When a Virgo's crude, you notice. Lyndon Johnson was rough around the edges. Huey Long, former governor of Louisiana, publicized his disgust for proper manners; it got him votes with the masses. Ambassador Joseph Kennedy was thought crude by the English, and his reputation for bad taste was recognized even in America. Too much breeding and manners can also present a problem. Peter Lawford (September 7) discovered this when he tried to join the Hollywood crowd. Virgos often find themselves at odds with society.

Virgos are transitional people; they bring us to a new place and they have the power to unite. J. William Fulbright said, "When Lyndon (Johnson) was majority leader he was master at managing the Senate and at reconciling people with diametrically opposed views. Nobody could match him. He knew every personal interest of every member of the Senate just like he knew the palm of his hand. He knew how to bring people together because he could appeal to their different interests." Johnson held the country together after Kennedy's assassination and inaugurated great social changes with the passage of the Civil Rights Bill.

Virgos dominate the professions of service, politics, and the creative arts. They adapt well to anything that requires organizational skills, perseverance, compassion, and creativity. When the need to serve is strong, they make wonderful nurses and social workers. If the Ego is strong, they should work for themselves and use their managerial skills to run companies or private businesses. Gifted in the fields of writing, politics, and finances, they easily rise to the top because they work hard and are dependable. Whatever they choose to do, their hearts and souls will be in it.

Virgo is the stage of the journey when the soul seeks spiritual nourishment. It yearns to unite with God. As it faces itself, it sees the consequences of its actions, the attachment it has to its desires, the fears and shame it has hidden. The challenge is to face and accept the whole self. Until this happens the Virgo often lives a lonely and separate life, relating to people and events in a compartmentalized way. However, it is through sharing that isolation ends and self-worth is gained. The Virgo soul sees the invisible thread that links one person to another, one spirit to all spirits. Brotherhood, service, and community are exalted here. Virgos are gifted with powerful charisma, unyielding will, superior analytical minds, and immense versatility. If, however, the spiritual dimension is ignored and the soul seeks its satisfaction in the physical world, success is achieved but without satisfaction. Until the soul surrenders to its spiritual calling, it lives in conflict with society, either judging it or serving it. The path of Virgo is not easy, but the rewards are strength, infallible faith, and the courage to proceed to the next phase of the journey where the birth of the individual—a whole and complete soul—will emerge.

THE VIRGO ENVIRONMENT

The Virgo environment demands a sacrifice. You must begin to let go of worldly attachments and learn the difficult lesson that you own and control nothing. The only possessions you can keep are the rewards of spirit—love and a sense of wholeness. The environment does not impede worldly success, but it will show you the consequences of your actions. Thus, you will face either the isolation and loneliness caused by your self-centeredness or the warmth and love that comes from unity and the rewards of community service. Responsibility will be yours at an early age; learn to accept it without becoming someone else's slave. Whatever you fear you will have to face, and the consequences of your thoughts and actions will be immediately experienced so that you can see the connection. The environment will often misjudge your behavior, praising you randomly, condemning you wrongly. Your challenge is to know in your own heart what's right and wrong and to follow your instincts. If you have trouble negotiating the complexity of your life, remember, you can accomplish everything by turning your will over to His.

Virgo/*One* (August 28, September 1, September 10, September 19) Mercury/Sun

PURPOSE: *To overcome your need for worldly success and control through testing your strength against the best and having faith in a higher power.*

"Let man be noble, generous and good! For this alone distinguishes him from all beings known to us."—Goethe. Virgo/*Ones* struggle with their need to shine in the world and their indifference to its rules or norms. These are innovative thinkers who follow their own imagination and instinct and then make the world take notice. Either ruled by strong, passionate desires, or able to deny all temptations, their will is strong, and so is their opinion. Perfectionists at heart, they are tough on themselves. If they don't accept their weaknesses, the negated part of them may become their problem. Their ability to categorize and notice detail makes them critical and judgmental. Freedom is an issue, and so is authority. In business they should be the boss. Personally, a commitment could be a challenge. They are charismatic and magnetic. They can lose themselves in someone else and worship a mate, then suffer the disillusionment of reality. Gifted with versatility, imagination, and talent, they know how to survive and use their strength to help others become independent. Caught between their desire for discipline and the need to be free, they face the challenge of balancing responsibility.

IF SPIRIT TAKES THE LEAD: With Spirit strong, the Virgo *One* is idealistic, imaginative, and prone to a perfectionistic nature. Challenges do not deter them, they see the world as filled with evil and they strive obsessively to do good and be right. They are rebels by nature and easily align with a cause. Against tradition and dogma, they see the pursuit of God in conflict with religion. Their minds are strong, their desire for knowledge is great, and their need to serve their community can make them put others ahead of themselves. Critical and tough, they need to love and remember that all things come from God.

IF EGO TAKES THE LEAD: With Ego in the lead, the soul is gifted, its talents many, and its morals questionable. These souls use either physical or financial strength to overcome their opposition. They can approach a problem from many different angles. Quick, strong, desiring success at all cost, no challenge is too great, no obstacle too large. Unrelenting in their will, they easily overcome most opposition. Cursed with a restlessness and an endless curiosity, satisfaction is something they will never achieve.

JOHANN WOLFGANG VON GOETHE. (August 28)

German poet, novelist, playwright, philospher, lawyer, biologist.

Goethe is said to be one of the most versatile figures in world literature. Virgo/*Ones* can do everything better than anyone else. Goethe is quoted as saying, "everything which rejoiced or troubled me (I turned) into a picture or a poem." Upon completing his law studies, he wrote *the Sorrows of Young Werther* in four weeks. It was a great success and inaugurated an aesthetic movement known as *Sturm und Drang* (Storm and Stress). Even the clothes that Werther, the hero of Goethe's novel wore became the fashion. Virgos know how to influence the masses. They also need to recreate themselves constantly. "I am like a snake, I slough my skin and start afresh." In the middle of his success Goethe moved to the court at Weimar and seemed to abandon his literary talents. His duties of state lasted for approximately ten years. It was the German philosopher Schiller who reconnected Goethe to the world of literature. With Schiller's prodding Goethe finished his monumental work, *Faust.*

KARL LAGERFELD (September 10)

Couturier.

"I would like to be a one-man multinational fashion phenomenon." The German-born son of a Swedish dairy tycoon, Lagerfeld was raised on an estate outside Hamburg. At fourteen he was sent to school in Paris and two years later he won a prize for the best coat design from the International Wool Fashion Office. Pierre Balmain was so impressed by Lagerfeld he made him his assistant. After three years of working in *couture,* Lagerfeld became bored and dropped out. Two years later he returned to Paris and worked for both Chloe and Fendi. In 1983, Lagerfeld signed with Chanel and the following year he had his own label. The fashion gazette *W* says that Lagerfeld "designs much in the way he talks, rapidly, mercurially, and with generous lacings of sharp wit." Lagerfeld revolutionized the way clothing is constructed. Particularly talented at layering clothes, he invented the scarf dressing, and has always encouraged women to create their own look. Lagerfeld says, "I may live in an ivory tower, but I have good glasses to look out. I see the world . . . from every century. I read. I read. I read."

Virgo/*Two* (August 29, September 2, September 11, September 20) Mercury/Moon

PURPOSE: To use your acute sensitivity, feelings of difference and fears of abandonment to gain insight into yourself, become creative, and bond with others.

"The spiritual self must never lose its sense of utter dependence on the invisible."—Jung. Powerful emotions rule here. Without self-acceptance and a creative outlet, there could be a problem. It's important for Virgo/*Twos* not to get stuck in the past, reliving old wounds; they must understand them and move forward, embracing all of themselves, even the parts that don't fit the norm. They are intelligent, analytical, and have great imaginations. Mood swings and depression can be a problem. Virgo/*Twos* should not spend time with negative people; they absorb their energy. *Twos* long for intimacy, but need to be able to set boundaries in order to have it. If they keep everything inside, they will be weighed down with a hopelessness that's difficult to release. Virgo/*Twos* must learn to discriminate, define, and say no; then, they're on their way to what their hearts desire. The way to heal is to share; if they want to end loneliness, they've got to be willing to take a risk.

IF SPIRIT TAKES THE LEAD: With Spirit powerful, so are fantasy, imagination, and idealism. These souls are obsessive, creative, and so emotional that they often deny their feelings in an effort to gain a sense of control. A yearning for intimacy, a desire to surrender, and a feeling of powerlessness leads them to spirituality or social and idealistic causes. Fear is strong, but so is courage; whatever they set their mind to, gets done. Restless by nature, they are a loner who comes out of their shell to help others heal. They have a magical quality that makes them irresistible and yes, different. They desire to please and to be loved. Unaware of the power of their persistence, they need to see this invisible asset in a new light.

IF EGO TAKES THE LEAD: Ego and the number *Two*, when not balanced with Spirit, can lead to self-absorption. They are narcissistic. Consumed with needs that were never met in childhood, they try to recreate the past. They can have great creativity, imagination, energy, and talent. They are a bit odd or unique in their appearance. A loner, they use their vulnerability and weaknesses to make others feel sorry for them. Great manipulators; their sensitivity and psychic ability help them become whatever you want them to be. Close to their feelings, yet unable to express them, they're difficult to deceive unless you're dealing with their personal issues.

MICHAEL JACKSON (August 29)

Singer, dancer, actor.

The youngest of nine children, Jackson was raised by a strong, abusive father and a warm, religious mother. The Jackson children began to sing when the TV broke and they needed something to do. Mr. Jackson recognized his sons' talent and quickly became their manager. Michael, the youngest, became the lead vocalist. As The Jackson Five, the boys won almost every local contest they entered and then took the biggest prize of all, amateur night at the Apollo. Motown signed the group and their career continued to soar. With his own creativity limited by his brothers, Jackson yearned to do a solo album. His father, anxious to quiet his son's rising discontent, agreed. Jackson hired Quincy Jones to work with him. The result was a hit album. His career as a soloist took off.

The scars of Jackson's childhood would not be erased. Creative, sensitive, shy and self-confident, Jackson is the perfect Virgo paradox. He lives in a *Two's* fantasy world. His twenty-seven-hundred-acre estate has its own zoo and amusement park. Jackson created the childhood he never was allowed to have. Persistent rumors of child abuse and homosexuality haunt him.

D.H. LAWRENCE (September 11)

Writer. Works include the novels *Sons and Lovers* and *Lady Chatterley's Lover.*

D.H. Lawrence, the fourth of five children, was born in Eastwood, England. From his mother, Lawrence experienced both rejection and extreme closeness. His brother George said, "We all petted and spoiled him from the time he was born—my mother poured her very soul into him." Lawrence's childhood was shadowed by poor health. Ridiculed at school by the boys because of his frailty, he also suffered from his parents' fighting.

Restless by nature, Lawrence became a wanderer, violently rejecting the materialism, stability, and social conventions of the middle class. He refused to acquire property, settle down, and become respectable. Lawrence was torn by his homosexual desires. However, his need to speak out against Victorian morality helped changed the climate of his time. Raised in a coal-mining town, Lawrence saw the mines as a symbol of his search for the essential, instinctual unconscious.

Virgo/*Three* (August 30, September 3, September 12, September 21) Mercury/Jupiter

PURPOSE: To pass the test of faith by believing in your talents and yourself and not letting desire keep you stuck and out of control.

"In quietness and in confidence shall be your strength"—Book of Isaiah. Strength is the key, and if Virgo/*Threes* have faith in themselves, they have it. If not, they become deflated and feel the need to surrender their strength to someone else. The challenge is not to give their power away, at least not to anyone but Him. The Virgo/*Three* is unique and has something special to offer. If they are too optimistic, they maybe using hope and faith to keep others at a distance or to balance the negativity of someone close. They may fear intimacy and prefer to idealize a mate. They have endless energy, charisma, and strong ideals. They have a desire to share their knowledge with those less fortunate. They must be careful not to let pride outrun humility. Foreign places and people attract them; philosophy and knowledge demand their attention. Experience is the best teacher; the Virgo/*Three* must step into the world and test her power.

IF SPIRIT TAKES THE LEAD: With Spirit at the helm, so is confidence, optimism; and strength. These souls love a challenge, are multitalented, and know how to deal with both the rich and the poor. Natural leaders, teachers, and spiritual gurus, they are driven by a need to serve and educate. Politics attracts them. They can fight long and hard for a cause. Their lesson is to not take on every impossible challenge or person that crosses their path. Intimacy may be a problem because they only know how to relate to large and grand things.

IF EGO TAKES THE LEAD: If Ego is ahead of Spirit, these souls are powerful leaders. They use force and their position to get people to agree with them. If they lack confidence, they may align themselves with someone powerful. The danger is becoming a dictator or being ruled by one. They need to use their talents according to the needs of the moment, rather than for control.

STEPHEN KING (September 21)

Best-selling author.

Stephen King has eighty-two million books in print and receives advances in the eight figures. Not bad for a kid who spent his life feeling depressed about his father's abandonment. King channels his obsessive nature into work. A perfectionist, he has been known to toss an entire novel in the trash because it didn't meet his expectations.

King wrote his first short story when he was eighteen. At twenty, he made his first sale of a short story, "The Glass Floor," to a magazine. His talent is his ability to bring the richness and power of his personal world into his fiction. "The Woman in the Room," from *Nightshift,* is his attempt to deal with his feelings about his mother's death. A keen observer, King is meticulous in his devotion to seeing how and why people and society work.

JESSIE OWENS (September 12)

Winner of four Olympic gold medals for track.

Virgo's ability to cross prejudicial social barriers found the perfect arena at the Eleventh Summer Olympic Games in 1936 Berlin. Hitler believed the Aryan race was superior and allowed no Jews or blacks on the German team. Jessie Owens, a black American youth from the South, held the world record in track. His superior talent won him four gold medals and his personal charisma won him the hearts of the world.

James Cleveland Owens was the son of sharecroppers in Alabama. Sickly as a child, he seemed frail and unathletic. But Charles Riley, the junior-high-school coach of the track team, asked Owens to run. Riley became like a second father. He taught Owens that the biggest obstacle anyone has to overcome is within one's own head. Gifted with the Virgo personality and charm, Owens was elected student body president of his 95-percent-white school. He went to Ohio State University and was blessed with another great coach, Larry Snyder. At the 1936 Olympics, Owens won four gold medals, breaking records in all events, an unprecedented feat by a track athlete. The German contender for the long jump, Luz Long, became friends with Owens before Hitler's eyes; Long hugged Owens when Owens won the medal. Although Hitler snubbed Owens, refusing to shake his hand, the boundaries of prejudice had been dissolved through courage, grace and talent.

Virgo/*Four* (August 31, September 4, September 13, September 22) Mercury/Uranus

PURPOSE: To keep your focus on a dream and manifest it, breaking free of outmoded restrictions, negotiating the crises placed to test your determination, focus, and ability to decide what is your responsibility and what isn't.

"Change is not made without inconvenience, even from worse to better."—Richard Hooker. The Virgo/*Four* either thirsts after change and finds it at every corner, or cowers, hoping it won't find him. But it always does. The Virgo/*Four* has a versatile mind; thoughts and actions come at superspeed. They see into the future and are fascinated with the past. They tend to overload or overstress. They either devote their lives to helping others, or pursue a desire with a tenacity that will make others step aside. If Spirit is strong, they'll want to fight for justice and human rights. They are unique, and loners. Their freedom and desire for change makes commitment difficult. Faith can be a wonderful anchor; it lets them believe that someone will take care of things when they can't. The danger is that they can withdraw for protection instead of learning how to say no. Maintaining individuality is a challenge; either they give it away for the approval of others, or are rebels and create disharmony just to maintain a sense of self. Virgo/*Threes* are gifted with more than one talent so finding a major thread to follow is difficult. Their challenge is to know their own limits and to keep on course. Natural problem solvers, they enter chaos and clean up the mess before most people get their bearing. They are easily bored and profoundly restless. They are always demanding more from themselves. They need to devote that endless supply of energy to helping someone in need.

IF SPIRIT TAKES THE LEAD: With Spirit in control, Virgo/*Four* takes on too much, too fast. They are hard on themselves and need to delegate their work. Attracted to a good cause, they are out front protesting injustice or prejudice. They have versatile, ingenious minds that get them into trouble; their curiosity never allows them to rest.

IF EGO TAKES THE LEAD: With Ego directing traffic, control and separateness come to the fore. These souls give orders well and rise to the head of their profession with ease. They are versatile, ingenious and probably unscrupulous. Inventive, they can take things apart and put them together, improving their function along the way. Nothing holds them back but their sense of isolation. Drawn to tension and controversy, their need to overcome conflict may keep them in a rut. They don't fit in many places, but then, that's by choice.

MEL TORME (September 13)

Singer, composer, arranger, drummer, writer.

"Mel Torme is the only white man who sings with the soul of a black man." Ethel Waters supposedly made that statement. Mel Torme lives up to the Virgo's reputation for versatility. The desire for variety also pervades his personal life; he has been married four times. In between, he dated such women as Ava Gardner, Marilyn Monroe, and Judy Garland. Of Russian-Jewish heritage, Torme's parents came through Ellis Island. Since Mercury, Virgo's ruler, represents youth, many Virgos have an early success. At the tender age of four, Torme sang on the radio and soon became a popular child star in Chicago. At fifteen he received attention for a love song he wrote, "Lament to Love." The Harry James Band wanted him, but child labor laws prevented Torme from touring with the group. Still, it wasn't long before Torme hit the road, and when he did, he never looked back. The restless nature of a Virgo feels at home without a home. Virgos are natural writers; Torme proved this by writing *The Other Side of the Rainbow,* a nonfiction book about Judy Garland. He also wrote an autobiography, *It Wasn't All Velvet.*

DOROTHY PARKER (August 22)

Writer, "Wittiest Woman in America."

Dorothy Parker had everything the world could offer. Parker knew everyone worth knowing. She had intelligence, talent, wit, and money. During the Depression, she and her husband were earning $5200 a week in Hollywood. But happiness for a Virgo does not come from fame and fortune, but from Spirit and doing for others. Apparently, Spirit was missing in Parker's life. She had many love affairs, two marriages, and attempted suicide several times. She lived with a hedonistic flair, lunched at the Algonquin Round Table, spent evenings at the theater, weekends at Long Island house parties that could rival those described in *The Great Gatsby,* and vacationed in France. Still, Parker had everything but happiness. After her death, Frank Sullivan wrote to a friend and said, ". . . she was at war with herself all her life."

Virgo/*Five* (September 5, September 14, September 23) Mercury/Mercury

PURPOSE: To harness your versatility into one goal, balancing your personal needs with your desire to help others.

"The wise through an excess of wisdom is made a fool."—Emerson. Virgo/*Fives* are no fools, but they are lovers of extremes. They bore easily, are never satisfied, and never give up. The other possible scenario is that they never try because life is too overwhelming; their perfectionistic nature prevents them from even attempting. Relationships are difficult because long-term commitments scare them. They like to keep things new and fresh. They're attracted to someone who is tough with them, someone with a powerful focus and strong roots. On the work front, they either burn the midnight oil or can't push the pencil across the paper.

IF SPIRIT TAKES THE LEAD: Spirit and the number *Five* get along too well. The result is obsession, perfection and self-judgment. These souls are hard on themselves and struggle with focusing on one goal. Trying to do everything right keeps them frustrated and caught up in self-punishment. Critical, they may hate their appearance. When they do direct their will and talents toward something they believe in, no one stands in their way.

IF EGO TAKES THE LEAD: Ego directs these souls to try and be in charge of every little thing. Whoever opposes them must be ready for a relentless fight. If they are filled with fear, they can appear helpless. Overwhelmed with the world, they don't know how to make things happen. Exhibiting either an inflated ego or none at all, they are a connector and know what's going on.

DARRYL FRANCIS ZANUCK (September 5)

Writer, founder and president of Twentieth Century-Fox.

Zanuck was born to a gambling, alcoholic father and a mother who had few moral values. Abandoned by both parents, it was his grandfather who gave him a sense of himself and taught him how to hunt, swim and fight. Most Virgos do things earlier than most. Zanuck lied about his age and joined the army, finishing his turn at seventeen. At this tender age he set out for Pasadena, California, with a secret desire to become a writer. A master strategist, Zanuck positioned himself close to the people he wanted to know. He sold his first story at his athletic club, where writers and producers hung out. Hollywood was new, but Zanuck was persistent. Soon, he was at Warner Brothers, writing scripts. His incredible speed—he could turn out a script over a weekend—and his wealth of ideas, brought him quickly to the top and kept him in demand. He is responsible for many firsts in Hollywood. Animals were seldom used in films, but Zanuck created the series *Rin Tin Tin*. He played a major role in producing the first talking picture, *The Jazz Man*. He introduced the gangster film, breaking with the tradition of sentimentality and happy endings. Known as a womanizer, Zanuck managed to stay married to the same woman, who served as his anchor. The Virgo health issue manifested in his need to stay in shape. Every day he worked out with a boxer. Over breakfast, he took French and Spanish lessons. His day didn't end until two or three in the morning. Few had the energy to keep up with him, physically or mentally.

MARGARET SANGER (September 14)

Women's rights activist.

Margaret Sanger experienced firsthand the bondage and suffering of women caused by their lack of knowledge about birth control. At the turn of the century, many women had six to fifteen children, and were often unable to feed and clothe them. With the senseless death of a client, a Mrs. Sachs, Sanger became an aggressive advocate of birth control. She gave up her nursing career and spent the next twenty-two years in and out of prison, fighting first for the right to gather information on birth control and then to dispense it to women in a proper and healthy manner. From the Netherlands, Sanger brought the idea of clinics to the United States, imported the diaphragm from Europe, and lectured untiringly on behalf of women and their right to choose when to be pregnant.

Virgo/*Six* (August 24, September 6, September 15)
Mercury/Venus

PURPOSE: To use your desire for truth and justice to either challenge society by opposing all it holds dear, or by immersing yourself within the system, keeping temptation and desires at bay while you use your great charisma and charm to persuade others to see your point of view.

"Let the universe handle the details."—Deepak Chopra. This is simple when you have faith, impossible when you don't. The Virgo/*Sixes* are perfectionists, either they take responsibility for everything and everyone in their life, or they ignore others and do their own thing. With the Virgo/*Six* there's seldom a middle road. Self-acceptance is the key here. They can easily be driven by desires. Style is a gift. If they've chosen not to fit in, they are crude and upsetting. If truth is their choice rather than beauty, justice and the law may attract them. They have a keen awareness of how things work and what makes people tick. The Virgo/*Six* should know that restlessness and divine discontent will always be present.

IF SPIRIT TAKES THE LEAD: When Spirit is ahead with the number Six, a very special soul emerges. They have the ability to connect with anyone, anywhere. Their adaptability allows them to go places others can't. A need to please could be a problem, particularly if they don't have a clear picture of themselves. Faith and a desire to be perfect keeps them restless and unhappy. Spiritual leaders, seekers of truth, or just plain charming, they slide through life. They need inner discipline; the world won't give it to them. They love beauty and seek it in all things. They must learn how to say no.

IF EGO TAKES THE LEAD: With Ego strong, there is a love of anything that brings pleasure. They can charm the snake back into the basket, and do it with a smile. Con men, salesmen, or just partygoers, society loves them when they're refined, and ignores them if they're crude. Either they play life's game extremely well, or are rebels who love to stir up trouble. They always get their way.

JOSEPH KENNEDY (September 6)

Ambassador to England, one of the wealthiest men in the world.

Joseph Kennedy was born at the top of the Boston Irish social ladder, to the "First Irish Family." The divine discontent of the Virgo/*Six* kept Kennedy unsatisfied, even with money, power, and fame. Pursuing things for their own sake, Kennedy lacked social conscience and participated in some of the most unsavory deals in the history of American business. It was said that he manipulated the stock market so as to depress the economy for his own gain.

It was at Harvard that Kennedy first experienced rejection from the social upper crust. Refused membership in the Brahmins, a prestigious social club, Kennedy spent much of his life proving he didn't need Boston society.

Kennedy chose not to fit into society; being crude was his calling card. He pursued women unabashedly and married Rose Fitzgerald, the prize catch of Boston. At the youthful age of twenty-five he became the head of a bank, the Columbian Trust. Eventually he became one of the eight wealthiest men of his time. His son Jack became the thirty-fifth president of the United States.

BOBBY SHORT (September 15)

Singer.

Often called the Fred Astaire of saloon singers, Bobby Short symbolizes the style and glamour of the Virgo/*Six*. He knows how to connect with an audience, charming them with his charisma, style, and voice. Invited to the White House, guest of the rich and famous, he personifies a luxury of this dynamic which does not go unnoticed. But it was not always there. One of ten children, Short grew up during the Depression. He started singing in saloons before he was a teenager. His talent was recognized by an agent, who put him in white tails and sent him off to Chicago. Once again, the restless nature of this sign was expressed by a man on the road. Like many black entertainers, Short got his real break in Paris, France, where race was less of a problem. There he made invaluable connections with society types, who would continue to be his fans. His return to New York brought him to the Carlyle, where his name will be remembered forever.

Virgo/*Seven* (August 25, September 7, September 16) Mercury/Neptune

PURPOSE: To conquer your need for perfection with faith and refine whatever you do, while at the same time helping those life has disowned and ignored.

"A morality without God is as weak as a traffic law when the policeman is on foot."—Will Durant. Vision and perfectionism are the gifts and the curse of the Virgo/*Seven*. They strive to improve themselves and the world. A bit judgmental and critical, their highly focused eyes see what others don't. They hate uncertainty and make quick decisions in order to end doubt. They are meant to strive for something greater than this world and must realize it's not possible to achieve and enjoy the moment. They are driven to accomplish their ideals and nothing stands in their way. They are capable of great success and great frustration. The danger is that they can give all their power to someone they believe is stronger and more perfect. There is no such person.

IF SPIRIT TAKES THE LEAD: With Spirit and the *Seven*, idealism gets distorted and what is left is too much sacrifice, and disappointment. They need a touch of Ego to keep them in the now. Others will disappoint them unless they learn to see their faults as well as their assets. This only happens if they can see themselves more clearly. Stop trying to save the world, but do spend time helping others. It's the only way to gain a sense of self-worth.

IF EGO TAKES THE LEAD: If Ego is strong, there's trouble. They can live a double life. They present themselves as saintly, while at the same time working behind the scenes robbing the homeless. They have no morals or scruples and are gifted with an iron will. If control is not their issue, they've given it away and are the victim of someone ruthless. They need boundaries and a belief in something more than themselves.

J.C. PENNEY (September 16)

Businessman.

J.C. Penney rose from a twelve-dollar-a-week clerkship to the presidency of a twenty-million-dollar concern. Born on his father's farm in Hamilton, Missouri, Penney was eight years old when he was told he had to buy his own clothes. His first job was as a clerk; he made $2.27 a month. There he learned to study the customers and their needs. Later, in Denver, he worked for a Mr. Callahan, became his store manager, and eventually was offered an interest in his business. He then started the first chain stores in the country, J.C. Penney's. Penney took the Virgo principle of sharing responsibility and wealth to its best expression.

BUDDY HOLLY (September 7)

Singer, musician.

Born in Texas to a strict Baptist family, Holly was one-quarter Cherokee. From the very beginning he was different. He wore glasses with narrow black frames. They set him apart from the usual good-looking performers, and he identified with black music. His friends included Little Richard, a black, gay musician. Gifted with a good mind, Holly worked his way to the spotlight by playing parties and doing his own radio show called *The Duddy and Jack Show.* Cocky, aggressive, and often reckless, Holly liked being on the edge. His break came with the song "That'll Be The Day," but it had to be released a second time before Holly made it to the top. The excessive side of the *Seven* revealed itself in Holly's alcoholism. In 1959, when Holly was only twenty-three years old, his plane went down in a storm.

Virgo/*Eight* (August 26, September 8, September 17) Mercury/Saturn

PURPOSE: To learn to balance your responsibilities, helping others but not depleting or limiting yourself; to use your faith and your Spirit to overcome obstacles and to teach others that nothing is impossible when you're focused and believe in yourself.

"There is enough for everyone's need but not for everyone's greed."— Gandhi. Strength, courage, and hard work are a piece of cake for the Virgo/ *Eight*. They easily take on tasks that make others cringe and perform them with little effort. Either they look for all answers from within, or don't trust their instincts. Few really know them. Control is important; to have it they will keep their world small. Gifted with either great faith or a lack of it, they have a talent for self-scrutiny which can translate into self-criticism. Gifted with insight into the human mind, they make great psychologists. When it comes to relationships, they want someone to be hard on them. Their challenge is to believe in themselves.

IF SPIRIT TAKES THE LEAD: The ability to be tough, strong, and determined, is the Virgo/*Eight's* gift. They have a critical eye and it's usually focused on themselves. They get things done, but at what cost? They always seek control and try to please. What they need is real faith, which gives them the ability to turn over some of their immense responsibility to others and a higher power. They avoid luxury and choose the difficult path. They believe that sacrifice and denial gives them control. My advice is to try kindness.

IF EGO TAKES THE LEAD: With Ego strong the cup is always half-full. Self-loathing can be a problem; These souls only see what's wrong with themselves. They work hard and have no idea how to nurture themselves. They value money, security, and position, and persevere with a diligence that makes even workaholics nervous. They are capable of cruelty; they are critical, never pleased, and always right.

MOTHER TERESA (August 26)

Nobel Peace Prize winner, founder of the Missionaries of Charity.

Agnes Gonxha made a decision to become a missionary when she was eighteen. Raised in a religious home, her choice was accepted and supported. She traveled to the province of Bengal, India, and stayed for thirty-four years. Her first job with the Sisters of Loreto was as a teacher of geography. On a bus to Darjeeling, she heard a voice tell her to go into the slums and serve the poor. To carry out God's wish she needed permission from her church. Gifted with patience and a strong will, she won the opportunity to try. They gave her one year to prove herself. "Our work," she said, "calls for us to see Jesus in everyone."

Mother Teresa immediately established an open-air school. She never demanded money for her needs; instead, she would say, "This is your chance to serve God." Her projects always came into existence quickly and naturally, with no campaigning friends and no public appeal.

PETER SELLERS (September 8)

Actor.

Born to show-business parents, Sellers hated the theater and, as a youth, wanted no part of the stage. He was sickly as a child, and, like many Virgos, he was spoiled by his mother. But his need for acceptance and approval eventually led him to the stage and film. He grew up in an adult world, without friends his own age, a loner in the tough and seedy world of the theater. "I had quite a unique childhood. I'm sure it's stood me in good stead. I mean it encouraged the resilience, the durability, it forged the humor. I suppose because without a sense of humor in those days we would all have gone under a dozen times a week." Sellers became a stand-up comic and paid his dues by playing strip joints. Big success came with his role as Fred Kite in *I'm All Right, Jack* and he won the British Academy Awards.

It was in the role of Inspector Clouseau that Sellers won international acclaim. The critics accepted him as a great impersonator and an inspired mime. Sellers often fought with depression. He gave outrageously expensive gifts to his friends but never gave to charity. A perfectionist, he was obsessive and very critical of himself, sometimes undermining his own success. Because his mother was Jewish and his father Protestant, he felt he never fit in.

Virgo/*Nine* (August 27, September 9, September 18) Mercury/Mars

PURPOSE: To use your will, your focus and your talents to impact the world with your unique point of view and to help others develop their own.

"Relinquish your attachment to the outcome."—Deepak Chopra. Not bad advice for anyone, but especially for a Virgo/*Nine*. The Ego tends to get in the way. This person knows how to get things done better and faster than anyone else. They tend to run over people rather than debate with them, though that is also a skill. They don't take no easily. The power of their presence is overwhelming. They have sharp tongues. If they lack self-confidence, others will overwhelm them. They may relinquish their power to someone they think knows more. There is nothing wrong with learning from others but they should not decide one's fate. The Virgo/*Nine* must learn patience. They tend to feel on top of the world or a victim of it; the middle road is never an option. They need self-discipline. Their challenges are to learn the power of humility, the value of waiting, the strength of surrendering.

IF SPIRIT TAKES THE LEAD: Spirit and the number *Nine* are strong and determined partners. Spirit wants its way, but is willing to wait for its reward. These souls see others through rose-colored glasses and because of this are often disappointed by friends or colleagues. They either resist others with incredible force or surrender to them. They are extremists and believe that nothing is impossible. They have trouble fitting in because they're one step ahead.

IF EGO TAKES THE LEAD: The Ego gets its way most of the time. After all, it has an incredible will and a sense of lawlessness that doesn't allow other people's limitations or morals to get in the way. These souls do what they want, when they want. Their endless energy is enough to bury most of their opponents, and the ones who still want to fight find themselves faced with a mind that can cut through any pretense. They're impatient, reckless, and passionate. They have trouble with loyalty because they lose interest in a very short time.

GRETA GARBO (September 18)

Actress.

Garbo was born to poverty in Stockholm, Sweden. Her father was an alcoholic but she adored him. When he had a few extra pennies he would buy her movie magazines. Her sister Alva had tuberculosis and was bedridden. Garbo's mother cleaned houses to pay for food and rent. She also made the family's clothes. Garbo's parents didn't get along and she was often beaten, but the abuse never suppressed her spirit. She got a break by hanging around the dramatic academy and the Mosebuche Theatre. The drama coach, Shemet Frans Enwall, offered her free lessons. But it was her encounter with Mauritz Stiller, an up and coming filmmaker, that made her famous. "I was the creation of Stiller and my future depended upon him."

Garbo left the film world at the height of her career. She was bisexual and lived a great part of her life in seclusion.

LYNDON BAINES JOHNSON

Thirty-sixth president of the United States.

Johnson's father was a member of the Texas legislature. Raised on a farm in Texas, Johnson preferred intellectual pursuits to physical labor. "A challenge is an opportunity," he said. At college, Johnson never got more than three or four hours of sleep a night. After graduation, he taught Mexican children in Cotulla, Texas. The students were poor and often came to school without breakfast. Johnson gave them something they'd never had, a chance. He developed a debating team and a basketball team. The kids loved him, and he loved them. Johnson also loved Washington because he could "smell the power." His enthusiasm was contagious. Myer Feldman said, "I think Lyndon Johnson had great virtues and great vices, depending upon whether that particular day he was emphasizing the vices or the virtues, you liked or disliked him." As a young New Dealer congressman from Texas, he was called "Roosevelt's boy." Soon, he was in the Senate as Senate Majority leader. Reluctantly, he accepted the position as vice president. The assassination of President Kennedy made him thirty-sixth president of the United States. Gifted with the ability to unite and bond, he rallied his country in a time of tragedy and went on to engineer the greatest domestic legislative programs in American history.

SUMMARY

Virgos are versatile and gifted with a confidence that intimidates as well as invokes awe. Their journey is not easy, for they must turn their back on the values of the world and find their own way. Their challenge is to accept all parts of themselves. As they begin to turn their attention inward and face their fears, shame, and darkness, they gain the strength of will they need to direct their entire being toward one goal. Faced with destiny and fate, they see how each of their thoughts and actions creates a response. They know that to survive they must begin to share their knowledge and their strength with others. As they embrace responsibility they begin to learn the true meaning of freedom. Gifted with incredible skills of organization and simplification, they improve everything they encounter. They seek a soul mate, a partner who will understand them instinctively. What they really want is spiritual union with God. As they accept good and evil as part of the same process, they begin to feel the unity and love that has always been waiting. Eager to meet themselves in the eyes of another, they move forward into Libra, the sign of relationships.

SELECTED SOURCES

Martine de Courcel   *Tolstoy: The Ultimate Reconciliation*   Hermann 1988

Eileen Egan   *Such a Vision of the Street: Mother Teresa, The Spirit and the Work*   Image 1986

Doris Kearns *Lyndon Johnson and the American Dream*   Harper and Row 1976

Paul I. Murphy with R. Rene Arlington   *La Popessa*   Warner Books 1986

J. C. Penney   *J. C. Penney: The Man With a Thousand Partners*   Harper and Brothers 1931

Bobby Short with Robert Mackintosh   *Bobby Short: The Life and Times of a Saloon Singer*   C. Potter 1995

Leo Tolstoy   *Anna Karenina*   Oxford University Press 1995

Leo Tolstoy   *The Death of Ivan Ilyich*   Bantam Books 1981

T. Harry Williams   *Huey Long*   Vintage Books 1969

PART III
THE CRISIS OF FAITH

*I*n **Libra, Scorpio,** and **Sagittarius,** faith gets tested. Spirit has felt the presence of God and once that happens the soul begins to see His presence, and the world as Ego once knew it begins to fall apart. With "reality" uncertain, and faith not yet tested, Ego and Spirit must join together, hand in hand, and take a leap of faith. The rest of the journey cannot be taken alone. From now on they need each other to survive. In Libra, the sign of relationships, they meet as equals. Ego has provided protection and the ability to fight the outside world; Spirit has given courage and the faith to take the risk needed to ascend and raise the consciousness of the soul. For the next three signs "reality" will begin to transform through crisis. As faith expands, certainty shifts and is felt in the ethereal instead of the "known." The soul begins to use its ability to create, and, with the gift of imagination, it turns inward, depending less on the outside world for support. As Ego and Spirit join forces, the soul becomes a formidable person indeed. In **Libra,** we encounter the superhero, the person capable of accomplishing the impossible thorough faith. Faith is only achieved through experience. Libra is the crisis of identity, the mask that Ego has provided gets cracked and the new and stronger spiritual self must emerge. In **Scorpio,** the psyche is attacked, the patterns and attitudes are altered and redefined so that old habits can be broken paving the way for unity to occur. In **Sagittarius** Spirit goes beyond the boundaries of the world and tries to demand that God show His face. Ego retracts and feels helpless, lost and alone, masking his failure with an expression of false faith and hope. Spirit also fails and returns resigned to having to work in unison with Ego. She accepts her fate and together Ego and Spirit work within the limits and boundaries of reality to achieve their goals.

CHAPTER EIGHT

Libra

(September 24–October 23)

When Libra arrives, autumn is here.
It's time to look into the mirror.
Don't be depressed, don't fake a smile
Accept it all, make it your style.
This is the mark of the truly great man,
He faces his truth, he does what he can.
So use your charm, your gift for pleasure,
Live every moment, life is a treasure.

Ruler: Venus   **Symbol: The Scales of Balance**
Element: Air   **Number: Six**

Libra is autumn, and like Nature, which sheds its pageantry as it turns inward, so does the Libra soul. The essence of life is all that matters now. Anything that distracts the eye or deters the soul from the truth must be let go of or ignored. The protective mask you have worn begins to shatter, allowing the new and stronger you to emerge. Libras are the new warriors of the zodiac; you use ideas to change the world, and, when they are coupled with bold and decisive action, you accomplish the impossible. You inspire others to reach heights they never thought possible. Part of your strength is your position. As a Libra, you've got a panoramic view. From the seventh house, the midpoint of the zodiac, you can see in one glance the past and the future. You are our historians and visionaries. Between the past and the future is the moment, and the moment is what Libra is all about. It is in Libra that the inner world of thought unites with the outer world of action. No more waiting for distant dreams or spending time healing old wounds. The ability to create is possible only in the present.

Don't be surprised if your Venus-ruled soul seems heroic and timid, bold and passive, determined and compromising. You are the scales of balance. From your position, the truth that all opposites are one is finally revealed. If you follow good far enough, it will lead to evil. The path is really a spiral, and everything on it is connected. From Libra's position on the zodiac, the distance between a point and its polar opposite appears shortened. Correspondingly, the hours that separate light from darkness diminish in October.

The pace of life quickens; beginnings and endings come so quickly, you begin to trust the pattern of change.

Libra is the outer limits of the self, the end of linear expansion of the Ego. The individual has experienced all that life has to offer. There is nothing new from this point on. You've explored and created your world and you've shared the world of others. Life has let you experience different perspectives and emotions. Change now occurs in the Spirit and in order for it to grow, consciousness must be raised. Your external world must be simplified so that attention can be placed on internal spiritual growth.

Ego has served its purpose well, providing protection and separateness. It allowed you to develop a sense of self and faith in your ability to turn mistakes and weaknesses into strengths. However, if you continue to depend on Ego, this great relationship could turn destructive. From now on, the more you hold on to it, the emptier you feel and the more of a burden your possessions become. Instead of giving you power and freedom, they bind you to them, restricting your actions and tightening their rein on your heart so that there is less of it to share with others. It's time to realize that a new dress, a Mercedes, or a country house will not give you lasting love or a sense of security. If you make the switch from Ego to Spirit voluntarily, the universe won't have to shake up your world to get your attention.

Faith is the helium of the soul, and the more you have, the higher you rise. No one achieves faith by reading a book. Faith is only achieved through direct experience. Faith is contagious, but it's never really yours until you've tested it. To do that, you must put yourself at risk. You've got to acquire a taste for the exhilaration of letting go and surviving. Each time you conquer fear you gain faith, and the power of the outer world diminishes. The two worlds, heaven and earth, begin to blend, and what they're creating is a new and lighter you. If it hasn't happened yet, you can get things moving yourself.

Realize that you have created your world from a point of view chosen in Aries, that throughout your journey you have fashioned every detail of that world, and with this knowledge a sense of power begins to awaken. Now you know you are the center of the universe, that you can have anything you want. All you have to do is create it. Instead of conquering the world, you can now transform it, unite it, and bring it peace.

Don't get upset if you lack faith. Unless you're a saint, you've probably misplaced your faith by desiring things of the world. Desire taken to the limit always leaves you feeling empty, disappointed, and alone. Until you hit bottom and lose all hope, you don't know the true meaning of faith. Nietzsche pronounced "God is dead." It is not until the death of faith—the faith we were born into, or the faith we were spoon fed—that true faith is possible. Libra is anyone who has experienced a loss and then a rebirth of faith.

Until you feel faith, the letting-go process is difficult. Libras fluctuate between depression and a great sense of hope. They live with divine discontent. Even God became disillusioned with his creation, destroying all but the most noble of souls, Noah. Then, He realized what He had lost. The flood destroyed His creation and Noah became the intermediary, the link between the old and the new. He is the hero who kept man alive.

Libras are heroes. They are souls who inspire us through their example to follow them to a new level of understanding. David Ben-Gurion (October 16), the first prime minister of Israel, said, "God or nature . . . endows the genius with sublime talents, not out of love for him, but from a desire to bestow upon the world sublime creations. He brings into existence an intermediary with the power to give, such creation to the world." Libras represent both sides of the chasm, and the means to cross it. They're the distraught people and the conquering hero. This is Oscar Wilde (October 16), gifted with genius and caught in the grip of his desires, dying alone and lonely. This is Christopher Reeve, (September 25) paralyzed after a fall from a horse, refusing to accept a wheelchair as his world, giving us all hope as he fights to walk again.

Life is here to teach lessons; learn the lessons and the crises are vanquished. Eleanor Roosevelt said, "There is no experience from which you can't learn something . . . The experience can have meaning only if you understand it. You can understand it only if you have arrived at some knowledge of yourself, a knowledge based on a deliberately and usually painfully acquired self-discipline, which teaches you to cast out fear."

Libra is a turning point. The soul turns the corner of the zodiac and begins its ascent above the horizon. As it enters Libra and the light, it completes the personal phase of the journey, the process of self-individualization, the final inward descent into your true nature. Once the self is harnessed, the soul is propelled into the world of others. All the essence of its experiences and beliefs will be used and shared. This is the meaning of the second half of the journey. However, the first half of this final phase requires courage and solitude. Solitude demands you contain your thoughts and ideas and not share them, either for attention or approval. Without containment nothing can come into being. This is not the lost, unconscious solitude of a Cancer. In Libra, you know how to express your feelings. You just need to use discernment on when and to whom you speak. When you can embrace and hold within you thoughts and fancies, rearranging them, combining some, discarding others, reducing the barrage of information into a simpler matrix, you access the process of creation and, in Libra, what bursts forth is an "idea."

A great idea has both heaven and earth as its parents. It has taken your instincts, your passion, your lofty dreams, and mixed them with reason, reality and the needs of the moment. A good idea has the power to gather the collective forces around it, drawing on the strength of each individual that embraces it, returning to them the hope they have invested in its symbol. Ideas have toppled monarchs and presidents. Their symbolic power speaks to both the hearts and minds of those who hear them, unifying individuals and propelling their passivity into action.

Ideas such as freedom or justice can cause war or peace. In the hands of a good man, a powerful idea can turn him into a myth, an archetype, or a god. In the hands of an evil man, a powerful idea can empower him to commit outrageous acts against others. Juan Perón (October 8), coined a word which threw him into the spotlight and onto a path that led him to the presidency of Argentina. The word was *descamisados,* or "shirtless ones," and around it he rallied the workers of Argentina, taking off his own shirt to show his allegiance with their cause.

This ability to attach your personality to the motivation and the power of a symbol, is a quick way to gain strength. Gandhi's (October 2) name became synonymous with peace, Alfred Nobel's (October 21) with excellence and Ben-Gurion's with Israel and the Zionist movement.

In the seventh house, the individual must learn to access universal power, for the tasks ahead are of the heroic kind. To conquer them will require that the soul give up its autonomy and share its power with others, thus enlarging its own. Libras know how to attach themselves to an ideal, a person, a symbol or a collective idea, and use its strength for their own end. If the ideal is a spiritual one, all will benefit and the person who represents the ideal will grow in consciousness. If the symbol is negative, as the Nazi swastika was, no one ultimately will gain because separateness leads to its own destruction. The quest to achieve perfection is accomplished through the choosing of a superior role model, merging with it, and stretching your limits by reaching above and beyond yourself. Once you do, you have the power to create your dreams in the now.

Libra is the sign of relationships. To have one requires you sacrifice your concept of independence and autonomy. Compromise does not mean relinquishing your individuality; it means you must contain the differences of someone else within you, and not be threatened. This ability to unite without losing a sense of self, is what Libra is all about. You're supposed to gain from a relationship, to improve yourself within it. In fact, you get to take on the other person's good stuff and call it your own. The reward of Ego is your partner's "assets" or social prominence. Through the union you enlarge your worldly persona. On a spiritual level, your partner's truth uplifts you by your union. This can happen in a marriage, with a guru, or even in a religious institution.

Of course, it is best to have both your soul and your status uplifted. To do that, you must first value both in yourself. You may look to a relationship to provide what you think is a missing piece of yourself. When you see that piece in someone else, you empower them through the projection and then reflection of your disconnected parts. You may become obsessed with the relationship and see it as the only way to be whole. The problem with marriages that provide a "missing leg" is that when that leg gets healed, the balance is thrown off. Both partners need to change for it to continue to work.

Sometimes, instead of projecting, you mirror yourself and then instead of balance, certain sides of you get lived to excess. F. Scott Fitzgerald (September 24) found his mirror in Zelda. ". . . Each reflected the other's impulses anticipated the other's thoughts, encouraged the other's most secret potentials, confirmed the other's intuitions, rivaled the other's boldness in their parallel conquests of their inner freedom. Zelda confessed her most sordid adventures, gave him her diary to read, as he gave her his novel. Even more than lovers, they were accomplices, twins going hand in hand to confront the world around them."

Equality is what a Libra seeks; it desires the perfect union. Until you can embrace all of yourself, you will not have control over whom you attract. If you have repressed anger, then you'll bring in someone angry. If you're too giving, you'll bring in someone selfish. Become as whole and balanced as you can, and everyone else in your life will improve. You are the creator of your world; it's an expanded, projected picture of you. If you don't like your world, paint a new picture.

Since Libra is the turning point, Libras often are born at a turning point within the family or the world. Eisenhower (October 14) was born as his father's world was collapsing. Alfred Nobel was born when his father went bankrupt. And Nietzsche (October 15) was raised by a house of women because his father was institutionalized for mental problems. If the turning point is downward, you are forced to reach bottom early and then come racing into the light, enjoying success in your early years. This experience is meant to build your sense of hope, and faith will be yours when you change your environment through your own effort. If the turning point is upward, be careful not to attach yourself too closely to possessions and things. Brigette Bardot (September 28) experienced success very early in life and it prevented her from trusting herself and her talent.

The wheel of fortune creates gain and loss; it keeps turning and so does the Libra's fortune. This turning point dynamics gives Libras a special skill. They know how to reverse a bad situation into something good. If you persist long enough, sooner or later the tide will turn in your favor. In his campaign strategy, Jimmy Carter (October 1) was able to turn "necessity into virtue and potential weaknesses into assets."

Of course, the Libra needs to be careful that he doesn't take something so far that it turns the corner and begins to fall. The *I Ching,* the Chinese method of divination, demonstrates this principle very clearly. The six lines that read your fortune are constantly changing and moving upward. When they reach the top there's only one place to go and that's down. Don't be in a hurry. Take your time to reach the top, and have more than one thing in your life going on, so when that first thing comes to completion, you have something else to which you can look forward.

Libra is the analytical process. Diderot (October 5), a Libra, was the founder of modern art criticism. "Good criticism, it is implied, has to be a two-stage enterprise: first a whole-hearted and generous, even credulous, response; and then a re-appraisal in colder blood." This is true for any relationship. First, it's embraced with love, then, the little things start to bother you. The man who could do no wrong now gets attacked for leaving the cap off the toothpaste.

Libra is also therapy, and the quest for self-understanding through the analytical process. Remember, truth is never static; it changes with each new perception. To seek the truth requires constant vigilance. Ego is the master of illusion; it makes you believe the world you live in is "real." Nietzsche changed the idiom of "having the courage of one's convictions" to having the courage to "attack one's convictions." He also believed in never automatically accepting an idea without challenging it. In Libra learning becomes a process of forgetting. The reduction of information is important now. New insights are acquired, not through more knowledge, but through the struggle to sort the information at hand.

The stronger the union the more powerful the child, and now that Ego and Spirit have united, the new addition is *reason*. Reason is the balance of heart and mind. In Libra, it becomes independent. It can sit above or beyond its competitive parents and see the whole picture. From this heavenly perspective you can easily discern and analyze the parts. Versatility is no longer limited; your accomplishments can have heroic dimensions. This is our desire to go back to our origins and to reclaim our past. It's David Ben-Gurion and Zionism. It's Gandhi, shedding the clothes and culture of England and returning to the ways of his people. Diderot turned to the beginning of knowledge by compiling the greatest thoughts and inventions and presenting them in several volumes of his *Encyclopédia*. In doing so, he provided everyone with the advantage of starting from a point at which the geniuses of the past had stopped. He battled the censors and endured a short prison term, but finally completed this tremendous undertaking.

The road to self-acceptance is always an inward one. To travel the passages of the mind and to face your demons, you need to become a shaman, a skilled warrior of the inner world. These magical beings know how to battle the illusive forces of shame, evil, anger, and hate. No sword of steel can cut the throat of illusion, no bullet can pierce the heart of fear, but humor or an idea can seep into the cracks of both, confront them and turn them away.

Anger, for many Libras, is a fearful emotion. The fear that anger will surface if the truth is revealed, keeps you feeling unable to move forward.

The ability to use anger properly is empowering. Repress it, and it is projected onto others. Then, the anger you demand gets voiced against you. Unexpressed anger prevents unity. In any relationship, you've got to be able to contain someone else's hostile feelings. If your garbage can is full, there's no room for anyone else's stuff. The Libra must learn to face anger and express it, not to automatically attack, but to choose a response appropriate to the situation.

The shift in consciousness in Libra creates a chasm. Nietzsche described this when he spoke of: "man as a rope . . . [caught] between two worlds and reach[ing] out for ideals he cannot attain short of crossing an apparently inseparable abyss." The abyss is the dead end one encounters before a new perspective is embraced. The soul is required to take a leap of faith in order to get to the other side. Without the leap, life becomes repetitive and boring. As the world outside stops offering something new, it is *you* who must change in order to grow. Oscar Wilde described the feeling of futility and exhaustion in the pursuit of something new. "I myself would sacrifice everything for a new experience and I know there is no such thing as a new experience at all." The feeling that life has nothing new to offer heightens the feelings of isolation. Sooner or later, you've got to be strong enough to expose your point of view to those of others and risk the negative results: rejection, anger, and abandonment.

Without a sense of wholeness, the critical analytical qualities of reason, so strong in Libra, become a negative force and instead of helping you to improve yourself, keep you depressed. John Lennon (October 9) said, ". . . every place is the same to a solipsist and life is 'Deja Vu,' the same old thing every time, the only difference being that as you grow older, the pace slackens to 'slow motion.'" Libra is the first sign to oppose its polarity. Therefore, the terrain is no longer new, the lessons all have a familiar ring. If your soul doesn't respond to the call to change, a sense of nothingness can overwhelm you.

A relationship can be the turning point. Here is when you start looking for someone else to improve your life. Of course, no one can fill your emptiness permanently, but by losing yourself in someone else's world, you bring excitement and newness into your life again. That is, until their world begins to feel like the same old routine. Sooner or later you've got to improve yourself through the association with an ideal. If you pick someone who challenges your spirit and your soul, you're on your way to happiness. If, however, you choose to be used by someone else to fill in their missing parts, you could become a codependent. The desire to use and be used is a Libra quality. Eleanor Roosevelt (October 11) felt her purpose in life was to be "used" to help others. She said we were "born to be used, [I] never mind being used by those who required help or support, or simple encouragement." However, if you allow someone to use you to keep their illusions alive, you're not helping them or yourself. This silent pact to keep the truth from being exposed, can also prevent you from growing. Perhaps a parent was never successful, and to keep them believing in their own greatness, you keep yourself from becoming successful. Bring your motivation to light and you can change it.

Once you allow yourself to grow apart from the old and familiar, you may feel a need to share your experiences and your knowledge. This is the beginning of discipleship. By giving, you learn to receive, and the continuous flow from one to another, the exchange of yin and yang, keeps you rising on the spiral.

Libra's desire to be used in the world for a larger purpose could be misinterpreted by the soul. With Ego as translator, you could easily feel as if you were destined to be famous. It's a touch of megalomania. When he was a child, John Lennon didn't understand why strangers on the bus didn't recognize him. David Ben-Gurion knew he was special. He believed his mother loved him so much because she knew he was a man of destiny. A phrenologist read his head and declared its unusually large size as an indication of incredible talents. His father told the village that someday "the entire world will talk of David."

Libras gravitate toward impossible situations which they then try to neutralize with their presence and the power of their will. It's one way of working out their inner struggle, but it's also a way of remaining stuck. Oscar Wilde said, "I was a problem for which there was no solution." It's easy to get attached to feeling torn apart and overwhelmed by fear. When chaos becomes the attraction, one becomes good at maneuvering in it.

Libras are great at playing both sides of an issue simultaneously—they make the best politicians. Juan Perón, the president of Argentina, was known for his masterful use of contradiction. Libras also make great negotiators. President Jimmy Carter is still trying to resolve hostile situations. Unfortunately, most Libras compromise too easily. It's part of their need to be of use to others for a higher purpose.

Libras are peacemakers, but there is nothing passive about their position. They know from experience that no one wins on the battlefront. With this knowledge comes a desire for peace, and a willingness to compromise. Libras are the bridge builders between the "real" world and the world of dreams. This is President Jimmy Carter bringing Egypt's Anwar Sadat and Israel's Menachem Begin together at Camp David. David Ben-Gurion was a leader who knew how to make hope a reality. After World War II, he traveled Europe, telling the Jewish people of a place where Jews could be strong and defend themselves. For their suffering, he promised they would have a Jewish state—Israel.

Hope does not need to be renewed if it has not first been slain. This is the end of illusion and reality. This is the dying process. Libra announces autumn, a time when leaves fall and nature begins to withdraw into itself. As Goethe said, "Everything that is created is worthy of being destroyed." And as much as Libra is associated with beauty, it is just as powerfully linked with decay. Truman Capote found a unique way of experiencing the dying process. In *In Cold Blood,* he intermingled his life with those of two murderers on death row. "The experience served to heighten my feeling of the tragic view of life which I've always held and which accounts for the side of me that appears extremely frivolous, that part of me that is always standing in a darkened hallway mocking tragedy and death. That's why I love champagne, and stay at the Ritz!"

The sense of dying or destruction is often associated with Libras. Lord Nelson (September 29), the English admiral who defeated Napoleon at Trafalgar, introduced a new concept in naval warfare. Its aim was total destruction of the enemy. Alfred Nobel invented dynamite and instituted the Nobel Prize for Peace. Susan Sarandon (October 4) received an Oscar for her role in *Dead Man Walking.* In the film, she plays a nun trying to save the soul of a man on death row.

Until you face death, you remain innocent and unaware of your true nature. In Libra, you must look death in the eye; when you do, your life is transformed. Interestingly enough, death is not at the end of the zodiac, but in the middle, because its acceptance gives us new life. Capote said of his experience of death row: "I came to understand that death is the central factor of life. And the simple comprehension of this fact alters your entire perspective."

With our greatest fear behind us we can move toward hope and the eternal. Anne Rice (October 4) has given popular culture another view of this quest for immortality. Through her vampire characters she explores the loneliness and emptiness of living close to death, of using others to survive, of shielding oneself from the light which represents hope and a new tomorrow. This is symbolic of the first half of Libra's journey.

Libra is an identity crisis. As the parts of the self become unraveled, the Libra identifies with each part as the whole. As the mask is removed and you are exposed, old habits, false virtues, and useless protection are discarded. With your lens cracked, the world appears as a mosaic or a collage. You walk the thin line of reality and madness. Without faith to unify all your personalities, fear may take hold and suggest negative means of escape. Drugs, alcohol, and even suicide become options. Some Libras, having crossed the veil of the real, stay on the other side and become mad. Nietzsche ended his life in an institution. Aimee Semple McPherson (October 19), the healer, had a nervous breakdown and lost contact with the "real" world for a while. John Lennon's mask was shattered when the Beatles broke up. For the rest of his life he struggled to bring the pieces of himself together. Lennon describes this process when he speaks of an experience he had in Hong Kong.

"I started taking off different layers of myself as if they were layers of clothing and setting them out about the room. I imagined my different sub-personalities as sort of ghostly forms . . . My goal was to get them all off and leave them in the room and not come back. I thought I could escape them that way, but of course, it didn't work." Unfortunately, just when he was about to gain control of himself and his creativity, an assassin's bullet ended his life. Many Libra artists write with collagelike images, or present their art is sharp, contrasting pieces. Lenny Bruce's (October 13) routines, according to Jonathan Miller, are like those of a "mad projectionist, cutting up and pasting together scraps of film in his booth atop the theatre."

When you fail to harness all the separate parts of yourself, then something other than Spirit is in charge. Ask yourself—who heads your chaos? If being popular and acting perfect is your traffic director, then you've made a big mistake. You've chosen a minor piece of yourself as your ruler and, sooner or later, it will fail. If kindness is your leader, what do you do when the moment calls for a harsh and painful decision? If intelligence calls the shots, are you at a loss when compassion and emotion are asked for? If the professor in you is in control, you're going to be in trouble when it's your turn to be the student. If you let Spirit, the unifier, take charge, she'll help you pull everything together. Nothing will be unloved or rejected.

When a piece of yourself takes over, decadence is the result. Libra leads in this field. This is the sign of F. Scott Fitzgerald and Jay Gatsby, his character who has become a symbol of the word decadence. *The Great Gatsby* portrayed a world of luxury where nothing was too extravagant or too outrageous. Unfortunately, excess in any form eventually becomes negative. Pleasure and happiness are two separate things. Pleasure does nothing to raise your consciousness or enlighten your mind; its multiplication does nothing to make you happier. The more you feed your pleasures, the larger their appetites, until it takes more and more to experience their fleeting pleasure.

In the sign of Libra you have a chance to become the total person. Nietzsche thought Goethe, the German poet and writer, to be the best example of the total man. He has "organized the chaos of his passions and integrated every feature of his character, redeeming even the ugly by giving it a meaning in a beautiful totality . . ."

The merging of polarities can create confusion. In Libra, good and evil are the same. Thus, an evil deed can easily lead to understanding and enlightenment and a good deed can lead you astray. Oscar Wilde said, "Personality is a very mysterious thing. A man cannot always be estimated by what he does. He may keep the law and yet be worthless. He may break the law and yet be fine. He may be bad, without ever doing anything bad. He may commit a sin against society, and yet realize through that sin his own perfection."

Another blend of polarities are reality and illusion. *Don Quixote de la*

Mancha, by Miguel de Cervantes Saavodra (October 7) expresses this dilemma perfectly. Quixote is a man whose dream is to right the wrongs of the world. He so strongly believes in his dream that it becomes real for him. This is the power of imitation. If you can imitate what you want, you can create it. Ben Kingsley says that playing Gandhi changed his life. Nick Carraway, the narrator of *The Great Gatsby* becomes his fantasy by watching and imitating Gatsby.

Besides imitation, Libra is the power of reflection. Don Quixote sees a barmaid as his lady-in-waiting, the beautiful Dulcinea, a woman of great virtue. Because he treats her like his ideal, she begins to see her herself through his eyes. Reach as high as you can and the dream can be yours if you have the strength and courage to create it.

If strength is not your virtue, and peace and harmony are what you choose no matter the cost, then you're the Libra of the perfect appearance. Everything matches—your panties with your bras, your umbrella with your raincoat. You make others feel their lives are in total disarray. But the truth is, inside you're a mess. However, there are some virtues of a perfect appearance, including being incredibly gorgeous. The perfect appearance Libra also leads the way in doing what's proper.

Perfect appearance Libras are gifted at hiding the truth and their feelings, in presenting a perfectly calm exterior. Libras of the perfect appearance are masters at molding themselves to become what others want them to be. They can present themselves so unobtrusively that they appear to disappear, or they can release their magic, and a whole room revolves around their sparkle. Truman Capote had the Libra magic. According to his biographer, when Capote walked into a room he was "the chemist's drop of volatile substance that changes the composition of any gathering from amity to effervescence."

Charm, magnetism, and style are Libra's natural gifts. Their ruler is Venus. When they're beautiful, they're sublime. Catherine Deneuve (October 22) is considered by many the most beautiful woman in the world, as was Rita Hayworth (October 17). Also Libras are Cheryl Tiegs (September 27), Heather Locklear (September 25) and, of course, Brigitte Bardot. In Libra, men are beautiful, too. Who could resist the charm and good looks of Marcello Mastroianni (September 28) or the aloof perfection of Roger Moore (October 14)?

If you happen to be born a Libra without harmonious features, then you're meant to learn what real beauty is all about. When you accept yourself, appearances don't matter, your actions do. Eleanor Roosevelt's mother was a beauty who made her daughter feel ugly. Eleanor spent the first part of her life feeling depressed and alone. It wasn't until her husband entered politics that Eleanor discovered her own talents and her mission. Eleanor Roosevelt had her fans and her enemies, but everyone acknowledged her charm and charisma.

Libras have the power to become myth, and they are attracted to those who possess this quality. Barbara Walters (September 25) became a superstar herself by interviewing the supermen and-women of our times. Anne Leibowitz (October 2) photographs them. Donna Karan (October 2) dresses them. Alfred Nobel honored them. John Lennon of the Beatles was one of them; eventually, he replaced his own myth with that of Yoko Ono.

If a myth helps you grow, then it's good. If it makes you live a false existence, then it's destructive. If your myth is the perfect family, then it's headed for a fall. If your myth is your relationship, sooner or later, he or she will disappoint you. Decide if you're attracted to a myth that puts you in conflict with your truth, or one that will help you achieve something greater within yourself. You have the power to create or destroy your myths; don't let a wrong set of beliefs dictate your life.

Libra's talent is not limited to the "real" world; they know how to navigate in the "other" world also. They're our shamans. They are able to cast out the demons of the tribe. The shaman offers a performance, when the "unspeakable" has been shouted forth, the tribe is purged and set free. Greek tragedy is a form of demon purging and symbolic of Libra's ability to heal through art and illusion, to effect a catharsis. Aimee Semple McPherson, was a healer and an evangelist who rose to national prominence early in this century. She drew incredible crowds of followers through her use of drama. Her church featured a fourteen-piece orchestra with a golden harp, a chorus of a hundred, and a brass band of thirty-six.

Once you've picked your hero and stretched yourself toward your ideal, it's time to learn how to keep your balance. Balance is achieved through the tension of two polarities. In Libra, it's your past and future. When you can stretch in both directions, you snap into the now and propel yourself out of your rut. Don't depend on the promise of Heaven or the glories of your forefathers. By undoing the blocks at both ends, you place yourself in the only location where things happen—the moment.

Libra is the sign of historians and visionaries. The historical part often finds expression in an illustrious family tree. Eleanor Roosevelt was the niece of Theodore Roosevelt, the twenty-sixth president of the United States. F. Scott Fitzgerald was related to Frances Scott Key, the composer of "The Star Spangled Banner." Ben-Gurion always said he was born a Zionist. Sometimes, the Libra uses his imagination to connect him to some great past. F. Scott Fitzgerald said, "I wasn't the son of my parents, but the son of a King, a King who ruled the whole world." Gore Vidal (October 3) became a well-known historian. His journeys into the past helped him find his own voice. Without healing and acceptance of the past, your success will be limited. Montgomery Clift (October 17), the actor, blocked his past and suffered. His brother Brooks said, "Psychologically we couldn't seem to take the memories, so we forgot. But at the same time we were obsessed with our childhood ... Monty once said the smell of boot polish reminded him of winter when he was a boy. He could get hysterical over the smell of boot polish.''

Reach beyond your pain to the strength of your ancestors. You can learn from all the great minds who have come before you. Reach for the future. A good vision can lift you from the mire of an unpleasant memory. Gandhi had a vision of independence for India through peaceful resistance. Christopher Columbus (October 12) set off to discover distant lands like America. Of course, you can get stuck in a vision just as easily as in the past. In her book aptly titled *Tomorrow is Now,* Eleanor Roosevelt says, ''There is no more liberating, no more exhilarating experience than to determine one's position, state it bravely and then act boldly.''

Free association is the easiest way to connect the inner world with the outer moment. Groucho Marx (October 2) was a genius at it. Psychologists use this method to help their patients discover their truth. Lenny Bruce used free association in his comic routines. Gifted with the ability to carry on a personal dialogue with thousands of people, he created a feeling of intimacy with his audience. Free association allowed the freedom to be intimate, and that's what Libras desire above all other things. Intimacy requires letting go of the ''I.'' Marcello Mastroianni made each woman feel as if she were the center of his world. Truman Capote's biographer, John Brennin, said of him, ''I soon found that Truman in a crowd or tête-à-tête could exist on no plane but that of intimacy.'' However, some Libras never learn how to connect. Thomas Wolfe (October 3), Nietzsche, and Alfred Nobel were all loners.

Truth, morality, and ethics are all unclear in Libra. The moral challenge of Libra is to reconcile the truth of man with the truth of God. Finding yourself caught between the two teaches the soul not to judge others. No man knows another man's truth.

Libra's answers are found solely within. In the outside world, they will seek things that inspire the soul—ideas, art, people who ask them to improve. Oscar Wilde said, ''Aesthetics are higher than ethics. They belong to a more spiritual sphere ... Even a color-sense is more important, in the development of the individual than a sense of right and wrong.''

For this stage of the journey, truth has become an illusive force. ''A truth ceases to be true when more than one person believes it?'' Wilde said. Kenneth Tynan, drama critic for *The New Yorker,* reviewed Lenny Bruce's London act by saying Bruce was the ''Sharpest denter of taboos at present active ... a true, iconoclast ... who breaks through the barrier of laughter to the horizon beyond where the truth has its sanctuary.'' Bruce said of himself, ''The world is sick and I'm the doctor. I'm a surgeon with a scalpel for false values.'' Speaking about Truman Capote, James A. Michener said, ''Artists are sometimes outrageously against the grain, that they expose unpopular causes, that they behave in ways that would be unacceptable to others, and that they can have waspish tongues. I've always had a strong suspicion that such artists help keep society chained up, or on its toes, and more civilized than it would otherwise be.''

The artist, like the Libra soul, divides and joins knowledge and intuition. Observe, select, associate, and then test. Both are looking for the moment of creation, for the moment of grace. Moments of grace almost never occur by chance. They result from focus and determined energy. The artist's task is to see that "the impossible is made to appear possible."

Who else but a hero would follow truth into pain and suffering to help humankind? From suffering, the desire for and appreciation of beauty is born. Nietzsche said, "I wanted to believe that the deepest sense of existence was to be found in suffering and that only art enabled us to face this suffering and not run away from it." Thomas Wolfe found beauty in his sorrow. In a letter to his friend Aline he said, "I've meant to lead a good life, and I've led a bad and wasteful one. But out of this waste and sin I believe in spite of all logic, that some beauty will come."

Illness and health are another polarity worth examining. Disease can be a catalyst; it can stimulate something new that causes you to change your life. When you have to fight to live, illness can make you strong. Nietzsche said, "Whatever does not destroy me, makes me stronger." Recent interest in holistic healing supports this theory. Those who have used their illnesses to change their lives, have healed themselves and reconnected with their personal truth. As with all opposites, pain and joy are inseparable. Nietzsche said, they are "so knotted together that whoever wants as much as possible of the one, must also have as much as possible of the other."

Libra is the scales of balance and all polarities are united through the power of the moment. Inner harmony is achieved at the sacrifice of the mask or exterior perfection. As false identity begins to shatter, the soul is forced to grasp the ethereal world of spirit. From that leap comes faith. It happens again whenever you have the courage to face your fear and to trust in the unknown. As you end the process of self-individualization and confront the world with your truth, you learn that truth does not need a hero to protect it, for it is invincible and transformative. Oscar Wilde said, ". . . No man dies for what he knows to be true. Men die for what they want to be true, for what some terror in their hearts tells them is not true." Know your truth. This is the power of Libra.

THE LIBRA ENVIRONMENT

◗ ☻ ☺ ☽

The Libra environment fluctuates between static and active. Libra desires to unify from within at the expense of appearances. When personal truth is honored, the exterior world is chaotic; if appearances are the priority, the inner world suffers. This constant state of flux is meant to teach you to rely on yourself and to know that you, are the creator of your world. The Libra environment will offer you many ideals from which to choose. Pick one and let it transport you to a new level of consciousness. If you're stubborn and hold on to the world of things and pleasure, you will find your inner needs in conflict with the world around you. This is the fork in the road. You must choose your own path, even if it means leaving others behind. The more you compromise your truth, the more powerless you will feel. By reaching above and beyond yourself, by allowing yourself be used for a higher purpose, you will find the strength and peace for which you have been looking.

Libra/*One* (September 28, October 1, October 10, October 19) Venus/Sun

PURPOSE: To take your own path, balancing your need for freedom with your desire for love.

"Let man be noble, generous and good! For this alone distinguishes him from all beings known to us."—Goethe. Goethe knew that to resolve conflict, one must surrender to his most noble side. Goals should have a higher purpose. In Libra, the fruits of fame and fortune leave a bitter taste. They demand too much of one's truth, and give little in return. The Libra/*One* must learn to accept themselves and to surround themselves with beautiful art, ideas, and people.

The Libra/*One* is charming, magnetic and a natural lover. The issue here is how and when to take responsibility. They love being surrounded by impossible odds, then proving to the world just how easily those odds are overcome. If Libra/*Ones* have faith, they're on their way. If they don't, they're in trouble. They either defy authority, rules, and tradition or surrender their individuality to their need for acceptance. A balance needs to be achieved; then, the peace they desire will be theirs.

IF SPIRIT TAKES THE LEAD: The *One* and Spirit are good friends. These souls are perfectionists, and can be unbending in their beliefs. Sometimes, they feel as though they're the only person with values. They fight for a cause or against anything that limits human freedom. The world is a demanding place and their great sense of responsibility sets them up to be used by others. Without good discrimination, they could feel depleted and fatigued.

IF EGO TAKES THE LEAD: Ego and Libra are not the best of pals. The pressure is on for Ego to fall into place and like any spoiled child, it rebels. Things that glitter attract them—fame, gold, luxury. The spiritual need to be used for an ideal allows them to manipulate the energy and use others for their own end. Their Venus flexibility can make them present any identity needed to gain their own end. Conversely, they can lean toward the *One* and be so rigid in their beliefs and righteousness they are impossible to deal with. Success is a possibility, but if it's only the worldly stuff they're after, they'll end up feeling empty. They hide from self-awareness. They can be lazy or a workaholic.

BRIGITTE BARDOT (September 28)

French actress, sex symbol.

Brigitte Bardot possessed the charm and sexual power of the Libra/*One* combination. However, this "bad little girl" never reached the independence of her number, *One*. She gave it away, first to Roger Vadim who created her public image. Her parents were against the marriage, but Bardot threatened suicide and they relented. She achieved stardom with *And God Created Woman*. The movie, about a freedom-loving young girl who acted without malice or thought of consequences, made her an international symbol of sexual desire. The laziness of Venus prevented Bardot from becoming a great dancer in her youth. Leslie Caron, her friend in dance school, said she could have been wonderful ". . . if she'd been willing to do the work." After her divorce, Bardot had many lovers and gave birth to a son whom she did not raise. Only when it came to animals did Bardot allow her higher self to take over. She lends her name and her fortune to taking care of lost animals. No matter what her faults, her childish pout, her natural elegance and her incredible charisma make her a legend in her own time.

JIMMY CARTER (October 1)

Thirty-ninth president of the United States, governor of Georgia, writer, humanitarian.

Jimmy Carter's autobiography, *Why Not The Best?,* sums up the Libra need to achieve greatness. Raised on a peanut farm in Plains, Georgia, Jimmy Carter was a hard worker and a good problem solver. Later, he attended the United States Naval Academy, Annapolis, Maryland, and married a local girl. His climb to success was slow but steady. After a commission in the navy, he retired to his farm and built the family business. Twelve years later he ran for office and became governor of Georgia. By the end of his last term, he had announced his candidacy for president. One of his greatest successes as president was the Sadat and Begin negotiations at Camp David, resulting in the Camp David Accords. A born-again Christian, Carter showed he could be a man of compromise.

Libra/*Two* (September 29, October 2, October 11, October 20) Venus/Moon

PURPOSE: To use your spirit to avoid the decadence and excess in life. To focus on your ability to help others without being pulled off your path.

"You are unique, and if that is not fulfilled, then something has been lost."— Martha Graham. The *Two* is always unique and matched with Libra, they've got a soul that has its own expression. Libra/*Twos* feel a great need to contribute something to the world. Their desire to be used for a higher purpose can make them great leaders or codependents. The keys here are a strong sense of self and a spiritual base. If Ego hasn't found its place, the need to please may inhibit the true talents of this soul and send them on a path of acquiring possessions instead of healing themselves and others. As a child, they were either spoiled and indulged or ignored, and they learned how not to expose their truth. Depression, mood swings, and an inability to trust could be problems. They are stronger than they appear and more stubborn than most. Their charm and ease with people masks a more complex person. At some time, they will be prodded to come out of their shells and shine. They have a great deal to offer the world if they can get beyond their fear and reach out to others.

IF SPIRIT TAKES THE LEAD: When Spirit is strong, this soul is indomitable. They can be a superman or superwoman who accomplishes the impossible. They know how to take a bad situation and turn it around, and they don't let despair get them down. They are very private, have great courage and compassion, but their personal lives are difficult. They may seek spiritual union with a mate, someone they can unite with in a mission, rather than on a physical level. Their physical health can suffer because their spiritual needs take priority. Self-nurturing is necessary, as well as a deep understanding of responsibility. They've got to learn how to let go.

IF EGO TAKES THE LEAD: If Ego is strong, so is excess and fear. These souls can suffer from highs and lows. Very manipulative, they use their intuition to read others and see beyond their masks. Masters at presenting themselves as weak or needy, they get others to give them what they want. Unable to express their feelings, they live a lonely existence, unable to connect. They may be attached to beautiful things and spend their lives on shopping sprees that only enlarge their feeling of emptiness.

ELEANOR ROOSEVELT (October 11)

First lady, author, human rights activist.

As the U.S representative to the United Nations, she was largely responsible for their Universal Declaration of Human Rights, adopted in 1948.

Eleanor, niece of President Theodore Roosevelt, was born into an aristocratic family. Her mother, who died when Eleanor was eight, considered manners more important than feelings, and beauty the most important of all. As a child, Eleanor felt ugly and unloved. Her father adored her but he had a problem with, alcohol. Before and after her marriage to Franklin Roosevelt, Eleanor was a classic Victorian woman: Her role was "to make him [Franklin] and all those she loved happy; to secure harmony; to remain patient and calm through all adversity and under any assault." Eleanor was in love with her husband and enjoyed three months of happiness on her honeymoon in Europe. When the couple returned, the groom's mother, Sara Delano Roosevelt, took over her son's home. In trying to please her mother-in-law, and be a good wife and mother to her six children, Eleanor suppressed her thoughts and ambitions. It was her husband's entrance into politics that changed Eleanor's life. Their move to Albany allowed Eleanor her own home. Without her mother-in-law's presence, she blossomed. Franklin Roosevelt found her an immense help in his career. When FDR was made assistant secretary of the Navy, Washington, D.C., became their next home. Eleanor's discovery of her husband's affair with her social secretary, Lucy Mercer, resulted in a loss of faith in her husband and her ideals but a gain of self-confidence. The pain gave her a stronger voice. By the time her husband was elected president, Eleanor was a leader of human rights. For the first time, the position of first lady was a platform for expressing bold, dissenting political ideas.

GANDHI (October 2)

Spiritual leader.

Gandhi began his adult life as a small-town lawyer and developed into a self-appointed champion of Indians, first in South Africa and then later in his own country—India. He married early and he became the chief wage earner and supporter of his family. To improve his earning ability, he was sent to England to study law. For the first time, Ghandi was free to explore life without the limitations of Indian tradition, and became westernized. Later, he cast off all traces of western influence and encouraged his people to speak their own language and regain their sense of self-respect. Gandhi referred to life as his laboratory for spiritual experience. His beliefs were that God could only be found within; that one must have a spiritual vision and be well disciplined in mind and body; that one must live a simple life that connects one to the truth, nonviolence, and love. Called Mahatma or Great Soul, Ghandi's policy of *ahima* or nonviolence led to the end of British rule in India. Ghandi the man of peace, was assassinated.

Libra/*Three* (September 30, October 3, October 12, October 21) Venus/Jupiter

PURPOSE: To live your beliefs and risk yourself through leadership, knowing that remaining close to the truth is the only protection you have or need in an ever-changing world.

"I believe that all of us have the capacity for one adventure inside us, but great adventure is facing responsibility day after day."—William Gordon. The Libra/*Three* is not interested in daily routine. Their dreams are of faraway places and impossible feats. But the truth is, the greatest challenge is living day to day, taking responsibility for the little things, seeing heroics in meeting everyday challenges. If Libra/*Threes* haven't had an opportunity to experience life firsthand and learn about themselves, they could be under the influence of someone with strong beliefs. It's time they take their power back and reconnect with faith and hope. If Libra/*Threes* are on the other end of the polarity, they are loners and rebels. Going against injustice or impossible odds is something they love. Charming, controlling, and willful, they make the rules. They need to stop trying to change the world and give themselves a new perspective. They need to accept their fate; only then can they transform it. The Libra/*Three* either takes on too much responsibility or not enough. Balance is the key to happiness. Intimacy may be a problem because they are attracted to the adulation of the many. Born leaders, they have their own unique way of approaching life, but authority issues may cause trouble. They need to take things one step at a time and value the small.

IF SPIRIT TAKES THE LEAD: If Spirit takes the lead, the soul will feel as if it has a calling or sense of destiny. They will ignore the simple things of life, and the desire to conquer some great obstacle to truth or justice will prevail. The challenge is to choose the right purpose and not become codependent. If they try to help those invested in staying crippled, they may find themselves in a dead-end situation. The key is to pay attention to their own needs, otherwise their self-esteem will suffer and someone else will own their power. They need to take risks and narrow the gap with those they love. Faith is revealed in the little things as well as through heroic deeds.

IF EGO TAKES THE LEAD: If Ego is powerful, watch out, world. These souls want to rule and have their presence known. Able to see the truth from a unique and personal perspective, their view is panoramic and their humor and wit as powerful as swords. They believe that their way is the only way. Obstinate and inflexible, they seem compromising because of their charm. Loners and leaders, they're rebels, not afraid of imposing their views on everyone else. It makes them angry when the world refuses to recognize their genius. Their challenge is to believe in their own talents and not worry about praise from others.

GORE VIDAL (October 3)

Writer.

Gore Vidal has expressed the Libra's love of history in his writing. He risked his career by breaking society's taboo on gay writing. His novel entitled *The City and the Pillar* opened the door for future gay fiction.

Born into a family both politically and socially connected, Vidal was the son of a pioneer in American aviation who was also a member of FDR's administration. Vidal was raised partly by his grandfather, who was blind. Vidal read to him often, and so developed his love of books. Vidal was educated at Philips Exeter Academy in New Hampshire. He joined the army after graduation and was sent overseas, where he began work on his first novel, *Williwaw*. He sold the book at the age of twenty. After the army, Vidal worked for a publisher, but the money wasn't there so he left for Guatemala, the first of his exotic hideaways. After publishing many novels, Vidal began to write for TV, theater, and movies. He is one of the most versatile writers of our century.

ALFRED NOBEL (October 21)

Established the Nobel Prize, inventor of dynamite.

In his last will and testament, Alfred Nobel established the coveted and prestigious Nobel Prizes. Nobel wanted to reward men and women who created something in an "idealistic" spirit. The prize would be given to the most deserving person, "without the slightest consideration if the person is a Swede or a foreigner, a man or a woman." Nobel was first and foremost an inventor. He explored a variety of fields: mechanics, engineering, optics, biology, and electrochemistry. The only person to file more patents than Nobel was Thomas Edison. His true dream was to be a writer, and he derived as much pleasure from words as he did from his laboratory. Nobel was fascinated with the newly discovered nitroglycerin. He knew if he could harness its awesome powers, the rewards would be great. Dynamite made him a wealthy man and earned him the nickname "The Merchant of Death." Desperately lonely, Nobel never married and had few friends.

Libra/*Four* (October 4, October 13, October 22)
Venus/Uranus

PURPOSE: To develop your inner world and personal truth well enough so that you can ignore the endless crises and distractions that will cross your path as you change and grow, pursuing truth and justice.

"Courage is contagious. When a brave man takes a stand, the spines of others are often stiffened."—Billy Graham. Brave isn't strong enough to describe the spirit of Libra/*Fours*. They have courage that can break through barriers and change the lives of others. They need to make sure they don't get hooked on the fast pace, the desire for tension, and the need to keep things exciting. Relationships are hard because they change from moment to moment, always reaching new insights. They seek unity, but unless they work from the inside and move toward wholeness, they'll find themselves still on the outside, trying to enter by breaking through. The Libra/*Four* can either be close to the truth or observe it from afar. If they choose the role of the loner, they'll be very analytical. If they position themselves in the center, then they become the negotiator of difficult relationships. They often enjoy the role of the rebel; they dislike tradition and authority.

IF SPIRIT TAKES THE LEAD: If Spirit has the lead, they are great in hostile situations and know how to bring two opposing factions together. They also know how to relate simultaneously to contradictory points of view. They seek truth, but they attract tension and hostility. Catalysts, they change the lives of all they encounter. Their desire to make the world a better place keeps them chasing after injustices, both large and small.

IF EGO TAKES THE LEAD: Ego doesn't avoid the crises of life, it creates them. These souls are unhappy unless the world around them is upside down. Able to maneuver in chaos, they do well when everyone else is clinging to life rafts. They are strong, and often brilliant. Because of their rigid point of view, they find themselves on the outside. They use their keen eyes and intuition to find fault rather than to unify. They need to know that true power and control are not found in opposition but in holding love and truth above all things, including their own convictions.

LENNY BRUCE (October 13)

Stand-up comic, writer.

Lenny was raised by an old-fashioned father and a stagestruck mother. When his parents divorced, Bruce's father gave him everything he wanted. The lack of discipline allowed the lazy side of Venus to emerge. Bruce dropped out of high school and joined the navy. He hated it so much he orchestrated a dishonorable discharge. Bruce's friendship with Joe Ancis, the original sick comic, helped him develop his comic style. Ancis was called the Marquis de Spritz because of his stream of consciousness and his absolute self-indulgence. Although personal intimacy was difficult for Bruce, he had the gift of making an audience feel as if they were in his confidence. His humor was based on shattering the facade of goodness, virtue and misrepresentation. Bruce was arrested many times for obscenity. He challenged the Constitution and polarized his audiences—they either loved or hated him. Bruce exhibited the Libra talent for writing. Unfortunately, Bruce died of an accidental drug overdose.

DWIGHT D. EISENHOWER (October 14)

Supreme Commander of the Allied Expeditionary Forces, president of Columbia University, supreme commander of NATO; thirty-fourth president of the United States.

Ike, as he was known to most of his friends, was a major figure of the twentieth century. He was the perfect Libra hero who guided America through World War II and then led the country down the road to peace.

Eisenhower's ancestors were Pennsylvania Dutch. The family was poor but religious. A strict disciplinarian, Eisenhower's father rarely smiled. His mother, on the contrary, was a joyful women and it was she who gave her sons the love and affection they needed. Eisenhower sought self-improvement rather than self-change. He was accepted at the United States Military Academy at West Point. He married Mamie Doud. As Supreme Commander during WW II, Eisenhower decided when to land on the beaches of Normandy. He was the most famous and successful general of the war, a symbol of victory over the Nazis and America's hope for a better world. Eisenhower wanted to retire in order to write and lecture. However, he was drafted by his country to run for president.

Libra/*Five* (October 5, October 14, October 23)
Venus/Mercury

PURPOSE: To realign your perspective and your identity so that it expresses your deepest truth and not the mask you show the world. To use your many talents and great diversity to provide a service to others that will facilitate them in expressing their truth.

"After ecstasy, the laundry."—Zen statement. Libra/*Fives* are divided between their need for the luxuries of the world and their need for truth. This is an identity crisis. If they don't discover who they are, they could spend their lifetime devoted to others. Libra/*Fives* are multitalented, which makes clarity and single-mindedness of purpose more difficult. Restless and on the go, they can suffer from depression and fear. They long for intimacy but are afraid of it, so they seek a partner who is distant and unattainable. They may even idealize a relationship. Their fear of losing their individuality and freedom keeps them chasing dreams. The Libra/*Five* should balance excess and perfectionism with faith.

IF SPIRIT TAKES THE LEAD: With Spirit strong, choices and temptations are ignored. There is only one way to do anything and that's perfectly. These souls idealize a role or image and live it as the truth. The here and now is something they try to avoid. Afraid of the truth, they seek new experiences and change constantly. They have a strong will and need to use it to unite the many facets of their being and focus them on a positive goal. An ability to connect with others and the masses gives them public appeal. People come to them with their despair and they give them answers as well as hope.

IF EGO TAKES THE LEAD: If Ego is ahead, the soul may lack self-confidence and an identity. Without a sense of self, the opinion of others can make them feel unworthy. They're too willing to do anything in order to get their way. They believe that the acquisition of things will end the emptiness they feel inside. Charming, and able to adapt to any situation, they make great salesmen or con men. They rationalize in order to avoid responsibility. Once they learn to face the truth, they're on their way.

DENIS DIDEROT (October 5)

Editor of the *Encyclopédie,* writer, founder of modern art criticism

The versatility of the Libra/*Five* combination is certainly evident in Diderot. A dramatist, novelist, and philosopher, he accomplished the monumental feat of compiling the first encyclopedia. Driven to gather all available knowledge into several volumes that the common man could access at will, he battled censorship, attacks from the church and government imprisonment in order to achieve his goal. Catherine the Great was his friend and at the age of sixty, Diderot traveled to St. Petersburg to discuss with the empress plans for the conversion of Russia into an ideal republic. Always in conflict with authority, Diderot spent much of his life under threat of exile and many of his daring and inventive novels did not reach the public until a decade after his death. His masterpiece *Le Neveu de Rameau (Rameau's Nephew),* was unpublished for two decades.

RALPH LAUREN (October 14)

Fashion designer.

Born Ralph Lifshitz, Lauren didn't become interested in clothes until the seventh grade. ''My friends were the hoods wearing motorcycle jackets, but I was wearing tweeds, bermudas, and button-down shirts.'' Lauren worked at Alexander's before serving in the army. Afterwards, he found it almost impossible to break into designing. ''I had no portfolio and no sketches. All I had was taste.'' In 1967, Lauren started the Polo neckwear division of Beau Brummel neckties. His tie was unique—wide, expensive, and opulent. Gradually, Lauren expanded his career and today, he is one of the most important of American designers.

Libra/*Six* (September 24, October 6, October 15)
Venus/Venus

PURPOSE: To have the inner strength to avoid temptation and luxury and reach for spiritual heights that will help you perfect and better yourself.

"When my enemies stop hissing, I shall know I'm slipping."—Maria Callas. The Libra/*Sixes* are perfectionists and feathers get ruffled wherever they go. Sometimes, the Libra/*Six* avoids their perfectionistic nature by giving in to desire and laziness. Honesty and the pursuit of truth and justice are important to them. Conversely, the Libra/*Six* can be a good liar. Moods are a problem; they battle with depression. The Libra/*Six* needs inner discipline. They've got to know how to say no to themselves first, then to others. Their strong love of beauty makes them surround themselves with art and antiques. However, the Libra challenge is to simplify life, rather than increase possession. The Libra/*Six* is a natural rebel. They are creative and shouldn't be afraid to take up a hobby or become a psychologist.

IF SPIRIT TAKES THE LEAD: Spirit with Venus accepts nothing less than a perfect picture. They strive incessantly to be better and greater. They are too tough on themselves. They are unaware that their striving keeps others away. They often achieve great success, but always at a cost to their health or their social life. Anxious to have a semblance of control, they remove temptation and deny themselves luxuries. They are disciplined and controlling. Others lean on them because responsibility is something they take seriously. They need to find the beauty in things just the way they are, and know that to be perfect is to love themselves.

IF EGO TAKES THE LEAD: If Ego is powerful, these souls want everything that life can offer. A lack of discipline creates the need for instant gratification. They are self-absorbed. Everything they see relates to them. Of course, what they're really looking for is love. However, because they desire it so badly, when it's offered they run away. They are strong-willed. They demand attention constantly and find fault with everything. Nothing will please them until they learn to love themselves.

FRIEDRICH NIETZSCHE (October 15)

Philosopher, psychologist, professor writer.

Nietzsche was born into a family of ministers. When his father died, Nietzsche was raised by women: his mother, sister, father's mother, and two maiden aunts. Nietzsche won a scholarship to the school of Pforta. From there, he went on to the University of Bonn. Appointed professor of classical philosophy at Basel, he became a professor at the age of twenty-four. He taught for ten years, until his health became poor. He spent a brief time in the military during the Franco-Prussian War. His friendship with Richard Wagner, the famous composer, influenced him greatly, but Nietzsche didn't come into his own until his split with Wagner. Nietzsche felt he had a strong mission in life. He never earned a great deal of money for his work, and tragically, spent his final days in a mental asylum. Nietzsche is best known for his concept of the Superman. The Superman represents the higher stage of humanity, a stage reached only when the masses are sacrificed to the elite in order for the collective to grow. Nietzsche continually struggled with issues of morality, religion, the individual, and the common man.

F. SCOTT FITZGERALD (September 24)

Writer.

Fitzgerald was born to a mother who spoiled him and a father who felt himself a failure. At Princeton he immersed himself in social life and the theater, to the detriment of his schoolwork. He said of himself, "I was convinced that I had personality, charm, magnetism, poise and the ability to dominate others. Also I was sure that I exercised a subtle fascination over women." However, Fitzgerald was a slave to his moods and felt he had no real courage, perseverance, or self-respect. According to his friend Edmund Wilson, whom Fitzgerald considered his intellectual superior and mentor, "Fitzgerald has been given imagination without intellectual control of it, he has been given the desire for beauty without an aesthetic ideal and has been given a gift for expression without many ideas to express."

Fitzgerald's wife, Zelda, was his perfect partner. Yet, he would make the mistake his hero Gatsby did, "of enclosing his highest aspiration in the frail vessel of a perishable creature who was subject to the law of her world of appearances." Zelda wanted to live life dangerously. An uncontrollable flirt, she smoked, drank, and eventually was institutionalized.

With World War I still raging, Scott set out to write a novel, something to leave behind if he died. He sold *This Side of Paradise* almost immediately. Although it sold 44,0000 copies the first year, Fitzgerald made little money. Magazines paid, however, and Fitzgerald faced a dilemma that was to last throughout his career. He could write for money or for his soul. His novel entitled *This Side of Paradise* broke the Victorian illusion of morality that existed in America. For the first time, a talented novelist had dared to describe the real morals of the new middle-class generation. Scott died of coronary occlusion, in poverty, and almost in total oblivion. However, his name lives on through his work.

Libra/*Seven* (September 25, October 7, October 16)
Venus/Neptune

PURPOSE: To find faith in the midst of despair or joy and become reborn. To use your new vision and strength to inspire others and help them overcome their sense of hopelessness.

"It gives me a deep comforting sense that things seen are temporal and things unseen are eternal."—Helen Keller. The Libra/*Seven* tries to solve the ongoing dilemma of philosophers—what is reality? They need to accept the fact that there is more than one reality. Their inner world needs to be strong and anchored in faith in order for them to be successful. The Libra/*Seven* is too idealistic and the only way the universe can ground them is with harsh reality. They need to remember they have the power to create anything they can dream. But they must be able to use their will to harness their whole self and direct it toward one goal. The Libra/*Seven* is a perfectionist, a dreamer, and a creative human being who feels the need to help others.

IF SPIRIT TAKES THE LEAD: If Spirit is strong, so are these souls. They have an unbending will and a perfectionistic nature that can drive others up a wall. If their will is directed toward a positive goal, they accomplish the impossible. The danger is that they can become stuck on saving souls who refuse to be helped. This is codependency, not healing. They must use discrimination. Mood swings and depression are a possibility. If they organize their inner world, the outside one will fall into place.

IF EGO TAKES THE LEAD: If Ego has managed to get ahead, then they are a demanding, judgmental, and dictatorial soul who wants things done "right." Of course, right means their way. They are perfectionists who battle a feeling of emptiness and keep striving for worldly possession when what they're really looking for is a spiritual connection. Able to live a double life, they can be very deceitful and afraid to show their true nature. Their need to please makes them present one face to the world while they wheel and deal behind the scenes. If they would open their hearts to others, that empty hole would start to fill up.

DAVID BEN-GURION (October 16)

First prime minister of Israel.

David Joseph Gruen identified himself with Zionism and the desire of the Jews to return to their homeland. He was gifted with an intense will, a phenomenal memory, the ability to concentrate, courage, and patience. He lived to declare the establishment of the state of Israel and became its first prime minister and minister of defense.

Born in Russia, he was doted on by his mother, claimed a genius by his father, and taught Hebrew and the Bible by his grandfather. In 1906, at the age of twenty, he arrived in Jaffa, Palestine, and four years later changed his surname to Ben-Gurion, to celebrate his second birth. It was here that he began his work toward the establishment of a Jewish state. "I have only one aim: to strive for the Hebrew worker in Eretz Israel, this is the fabric of my life . . . the sacred mission of my life, and in it I shall find my happiness."

BARBARA WALTERS (September 25)

ABC news correspondent, interviewer, author.

Walters was born in Boston. After graduating from Sarah Lawrence College, she moved to New York. There, she worked for an advertising agency, then landed a job writing material for Dick Van Dyke, Jack Paar, Anita Colby, and the NBC news bureau. It was her position as the hostess on the *Today Show* that brought her celebrity status. The author of a best-selling book, *How to Talk to Practically Anybody about Practically Anything,* she has become famous by interviewing the rich and powerful. The impossible interview is her specialty. She is able to get inside a person's life and reveal to the audience the most intimate personal details of the interviewee's life. Her TV specials are famous and even the reruns attract an audience.

Libra/*Eight* (September 26, October 8, October 17) Venus/Saturn

PURPOSE: To strive for spiritual and worldly balance through your actions, thoughts and deeds, unafraid to oppose injustice, eager to embrace the truth, and always providing a haven for those who have lost their voice and their way.

"I never thought of stopping, and I just hated sleeping. I can't imagine having a better life."—Barbara McClintock, 1983 Nobel laureate. The Libra/*Eight* can be obsessive, particularly when it comes to work. They may tend to analyze everyone and everything a bit too much. They've got a great eye for detail and know how to package and sell anything. Depression may be a problem because they can't always get off the spot and see the bigger picture. When they can, nothing is impossible. Their world will remain small unless they learn how to trust. Relationships can be a problem unless they stop testing them again and again. The Libra/*Eight* needs faith. They are talented, have concentration, and take responsibility. Those are winning qualities.

IF SPIRIT TAKES THE LEAD: If Spirit is powerful, then these souls are idealists who are also proficient in the business world. They are masters at using the ideals of others to get a job done. Strong and willful, they can risk everything for what they believe. They need to learn to value the power of the "real" world so that they can present their truth in a way that others can accept. Too responsible, always overloading their life with challenges, they find peace a distant stranger. Learning how to set limits is important or they could have a nervous breakdown.

IF EGO TAKES THE LEAD: With Ego in the lead, security is a major issue. These souls don't trust anyone or anything. They must realize that their feelings of emptiness won't go away without faith. They are constantly afraid that their world will crumble. They need to believe in themselves. They are perfectly capable of handling anything that comes their way. Tough on everyone, they like to be shown their mistakes, even though they're difficult to work for because they're hard to please. Success in business is likely, but their personal world requires some love and self-acceptance.

JUAN PERÓN (October 8)

President of Argentina.

Perón was a master at using others to gain political power. He harnessed the votes of the country's workers and rode them to the presidency. He encouraged the unions to organize, knowing they would depend on the government. In the end, he destroyed the independence of the unions forever. He married a woman who became a myth in her own right and gave her powers no Argentinian woman had ever had. With Eva Perón by his side, Argentinian women gained the right to vote.

Gifted with great charisma and an ability to improvise on the spot, Perón brought political ambiguity to an all-time high. Some called him a saint; others believed him to be the devil himself. Perón himself felt he transcended good and evil. Controversial to the end, he was cynical, disdained the truth, lacked principles, and advocated violence to suppress opposition.

JESSIE JACKSON (October 8)

Minister, presidential candidate.

Born out of wedlock, Jackson experienced being poor and shut out. His involvement in the sit-ins during the sixties brought him to the attention of Dr. Martin Luther King. King became his mentor and in 1968, Jackson became an ordained minister. A prominent political figure, Jackson has met with Castro, Arafat, and other world leaders. He has also made several bids for the White House and has written several books. Jackson is one of the most powerful African-American leaders in America. He founded PUSH (People United to Save Humanity), an organization dedicated to economic betterment of black communities and black-owned companies.

Libra/*Nine* (September 27, October 9, October 18)
Venus/Mars

PURPOSE: To have developed your sense of self and your personal perspective to a point that you cannot be seduced by the pleasures and luxuries of the world around you. To use your strengths and vision to help those who are stuck and unable to move forward.

''An idea can turn to dust or magic, depending on the talent that rubs against it.''—William Bernbach, advertising executive. If anyone can turn a simple idea or project into a major happening, it's the Libra/*Nine*. Their touch is magic. Charismatic, prone to excess, a bit idealistic, they strive to show the world the truth while working for peace and justice. They can easily become a symbol of a cause or an ideal, but they must be careful because they can too easily lose themselves in someone or something. A strong identity is important and so is a developed spiritual nature. If these two things are in place, success is guaranteed. More than anything else, the Libra/*Nines* need to trust their instincts. Passive and aggressive, they switch between giving orders and not taking responsibility for their actions. The Libra/*Nine* is assertive. They become frustrated when they don't get their way. Their desires are strong and they can keep others off-balance by indulging their need for pleasure. They need to work on self-discipline and patience.

IF SPIRIT TAKES THE LEAD: When Spirit is strong with the *Nine,* the body suffers. They don't pay attention to physical needs. They are idealistic and get caught up in what the world should be, rather than what it is. They push themselves relentlessly, seldom thinking of the consequences. Gifted with vision and a lust for life, they can become leaders with immense impact and strength. They need to find a balance between their spiritual side and their earthly needs, between their aggressive behavior and their passive responses.

IF EGO TAKES THE LEAD: If the Ego is strong, they are self-absorbed. They believe they were born for greatness and set out to prove it to the world. Riddled by an inability to take action, and a lack of faith in themselves, they also have superhuman strength. They are capable of extreme behavior and battle mood swings and excessive behavior. Cursed with divine discontent, nothing makes them happy and so they seek satisfaction in the pleasures of the world: love, sex, money, fame. They can be successful because they're charming.

JOHN LENNON (October 9)

John Lennon was born into chaos. His parents abandoned him, and he was raised by his Aunt Mimi. Emotionally damaged, John found an outlet in his music. Elvis Presley's song ''Heartbreak Hotel'' inspired Lennon to buy a secondhand guitar. It was in Hamburg, Germany, where Lennon's rock-'n'-roll band, the Beatles, developed their style and a serious following. Brian Epstein, who recognized their special gift, became their manager. Lennon's life changed dramatically when he met Japanese artist Yoko Ono. To him, she had wisdom and magical powers. They married and eventually, she gained control of much of his life. After years of trying, they finally conceived and gave birth to a child named Sean. Just before Lennon's assassination in 1980, he recorded an album entitled *Double Fantasy*. Lennon's ability to touch the hearts and souls of people all over the world was unprecedented.

AIMEE SEMPLE McPHERSON (October 9)

Aimee McPherson was an evangelist and healer who had the power of faith, an incredible presence, a knack for showmanship, and the ability to heal. McPherson and her first husband became missionaries to China. McPherson's second marriage was not happy. However, by then she was hearing voices telling her to take up the calling of preacher. She ignored the voices until one day she broke her ankle and the doctors declared they were unable to properly sew the ligaments. The voice came again and told her to see a healer. McPherson followed its advice and the ankle was miraculously healed. Aimee took up her calling. Her fame grew as she traveled across the United States in a Packard, preaching and healing whoever came to see her. Ministers began to warn their flocks against her. They accused her of hypnotizing the audience. In her presence, people would begin to speak in tongues and cast away their crutches, opening arthritic hands to the Lord. By the time she arrived in Los Angeles, she was famous. With a gift for raising money, she began building a temple that would cost nearly a million dollars. She didn't have close friends, and many looked upon her as immortal, or beyond human needs. Following her mysterious kidnapping, which many believe she orchestrated, 10,000 people convened at the temple, women tried to kill themselves by throwing themselves into the sea where she was first thought to have drowned. Discovered in a hospital in Arizona she was later charged with corrupting the morals of the public, obstruction of justice, and conspiring to manufacture evidence. After much notoriety, the charges were dismissed. Aimee suffered a total mental and physical breakdown. Eventually, she died from an accidental overdose of barbiturates. Her son Rolf took over her four hundred churches and two hundred missions.

SUMMARY

In Libra, the phase of individualization ends and the soul reverses its priorities. No longer can you think just about yourself. You must think about giving, and the need to rise above the glitter and empty offerings of the world. The soul is wise. It knows that the true gifts of the world are in the seeking of an ideal, not in achieving results. It also knows that all knowledge must now be found from within. In a last effort to complete the process of self-awareness, it struggles to unite all parts of itself. The mask it has been wearing for protection is shattered and the soul exposes its truth unafraid of how it will be received. It has learned how to protect itself; its skills can turn mistakes and failures into strengths. Armed with this kind of experience it is unafraid of the unknown. Reason is its authority and the desire to share begins to emerge. This is the sign of relationships. As the soul ends the first half of the journey, it passes through the depths of despair then soars to unbelievable heights. It seeks clearly that life is not about being alone, but about letting others use you for a higher cause. The old turns to ashes and it feels reborn. This process will be perfected in the next sign of Scorpio.

SELECTED SOURCES

Patricia Bosworth   *Montgomery Clift: A Biography*   Limelight Editions 1990

John Malcolm Brinnin   *Dear Heart, Old Buddy* Delacorte Press 1986

Blanche Wiesen Cook   *Eleanor Roosevelt*   Penguin 1993

David Herbert Donald   *Look Homeward: A Life of Thomas Wolfe*   Little Brown & Company 1987

Kenne Fant   *Alfred Nobel: A Biography*   Arcade 1993

P.N. Furbank   *Diderot: A Critical Biography*   Alfred A. Knopf 1992

Betty Glad   *In Search of the Great White House*   W.W. Norton & Co. 1980

Albert Goldman   *Ladies and Gentlemen-Lenny Bruce!!*   Random House 1972

Albert Goldman   *The Lives of John Lennon*   Bantam Books 1989

Walter   Kaufmann   *Nietzsche.   Philosopher,   Psychologist,   Antichrist*   Princeton University Press 1989

Andre Le Vot   *F. Scott Fitzgerald*   Doubleday 1983

Joseph Page   *Peron: A Biography*   Random House 1983

James Pada   *Peter Lawford: The Man who Kept the Secrets*   Bantam Doubleday 1991

Joy Parini, ed.   *Writer Against the Grain*   Columbia University Press 1992

Shabtai Teveth   *Ben-Gurion: The Burning Ground 1886–1948*   Outlet 1988

Scorpio

(October 24–November 27)

Justice, power, sex and money,
This is Scorpio's food and honey.
Extremes are what they know about,
All or nothing is their route.
Collective guilt, weighs them down,
Pain and suffering is their crown.
Their gifts are energy and great passion,
Their genius puts them ahead of fashion.

Ruler: Pluto   **Symbol: Scorpion**
Element: Water   **Number: Zero**

The soul enters Scorpio focused and centered within, sensitive and vulnerable without. This is the sign of contradictions and extremes; of polar opposites contained by powerful emotions that are either rising to the heights of ecstasy or falling into the depths of despair. Restless, self-taught, and ambitious, Scorpios strive for stability and permanence in a world they have created by the sheer power of their will. Answering only to themselves, Scorpios question even God's authority. As they bring their lives to the edge over and over again, creating one crisis after another, they are able to shed the habits and restrictions of their past, access the essence of their soul, and be the catalysts of monumental change. This is a process that integrates all opposites, including good and evil, Ego and Spirit.

In Cancer, the previous water sign, the past was accessed through memory, a process that blended fact with fiction. Scorpio adds the future, and projects itself into an ideal world it prefers to the moment. Your challenge is to create that world in the now, not to get stuck in nostalgia or dreams. Vivien Leigh (November 5), the actress best known for her role as Scarlett O'Hara, "molded her days from dream and fantasy which never contained defeat, and she had lived in the future where almost anything could happen." When you can be in the moment and draw strength from your past experiences and your vision, you're ready to create your perfect world. Don't wait for circumstances to be ideal; make do with what you've got. You're a genius at recycling, restructuring, and reorganizing whatever you get your hands on. This ability to intermingle what *was, is,* and *could be* into form is the gift of creation and transformation. Within you are the means and confidence to overcome any obstacle in your path. You have the secret of transcending the moment, and this is true power.

Like your ruling planet Pluto, your small stature wisely masks the magnitude of your strength. You mingle with others without them knowing just how ambitious you really are. Your delicate and refined physical nature is what reflects your power, not according to Ego's measurements, which are bulk and muscle, but in alignment with Spirit and Nature's laws. Harmony and symmetry are what count here. In Nature, exterior perfection reflects good health and the ability to survive. Scorpio produces classical beauties such as Princess Grace of Monaco (November 12) and Linda Evans (November 18) of *Dynasty* fame.

Scorpios are not just beautiful, they are mighty creatures with great magnetism and a personality that struggles between extreme contradictions. You're the young genius and the adult child; the cold, indifferent heart and the compassionate healer. Shy at times, you can also be recklessly courageous. You believe yourself to be everything and nothing. Either spiritually pure, or the rebel overthrowing heavenly authority by becoming your own moral law, you walk a thin line between saint and criminal.

Scorpio is about the unity of all points of view contained in one person, giving the Scorpio great talents but no escape from a life of inner struggle. The obstacles of the outside world are nothing compared to the battles that rage within. Even the cool analytical force of reason, so powerful in the previous sign of Libra, hasn't a chance against unbridled emotion. When it rises, so does panic, because you lose control. But if you don't let go, you can't fall in love, or truly enjoy sex, or be totally in the moment. Scorpio is about surrender, opening yourself up to life, love, and God. Don't fight the pull to trust in faith and loosen your grasp on your possessions. If you don't, sooner or later the universe will give you a kick and you won't have a choice. You need to experience your feelings in order to achieve objectivity. With objectivity, feelings can be used for personal gain or for social change.

If you're still in your selfish mode, be careful. Power that's not shared, becomes destructive. When you shut down the process of evolution, pressure builds—the kind that can explode like an atom bomb, or launch a soul high enough to look God in the face. Both are deforming and destructive experiences.

Don't dismiss emotions as inconsequential; they are the essence of power and spirits way of connecting us to others and God. In Scorpio, even hate and anger are preferable to indifference. If this is your sign, you will experience the highs and lows of moods and feelings, establishing their limits so that you will know once and for all you can surrender and survive. It's understandable that you may feel the need to temporarily shut down to gain a semblance of control. Georgia O'Keeffe (November 15) said, "Self-control is a wonderful thing—I think we must even keep ourselves from feeling too much—often if we are going to keep sane and see with a clear unprejudiced vision." A constant fear of being overwhelmed by feelings can make you prefer the reputation of being cold-hearted to the experience of powerlessness that comes when emotions prevail. Turgenev (November 9), the Russian writer, became obsessed with a married woman who refused to leave her husband or become his mistress. The attraction is to rejection. This is not uncommon for a Scorpio. You often pick a partner you can never have. This places control in the hands of someone else and allows you to experience the process of surrender without having to worry about the next step, which is merging and transforming. As long as you remain caught in the battle of polarities, love will be a roller-coaster ride from ecstasy to pain. However, it is only through experiencing your emotional extremes that you will gain faith and confidence in your ability to live through them and achieve objectivity. As you gain faith in yourself and begin to rise above your emotions, they find their proper place in your psyche.

Beauty, both inner and outer, is important to a Scorpio. You're either totally consumed with your appearance, presenting a perfect picture like Princess Grace, or you sleep in your clothes, like Bill Gates (October 28). If the inner world of truth and spirit is ignored, exterior beauty will become too important. Vivien Leigh was a perfectionist. Her personal "fastidiousness edged on being a fetish. Dozens and dozens of white gloves (at one time about seventy-five pairs) freshly cleaned and meticulously wrapped in tissue, occupied her top drawer."

Your need to have things perfect can make you turn your world into a brilliant jewel. As the alchemist of the zodiac, you have the power to bring something to perfection and you're given all the talents to make it happen. Insight gives you the vision to recognize the essence of anything, and your great discerning ability allows you to chisel away any superfluousness that hides true beauty or meaning. You love things simple, pure, and perfect. Your talent is to create form from the formless. You mold emotional content into a creation that seems to live with a vitality of its own. This is the house of sex and from this magical emotional expression a new being is often brought into the world. Scorpio contains the qualities of a great teacher, the ability to recognize the students' potential and bring it out through the right challenges.

Success in Scorpio is not a mysterious thing. Hard work brings rewards. You're not afraid of getting your hands dirty. Mistakes don't bother you, either; you have the confidence to jump in and move things around until you get them right. You recognize opportunity and you have the courage to risk yourself by going after it. Field Marshal Montgomery (November 17), the English WW II military commander, said, "At certain moments in life an opportunity is presented to each one of us; some of us are not aware of the full significance of what has happened, and the moment is lost. Others, alert and enthusiastic seize the opportunity with both hands and turn it to good advantage; these have ambition; as every man worth his salt should have . . .''

The Scorpio's confidence is based on experience. You survive one crisis after another. You love them; they make you come alive. Ted Turner's (November 19) chief financial officer Will Sanders says, ''Every project he took on had the potential to sink him. No sooner did you feel like you were comfortable and able to breathe a little bit than we'd take on some other impossible task.''

The need to risk builds faith in oneself and in a higher power. But it requires courage and a desire to do the impossible. Thomas Corcoran said of Robert Kennedy, ''He obviously enjoyed approaching the brink of the impossible.'' Jodie Foster (November 19) chose to continue with a stage performance after being informed that a man who wanted to kill her was in the audience.

Danger, difficulty and the impossible are attractions. Whether riding the rapids in Colorado or risking a fortune on a new idea, you only feel your blood flowing when you've pushed yourself beyond earthly limits.

The ability to be spontaneous and take a risk demands you be in the moment—and that means you must take responsibility for where you are and who you are. You've got to immerse yourself in pain and discomfort. Don't avoid life by living in your dreams. If their past is too painful, many Scorpios sever it from their memory and focus on the future.

Of course, repressed feelings work on our unconscious and broaden our shadow. Scorpios can have deep shadows and dark moods. They struggle with depression and sometimes contemplate suicide.

The avoidance of pain and suffering causes them to retreat from life and retract within themselves, but this only leads to more suffering. However, by surrendering to pain, one passes through it and reaches pleasure. Despair follows a Scorpio until he or she finds the courage to surrender to it. When you stop avoiding the pain of separateness, alienation and aloneness, you allow yourself to be carried beyond emptiness to fullness and unity. Scorpios need to rid themselves of the old feelings by going through and beyond them. This is difficult because Scorpio is a water sign which absorbs, giving the Scorpio an amazing ability to memorize and remember. This great memory makes the Scorpio child seem adultlike and gifted. Jodie Foster spoke full sentences at one year and taught herself to read at age three. Dick Cavett (November 19) was smarter than all the other kids at school. Bill Gates put his high school's schedule on a computer program he invented.

This powerful memory is both useful and damaging. It can do horrible things to relationships. You never give someone a chance to change. You're always reliving the past hurt unless, of course, you've developed the skill of emptying yourself. The process of emptying and receiving anew will keep you growing and transforming. Without space in your heart, God cannot enter.

The Scorpio environment is often extreme. Georgia O'Keeffe was born in Wisconsin, where the landscape was sparse and abstract. This water sign is attracted to places that jolt the senses, for example, the beach. Besides the powerful experience of sand, sun and water, the beach allows the Scorpio to go naked, something they love to do. In fact, many are shameless. They seek freedom to express and enjoy the gifts of nature. Nature itself is Scorpionic. Its surface beauty hides a deep and intense struggle to survive. Seagulls floating in the sky make a lovely picture. However, they are hunting, searching the waters below for fish.

In Taurus, Scorpio's opposite sign, desire emerged in the form of "I want." In Scorpio, you feel the desires and yearnings of others. Instead of being concerned about self-nourishment, you may feel depressed about the hunger of the masses and want to do something to change their plight. This is the beginning of guilt. From this point on the soul cannot exist solely for itself. It feels the connection to all things and it knows that one person has the power to effect change in the world. It's time to use your energy and wisdom to make a difference. These are the social reformers and politicians. Our institutions are developed to protect us from the unreasonable demands of others on our possessions, our ideas and our freedoms, and to guarantee fairness and justice for all. Scorpio rules either the establishment of these institutions or their destruction, which occurs when they fail to achieve their purpose. In Scorpio, the law is often taken into one's own hands when society or government doesn't provide enough protection, or if it tries to limit personal freedom. Robert Kennedy found the system lacking when he finally nailed Jimmy Hoffa. Even his overwhelming evidence against Hoffa was not enough to keep the union leader from returning to racketeering. Kennedy sought to establish new laws to deal with the unions and the Mafia. Hillary Rodham Clinton (October 26) is frustrated by the court's inability to protect children. A large part of her law practice was dedicated to the protection of children.

Scorpio is the perfect breeding ground for revolution, this is the sign of the rebel. This is where creative ideas and energies meet the resisting wall of rules and regulations and narrow minds. If you're a Scorpio who has opted for repetition instead of transformation, you may struggle with depression and the feeling of being stuck in a life without a purpose.

Getting close to a Scorpio is either the easiest thing in the world or the hardest. However, you can glimpse their truth through their incredible eyes. Their stare is direct and reveals the intensity of their inner nature. Richard Burton (November 10) and John Keats (October 31) had the Scorpio eyes. Robert Kennedy's eyes were, "Like pale blue razor blades, they pierced through anyone in conversation.'' The Scorpio's eyes also reveal the paradox of their personalities. Vivien Leigh got the part of Scarlett O'Hara in *Gone With the Wind* because she could project the heroine's dual nature. ''There was about her a wildness that flashed in her eyes, and yet few women had more outward composure, elegance, or style.''

The Scorpio is an eccentric and a loner. You don't want to fit in. When you accept your desire to stand apart you will find others accepting you. Georgia O'Keeffe dressed like a man. Marie Curie (November 7) took an apartment in Paris alone at the turn of the century. When Scorpios are true to themselves, they're not concerned about what others do or think. Yet, their indifference is seldom returned. Scorpios never get ambiguous reviews. Others either love or hate them.

Scorpio is a fixed sign and so the process is what's important here, not the end results. Don't worry about where you're going—just get going. By doing, you learn. Hard work helps you focus on the moment. Work is holy. It helps put your beliefs into action, and this is true power. The common man is the hero in Scorpio. Dignity and nobility are gained through struggle. The poor come closer to following in Christ's footsteps, embracing pain and suffering as a part of the process of redemption, forgiveness, and reconciliation.

Scorpio learns by absorbing. You have confidence in your ability to size up a situation and quickly reduce its complexity. Brigadier Essame said of General Montgomery, ''He could describe a complex situation with amazing lucidity and sum up a long exercise without the use of a single note. He looked straight into the eyes of the audience when he spoke. He had a remarkable flair for picking out the essence of a problem, and for indicating its solution with startling clarity.'' This ability instantly to problem solve, to go to the essence, ignoring the superfluous, makes you leaders. Your courage can often seem foolish. Robert Kennedy taught himself how to swim by jumping into the Nantucket Sound! But by immersing yourself, you force yourself to open up to life, allowing it to reveal its secrets.

To do this requires that judgment be left by the wayside. Keats surrendered to nature and it spoke to him. Dostoyevsky (November 11) believed that ''whoever approaches things with openness and sympathy (love) will also receive an answer. Things will begin to talk to him, to speak within him.'' Scorpios have an incessant need to understand whatever it is they are doing. But since they only learn from the inside out, they must first absorb it, possess it, and become it. When they know it all, they're ready for action. Don't touch their work. Don't teach them. They'll learn their own way through experience, trial and error. They avoid input from others. Rodin (November 12), the famous French sculptor, was self-taught. Madame Curie was educated at home by her father. The normal route of school doesn't always work for a Scorpio. They're often late bloomers who don't come into their talent until they immerse themselves in life. The sooner you throw yourself into life, the sooner you'll discover yourself and God. Dostoyevsky's Father Zosima said "You must love all that God has created, both his entire world and each single tiny sand grain of it. If you love all things you will also attain the divine mystery that is in all things."

The desire for unity highlights the discrepancy between what you feel inside and what exists in the world. Art struggles with this all the time. Georgia O'Keeffe felt the discrepancy between the color of things as they are known and as she perceived them. The awareness of this division can drive a perfectionistic Scorpio crazy. Camus (November 7), called this division *the absurd*. "... this mind and this world, straining against each other without being able to embrace." This chasm or division is particularly harmful when ignored. Instead of striving to bridge the gap by changing and transforming your perceptions, you attempt to impose the past on the present. This happens a lot in relationships. You meet someone charming and new and immediately your old emotional baggage comes into play. You know he's going to betray you, just like your first husband did. The ability to empty yourself emotionally is a Scorpio challenge. The more often you do it, the more rewarding and creative your life becomes.

This Scorpio chasm is the new you meeting your old habits and routine. Without change, your life will lack a sense of purpose. Only by taking a leap of faith can you experience something new. Scorpio is the sign of metamorphosis, of death and rebirth. The Scorpio tries to bridge the gap of faith by living their belief, not just talking about it.

Hillary Clinton said "... the practical method of trying to live as a Christian in a difficult, challenging world, was very appealing to me."

The continuous dance between Ego and Spirit comes to a dead end in Scorpio. Ideally, Ego should surrender to Spirit. This happens during the moment of sexual orgasm. This surrender should occur in other places, too, but Ego is not so eager to give up its power. Instead, it allows Spirit to take the lead, but it tries to sabotage any growth, spiritual or otherwise. But Spirit is not afraid. Now at the helm, it starts making an impact. The soul feels the pull to detach from possessions and experiences the need to help others. If, however, faith has not yet been implanted in your soul, you may panic at this point and cling more ferociously to things. To counteract the need to surrender, you strive for more worldly power, hoping to acquire enough resources to hold fate at bay. Superstition is another way to feel in control of your environment. By repeating an act or a ritual, you believe you have the power to repeat a response; you gain control over your environment. This is the beginning of tradition and religious dogma—the striving for control through repetition of the old.

Ego now has a new plan. Since Spirit gains its power over man through faith in God, all Ego has to do to take back control is cast doubt on faith.

How can God exist if children and the innocent suffer? Ted Turner asked this question when he had to witness his beloved little sister die a painful death from lupus erythematosus. When Robert Kennedy was asked about God he said, "If God exists, why do poor people exist? Why does a Hitler arise? I can't give an answer for that, only faith."

If your faith is wavering, start piling up the sandbags. In Scorpio, faith will be tested over and over again. Nothing less than a leap of faith is required in order to continue the upward swing of the spiral. Scorpios who take this leap become our inventors, our psychics, and our spiritual leaders.

Scorpio is the desire to have God use your voice. This is Billy Graham (November 7), preacher. In accepting the Nobel Prize, Albert Camus said, ". . . the silence of an unknown prisoner subjected to humiliations at the other end of the world is enough to tear the writer from exile, at least whenever he manages, amid the privileges of freedom, not to forget that silence but to give it voice by means of art."

Oscar Wilde said that there are two great tragedies in life, never getting your wish, and getting it. Only God can see the whole picture, so it's better to leave things in His hands. Scorpios are the intermediaries between His will and the people. These are the physicians who heal through God's power. However, if you're not ready to turn your power over to the real source, you could opt for a more tangible individual like a guru, a boss, a lover, or your mother. If you make the wrong choice, you take on all their baggage and you end up living their lives, not your own. The surrender will happen; it's up to you to make it positive. There is nothing wrong with temporary surrender; it's how a Scorpio learns and grows. Life is a cycle of giving and receiving, of going and returning. Give yourself over and come home to the source.

If you don't have faith and you want to play God, then you'll only be interested in having your way—no rules, no laws, no moral guidance but yourself. Dangerous? Absolutely. For without something higher and greater than yourself, the tyrant within emerges and refuses to tolerate other points of view. Negative power looks for a scapegoat, somebody upon whom they can feel superior or place the responsibility for their actions. In Scorpio, forgiveness can be a form of revenge. If someone does something against you, this gives them power over you. However, if you thank or forgive them, you take back the power. To hurt someone gives you a sense of power. And, "To want pity is to want others to suffer with us." Self-sacrifice also brings increased feelings of power and superiority. Self-respect is an issue. According to Nietzsche, "our self-respect depends on our ability to repay in kind both the good and the bad." Scorpios lead the way here. Don't step on their toes; you'll lose your foot. You hurt them today and when you return in ten years, they'll be waiting.

Scorpio rules death. The most powerful catalyst for change is the fear of death. Facing death shocks the psyche into a crisis and begins the process of disintegration, which must occur in order for the new self to emerge. "In many cultures and religions members must be willing to confront not only physical death but also ego death. This is the death of an old identity no longer appropriate to one's current stage of development. The old sense of self must die and out of its ashes must blossom a new identity appropriate to one's developmental or spiritual goal."

Marshal Montgomery experienced a mental breakdown when his wife died. Picasso (October 25) was believed to be stillborn and would have died if his uncle hadn't blown cigar smoke in his face, causing him to stir. Ted Turner lost his sister and his father when he was a child. Richard Burton and Dick Cavett were children when their mothers died. Robert Kennedy lost his two brothers. Bill Gates's best friend in high school died in a hiking accident. Hillary Clinton says the death of John F. Kennedy was a turning point in her life. Dostoyevsky faced death himself. Arrested for conspiring against the government, he actually stood on the scaffold before he received a pardon. "Imagine if I am turned back to life, imagine how endless it will seem. A whole eternity and this eternity will belong to me! Then I will live each minute as a century without losing any of it, and I will keep an account of each minute and not waste a moment!"

Scorpios can put themselves in the now more powerfully than any other sign. Because of this, they have access to unlimited power and charisma. Scorpios desire to own their power. Georgia O'Keeffe said, "I had a sense of power. I always had it." Truman Capote said that Robert Kennedy had the power to make people jump.

If power is your thing, and you like playing God, then you might be an evangelist or a revolutionary. They both collect the power and emotions of the masses and they both are seeking a transformation. A great deal of their power is their ability to focus. A friend of Georgia O'Keeffe said about her that "Everything is done with full attention." For the sign ruled by Pluto, every small detail becomes important when you're totally present in the moment. Simple things glow with a brilliance, life is filled with intensity, colors and objects come alive through the power of the Scorpio eye.

Scorpio is the midlife crisis of the zodiac. It's time to reevaluate your life because you see the end is near. In Libra, what died was the mask, or your identity. In Scorpio, the process of destruction continues, and what collapses is the psyche. Mental habits, attitudes, and the limitations of perceptions decay. The blocks formed by emotional garbage are collapsed. The psyche, tired of stagnation, creates a crisis to facilitate the process of transformation. "What is destroyed in this process is the old, limiting concept of oneself and the corresponding restricting view of existence and of the universe." The process can be dangerous in the body and soul of a weak, negative, and spiritually devoid person. A history of anger, abuse, and violence can keep the soul stuck in the process of disintegration and dismemberment and prevent it from completing the process. The yearning to merge with God is symbolized in the sacred mass. The need to absorb another person or ideal, to possess it so completely that their is no separation between you and the object is a Scorpio desire.

The containment of opposites in Scorpio leads to complex individuals, even split personalities. Grace Kelly seemed cool and aloof, but was really passionate. Bill Gates, called "Binary Bill of polar contradictions," can be charming and rude, shy and aggressive. Barbara Gelb of the *New York Times* said of Richard Burton, "He is simultaneously the dark and self-destructive Celt and the glossy idealization of classical actor, circumspect and disciplined." Robert Louis Stevenson (November 11) created the characters of Dr. Jekyll and Mr. Hyde. Dr. Jekyll cannot accept his baser instincts and so they are lived out without restrictions in Mr. Hyde, a split-off part of himself. Stevenson masterfully depicts the hate and ecstasy that surrounds the struggle to unite good and evil within oneself.

In Scorpio, evil is overcome by good. However, when the two worlds cannot unite, when the mask refuses to integrate the whole being, a mental breakdown can occur. Vivien Leigh was diagnosed as a manic-depressive. Some even thought she was schizophrenic.

Evil, or your baser instincts, cannot be avoided. If you run from them, you'll run right into them. Mr. Hyde eventually commits murder and Dr. Jekyll must deal with the consequences. Jesus said, "All things evil come from within." Paracelsus, a Sagittarius, and a sixteenth-century physician and philosopher said, "He who knows no repentance and no suffering can offer no resistance to the devil. You must know your enemy and your weaknesses, it is the only way to self-mastery . . ." In Scorpio, evil exists as a path to forgiveness and goodness. Sin is inevitable in a world of choice; man pays for his sins through suffering. Suffering leads to happiness because one has earned the right to forgive oneself. Suffering purifies the soul. Therefore, sin is both necessary and productive.

In Scorpio, nothing goes to waste. That means they're great at transforming leftovers into gourmet dishes or redesigning old clothes into new fashion. The coffee grounds fertilize the plants, paper is used on both sides, and they've been recycling long before it was a law. If you show them that you've got a talent or a resource, they'll tap it, use it and often abuse it. If your skills are mechanical, you'll be fixing their washing machine at two in the morning and wondering how in the devil they got you there. On the positive side, they know how to get the most and the best out of anything or anyone. They'll bring out talents you didn't know you had. They know how to make money multiply. They're great on Wall Street, which combines this talent with the element of risk they so love.

Scorpio rules excrement. It's the first gift we give to the world and how it's received is important. If you want your child to be a financial genius, don't make potty training a negative event. Be excited about his simple offering and he'll be on his way to a successful career. Of course, the other extreme is always a possibility and a Scorpio can be wasteful.

Mystery, secrets, and the unknown attract a Scorpio almost as much as sex. They love unlocking the secrets of the world or your diary, or solving a murder or a riddle. They make great detectives, occultists, spiritual leaders, and healers. They're methodical in their approach to a problem and refuse to give up until they understand what's going on. They plow ahead with phenomenal confidence. Don't try to hide anything from a Scorpio. Don't cheat in a relationship unless you want to get caught. The one strand of blond hair on the bathroom sink will catch their discerning eye.

Scorpio represents the abandonment and exile of Adam and Eve. Scorpios experience some form of abandonment or exile during their lives. It's part of the pain and suffering that comes from choosing their own path, from the loneliness of choosing consciousness instead of instinctual response. Most experience abandonment in subtle ways. A parent can favor one child over another. Friends might leave when you exercise your individuality. Exile is abandonment in the extreme. Dostoyevsky was exiled to Siberia. Lise Meitner (November 7), the great physicist, lived in exile in Sweden during World War II. Hillary Rodham Clinton had to move to Arkansas when she married. However, the other side of abandonment and exile is reconciliation and forgiveness, the return to Eden and to God.

Scorpios have access to universal knowledge, this makes them seem like geniuses. That access brings with it the pain and suffering of the collective. They're the champions of the poor and helpless. Without much prodding, the Scorpio can take responsibility for the poor, the hungry, your mother's depression, and the fact that your sister didn't go to the senior prom. It doesn't matter what it is; if they feel it, they are responsible. In a metaphysical way, they are not wrong. Each of us is linked to the other and if one person is hurt or hungry, it affects everyone. In Scorpio, it's important to become a shining example for others to follow. Dostoyevesky's Father Zosima says, "Instead of passing judgment on others you must suffer for their misdeeds— as if you yourself had performed them." Scorpio is the sign in which we become aware that what we do influences others, that we're all connected and everything we do comes back to us. In Camus's *The Plague,* Tarrou says, "I learned that I had had an indirect hand in the deaths of thousands of people; that I had brought about their deaths by approving of acts and principles which could only end in that way." When Scorpio guilt is strong, happiness is never quite achieved.

Scorpio is a loner, an individual who learns through experience. As a result, you can be selfish and even a bit narcissistic. One needs solitude and self-involvement for the spiritual journey and the creative life. Speaking of

Picasso, Norman Mailer said, "One's narcissism can be a handmaiden to one's art. Sometimes it takes no less than a long immersion in oneself to deliver the artist within." Realize that you have to be both selfish and selfless. Eventually, the gap will narrow and unity will be achieved. You'll be able to choose the appropriate response to any situation.

Art, as usual, plays an important part in this sign. Here the artist attempts to present all points of view. Picasso did this with Cubism. Art in Scorpio has a powerful emotional impact. For Georgia O'Keeffe, "the entire visual world was dependent on the emotional world. The power of a painting depended not only upon technical skill but also upon emotive powers." The artists of this sign merge, absorb, and surrender to their art, desiring also to possess it. The need to play God is part of the experience. A desire to impart life to inanimate objects is the challenge. Picasso said, "One should be able to take a piece of wood and turn it into a bud." He also said, "God is really another artist like me," and "I am God."

There is such a thin veil between the Scorpio's inner world of magic and the outer world of reality, that sometimes they lose sight of which is which. This water sign rules hallucination. Dostoyevsky said, "What didn't I find to dream about in my youth? What didn't I live with my whole soul in golden and blazing daydreams that merely resembled opium hallucinations!" When they work, they can go for days without sleep, consumed by their creation. It feeds them as they create it, surrendering, possessing, transforming themselves as they reproduce for the world that which lives within them.

Love and relationships are not easy for a Scorpio. They have more than a few control issues to deal with. To begin with, if the relationship is not intense, a Scorpio is not interested. He would rather settle for a friendship or no relationship at all. Nothing less than extreme intensity brings the Scorpio to the surface to connect. They either appear detached and cold, or lustful, eager to express their sexuality at the spur of any moment. At a party or in a crowd, they can be aloof or the center of attention. They stand out no matter what. The need to surrender is always present, as well as the fear of losing control. But each time you surrender and return to yourself, you're different and the process becomes easier.

Some Scorpios are romantic. They can lose themselves in their dreams and desires. At the other extreme is the primal Scorpio, the one who has little restraint or finesse. Sex is very important. They need the physical connection, the intensity of surrender and control. When they lean toward the ethereal, then the relationship can have a heavenly basis. They desire a spiritual bond, a union of souls. Madame Curie and her husband had a wonderful marriage because they had a common goal and a purpose that was greater than them both: a desire to contribute something to humanity. If God has nothing to do with the Scorpio's union, then it can be a struggle for power and dominance and the dark feelings of hate and abuse can be as much of an attraction as love. Turgenev was attracted to negative women because of his violent mother. He said, "I'm not happy until a woman has her heel on my neck and is pushing my face into the mud."

When it comes to being a lover, no one is better. Richard Burton had an insatiable sexual appetite, in spite of his love for Elizabeth Taylor. He was known to sleep with any woman who was willing, yet the rumor was he was not an indifferent participant. Ted Turner was also known to fool around. His friend Lawrence Brenner said that where women were concerned, "he had a sort of trophy mentality." A woman had to sacrifice not just her body and her will, but her peace of mind to live with Picasso. Many did so, willingly.

When it comes to professions, there is not much a Scorpio cannot do. However, they are particularly gifted as physicians. They like pressure and being on the edge. They make great psychologists because of their keen insight into the essence of a soul and their ability to bring others out, allowing them to shine. Their eye for the beautiful gives them talent as decorators, jewelers, or fashion designers. Their ability to impart knowledge makes them wonderful teachers. When it comes to using resources, they're the best. Wall Street has a long list of famous Scorpios. Politics intrigues even the most passive because they believe so strongly in social reform. Gifted with great voices, Scorpios make good actors or singers. They're master creators, and whether it's as a painter, writer, or poet, they shine.

Scorpios are living contradictions. They're the Bill Gateses, the Ted Turners, the Madame Curies of the world. They persevere when others have long ago given up. They see solutions in a blink of an eye. They seem to channel their information rather than process it, and just when you think they're down and done for, they regroup and outrun you by leaps and bounds. All these gifts make them great achievers but the price they pay is high. For the Scorpio, peace is not resting by the fire. It is being in the midst of a crisis when every part of their being comes alive. They have presence, strength, courage, and compassion and when they put that together with faith, the world is never the same.

THE SCORPIO ENVIRONMENT

The Scorpio environment is extreme. It either possesses you entirely, trying to absorb the essence of your being, demanding everything you have to give and more, or it cuts you off, leaving you feeling abandoned, isolated and alone. Life is sprinkled with crises, events that seem beyond your control. Your challenge is to face them straight on, using your knowledge and your experience as your resources, your vision of the future as your guide. The extreme environment hones your creative power and teaches you how to transcend the moment by being fully present in it. You have looked the illusionary demon in the eye and it has lost its power. Now, you know for sure that faith in yourself and a higher power is all that you need to be happy.

Scorpio/*One* (October 28, November 1, November 10, November 19) Pluto/Sun

PURPOSE: *To balance independence and freedom with the need to make a difference in the world through helping those who have no voice.*

"What doesn't kill me only makes me strong."—Nietzsche. The Scorpio/*One* is strong, secretive, and competitive. When they're spiritual, they are perfectionists and may refuse to bend even on the smallest detail. If they do not believe in a higher power, then anything goes. Lying becomes a talent and they are capable of molding reality to fit their needs. Their childhood was not easy. Either their father was missing or he ruled with an iron hand. They need to learn to take their power and walk their own path. Obstacles are there to hone their strength and their emotions. Feelings are either controlled and hidden or out of control. If they choose a cause to fight for, it will be freedom and justice. Their persistent nature, their ability to observe and absorb, give them great artistic ability or people skills. With their great charisma, they find themselves either as the center of the party or they play the role of rebel and provoke authority, refusing to be a part of the group. Their desire for excellence can make them strive for physical and moral perfection. Intimacy is a problem, they avoid closeness, while at the same time long for someone who can intuitively understands them. The Scorpio/*One* loves the mysterious and the unknown. They make great psychics and occultists, and some see spirits or hear voices from the other world. Authority will always be an issue. Faith is the key. Life tests their beliefs and shows them exactly how far they're willing to go to hold on to their dreams. Hard work helps to center the Scorpio/*One*. Travel and just plain experience is what they need to center themselves and find their path.

IF SPIRIT TAKES THE LEAD: With Spirit strong, the Scorpio/*One* has high principles. They are righteous and difficult to please and to work for. Their lives are not easy because they refuse to disguise their truth in any way. They need to learn how to present their beliefs without alienating the world or setting themselves up for attack. They have a desire to save the world. They need to love themselves as much as their truth. In this way, they can protect themselves from abuse.

IF EGO TAKES THE LEAD: Without a balance of Spirit, the Scorpio/*One* may experience abuse, either physically or emotionally. The world is tough, demanding, and cold. They are loners who don't trust because as a child their boundaries were invaded. They seek control. Either they feel helpless and give their power away, or they are tyrannical and impose their will on others. They are uncertain about their beliefs, and change their values to get their way. Success is a possibility, but happiness will be harder to attain because love requires faith and the experience of surrender.

WILLIAM HENRY GATES (October 28)

Cowriter of Microsoft BASIC; inventor of the WINDOWS operating system.

Gates is the youngest self-made billionaire in history.

Born in Seattle, he is the only son and the second of three children. As a child, Gates was considered a nerd. He didn't fit in until he found computers. He put his high school's scheduling program on computer and became a legend at Lakeside High. At Harvard, he started his own company, Traf-O-Data, with his best friend, Paul Allen. After selling his software program, Microsoft BASIC, he dropped out of school. At the age of twenty-five, he offered IBM a program called DOS which would become the essential operating system for over a hundred million computer users and the basis of the Gates empire. Known as "Binary Bill," he exhibits the many-faceted personality of a Scorpio. With a company now worth more than seven billion dollars, he has proven that when you believe in your vision, you can make it happen.

JODIE FOSTER (November 19)

Actress.

A child genius, Foster was speaking at nine months, using sentences at one year, and teaching herself to read at three. She hardly knew her father; her parents divorced before she was born. Foster's mother managed her career. As a child, Foster did TV commercials and movies. At age thirteen, three of her films were shown at the Cannes Film Festival: *Taxi Driver, Bugsy Malone,* and *The Little Girl Who Lives Down the Lane.* Like most Scorpios, Foster is self-taught; she never studied acting. In 1985, she graduated from Yale, where she majored in creative writing and literature. In 1989, she won the Academy Award for Best Actress for her performance in *The Accused,* a story about a young woman who is gang-raped. In 1991 she won again for *Silence of the Lambs.* The ability of a Scorpio to attract obsession was evident when John W. Hinckley, Jr. tried to assassinate President Ronald Reagan to get her attention.

Scorpio/*Two* (October 29, November 2, November 11, November 20) Pluto/Moon

PURPOSE: To experience your emotions allowing the highs and lows to come and go so that you can gain confidence and control in your life without losing the passion.

Scorpio/*Twos* struggle between wanting to be alone and wanting to communicate their feelings. Sometimes, they are prolific writers or creative artists with a unique approach to life. Fantasy is strong; Scorpio/*Twos* have the power to visualize and manifest their vision in the now. The danger for them is becoming nostalgic about their past. They make good psychologists, healers, and physicians. The pain and weaknesses of others affects them. They are strong and resilient. They have incredible courage, the kind that can make a difference in the world. Their life is full of drama; they're emotional, creative, and unique. If they conform too much, it can lead to depression and mood swings. If their emotions are blocked, they may struggle with a physical handicap or an unusual illness. They need faith in themselves and a higher power. Their attraction to the occult can lead to God or to an insane guru. If they stay centered, their power and sense of compassion can be a great help to all who know them.

IF SPIRIT TAKES THE LEAD: If Spirit is strong, the Scorpio/*Two* can lead a revolution or topple the government. They are persistent and resilient. They have a tendency to want to heal others, and to help them overcome insurmountable odds. They should use their faith in allegiance with their instincts; otherwise, they could enslave themselves to someone else's desires.

IF EGO TAKES THE LEAD: If Ego is strong, so are superstition, ritual, and tradition. The Scorpio/*Two* is attracted to the mysteries of life and strives for constant emotional control. They either isolate themselves or create a series of emotional dramas that keep the attention on them. They need to be careful that they don't use the image of martyr or victim as a means to control and manipulate others. They're incredibly intuitive and when they want to hurt, they go right for the jugular. Seductive and charming, they get exactly what they want.

FYODOR DOSTOYEVSKY (November 11)

Writer.

Dostoyevsky was born into a religious family. His first novel, *The Poor,* was a huge success and he was immediately invited into the homes and circles of the elite. But his ego was not mature enough for such acclaim, and he aroused as much animosity as he did praise. Dostoyevsky suffered loneliness and isolation; he longed for the unity of all people and for universal oneness. This desire to better the world brought him to join the Petrashevsky Circle, in which questions of freedom, social injustice, and the suffering of the common man were discussed. His association with these free thinkers brought about his arrest and he was sentenced to death. While standing on the scaffold, he was pardoned by the tsar and sent to Siberia, where he worked alongside criminals. Dostoyevsky saw goodness in all men. All of Russia mourned his death. Gone was a voice that posed the right questions, a voice that believed in God and the ability to transform life through suffering.

ROBERT KENNEDY (October 29)

Attorney general; presidential candidate.

The seventh of nine children, Robert Kennedy had to fight for his father's attention. Shorter than his brothers, he felt inadequate and insecure. Attending six different schools in ten years didn't help develop his self-confidence. Like most Scorpios, Kennedy's true genius was nurtured by experience and his keen sense of observation. After graduating from Harvard, Kennedy helped his brother Jack in his bid for a seat in the Massachusetts House of Representatives and his own political career began. Kennedy's work for a Senate select committee investigating racketeering gave him a reputation of being someone to reckon with. The organizational genius behind Jack's campaign for president, Kennedy became attorney general.

Ramsey Clark said of Kennedy that, "He just had this burning passion to help people who had been denied justice." Kennedy was assassinated during his California campaign for the presidency. His legacy is carried on through his children, several of whom have entered politics.

Scorpio/*Three* (October 30, November 3, November 12, November 21) Pluto/Jupiter

PURPOSE: To overcome your defiance of authority by dedicating your experience, knowledge, and leadership ability to a higher cause, knowing that through service to others you will achieve the perfection and greatness that you desire.

"Human beings, by changing the inner attitudes of their minds, can change the outer aspects of their lives."—George Bernard Shaw. The Scorpio/*Threes'* beliefs are what give them confidence. They've tested the beliefs in the world and know they work. Their attraction to difficult, even insurmountable projects or people is a problem. Their life becomes a never-ending quest for an impossible goal. If life chooses to reward all their efforts, they might face another dilemma— how to deal with receiving instead of conquering. However, if they experienced defeat too early in life, before having gained self-confidence, they will doubt their ability to do great things. It is important that the Scorpio/*Threes* realize their need to accomplish things of an heroic nature, and make themselves aware of the difficulties they create through this desire. The Scorpio/*Three* is a loner, and intimacy is a problem. They love freedom and live by their own rules. Loyalty, truth, and justice are important. Authority is always an issue. The Scorpio/*Three* should be his own boss. They use their ironic sense of humor to keep some people at bay and everyone laughing. A love of travel and foreign things is common, as well as a feeling that fate is closing in on their freedom. The Scorpio/*Three* is a born leader. They can either be rebels or persons who want to be recognized as important by society. What they need more than anything else is faith in themselves, based not on impossible dreams but on actual experience.

IF SPIRIT TAKES THE LEAD: If Spirit is strong, so are the Scorpio/*Threes*. They have a need for justice. Their mission is nothing less than changing the world. They believe that good conquers evil and the soul can endure any opposition. They are good with powerful people and politics may attract them. Regal by nature, they have no trouble working with the best, either on a project or as a spiritual advisor. Because of their intense focus, they can forget to take care of their appearance. Intimacy may be a problem, because they choose relationships with persons who are either superior or inferior. Their hope and faith is inspiring to others, but they need to learn to be in the now.

IF EGO TAKES THE LEAD: If Ego is in the lead, the Scorpio/*Three* can be riddled with insecurity and depression, or they are king of their turf. When ambitious, there is no limit to their desires. They don't take orders well. If they do, they're hiding their truth to get ahead. They are a rebel, someone who doesn't care what others think or feel. They tackle large problems and are their best when they go right to the top. They need faith in themselves and a sense of detachment from material things.

GRACE KELLY (November 21)

Actress, princess of Monaco.

Grace Kelly was the classic beauty who became a princess. Like that of most Scorpios, her personality was paradoxical. She appeared cold and aloof, yet sexually she was warm and passionate. The third of four children, Kelly never really felt special in her family. She had one desire—to be an actress. At age eighteen, she auditioned for the prestigious American Academy of Dramatic Arts and was accepted. Kelly's beauty got her modeling jobs; her first job put her on the cover of *Redbook* magazine. Her acting breaks came almost as easily. A small part in a play led to television and television led to the movies. In her first picture, *High Noon,* she costarred with Gary Cooper. On location for *To Catch a Thief* in Monaco, she met Prince Rainer and sent him a thank-you note for the afternoon they spent together. He returned her note and a correspondence ensued. After a visit to America, he proposed. The fairy-tale wedding was world news and the obscure principality became an "in" spot. Kelly's new position did not permit her to act. The independence she had fought so hard for was now surrendered to a life of obligations and rituals. Kelly had three children and found her purpose in charities and beautifying the place she now called home. Her early death was a tragedy felt around the world.

CHARLES BRONSON (November 3)

Actor.

As with many a *Three,* foreign places are advantageous. Bronson has been a bigger success abroad than at home. In Spain he is considered a sex symbol. In Italy, he received the Gold Star Award as the film industry's top international star. Born in Pennsylvania, Charlie Buchinsky worked the coal mines with his father near his hometown of Ehrenfield. He was drafted into the army during World War II and became an actor at age twenty-seven. He was spotted at the Pasadena Playhouse and earned a small part in a film with Gary Cooper. Success was slow. It took the filming of the "spaghetti western" *Once Upon a Time in the West* to bring Bronson the success he deserved. Bronson often plays a vigilante, a perfect Scorpio role. During the filming of *The Great Escape* he met his wife, Jill Ireland. They acted together in several films until her death from breast cancer.

Scorpio/*Four* (October 31, November 4, November 13, November 22) Pluto/Uranus

PURPOSE: To learn to use your strong sense of individualism to unite rather than to keep you isolated and alone.

"Change your thoughts and you change your world."—Norman Vincent Peale. The Scorpio *Four* loves tension, change and crisis. *Fours* have a strong need for excitement and a desire for unity. They are catalysts in the lives of others and their own world goes through many changes. They take things to the limit, and then, miraculously, a new point of view is achieved. They make great negotiators in intense and powerful situations. They need to be put on the edge; danger is an attraction. In a relationship, this can be disaster. The Scorpio/*Four* is restless and needs someone who can relate to them as they constantly evolve. They are great diplomats, able to see what diverse people have in common. If their spiritual side is missing, they may find themselves on the outside, looking in. They need to guard against becoming isolated and alone. Solitude is good if it puts them in touch with their inner nature; it's not good if it keeps them eating dinner with the evening news. To bring themselves into the mainstream of life requires they access their desire to help those who need support.

IF SPIRIT TAKES THE LEAD: If Spirit leads the way, rebellion is strong. The Scorpio/*Four* works toward peace and bringing people together. The danger here is that they forget that peace is what they seek, as they constantly allow themselves to be drawn into tense situations that challenge them to resolve the problem. In this way they can chase issues instead of creating solutions. They need to value their own lives and emotions.

IF EGO TAKES THE LEAD: Ego and the number *Four* get along very well. They agree that nothing or no one can tell them what to do. These souls are only good when they're the authority. They can't stand to be restricted or contained. Often a loner, they feel as if they don't fit in; the truth is, they don't want to. They're inventors who like to strike out into new territories. Intimacy is a problem because they have a wall around their emotions. More concerned with discoveries, change, and excitement, they find that harmony eludes them and relationships come and go.

WILL ROGERS (November 4)

Comedian, writer, movie star.

Few private citizens have impacted the country and the world as Will Rogers did. He used humor to deal with controversy and through the power of laughter the world saw a new point of view. Part Cherokee, Rogers's main love was his lasso. His mother died when he was young and Rogers felt her absence until he married his wife, Betty. His career started by accident, as with most *Fours*. Tired of roping contests, Rogers took off for Argentina to work with the gauchos. Eventually, he landed on a boat to South Africa. In Johannesburg, Rogers met Texas Jack and his Wild West Show and was hired for his skill with the lasso. Texas Jack taught Will the fundamentals of show biz. On his return to the states, Rogers joined the world of vaudeville. Vaudeville led to the Ziegfeld *Follies*. Rogers's act was not a success until he started to use the daily news as the basis of his humor. With fresh material every day for his keen insight and satirical comedy, it wasn't long before fame caught up to Will. Soon, he was writing books, his own column, and even contributing to the *New York Times*. Politicians took him seriously and he campaigned for several presidents, including Franklin Delano Roosevelt. His trip to Europe was the most publicized tour in history. Wherever he traveled, he was the guest of kings and notables. The *New York Times* wrote "... Will Rogers has done more to educate the American public in world affairs than all the professors who have been elucidating the continental chaos since the Treaty of Versailles." His accidental death in an airplane crash in Alaska was a cause for national mourning. Congress appropriated one and a half million dollars for his memorial.

ROBERT LOUIS STEVENSON (November 13)

Novelist, poet.

Robert Louis Balfour Stevenson was born in Edinburgh, Scotland. His father was a lighthouse engineer and Stevenson was expected to follow in his father's footsteps. His desire to become a writer required a showdown with his parents, who eventually yielded. For a while, Stevenson explored the bohemian life of Edinburgh. However, it was his stance on religion and morality that finally made his father sever the family relationship. Stevenson's health deteriorated and he was forced to go abroad. There he fell in love and married, which helped him reconcile with his parents. A voyage to the South Seas spiritually renewed him and he fell in love with the freedom and beauty of the islands. His *Dr. Jekyll and Mr. Hyde* depicts the Scorpio battle between good and evil. In Stevenson's story, the baser side of man does not get integrated but emerges as a separate person.

Scorpio/*Five* (November 5, November 14, November 23) Pluto/Mercury

PURPOSE: To use your many talents to acquire a great goal, always keeping yourself centered and detached from the games of life that are there to entice you and keep you from success.

"Most powerful is he who has himself in his own power."—Lucius Annaeus Seneca. The Scorpio/*Five* is gifted with a powerful will. If they use it to direct their many talents toward one goal, they can achieve great things. Their voice can easily speak for the collective. Compassion for the poor, the lost, and the abandoned is strong. If it's not, they are selfish and self-consumed. There's no middle ground here. The Scorpio/*Five* must detach from the material things of life in order to achieve true happiness. Otherwise, possessions can enslave them. Relationships are difficult because intimacy is a problem. They tend to idealize the souls they love, preferring to dream about them rather than marry them. Scorpio/*Fives* need to take responsibility for themselves and use their many talents in the service of others. When they heed the call to surrender the Ego, they begin to receive the rewards of peace and happiness.

IF SPIRIT TAKES THE LEAD: With Spirit at the helm, others become more important than the self. A feeling of unity pervades the Scorpio/*Five* and a need to experience the simple things in life. The poor—their hunger and their pain—affects them. They must be careful of martyrdom. If they are not strong, they will be depleted. Learning to give and receive equally is their primary challenge.

IF EGO TAKES THE LEAD: Ego can be very powerful in this combination. It gets stuck on an infantile sense of self, it feels deprived and nothing it receives is ever enough. Possessions, position and money are important to them, as is a sense of superiority. Instead of harnessing their pride, they try to knock down or surpass those whom they perceive as above them. They need to feel special.

PRINCE CHARLES (November 14)

Born to Princess Elizabeth, and immediately attended by two nurses, a staff of maids and footmen, Charles entered the world destined to be the future king of England. Shy and lacking self-confidence, Prince Charles did not meet the standards of his father, the duke of Edinburgh, who constantly criticized him. Their only avenue of communication was through the sports that Charles loved, mainly, hunting and fishing. His sister Anne, a precocious and outgoing child, was easily her father's favorite. Charles wasn't allowed to experiment with life until he was much older. His fate was decided by others, not good for any Scorpio. Sent away to school, he found himself with no one to confide in. Charles longed for a purpose in life. He loved nature and had a growing need to explore his spiritual side outside tradition and the Church. He was drawn to metaphysics, Eastern philosophy, healing, and Paracelsus's return to nature. As the most eligible bachelor in the world, the prince had his pick of beauties. Pressured to marry, he chose Lady Diana Spencer. Their marriage produced two wonderful heirs to the throne, but not much happiness. The couple is now divorced. Through all the publicity, Prince Charles has managed to continue working for the people, supporting environmental programs, organic agriculture, architecture, and homeopathy.

VIVIEN LEIGH (November 5)

Actress.

Vivien Leigh, destined to play one of the most sought-after leading-lady roles in the world, that of Scarlett O'Hara in *Gone With the Wind,* was born in India. Her Catholic parents were concerned about bringing her up in a foreign country, so she was sent off to boarding school in England. Leigh's father was an actor and she chose to follow in his footsteps. With her remarkable beauty, talent, and personality, acting breaks came easily and in no time at all, she had a film and stage career. Leigh married young, but her passion for a man was not awakened until she met Laurence Olivier. Determined to win him even though he was married, she befriended his wife, learned his every desire, and finally won his heart. Their love affair was world news. Together they traveled to Hollywood for her to audition for the part of Scarlett. Unfortunately, Leigh's latter years were not so happy. She became a manic-depressive. Olivier left her and she died of tuberculosis.

Scorpio/*Six* (October 24, November 6, November 15)
Pluto/Venus

PURPOSE: To take your dreams out of the future and create them in the now, using all your resources, charm, knowledge, and personality.

''Character is formed in the stormy billows of the world.''—Johann Wolfgang Von Goethe. The Scorpio/*Six* needs discipline and experience to make the world theirs. Driven by intense emotions and desires, they are perfectionists with a strong drive to create and control their yearnings. The Scorpio/*Six* can connect with the king of Siam or the beggar on the street. They worry about the poor and the needy, but at the same time they manipulate others for their own end. Money is a powerful force in their life. Either they are very good with it, or they ignore its rewards and prefer to seek truth, beauty, and love. Balance is preferred here.

The Scorpio/*Six* knows how to bring out the best in everyone. They demand unconditional loyalty and love. They need to have faith in a higher power and do things for their own sake. Then they will find the peace and happiness they seek.

IF SPIRIT TAKES THE LEAD: If Spirit is strong, the Scorpio/*Sixes* are perfectionists, seeking to improve themselves constantly, never accepting that where they are is the place to be. They can transform the lives of others. They go right to the essence of whatever they see, removing the debris that keeps the essential from shining. They are a rebel, willing to fight for truth.

IF EGO TAKES THE LEAD: If Ego is strong, the Scorpio/*Sixes* are attached to money and worldly power. They desire position, respect, and all the beautiful things that money can buy. Either they deprive themselves in order to gain self-control, or they overindulge, in an effort to fill the emptiness they feel inside. They seek security and control, and are obsessed with protecting themselves and their possessions. Only the things of the Spirit can never be taken away.

ERWIN ROMMEL (November 15)

German field marshal during WWII.

A pale and sickly youth, Rommel aspired to be an aeronautical engineer. It was his father, a hard and overbearing man, who placed Rommel on his path of destiny by enrolling him in the Württemberg army. Rommel found he had little in common with the other lieutenants. Like most *Sixes,* he found his way to the top early. Hitler was impressed by his ability to execute orders to the letter. Their relationship was a source of Rommel's power and the creation of a jealousy that would later lead to his defeat. His victories, as well as his unconventional tactics, created a myth, not just a hero. Even the enemy thought of him as invincible. Never happy with just giving orders, Rommel led his men into battle. His troops adored him. A self-taught strategist, Rommel did not have the fine military training some of his comrades possessed. Rather, his genius came from his bold and creative approach to a challenge. His habit of going over the heads of his superiors, to Hitler himself, angered many. When he needed the support of those he had offended, they withheld it. His greatest achievement was in North Africa, where he survived for two years with only one Panzer division. Ironically, in the end he was accused of being a part of a conspiracy to kill Hitler, and was reduced to accepting the honor of committing suicide by poison.

GEORGIA O'KEEFFE (November 15)

Artist.

Born on a farm in Wisconsin, O'Keeffe had an early introduction to the extremes of nature. The landscape around her was sparse and abstract. O'Keeffe grew up independent and free-spirited. She said, "It may have come from not being the favorite child and not minding that—it left me free." Like most Scorpios, she hated school; instead, she learned through experience. Drawing classes began at home when she was eleven but her great talent was not immediately obvious. The visual world would be her teacher, as well as her ability to observe the discrepancy between the color of things as they are known and as they are perceived. Eccentric in many ways, O'Keeffe was also set apart by her appearance. She often dressed like a man. In her art, she experimented with perspective and design. She used bold color, voluptuous contours and a sophisticated manipulation of space, but the real power of her painting was its spiritual and emotional context.

A feminist in a male-dominated world, O'Keeffe became a heroine of the women's movement in the 1970s. However, it was her encounter with Alfred Stieglitz, whom she would eventually marry, that led her to the Arthur Dow approach to art. "A pictorial composition," Dow wrote, "is not merely an assemblage of objects truthfully represented, it is the expression of an idea, and all the parts must be so related as to form a harmonious whole."

Scorpio/*Seven* (October 25, November 7, November 16) Pluto/Neptune

PURPOSE: To use your exceptional visionary ability to raise the perception and consciousness of others through your unique ideas and creations that you present to the world.

"Lord, grant that I may always desire more than I can accomplish." —Michelangelo di Lodovico Buonarotti Simon. The Scorpio/*Seven* has such high expectations he lives either in the clouds or in extreme despair. Mood swings are prevalent. *Sevens* are either master manipulators who know how to use everything for their own ends, or they are used and abused. The desire to sacrifice for others is strong. They need to help those who cannot help themselves, but beware of getting caught in a codependent relationship. They have a vision of a better tomorrow and the will and courage to make a difference in whatever they do. The Scorpio/*Seven* is gifted with a unique perspective; others seldom understand them. They need to develop boundaries. The mysteries of life intrigue them. They have the capability to dream and manifest dreams. Perfectionistic and restless, they drive themselves crazy. They are also judgmental, because they feel so vulnerable, they cannot imagine why others think them so difficult. They are either attracted to chaos and confusion or avoid it like the plague, making black-and-white decisions in order to put things in their proper place. They need to believe in something greater than themselves. Ideals, dreams, romance, music, and fantasy are their strengths. They need to guard against deception or negative means of escape like alcohol or drugs. Life can be wonderful, if they learn how to blend their fantasies with the real.

IF SPIRIT TAKES THE LEAD: If Spirit is strong, the Scorpio/*Seven* lives in the future and their vision can change the world. However, too much dreaming and not enough hard work or practical application of ideas, can keep them in the clouds and open to abuse. They are not present and so others can move into their space. This is dangerous. They need to be in the moment and learn to protect themselves. They have a unique vision and can be an inventor or a problem solver. Unyielding in their beliefs, they can place unreasonable demands on themselves and others.

IF EGO TAKES THE LEAD: If Ego is strong, the Scorpio/*Seven* is a dictator and perfectionist. Materialistic and security conscious, they find it hard to trust anyone. They live with divine discontent. They believe that worldly acquisitions will fill their emptiness. Personal happiness is difficult. No one is ever good or loyal enough. They are a master manipulator. They have an ever-changing moral system; they rationalize to justify their needs and actions. They need to root themselves in solid principles and life will began to treat them more kindly.

MARIE CURIE (November 7)

First woman to win the Nobel Prize, one of the few scientists to win it twice.

Born Manya Sklodowska in Poland during the Russian occupation, Curie was tutored by her father, a teacher who made learning at home fun. Her mother died of tuberculosis when Curie was ten; it was a loss that would take her years to overcome. From the very beginning, Curie paved the way for women's equality. As a young woman at the turn of the century, she attended the Sorbonne, where most of her classmates were men. While in Paris, she lived alone. Exhibiting in an extreme way the Scorpio ability to concentrate, she spent all her time on her studies. Finally, she graduated first among her colleagues. Her plans to return to Poland to teach were abruptly changed when she met Pierre Curie, a fellow scientist. They soon developed a friendship that led to marriage. Together, they worked on the cause and nature of radioactivity. Madame Curie isolated radium and named a new element, polonium. The couple received the 1903 Nobel Prize for their work. The fact that a woman had worked side by side with her husband, created quite a stir. Curie was accused of being unfeminine, cold, and unnatural. Others said she had only assisted her husband. In 1911 Curie won a second Nobel Prize, (for isolating pure radium) after her husband's death, eliminating any doubt that she was not an equal contributor and a brilliant woman.

PABLO PICASSO (October 25)

Artist.

Picasso was born into a middle-class family. His father was an artist without talent, more of a gentleman than a breadwinner. His sister Conchita's death at age seven, had a profound effect on the thirteen-year-old Picasso. To save her life he promised God he would give up painting. Picasso carried the guilt of her death all his life. As a child, Picasso was obsessed with drawing. His early years as a painter were plagued with poverty and a passion for women and sex. He was a frequent visitor to the brothels, and each phase of his painting reflected a major new relationship. Picasso had a melancholy nature. He worked all night and never cared how he looked or dressed. As a painter, he discovered more new styles—for example those of his Blue Period and Cubism—than any artist who had come before him. Endowed with a huge ego, he often thought himself godlike, and like God, he often concealed his true nature. "The painter no longer has to limit himself to depicting the object as it would appear from one given viewpoint, but when necessary for fuller comprehension, can show it from several sides from above and below."

Scorpio/*Eight* (October 26, November 8, November 17) Pluto/Saturn

PURPOSE: To use your power to transform yourself—first by accepting your fate, then by transcending it.

"Alas, after a certain age, every man is responsible for his own fate."— Albert Camus. Scorpio/*Eight* is the dynamics of obsession. Their challenge is to love themselves and have faith in a higher power. If they are not perfectionists, they act cool and detached; the truth is, this is a facade. The Scorpio/*Eight* wants and needs control. This makes their world small and they miss out on much.

They work too hard and take on too much responsibility. They are attracted to difficult people and situations. They hold in tension, or, someone else in their life is very controlling. This other person may make the Scorpio/*Eight* feel safe, but the Scorpio/*Eight* is giving up far too much. They need to learn to love themselves. They are talented and strong and must learn to choose the problems and the people in their life.

IF SPIRIT TAKES THE LEAD: If Spirit is ahead of Ego, the Scorpio/*Eight* is an idealist who strives for personal perfection. The danger is they may surrender all their power to someone else and let this strong, smart and powerful person take over their lives. They'll never get the satisfaction they're seeking from someone else. They must take back their power and follow their own vision.

IF EGO TAKES THE LEAD: If Ego is strong, the Scorpio/*Eight* is into control. The result is a small, well-managed world. They have a great eye for scrutinizing things. They seek safety and protection, but can still be deceived because they don't trust their instincts. They are obsessive and can be cruel, dictatorial, and punishing. They try so hard they make mistakes, and get angry. The cycle of discontent and anger keeps growing. Their inability to compromise or trust makes them a prisoner of their own lack of faith.

LEE STRASBERG (November 17)

Teacher of the Stanislavsky Method of acting, founded the first ensemble group of trained actors.

Lee Strasberg had a powerful effect on the art of acting in the United States; he took Stanislavsky's method and added something of his own. Born in Austria in 1901, he immigrated with his family to the United States in 1909. As a child he had an insatiable appetite for reading and was gifted with phenomenal retention. Interested in acting, he joined the Students of Art and Drama. For a while, he made a living making women's hairpieces. And then he encountered the Laboratory Theatre and Richard Boleslavski and Maria Ouspenskaya. These were the two best teachers of the Method, a means of training the actor to produce consistent quality of performance. Strasberg studied the Method for several years and eventually in 1931, founded the Group Theatre in 1931. He was the first to develop an ensemble group. Strasberg added an "inner technique" to the Method. It helped the actor break through "habits" and use his or her natural body movements and impulses. Strasberg worked with the likes of Marilyn Monroe, Marlon Brando, Robert DeNiro, James Dean, and Dustin Hoffman.

HILLARY RODHAM CLINTON (October 26)

Lawyer, first lady of the United States.

The first child in her family, Hillary's inquiring mind was recognized early. An A student, she was a natural leader, an articulate speaker, and felt passionately about the poor and social issues. Her first interest was medicine, a typical Scorpio profession. Persistent, dedicated, and analytical, she was always noticed and hard to ignore. Hillary Rodham attended Wellesley, and then Yale, to study law. At Yale she met Bill Clinton, a man who wasn't afraid of or intimidated by her. One year after they graduated, he proposed and Hillary was thrown into a dilemma. She had plans for her own career. Marrying Clinton meant moving to and living in Arkansas. Before she made her decision, she joined John Doar's team in preparing to impeach Richard Nixon. Her assignment was to write the procedure rules of impeachment. With her work completed after Nixon resigned, she accepted Clinton's marriage proposal. With his election to governor, she became the first lady of Arkansas, and began to meet the public's resistance to a woman of her strength and intelligence—a problem that has followed her to the White House.

Scorpio/*Nine* (October 27, November 9, November 18) Pluto/Mars

PURPOSE: To use the power of your ego to persuade others to follow your path, your dreams, and your desires, which include a vision of helping those in need.

"Wickedness is always easier than virtue, for it takes the short cut to everything."—James Boswell. The Scorpio/*Nine* likes to have things their way and with the least amount of fuss. They are direct and honest, even when they are doing something wrong. They know how to create their world and when they're confident, no one can stop them. They also have charm and lots of sex appeal. Of course, they know how to use both to their advantage. If they lack faith and a strong sense of self, the reverse is a possibility and others may overwhelm them. Protection and the ability to confront and fight are important. Impatient and restless, they seldom stop to reflect. They need to learn not to be afraid of solitude. Once they discover their true nature, their strength will be real and long-lasting. Hard work is needed to develop their talents.

IF SPIRIT TAKES THE LEAD: If Spirit is strong with the number *Nine,* the Scorpio/*Nine* gets what they want. They're persistent to a fault. They should worry about being overwhelmed by someone else's goal or desires. Spirit's need to serve can make them care too much about others and not enough about themselves. They can love too strongly, give too generously and are always disappointed when others don't reciprocate in kind. It's impossible to find a balanced relationship when you put too much of yourself into it.

IF EGO TAKES THE LEAD: If Ego is more powerful than Spirit, the Scorpio/ *Nine* becomes aggressive, angry and persistent. They want things immediately and rarely think of consequences. A great manipulator or salesman, they are able to convince others that what they think is right. they plunge ahead, unconcerned by feelings and with no respect for the space of others. The goal is all that counts. They create animosity and don't even know it. When they need help, enemies rise to stomp on them. You need to realize the impact you are making on others.

IVAN TURGENEV (November 9)

Writer.

A compassionate child, Turgenev developed a concern for the serfs, whose pain and suffering he felt keenly. And because of his violent mother, he developed a love for obsessive and domineering women. His love for a married singer named Pauline Viardot was obsessive. He devoted his life to her, even though she refused to be his mistress and never left her husband. His life was a struggle of opposites. He took a minor part in the revolutionary movement to free the serfs. Although Russian down to his toes, he only seemed happy abroad.

LINDA EVANS (November 18)

Actress, producer.

Evans is best known for her role as Krystle Carrington in the TV show *Dynasty.* Born in Hartford, Connecticut, Evans moved to Hollywood with her parents as an infant. She attended Hollywood High. A friend took her to a casting session for a television commercial and she got the part. This break was followed by an appearance on TV's *Bachelor Father.* She studied with Lee Strasberg and landed a part on *The Big Valley.* However, real fame came with her role in *Dynasty.* Her success led her to form her own production company. Evans has been married twice. Her first husband, John Derek, is known to have an eye for beautiful women. After their divorce, she married real estate tycoon, Stan Herman. This marriage didn't work, either. Evans says, "In doing the thing that I least wanted to do—be by myself—I've discovered something really beautiful, which is I'm going to make the best partner for someone in the whole world now because I've found myself."

SUMMARY

Scorpios are the magicians of the universe. What's their secret? Their ability to use resources—all of them. They draw from their experiences, their dreams, and their environment. As God's intermediaries, they bring his heavenly knowledge to the common man. These are the physicians, healers, writers, artists and psychics. Their voice often represents the silent, those unable to speak out against injustice, cruelty, and greed. They rule transformation. They are particularly drawn to anything hidden, forbidden or impossible. They like to shock the world and prove what a simple person can do if he focuses all his energy on the moment. They must face their baser instincts, once they do, they're undefeatable. Scorpio is the power of the emotions. Once they have learned how to use them, they are ready to enjoy all the drama, and texture that life has to offer. Through them we will learn the power and resilience of faith and hope which although developed in Scorpio, will not be perfected until the next sign of Sagittarius.

SELECTED SOURCES

Hollis Alpert   *Burton*   G.P. Putnam's Sons 1986

Roland H. Bainton   *Erasmus of Christendom*   MacMillan 1969

Donald Day   *Will Rogers: A Biography*   David McKay Company, Inc. 1962

Anne Edwards   *Vivien Leigh: A Biography*   Simon & Schuster 1979

Robert Goldberg and Gerald Jay Goldberg   *Citizen Turner: The Wild Rise of an American Tycoon*   Harcourt Brace 1995

Walter Kaufmann   *Nietzsche, Philosopher, Psychologist, Antichrist*   Princeton University Press 1989

John Keats   *The Complete Poems*   Penguin Books 1973

Geir Kjetsaa and Elisabeth Sifton   *Fydor Dostoyevsky: A Writer's Life*   Viking 1987

Ronald Lewin   *Montgomery as Military Commander*   Stein and Day   1971

Norman Mailer   *Portrait of Picasso as a Young Man: An Interpretive Biography*   Atlantic Monthly Press 1995

Stephen Manes and Paul Andrews   *Bill Gates: How Microsoft's Mogul Reinvented an Industry and Made Himself the Richest Man in America*   Doubleday 1993

Paracelsus   *Selected Writings*   Edited by Jolande Jacobi   Princeton University Press   1951

Susan Quinn   *Marie Curie: A Life*   Simon & Schuster 1995

Donnie Radcliffe   *Hillary Rodham Clinton: A First Lady for Our Time*   Warner 1994

John Richardson and Marilyn McCully   *A Life of Picasso: 1881–1906*   Random House 1991

Roxana Robinson   *Georgia O'Keeffe: A Life*   Harper & Row 1989

Arthur M. Schlesinger, Jr.   *Robert Kennedy and His Times*   Houghton Mifflin Company 1978

David Sprintzen   *Camus: A Critical Examination*   Temple University Press 1988

Robert Louis Stevenson *Dr. Jekyll and Mr. Hyde and Other Stories* Penguin 1979
Roger N. Walsh, M.D., Ph.D. *The Spirit of Shamanism* Tarcher 1991
Alan W. Watts *Nature, Man and Woman* Vintage 1991

Sagittarius

(November 23–December 21)

God is the quest for the sign of Sadge
The Word, its power, is their badge.
Here, man must meet what he has sowed,
His fate awaits just down the road.
No, he yells, I'll fight you Lord.
I'll use my wit, the Word's my sword.
So Sublime will my mastery be,
All of Heaven will bow to me.

Ruler: Jupiter   **Symbol: Archer**
Element: Fire   **Number: Three**

Sagittarius completes autumn and carries the spirit into the cold, harsh reality of winter. The essence of life must now be met directly, with no tempting distractions from Ego's versatile palate. Nature is devoid of warmth and its usual visual delights. In Sagittarius, your environment mirrors the stark simplicity of your soul. Spirit must pass a test. It must survive without Ego's mask, the part of your personality that feels protected by money, labels, and possessions, all the things that separate one person from another. Your new and stronger shield is faith, hope, and confidence in your talent, and the ability to reason and discern. This is about the higher mind and artistic survival. What's important now is poetry, humor, and mental games that challenge the intellect and stretch the reason. In the world of the word, the only limitation is your imagination. True freedom is found in the mind, in unlimited responses to the uncontrollable events one meets along the path.

This part of the journey must be traveled alone. Sagittarians are self-sufficient loners. They desire to achieve great heights through their own powers, talents, and instincts. They carry a seed, a sacred part of themselves they refuse to share with the world. It's the only way to assure that their uniqueness will survive. To strengthen the protection of this inner purity, Sagittarians refuse the input of others, praise and rejection are ignored. Woody Allen (December 1) says, "It's important to keep your own criteria and not defer to the trends of the marketplace."

Sagittarians have learned through hard experience the important lesson of following their own path. The gift of hard experience is self-reliance and confidence. If the Sagittarian has been over-protected, they will be drawn to challenges, to situations that force them to rely on nothing but their wits and stamina.

Being the underdog is a Sagittarians favorite position; they love having to fight to the top. They seek resistance in order to expand. They never accept boundaries set by others. This is Spirit and its desire to see nothing less than God's face. The soul seeks nourishment in things that inspire and uplift. This nourishment is found in the *word*. Armed with wit, humor, and intellect, their sharp, dexterous mind uses syntax to wound an opponent, irony to shatter pretense, and laughter to expose excessive pride and vanity.

In this new and exciting world, answers are not sought, because they confine one to reality. Questions are the key; they form the ethereal perimeters of the unknown. The right questions can rise above knowledge, dogma, and the Ego, allowing new ideas, solutions and possibilities to unfold. This is unity. No point of view need be discarded. Thus, the dilemma of choice, presented in the opposite sign of Gemini, is resolved in Sagittarius. Opposing points of view are taken inside to be studied and scrutinized. Here, the essence is discovered through the systematic discarding of the unnecessary. Unity has replaced division; everything is a reflection of Him.

Sagittarius is the seed of a new beginning. Within the seed lies all potential. The average man follows the masses and cannot grow because there is no seed-center. According to De Casseres, ''A genius is born with a secret. Its mind exfoliates. It sheds instead of taking on. It attracts the thing buried in its own depths and militantly repels all objects foreign to it.'' Originality is the Sagittarian ability to form ''new clusters of mental dissociations.'' According to John Ardoin, Maria Callas (December 2) was great because ''All that was useful to her was the kernel . . . she watered the seed and let it grow. Out of that little nothing came the incredible multifaceted amazing, transfigured creation.''

Sagittarians have a talent for taking something in the formative stage and bringing it to fruition. The hidden essence of Scorpio is now a seed or a bud, and with the Sagittarius ability to nurture and shape that bud, the seed begins to grow and blossom.

Unity is attained, the goal is achieved, and Sagittarians have arrived at their destiny. They are the men or the women of their times. Many have called Winston Churchill a man of destiny. No one else could have rallied the English people so powerfully or so eloquently during the German invasion of England. His words ''Never give in, never, never, never, never, give in'' are the Sagittarius motto. Churchill himself proclaimed to Lord Moran, ''This cannot be accident, it must be design.''

Your moment may not be so dramatic, but nonetheless it is yours, and through your ability to defy it, you are able to overcome a sense of defeat or limitation. In his autobiography Kirk Douglas, (December 9) shared his private victory over the feelings of nothingness that were a product of a father who persistently ignored him. Sitting in the kitchen with his sisters, watching his father eat a meal as if none of them existed, was more than Douglas could endure. He flicked a spoonful of tea across the kitchen table, into his father's face. Enraged, his father threw Kirk through the door and into the next room. "I was triumphant. I had risked death and I had come out alive. . . . I have never done anything as brave in any movie."

Steven Spielberg's (December 18) *Back To The Future* shows us how one moment can change a life. The lead character goes back in time and helps his father stand up to a bully and rescue his mother. This one heroic act reverses the process of helplessness to one of hopefulness, and when he returns to the present, his parents lives are happy and successful, instead of despairing.

However, this connection to the moment threatens the freedom of the Sagittarius who resists the forces of destiny through defiance. Thus, Sagittarians hold on to the moment and want to mold it to their own ends. Their motivation is fear of fate, which lies just ahead; they believe they can avoid the consequences of their actions through the sheer power and force of their being. The challenge of Sagittarius is twofold. First Sagittarius must defy the moment and rise above it, achieving the impossible, stretching the spirit and imagination to its limits. From that height they can see that they cannot command God to reveal Himself, that their desire to be with Him has weakened the body and the Ego, as well as the soul's ability to complete the journey. Sagittarius then understands that it is through acceptance, not resistance, that the goal is achieved. This acceptance is not defeat but a return to humanness and humility—and the beginning of transcendence.

How we perceive God is a reflection of our consciousness. The God of Sagittarius is both loved and feared, desired and hated. Since He is responsible for fate, and fate is the enemy of freedom, then God is also the enemy to be sought out and challenged. He has deserted man; he punishes and wounds; he hides, instead of revealing Himself. His gift of free will was nothing more than an illusion. The world of cause and effect demands we pay a price for everything we have thought or done. Freedom, so valiantly fought for in the previous signs, is now slowly being taken away. Only the realm of the mind and the imagination offer refuge. Here is the seat of all creation. The Sagittarians' talent becomes the focus and the means of maintaining their freedom. If they protect it, they remain masters of their universe. Most Sagittarians have an amazing confidence in their work; it transcends the limitations of their personalities.

Sagittarians are versatile beings and backed by great resilience and persistence, they eventually get to where they want to go. Poetry, music, art, and the word uplift their spirits. They have a passion for language, harmonics, rhythm and music, vibrations that link heaven with earth.

With fate around the corner, and freedom becoming more and more restricted by uncontrollable events, the first response of the Sagittarius soul is defiance. Beethoven (December 16), who created some of his greatest music after going deaf, cried out in the crisis of losing his hearing, "No, I cannot endure it. I will take Fate by the throat. It shall not wholly overcome me." Eventually, his suffering brought him to a place of surrender. "Fate show your face! We are not lords over ourselves. What is determined must be, and so let it be."

Spirit needs to rise as high as it can go, reach the limits of its capacity to love, give, imagine, and create. From that place, it will see that from that height no human being is capable of surviving unscathed. John Milton's (December 9) poetic masterpiece, *Paradise Lost,* was written when he was blind. The power of the senses diminishes in the presence of the Lord; Sagittarius must be careful of an audience with Him. The apostle Paul encountered God on the road to Damascus. The brilliance of the meeting blinded him. Paul was three days without sight; he regained it only after he had submitted himself entirely to the Lord's direction. The desire to confront God is a powerful theme in Emily Dickinson's (December 10) poetry. Her dilemma was twofold—"to seek out the hidden God so that an attack might be mounted and to find some weapon adequate to pitch against the mighty force of the godhead. As a solution to both of these Dickinson returned to the power of the Word." God told Moses, "Thou canst not see my face, for there shall no man see me and live." (Exodus 33.20).

When the senses and the body are weakened, Spirit is able to reach higher. Only Spirit can rise above fate, but when it does, the body suffers. Many Sagittarians struggle with physical ailments. As a child, Churchill was sickly and overweight. At age seven, he set out to prove that biology need not be destiny. He "was to a marked extent, forcing himself to go against his own inner nature."

Physical limitations don't exist in the world of magic. However, it's important for Sagittarius to see that the need to return to the divine is selfish. It hinders the attainment of the goal because it weakens the Ego and the soul's ability to negotiate the world.

As the hand of fate slowly tightens its grip on the Sagittarius, the soul responds in one of several ways. If fear is greater than courage, they may try to avoid responsibility entirely by giving away their power to someone believed to be stronger and more capable of protecting them. Maria Callas turned over her destiny to two men. Battista Meneghini, her husband and manager, stole her money. Her lover, Aristotle Onassis, the richest man in the world, had no respect for her talent. Callas's passion for this man led to a loss of confidence and the destruction of her opera career.

Surrender doesn't mean turning over a life to someone else. It means allowing yourself to be led by God. Human beings should never control each other. They should educate and pass on experiences and knowledge to those who come after. The negative use of education leads to mind control. When this occurs, enlightenment gives way to fanaticism.

Sagittarius rules anything that expands the mind—religion, education, philosophy, and travel. If however, the Sagittarius is determined to hand over their power, they might safely choose established rituals and traditions. An attraction to dogma can be good or bad, depending on whether it enhances your life or limits it. Margaret Mead (December 16), the famous anthropologist, saw ritual as "the outward signs of community. A good ritual is very like a natural language, one which has been spoken for a very long time by very many kinds of people . . . a ritual must be old . . . otherwise it will not be fully available to everyone born within the tradition: yet it must be living and fresh, open to new vision and changed vision."

It's not uncommon for a Sagittarius to change his or her religion. The famous philosopher Spinoza (November 24) was excommunicated from the Jewish congregation at Amsterdam for heresy. He changed his name to the Latin Benedictus. Disraeli, the prime minister of England, renounced his Jewish religion and became a Christian.

Nothing is imposed on the Sagittarius. They need the freedom to explore the world through their minds and imaginations. In fact, many are not interested in religion at all. Woody Allen said, "I was unmoved by the synagogue. I was not interested in the Seder, I was not interested in the Hebrew school, I was not interested in being Jewish." Some Sagittarians may try to escape the grip of fate by outrunning it. They may climb the mountains of Tibet, visit the Great Wall of China, trek through the rain forests of South America in an effort to hide from fate. A second motive behind the love of travel is the desire to conquer the distant unknown. A third is that many Sagittarians have better luck in foreign countries (God sent Abraham into a foreign land to make his fame and fortune) or outside their community. Margaret Mead documented the behavior of primitive cultures and brought her discoveries home, challenging our views on sex and guilt. As a young man, Mark Twain (November 30) traveled throughout the United States, making a name for himself as a reporter who spoke out against injustice, such as crimes committed by the police, judges, and institutions.

However, the Sagittarius does not have to leave home to travel unchartered territory. The greatest and most challenging journey of all can be made in the realm of the mind. Through poetry, Emily Dickinson challenged God and confronted her feelings of isolation and loneliness.

Most Sagittarians get stuck in the first stage of this sign—defiance, and the desire to retain total freedom. Oppression of any kind enrages them. Winston Churchill said, "it's when I'm Joan of Arc that I get excited."

Mark Twain said of his mother, "When anybody or any creature was being oppressed, the fears that belonged to her sex and her small stature retired to the rear and her soldierly qualities came promptly to the front." Mark Twain, himself, was a champion of justice. "He had expressed anger at injustices toward the powerless many times . . . that anger was . . . extended to include those who were powerless because of the color of their skin."

Evil in Sagittarius looms large; it encompasses the whole universe. Everything but the Sagittarians' truth is the enemy, because everything threatens to limit their freedom and self-expression. Woody Allen said, "It's very important to realize that we're up against an evil, insidious, hostile universe." However, it's important to remember that truth is found in both the great and the small. The Sagittarian must guard against getting stuck in asking only the ultimate questions. Who am I? Is there a God? What is my relationship with Him? Through the voice of Brother Leo in his novel *Saint Francis,* Nikos Kazantzakis (December 2) takes a more encompassing view. "That evening I understood for the first time that all things are one and that even the humblest everyday deed is part of a man's destiny. Francis too was deeply roused; he too felt that there is no such thing as a small deed or a large deed and that to chink a crumbling wall with a single pebble is the same as reinforcing the entire earth to keep it from falling, the same as reinforcing your soul to keep that too from falling."

To reach the higher mind, a person must have learned the lessons of the previous signs. He must have contained all conflicting points of view within to be studied and scrutinized. The whole picture must be embraced, and then, the process of disassociation begins. The mind of Sagittarius eliminates rather than adds. They dissect, discard, and separate, arranging the facts according to their priorities. All facts will begin to find their own level, according to the way the Sagittarians have developed their priorities.

This is the Sagittarians' ability to detach from their emotions, goals and priorities. All they have to do to reach an answer is take in the facts and let them automatically sort out. The final stage is accomplished through the Sagittarius imagination. It adds the missing pieces to the puzzle. To manifest their dreams, they need to blend imagination with reality. This happens through the encounter with a harsh environment. The shock that comes from the need to survive forces them to unite all possibilities. When the mind can take into consideration both the real and the possible, the needs of the moment, the goal ahead, past experiences, and the cosmic law of God, it is ready for anything.

In the Sagittarius mind, one opposing view is pitted against the other with equal force. One takes the lead, the process is repeated, and the information gets reduced and redefined. To do this well requires Sagittarians to be masters of their emotions and desires, and to have objectified them, to see them as separate and apart from them. The more the Sagittarian can observe their emotions, the higher they can raise them and incorporate them into mind and reason. Then, wisdom is not far away.

Sagittarians are able to draw from what there is and reshape it to fill a need. They make things work. Through their ability to choose an infinite number of solutions to a problem, they have no reason ever to be stuck. As Jane Howard, Margaret Mead's biographer said, "She was convinced that there always is a way, it's just a matter of figuring out what it is."

Sagittarians are totally intuitive; the process of assorting facts and options is all done by intuition. Field Marshal Alanbrooke, Churchill's chief of the Imperial General Staff, was constantly astonished by Churchill's "Method of suddenly arriving at some decision as if it were by intuition without any kind of logical examination of the problem ... He preferred to work by intuition and by impulse." To do this, the Sagittarians must trust themselves. Attitude has power here; it either moves them along or keeps them in a rut. Sagittarians must allow their minds to play. They love to tease, tempt, lure, and amuse, while at the same time informing, teaching, and sharing their experiences through the infinite choices they have at their fingertips.

The gift of the higher mind is not without its dark side. To soar also means to fall, and many Sagittarians struggle with dark moods or depression. Churchill did, and so did Beethoven. The individual, formed and forged in the last two signs, now sits between the two worlds of Spirit and Ego and wrestles with them both. Spirit first seeks to transform Flesh to Spirit, ignoring its presence in the physical form. Once Spirit is tamed, balance is achieved. Actual results in the mundane world can be less harmonious. Caught between spiritual yearnings and worldly luxury, Sagittarians often feel a need to choose between the two. Rossi Lemeni said of Maria Callas, "She started to lose her voice when she lost confidence in herself as a performer and lost it altogether when she decided to fulfill her ambition to be the First Lady of European society." Spinoza lost his love when she married a man who gave her an expensive necklace. His heart broken, Spinoza never married.

Religion is ruled by Sagittarius, but it doesn't rule these Jupiter souls. Most Sagittarians struggle with the concept of being spiritual, but not religious. Religion limits. Often, the Sagittarian wants to find his own personal way of relating to God. Mark Twain believed in God, but not in religion. He said, "I cannot see how a man of any large degree of humorous perception can ever be religious."

Margaret Mead expressed a typical Sagittarian view when she said, "A great religion provides an image of all humankind, an image sufficiently universal so that it can cross national, linguistic and racial lines." Religion has to include everyone. Tolerance of the beliefs of others is essential. Tolerance is born of the Sagittarian ability to contain within himself contradictory emotions and ideas. To do this successfully, the Sagittarius mind must be stretched and challenged.

The Sagittarius soul walks its own path, their methods of reaching their goals are unique. They're inventors and innovators because they never accept the limitations and boundaries of others. Chaplain Junker said of Beethoven, "his style of treating his instrument is as different from that usually adopted, that it impresses one with the idea that by a path of his own discovery, he has attained that height of excellence wherein he now stands." William Blake (November 28) the visionary poet, prophet, and artist said, "O why was I born with a different face? / Why was I not born like the rest of my race?" Sagittarians walk their own path, unaffected by the rejection they receive for daring to be different. Bette Midler spoke of her early rejections. "It didn't faze me, Okay. I'd think to myself, Go ahead, shut the door in my face! Be out to lunch! Hang up on me!. I don't care. I'll be back!"

Sagittarians believe in their talent more than they believe in themselves, and they'll keep going until someone else acknowledges what they can do. The desire of Spirit to test itself and overcome any odds often manifests in a childhood of poverty and conflict. Faced with racism, discrimination, abandonment, class differences—anything that separates and makes one feel alone—Sagittarians learn early in life to walk their own path. Sammy Davis Jr. (December 8) was thrown from the world of entertainment, where his father and uncle had shielded him from racism, into the first integrated United States army division, where he was abused, attacked, and demeaned. Davis came through the experience more determined than ever to be the best. Kirk Douglas was Jewish and poor and felt both down to his very bones, but it didn't stop him from going to college, being elected president of his senior class (the first time a Jewish, non–fraternity member received such an honor) and dating the most beautiful girl on campus.

Sagittarians must remember not to let the tests of Ego make them feel less than they are. If they feel lonely and rejected, they are accepting Ego's reality, not the one they are capable of creating. Sagittarians must choose the thoughts that surround and protect them. They must let those thoughts be uplifting ones.

If Sagittarians are fortunate, the gift of specialness will be given to them at an early age. However, some may have to discover it themselves. But once they have found self-worth, nothing else really matters. Kirk Douglas received the Sagittarian gift of specialness from his mother, who barely had enough money to provide food and clothing for her children. What she did have was love and faith. She told her son she found him outside in a beautiful gold box, shimmering in the snow. When questioned about the box itself, she said. "Son, when I found you, I was so happy that I couldn't think about anything else." Douglas said, "I was disappointed that my mother had let the beautiful gold box disappear. But I was also very happy, because I was more important to my mother than even a beautiful gold box with silver strings attached to it, going all the way up to the sky. From then on, I always knew that I would be somebody." In Sagittarius, one seeks nobility of heart and mind. Those fortunate enough to acquire these qualities become the new heroes of the zodiac. They still seek justice, freedom and human dignity, but they accomplish it with inspiration and the power of the *word*.

The secret weapon of a Sagittarius is the power of positive thinking. They have the ability to see something good in everything and everyone. Mark Twain's mother "always found something to excuse and as a rule to love, in the toughest of them—even if she put it there herself." This is the ability to mirror God, to reflect his image—that is, to see the divine in all human beings. The power of this gift is limitless. To see good in others is to help it grow. In *Paradise Lost,* Milton proclaims that through the fall of Adam and Eve something greater will be gained, the redemption of man. Paracelsus, the famous philosopher and physician, said, "Hope is one of the loftiest emotions we can experience; we must trust in our art and hope that it will not fail. For wherever we lack hope, our fruits will be also lacking."

This sense of hope is assisted by the Sagittarius who knows how to select from the environment thoughts and events that support Spirit. Kirk Douglas said, "Every night, before going to bed, I tried to think of a happy thought, like a dog that has hidden a bone. If I had a pleasant thought during the day, I would lock it away with the reminder 'Oh yes, I must think of that tonight.' "

The intellect is the key to Sagittarius, it is about a mind daring enough to break through tradition, limitations, distortions, and untruths. The mind is where true freedom lies. Only in the realm of reason can you achieve the freedom to explore, create, imagine and live life to its fullest. What the Sagittarius believes to be true, they make special, and give life. Around that belief they select other thoughts that support it. Positive thinkers value beautiful moments and use them as a shield to protect against depression, ignorance, separation, and evil.

A certain vigilance is necessary to maintain superior intelligence, reasoning power, and a positive attitude. Skepticism of emotions and even of intelligence is essential to the higher mind. Emotions need to be raised to the level of reason. If they aren't, the Sagittarius will be tossed and battered by their pursuit or denial. Internalizing emotions allows them to be studied. A Sagittarius who refuses to digest and examine the views of others becomes a tyrant and a racist.

Sagittarius demands that we discover through dissociation, through removing the impediments that keep the truth from blossoming. This is the sign of expansion, and it is achieved through the shedding of outmoded ideas, habits, and patterns. This is also the sign of the attitude. The Sagittarius voice breaks through outmoded tradition. Mark Twain spoke against racial discrimination. Margaret Mead challenged sexual taboos. Spinoza freed God from man's limitations. Paracelsus revolutionized the world of medicine. Sagittarians know the power of the word and they seek to master it. Churchill said, "It was my only ambition to be master of the spoken word." Through the use of language they transform their emotions. Anger becomes irony. Even humor and insight become weapons that advance the speaker toward a goal. Sagittarians wound with the truth encased in syllables and well-honed paragraphs. In perhaps his most famous public adress, Winston Churchill rehabilitated a beleaguered nation. "We shall go on to the end," he said to the people of England. "We shall fight in France, we shall fight on the seas and oceans, we shall fight with growing confidence and growing strength in the air, we shall defend our island, whatever the cost maybe, we shall fight on the beaches, we shall fight on the landing grounds, we shall fight in the fields and in the streets, we shall fight in the hills; we shall never surrender."

In Sagittarius, defeat is not an option. Through their fearlessness, their love of controversy and conflict, their humor and their style, we learn from them, follow them, attack them, and love them, for they are our leaders. When their goal is to elevate the spirit of mankind, we stretch ourselves to do the impossible because they believe in us.

Gifted with strong egos, pride and vanity are the enemies of Sagittarius. They sense their own greatness; the divine living within. If this is not translated into a higher mission, the Ego can become greatly inflated and carry with it a sense of self-importance. These souls have presence and a passion for life. Their energy can fill any room or auditorium. Exceptionally generous, the Ego gives but demands adulation and loyalty in return. These are the sugar daddies and the politicians, who promise everything and then use your faith and your support for their own ends. When the Sagittarius faith is used for the right reasons, they become the prophets, spiritual leaders and gurus of the zodiac. These are the men and women dedicated to preaching the glory of God, those who feel chosen to pass on His message. They are the translators of divine knowledge into words all can understand. Mark Twain said, "My books are water; those of the great geniuses are wine. Everybody drinks water."

The ability to translate the divine into the basic nourishment of life truly requires the mind of a genius. These Sagittarians channel their knowledge through their instincts and the inner voice. Catalysts, they push those they meet to go beyond their limitations, to stretch their minds where comfort and complacency have threatened to stunt their growth.

The primal instincts of Aries are mature and developed in Sagittarius. Right and wrong are weighed by contemplating the consequences of actions and the degree of the threat to survival. All that's important now is the Sagittarius goal, and staying alive long enough to get there. Morality must be based on the moment. The Sagittarius must be able to act quickly and intuitively. They must be able to integrate their emotions, experiences, goals, God's laws, and the needs of the moment. Versatility is their gift. They are masters at temporarily distorting the truth to achieve a desired result. Fact and fiction get thrown together the better to represent their point of view. It is said of Mark Twain that. "Throughout his career as a reporter Sam [Clemens] would often show a remarkable indifference to the facts. If the facts sounded better mixed in with fiction, then Sam threw in the fiction."

Twain also said, "Don't part with your illusions. When they are gone you may still exist but you have ceased to live." When it comes to fantasy, few could match the creative mind of Walt Disney. Disney (December 5) developed his imaginary world to escape from a fanatical, abusive father and a hard childhood. His movies, characters and theme parks are modern-day classics that delight all generations.

Able to arrange facts in any order, Sagittarians can see things from others' perspectives, while never losing sight of their own. This is the beginning of compromise and the ability to coexist with others. In the world of survival, Sagittarians succeed because they have the ability to bend the rules, using reason, and to make decisions that walk the narrow line of good and evil, right and wrong. If the Sagittarian has faith, God will help them. If there is no one above them, they run the risk of becoming a law unto themselves. If the Ego is not tamed and the faculties of reason not developed, the Sagittarius could run into trouble with the law. This is where cosmic law meets collective values, personal needs, and goals.

The order of things is important in Sagittarius. They need to create a hierarchy. This system of priorities can lead to the master and slave relationship. However, it is ideas, rather than chains, that enslave. The Berlin Wall came falling down without a shot being fired once the collective spirit of the people refused to be contained. In Sagittarius collective belief systems battle for position. The challenge is to recognize the similarities of men's minds and live comfortably with the differences. One way Ego and Spirit deal with inequality is through the contrivance of unity. Education is an equalizer, if someone has knowledge it can raise them above the limits of their pocket books and equalize the discrepancy. Another way to expand the mind and thus equalize the differences between men, is through travel. Learning about different cultures and people allows the Sagittarius to adopt a broader perspective. This new perspective makes easier the acceptance within themselves of more than one point of view.

Religion and spiritual teachings demand the Sagittarians use their higher minds. The more their mind expands, the more opportunities they attract, and the more choices they create for themselves.

Since Sagittarius carries the soul from the overwhelming powerless feelings of emotions to the soaring freedom of the higher mind, many Sagittarians come to prominence during times of great transition. Mark Twain wrote *Huckleberry Finn* after the Civil War. Through the characters of a young white boy named Huck and a slave named Jim, Twain showed their common humanity. John Milton was a powerful voice on the issue of Church reform.

Milton wrote militant prose attacking those who favored Episcopacy, accusing them of stopping the course "of the Reformation."

Sagittarius can be a bridge between what appears as irreconcilable feelings, people, or issues. If the Sagittarius mind has not expanded enough to contain more than one perspective, then the Sagittarius will be pulled between two points until both *can* be contained within. Sagittarius energy unites, heals, and expands the consciousness, allowing for new and more encompassing perceptions. Whenever Sagittarians can rise above an issue and take a panoramic view, they can see the threads that connect instead of separate.

The masking of truth is essential to survival. Truth is a weapon that must be kept out of the hands of those not ready to use it properly. Thus, the discrepancy between the Spirit and the Ego begins to manifest. In order to make others see what they want them to see, the Sagittarius must know how to mislead the eye. It takes great skill not to duplicate something exactly. Carbon copies are a dime a dozen. They fail to invoke the truth. The ability to present the truth so that the world *can* recognize it, is not so simple. It requires the more complex skill of mixing facts and fantasies to make the viewer *See* the truth from the Sagittarian perspective. This discrepancy between appearance and reality is sometimes observed in the way their spirit or talent is not apparent in their appearance. Woody Allen is always seen in baggy corduroy trousers, frayed sweater, black-rimmed glasses, and sensible shoes. At the height of his fame, Beethoven was still so poorly dressed he was once picked up as a vagrant.

Sagittarians hold their truth safely inside. Only someone who has proved their worthiness is allowed to know it. Loyalty and trust are two important qualities a Sagittarius seeks. They don't give either easily, but when they do, they give their support for life. Winston Churchill expected total, uncritical loyalty and he reciprocated in kind. For his entire life, Walt Disney was plagued with issues of loyalty. He offered his cartoonists double their salary in order to keep them. Those who stuck with him during the difficult times had a job for life.

Art and the artist, like Ego and Spirit, are somewhat separate in Sagittarius. The creation often exceeds the power and freedom of the creator. Spirit is not limited by the fears of Ego, but works independently, soaring to great heights, while the body often remains locked in despair and hopelessness. Difficulties and hard times help the Spirit separate from the body and create new and imaginative worlds. Art is now used, not expressed; it becomes a means of escape. In art, the soul can maintain total freedom and control. Maria Callas, ". . . was interested in everyone's part. After a while the role became like a second skin. Her interpretation gradually took hold of her and became totally instinctual." Emily Dickinson thought poetry and the poet allowed the mortal and the eternal to unite. Kirk Douglas thought art "can only be obtained from hunger—hunger for beauty or harmony or truth or justice.'' This is Spirit when it races ahead, thirsty for a chance to express itself. Beethoven regarded art as a way of communicating knowledge about reality.

Relationships are not easy for the Sagittarius. They are loners, but they're also passionate, generous, and have very sexy minds. Some Sagittarians never marry and prefer to remain alone, in order to protect their individuality. Without the ability to contain more than their own point of view, it will be difficult to accept love. Woody Allen solved this problem; he and Mia Farrow each had their own apartment. Maria Callas made the mistake of turning her individuality over to the men in her life. Onassis made her sacrifice her talent for him and, for a Sagittarius, this is a fate worse than death.

Sexually, the Sagittarius is either promiscuous or loyal. It depends on how much they let someone else into their private world. Once they do allow someone in, they are committed for life. With their great talent for imagination, the Sagittarian can easily fall in love with someone totally unavailable, someone they can long for, someone they keep above them and out of their world. When love is found in the moment they can have the perfect union, one that lasts for life. Winston Churchill's family was the center of his life. When he met the woman he loved, Mark Twain gave up his adventuresome ways to settle down and he never regretted it for a moment. So, if your lover is a Sagittarius, don't let him or her keep you on the sidelines of their life. Sometimes, they need you to push beyond their resistance.

As far as career is concerned, Sagittarians excel in almost any endeavor. However, they lead the way in the fields of writing, law, politics, teaching, and philosophy. They dominate the halls of universities and religious institutions. Their love of travel and foreign cultures makes them good with anything international; they also have a knack for languages. Whatever they do, they strive to be the best. They are constantly learning, changing and bringing new ideas to their work.

Sagittarians are natural leaders, gifted with unlimited energy and spirit. Their ability to inspire and transfer their beliefs gives them power to influence the course of events or the lives of others. Their personal lives can suffer. When intimacy is not their strength, a quest for knowledge and truth often is. Loners and staunch individualists, they put their mission first, above and beyond their personal needs. They love their freedom. They need to create, to challenge others, and to transform what is into what could be. They have vision and the gift of prophecy. When they connect with their divinity, they are invincible. Pride and vanity are their enemies; they want things their way or no way. Advice is not something they seek, but they are open to learning and guidance. This is the sign of the professor, the soul who desires to know the highest truth. Don't try to understand them. Know, however, that you can count on them, for they value loyalty above all else. A Sagittarian has the qualities that make a great friend, a brilliant advisor, or a heroic leader.

Once they believe in themselves, it's only a matter of time before the world sees things their way.

THE SAGITTARIUS ENVIRONMENT

The Sagittarius environment either overprotects, wrapping loving arms around you in support, making you feel special, or it casts you out into the cold, harsh reality of life so that you can learn to survive against all odds. Either way, the Sagittarius has to take a risk. This is the sign of hard experience. True confidence and knowledge is gained through their capacity to survive by their wits alone. Here, the higher mind prevails: the ability to intuit, reduce a problem to simple choices, to see the whole picture and fill in the missing pieces of a problem with reason and imagination. These are the only weapons they need to stay alive and to reach their goal. With Spirit strong, it seeks things that uplift it—poetry, music, the arts, inspiration and words. These things fortify the Sagittarius against formidable enemies. The environment provides the shock the soul needs to unite faith, imagination, and reality. Once the higher mind has all its resources at its fingertips, it's ready to pull everything together and allow Sagittarians to take their place in the world.

Sagittarius/*One* (November 28, December 1, December 10, December 19) Jupiter/Sun

PURPOSE: To develop your individuality and express your unique talents without compromising yourself to authority but allowing yourself to surrender to love.

"To be what we are, and to become what we are capable of becoming is the only end of life."—R.L. Stevenson. The challenge of the Sagittarius/*One* is faith in themselves, the ability to walk alone, make their own rules and survive in spite of the pressure to surrender their uniqueness to the crowd. They are either very powerful, with a definite point of view, or they can be overwhelmed by someone they see as powerful. Sagittarius/*Ones* must learn to own their strength and always be open to new and different ideas. When they do, they're undefeatable. Persistent and driven, they like things difficult and may seek out tough experiences that will hone their nature and strengthen their self-confidence. Talented, charming, and charismatic, they have the ability to mesmerize a crowd, but one-on-one dealings can be difficult. They are loners and their love of large experience makes it difficult to settle for intimacy. Loyalty is the key. Once they can trust someone, they begin to open up and let them in. The Sagittarius *One* should be aware that when things go too well, they can become upset because they've lost their challenge. The Sagittarius *One* rebels against authority. Their principles can be so high and lofty they can't bend, which causes unnecessary problems in their lives. Sagittarius *Ones* need to look at the whole picture; they need to step back and become good observers. Then life becomes fun.

IF SPIRIT TAKES THE LEAD: If Spirit is in the lead, the Sadge/*One* gives the orders. They are natural-born leaders who are never content to be second-best. They have faith in their talents and rejection never discourages them. They are loyal and unrelenting. They often persist to the point of being self-destructive. If they are too rigid in their principles, they can create unnecessary obstacles and invite abuse. Intimacy may be a problem because they are seeking something inspirational and grand, not personal and private.

IF EGO TAKES THE LEAD: With Ego out front, the Sadge/*One* wants to rule the world. Incredibly charming and generous, they give a lot but want power, loyalty, and support in return. They are the politicians and authority figures who believe their way is the only way. They are stubborn and persistent and so is the opposition they meet. Without a strong sense of self, they can be overwhelmed by someone else.

BETTE MIDLER (December 1)

Singer, Actress.

Midler was born in Hawaii. Endowed with an overdose of persistence and ambition, she landed a bit part in the made-for-TV version James Michener's *Hawaii* and was chosen to return to L.A. to help finish the picture. Without sharing her plans with her parents, she set off to become an actress. She saved every penny she made in L.A. to finance a trip to New York. Midler's determination paid off. When she landed in New York, she auditioned for any part she could. Finally, she was hired to play the prize role of Tzeitel in *Fiddler on the Roof.* However, a spontaneous act at a local bar changed her life. Midler sang "God Bless the Child" and turned the place upside down with excitement. From that moment on, she knew she wanted to be a singer. She took a job at the Continental Baths and hooked up with Barry Manilow, who became her partner for four years. Finally, Johnny Carson gave her a break. They played off each other brilliantly and their friendship endured until his last show, where she sang a farewell song. Midler went on to world tours, award-winning albums, movies, and finally, a husband and child. Her strength is in her versatility and intelligence.

EMILY DICKINSON (December 10)

Poet.

Emily Dickinson was a woman devoted to her art. She lived a quiet, secluded existence; her religious background was, New England Puritan. Extremely intelligent, Dickinson felt the limitations imposed on women of her time and battled with her personal religious convictions. Unable to reconcile herself with a punishing and distant God, she used her poetry to seek Him out and challenge Him. Living the inner life of a *One,* Dickinson used the Sagittarius energy to explore the world of ideas, instead of distant lands. Her poems are not personal but panoramic. She identified with large themes: isolation, fate, a deity indifferent to the world, and death. Dickinson wrote almost two thousand poems but only seven were published in her lifetime.

Sagittarius/*Two* (November 29, December 2, December 11, December 20) Jupiter/Moon

PURPOSE: To learn how to use your sensitivity and your vulnerability to overcome great odds, transforming them into inspirational strengths that get you to your goal and allow you to help others along the way.

"Until you try, you don't know what you can't do."—Henry James. Once the Sagittarius *Two* has accepted the fact that they can't do everything and accept their talents, which are many, they're on the way. The danger is their desire to have someone else protect them; giving power away always leads to trouble. Sagittarius *Twos* must conquer their fear of abandonment and choose someone loyal, not a showman who knows how to amuse and abuse. They like the razzle-dazzle of life, but they're not always prepared to hold their own. Psychic and creative, they can be visionaries. A bit dramatic and obsessive, they are afraid their needs won't be met. They are loners who trust with difficulty. They can refuse to budge once they make up their mind, but their defiance can work against them. Their challenge is to express their feelings and take events less personally. Once they do, they'll find they get hurt a great deal less and that the desire for vengeance is gone from their hearts.

IF SPIRIT TAKES THE LEAD: If Spirit is out front, then healing is, too. Whatever their gift, they have the power to effect change in others. The Sadge/ *Two* is a catalyst in life, and through their sensitivity and creativity they give the world something inspirational and divine. They are obsessive and once they get an idea in their head, it never gets out. They love too deeply, feel too passionately, and are truly very much alone. No one soul can fulfill their desires and needs. They need a spiritual quest.

IF EGO TAKES THE LEAD: If Ego is ahead, then selfishness and obsessiveness will dominate. The Sadge/*Two* knows how to influence the beliefs of others, preying on the needs and weaknesses of people who are looking for someone to take care of them. They are dramatic; they create problems, always desiring more than what someone is willing to give. Plagued with a sense of separateness and loneliness, they strive for recognition and adulation, but even when they get it, it's not enough.

MARIA CALLAS (December 2)

Diva.

Callas, born Maria Anna Sofia Cecelia Kalogeropoulos was an overweight child with thick glasses and a beautiful voice. From Queens, New York, Callas's mother left the father and returned to Greece with her two daughters. When the war broke out, Callas's sister's wealthy fiancé helped the family and her music studies continued. Her career took off in Italy, where she met and married Battista Meneghini, who became her manager. All her life, Callas struggled with her weight, and, early in her career, it was a terrible embarrassment. Eventually, she lost the weight and learned to dress in the latest fashion. Callas was an intuitive singer. Her voice was unique, filled with drama and emotion. Audiences adored her and in a short time she became the greatest diva of the century. Her romance with Aristotle Onassis, the richest man in the world, brought her both great happiness and pain. When he dropped her for Jacqueline Kennedy, she felt betrayed. As Callas immersed herself in society and turned her back on her career, her voice began to fail. But Callas retained a strong ego and the ability to mesmerize her audiences. Her sudden death shocked fans around the world.

ADAM CLAYTON POWELL, JR. (November 29)

Congressman from Harlem, the first African-American congressman from the Northeast.

Brilliant, flamboyant, and controversial, Adam Clayton Powell was a tireless crusader for racial equality. Born the grandson of a slave, Powell was raised across the street from the Abyssinian Baptist Church. At age twelve he started a group in the basement of the church called the Young Thinkers, to talk about local and national issues. His illustrious career, which included being the first elected African-American congressman from Harlem, was tainted by his love of the good life. In 1956, Powell left the Democratic party, because Adlai Stevenson, the Democratic candidate for President, was indecisive on the issue of race. As an unofficial representative of the United States, Powell visited Indonesia, which was hosting a conference about international racism. He was well received by the press and world leaders. Under President Lyndon Johnson, he became the chairman of the Education and Labor Committee of the House, and was a central figure in passing laws against poverty. Personal scandals and his reluctance to pay attention to the rules cost him his seat in Congress. Harlem reelected him, but he was not reseated until the Supreme Court backed him.

Sagittarius/*Three* (November 30, December 3, December 12, December 21) Jupiter/Jupiter

PURPOSE: To use your courage, strength, and perseverance to go beyond the limitations of the thoughts and ideas of those in power, creating your own unique beliefs that challenge the old and uplift the spirits of those who meet you.

"Some men see things as they are and say, 'Why?' I dream things that never were and say 'Why not?' "—Robert F. Kennedy. Sagittarius/*Threes* love a good fight. They seek out adversaries strong enough to challenge their souls. Without them, they don't reach their potential. The best way to use their energy is to pick a lofty goal, one that affords them the challenge they need to rise above their environment and know that only they determine their identity. Passionate and inspiring, they attract attention. They have great wit and charm, but their goals are more important than their relationships. Intimacy may be a problem because they love space and don't want love to hold them down. If they find loyal soul mates who allow them to be who they are, they can be faithful for a lifetime. If they are still fighting for freedom and individuality, closeness is not the thing they want. Different cultures and the past intrigue them. They take on too much responsibility and overburden themselves at work. Once they own their own strength, they won't misuse it; once they find their path, they'll help others on theirs.

IF SPIRIT TAKES THE LEAD: If Spirit is strong, the Sagittarius/*Three* is a leader and the tasks they attempt to accomplish are nothing less than heroic. They need to be careful they don't overwhelm their life with attempting impossible feats that keep them from enjoying everyday things. They need to fight for freedom and against injustice; they might even risk all they have to make a point. They're extreme, passionate, and inspiring. They can make a difference; don't waste time by showing off.

IF EGO TAKES THE LEAD: If Ego is predominant, they are nothing less than an egomaniac. Brilliant and manipulative, instinctual and courageous, they go after what they want fanatically. If they are afraid of owning their power, they may give it away to a religion or someone else with strong beliefs. If they do, they'll always feel powerless and overwhelmed by life.

MARK TWAIN (November 30)

Riverboat pilot, newspaper reporter, adventurer, satirist, writer.

The power of the word found its way into the Sagittarius soul of Mark Twain, born Samuel Clemens, who believed that laughter was the "one really effective weapon humankind possessed to struggle against injustice.'' A natural adventurer, he traveled the world until he married and settled down with a woman he had loved all his life. As a young reporter, Twain achieved recognition for standing up against injustice, speaking out against the clergy, corrupt politics, and racism. He protested and criticized with humor. ''Against the assault of laughter nothing can stand.'' Twain was a man of contradictions: he believed in God, but not religion; he hated capitalism, but desired to be wealthy; he abhorred violence, but believed in revolution as the most effective way to end injustice.

SIR WINSTON CHURCHILL (November 30)

Prime minister of England, writer, historian.

The son of an English duke and an American mother, Churchill had a difficult childhood. He was ignored by both parents and sent away to boarding school, where he endured ridicule and humiliation. As William Manchester put it, Churchill's only weapon was an *unconquerable will and an incipient sense of immortality*. Churchill seemed to be a man of destiny. World events challenged him to meet impossible odds. As prime minister, he had the magnitude and power to rally the spirit of the English people to defy the invasion by Germany. Churchill united a country and gave England courage to survive. Unfortunately, Churchill's great spirit was tempered by deep bouts of depression. Churchill loved tradition and wrote fifty-six books, half of them on war and warriors. His mastery of the English language and his wit were unequaled.

Sagittarius/*Four* (November 23, December 4, December 13) Jupiter/Uranus

PURPOSE: To use your perseverence, and faith to break free of outmoded ideas and behavior; to unify through your ability to see beyond the differences of others and into what is true and real.

''Things do not change, we change.''—Henry David Thoreau. The Sagittarius/ *Four* is a catalyst in the lives of others. Freedom is their true love, and nothing will ever come between them and its quest. A relationship is important, but difficult; they don't allow people to get very close. When it comes to friends, the Sagittarius/*Four* is not wanting. They value the friendship of many types of people. Drawn to faraway places and different cultures, they may lead a nomad's life. If not, they dream about it. They have a talent for bringing others together and make great negotiators in business or politics. Whatever they do is innovative and change is on the agenda. True loners, they prefer their own company. Loyal and steadfast, they demand the same from others. Their minds are like calculators, quick and adept at solving problems or seeing solutions almost instantly. They are also instinctual. They like to do several things at once. Attracted to controversy and problems, they need to be careful they don't lose peace of mind trying to diffuse the hostility around them. Their moment to shine is always close at hand; they must be prepared for it.

IF SPIRIT TAKES THE LEAD: If Spirit is in the lead, they believe they have all the answers, and they may, but ramming them down someone's throat will not get the job done. They want to improve the lives of others with or without their consent. Drawn to the underdog, they could get stuck helping those who refuse to help themselves. Freedom and justice are what drive them, just make sure you don't drive yourself into poor health.

IF EGO TAKES THE LEAD: If Ego is strong, then so is the sense of isolation. If they are not tough, then they can be overwhelmed by someone who restricts their freedom and dictates their life. Controversy attracts them. Original thinkers, they need to be careful they don't become a bully, ignoring rules and regulations, insisting on having things their way. Authority is an issue; they need to learn how to live in a world with other people.

DICK VAN DYKE (December 13)

Actor, singer, dancer, comedian.

Born in White Plains, New York, Van Dyke grew up in Illinois, where his father worked as a salesman for Sunshine Biscuits. Attracted to radio, Van Dyke did mike duty at an Oklahoma army base during WWII. After his discharge, he set off with a friend to make his fortune. They developed a lip-sync act called the Merry Mutes. Eventually, Van Dyke sent for his high-school sweetheart, Marjorie Millett, and married her on a radio show called *Bride and Groom.* It was the only way they could afford a ring and a honeymoon. The couple lived a nomad's life until Van Dyke's luck changed when they settled in Manhattan in 1956. Four years later, Van Dyke got his first big break in the musical *Bye Bye Birdie.* His biggest television hit was *The Dick Van Dyke Show,* starring Mary Tyler Moore. It won five Emmy Awards and was on the air from 1961 until 1966. Since then, Van Dyke has starred in several successful television shows.

GUSTAVE FLAUBERT (December 13)

Writer.

Flaubert's father was a surgeon at a hospital in Rouen, France. To the little boy, this man was larger-than-life. Flaubert was shy; his father considered him dull-witted. Flaubert's dreams became his refuge. He began to write at an early age. School was more a prison than a place to learn. "From the time I entered school," he said, "I was melancholy, restless, seething with desires.

I yearned ardently for a wild and turbulent existence, I dreamed of passions and wanted to experience them all." Flaubert's *Madame Bovary,* a novel about an adulterous woman, was considered "an outrage to public morals." It was very successful; nevertheless, he had to defend the novel in court. Flaubert won and the scandal of the trial made the book even more successful. His next book, *Salammbo,* was about a Carthaginian heroine, daughter of the general Hamilcar and priestess of Tanit. Some loved it, others were outraged. The critics attacked it unmercifully and still it was a success. Flaubert had friendships with other great writers of his time, including Guy de Maupassant, George Sand, Maxime Du Camp, Ivan Turgenev and Emile Zola. His life depicts the duality of the Sagittarius, who desires to be alone but who always seems to be attracted to controversy.

Sagittarius/*Five* (November 23, December 5, December 14) Jupiter/Mercury

PURPOSE: To see the great in the small, the details in the large. To take a leap of consciousness using your mind and imagination to create something no one has ever done before.

"The absence of alternatives clears the mind marvelously."—Henry Kissinger. Sagittarius/*Five* is a very versatile combination; being able to choose one path or one direction as a goal may be a challenge. These souls have the gift of imagination and the ability to see things from many points of view, but this doesn't do them any good unless they have the courage to manifest their perceptions by taking a risk. Prone to worry and restlessness, they need to access their faith and let God do some of their work. They are comfortable with kings or the common man. They can be perfectionists, and obsessive workers. Relationships may be difficult because of this. If they are interested in the opposite sex, they could prefer many partners. Their will is unbending. Judgment, religion, and justice could all be strong issues. Sagittarius/*Fives* must remember their ability to contain all points of view within themselves. Tolerance of the perspectives of others is the challenge of this combination. When they open up, they have great ability to influence the lives and choices of others.

IF SPIRIT TAKES THE LEAD: If Spirit is strong, these souls feel they have a mission to give a voice to those who feel powerless. They are perfectionists. They worry about endless details, forgetting that faith is the ability to let go. They overdo everything, but their persistence usually pays off and success is not a distant stranger. Health can be an issue, for they easily forget the needs of the body. If they're religious, they're fanatical. Slow down and learn the process of acceptance. It's the path to peace and happiness.

IF EGO TAKES THE LEAD: Ego takes the lead, morals are worthless and anything goes. They are not to be trusted. They know how to present themselves in any guise. If they're too far off-center, the law could be looking for them. In spite of their faults, people love them and are willing to give them what they ask for.

WALT DISNEY (December 5)

Creator of animated films and characters.

The imagination of Sagittarius becomes genius in Walt Disney. His career was and still is, even after his death, full of innovative successes. But new ideas seldom find an easy road. Disney's father was a fundamentalist, and he and his older brother Roy worked the family farm before they were ten. Beaten with a whip or leather belt at the slightest provocation, Disney survived the cruelty through his imagination and hung tightly to the fairy tales his mother read to him at night. Gifted with an ability to draw, he used what little money he had to buy crayons or chalk, but more often than not he sketched with coal on toilet paper. Eventually, Disney gravitated to advertising, and then to animated cartoons. He took a risk and moved his company to Hollywood. Eventually, Disney had a winner in Oscar the Lucky Rabbit. However, the larger companies with whom he had a contract stole his creation. The lesson was not lost on Disney. When Mickey Mouse became a success, he refused to sell his rights. In fact, he was the first really to capitalize on merchandising. Disney's married life was not blissful; nor was he without sexual problems. His early childhood trauma contributed to a problem with impotence. Although he was regarded in high esteem as a man who upheld the higher principles of society, he was also a prejudiced man. An anti-Semite, he joined forces with Hoover as an FBI official informant, helping root out communists, subversives, and Jews. His ego was strong and needy, and he took credit for more than his share of the Disney creations. He demanded long hours and hard work, and of course excellence, of his employees. In spite of his faults, his legacy is monumental.

MARGARET CHASE SMITH (December 14)

First female United States Senator.

Smith was one of the most influential women in the history of American politics. She served thirty-two years in Congress. Twice she was considered a vice presidential possibility, and in 1964 she launched the first campaign by a woman for the presidential nomination of a major party. Smith never revealed how she would vote. Often, her stance was against the party establishment.

At age thirty-two, she married Clyde Smith whom she had known since she was sixteen. Twenty-one years older and a man with a shady past, he was linked to highway fraud and an illegitimate pregnancy. Smith followed him to Washington where he was a member of the House of Representatives and became his secretary. When he died, she ran for his seat. Tutored by Bill Lewis, she learned how to develop a national constituency. Lewis directed her first senatorial campaign in 1948, and she won an upset victory. Overnight, she became a heroine of women everywhere. As a senator, she immediately took on Joseph McCarthy and courageously confronted him long before the Senate majority censored him. She was elected to three more terms and sat on the powerful Armed Services, Appropriations, Space, Government Operations, and Intelligence Committees. She was defeated only at the age of seventy-four.

Sagittarius/*Six* (November 24, December 6, December 15) Jupiter/Venus

PURPOSE: To use your charm to make your rebellious nature and your desire to create change a process without opposition.

"Without deviation, progress is not possible."—Frank Zappa. The Sagittarius/*Six* is a rebel by nature, and is attracted to other rebels. These are men and women who are not afraid of seeking the truth. Charming and charismatic, they love beauty and may have deep and passionate desires. They are unique in every way. Discipline may be a problem; excess could be an issue. Society attracts them and at the same time, their love of privacy may force them into seclusion. They are gifted as writers or as poets. Music is also important to them. Challenges attract them and so do change and controversy. They protect their beliefs, either by keeping them quiet or by fighting openly for them.

IF SPIRIT TAKES THE LEAD: If Spirit is strong, the love of justice and equality are important. The Sagittarius/*Sixes,* are rebels and they like a good fight. They need to be careful they don't get in trouble with the law, even though they're fighting for the underdog. They are restless and filled with passion and desire. They know they are special, and they strive to make sure that others feel that way, too.

IF EGO TAKES THE LEAD: With Ego strong, so is an excessive nature. These souls are obsessed with the beauty of their own voice, words, and ideas. Their loyalty fluctuates with the present truth; their truth fluctuates with the needs of the moment. Smooth, charming, and generous, they are proud and vain and, yes, often successful. They surround themselves with people who adore them, as well as with beautiful possessions.

WILLIAM F. BUCKLEY, JR. (November 24)

Writer, columnist.

Founder of the *National Review,* a journal of conservative opinions, Buckley's column is syndicated in more than three hundred newspapers. His opinions and wit are sought among intellectuals around the world. Buckley's television show, *Firing Line,* won an Emmy after it first aired in 1966. His guests have included Presidents Ronald Reagan, Jimmy Carter and Gerald Ford and British Prime Minister Margaret Thatcher.

Buckley was born in New York, but went to school in France and England. He returned to America for prep school, the army, and Yale, where he became chairman of the *Yale Daily News.* His first book was a controversial bestseller, *God and Man at Yale.* He is author of some twenty books and hundreds of articles. Buckley is married to the former Patricia Taylor, who is known for being one of New York City's best hostesses and its most sought-after benefit chairman.

RON DELLUMS (November 24)

Democratic Congressman.

Dellums was born in Oakland, California. He joined the Marine Corps after high school and on the G.I. Bill, graduated from San Francisco State. In 1962, he obtained a master's in social work from the University of California at Berkeley. He started out as a psychiatric social worker and soon found himself director of various Bay Area community social-service agencies. "I got talked into going to a meeting to tell people why I didn't want to be a (Berkeley) city council candidate, and wound up being the candidate." Dellums won with the backing of left-wing African-Americans, Asians, and whites. Three years later, Dellums unseated a white congressman and went to Washington. Dellums protested the Vietnam war by holding his own war crimes hearings against U.S. military officials, and in 1971 participated in a rally on the steps of the Capitol. More than one thousand people were arrested. Dellums also spoke out against racism in the armed forces and forced the government to confess that prejudice existed in U.S. bases in South Korea and Iceland. In 1983, Dellums was arrested for buying cocaine and marijuana. The charges were later dropped by reason of insufficient evidence. Dellums defends his title of radical African-American public official. "If being an advocate of peace, justice and humanity toward all human beings . . . [and being opposed to] the use of 70 per cent [sic] of federal moneys for destruction and war [is radical] . . . then I'm glad to be called a radical."

Sagittarius/*Seven* (November 25, December 7, December 16) Jupiter/Neptune

PURPOSE: To create through the power of your beliefs something divine, something that uplifts the soul of man.

"You have in your composition a mighty genius for expression which has escaped discipline.''—H.G. Wells. The Sagittarius/*Seven* lives in a world of beauty, imagination and fantasy. When they learn how to ground themselves, they can be geniuses. The Sagittarius/*Seven* either effects change in the world, or follows some great idea or person who they believe has these powers. They need to remember it is always dangerous to give away personal power. They feel the need to contribute something meaningful to the world. However, the other extreme is possible; the Sagittarius/*Seven* can be a dictator. They are psychic and may have vivid predictive dreams or even experience visits from angels. They need all the reality they can get. Once their feet are on the ground, their spirits are free to soar.

IF SPIRIT TAKES THE LEAD: With Spirit in the lead, so are perfectionism, truth, justice, and determination. These souls are headstrong and impossible to ignore. Their challenge is to see the whole picture, not just their own point of view. When they can choose who needs their help, instead of giving to anyone who asks or is in trouble, then they're ready to make a difference in the world. Without faith, they have trouble finding balance. They take on too much responsibility and drive themselves and their body to ruin. Learn when to say no and life will take on new meaning.

IF EGO TAKES THE LEAD: If Ego is strong, a dictator emerges, someone who doesn't care how or why the job gets done. Able to live a double life, they are manipulative and deceptive. They love to reach for the impossible, but their greed, pride and feelings of inadequacy keep them unhappy and striving for something more. They seek adulation, but whatever they get is not enough.

LUDWIG VAN BEETHOVEN (December 16)

Composer.

Beethoven's legacy is so monumental, it is hard for some to believe his works were created by a human being. Beethoven's life, however, was not without human struggle. He was born into poverty. His father was an alcoholic, so Beethoven assumed responsibility for his younger sister and brother, and when his mother died, his father. Beethoven studied piano during the Mozart frenzy spreading across Europe. His father noticed his gift, and greed led to cruelty—Beethoven was punished for not practicing. However, the music was more powerful than the cruelty, and Beethoven soon surrendered to it. He received some help from his mentor, Niefe, who introduced him to the music of Bach, which greatly influenced Beethoven's piano techniques. Considering himself a concert pianist, Beethoven didn't turn to composing until he learned he was going deaf. He broke with the style of Mozart and opened music to a broader, more grand style, orchestral in manner, one that allowed for color, bright outlines, and deep shadows. His personal tragedy contributed to his triumph. He struggled to see God in his music. His legacy is his ability to transport the human soul to a lofty and higher place.

MARGARET MEAD (December 16)

Anthropologist, writer, filmmaker.

The great adventurous spirit of Sagittarius found a perfect mate in Margaret Mead. At the age of twenty-three, she set off for the South Seas and then wrote *Coming of Age in Samoa.* In it, she described the guilt-free love of adolescent sexuality. The book was considered scandalous and from that point on, Mead was associated with sex and freedom, provocative ideas and inexhaustible energy. Like most Sagittarians, she was always on the move. By the time she was in junior high, she had lived in sixty houses. Her desire for knowledge was ever present. Her view of God was all-inclusive. Not surprisingly, she chose to teach, a favorite Sagittarius profession. Mead was married three times. Her profession as an anthropologist allowed her to travel and to experience life from many points of view. Her ideas on sex, culture, education, and child rearing affected several subsequent generations.

Sagittarius/*Eight* (November 26, December 8, December 17) Jupiter/Saturn

PURPOSE: To transcend your destiny through acceptance. To balance hope and despair, success and defeat, using all as sources of strength.

"Nothing would be done at all if a man waited until he could do it so well that no one could find fault with it."—Cardinal Newman. The Sagittarius/*Eight* is a perfectionist. They scrutinize everything in their path. They demand trust and loyalty from others because they give them back. Hard workers, Sagittarius/ *Eights* take on unnecessary responsibility in an effort to make everyone's life better. It's the process that's important now, not the end result; the journey, not the goal. But unless they set boundaries, the overload could bring them close to a nervous breakdown. Depression or dark moods are also problems. *Eights* swing between hope and despair, all in the same hour or day. Authority issues are alive and well in this combination. Their will is strong. They're stubborn. They are caught between an expansive mind and a love of freedom, and the fear of losing control if they open up their world and make it larger. The Sagittarius/*Eight* must learn to risk. This develops faith and allows expansion. With confidence, the world opens up. Sagittarius/*Eights* have had tough lives, but it's taught them the power of perseverance and faith.

IF SPIRIT TAKES THE LEAD: If Spirit is ahead, these souls are strong, disciplined and too responsible. They seek power to help those in need, but their need for control often undermines their effort. Attracted to tough situations and people, they are hard workers who seldom take a break or give one. They need to allow their faith to let them open up and trust something beyond themselves. They need to know that if they don't do the job, it will get done anyway.

IF EGO TAKES THE LEAD: If Ego takes the lead, the Sagittarius/*Eight* becomes a leader in the world of business. They have strong goals, but little compassion for pain or suffering. The work is more important than the worker. They are perfectionistic and only see what's wrong, not what's right.

KIM BASSINGER (December 8)

Model, actress.

Bassinger began her career as a model but soon found herself in Hollywood. Her leading men have included Sean Connery, Burt Reynolds, Robert Redford and Dan Aykroyd. It was her part in the James Bond movie *Never Say Never Again* that brought her instant notoriety and other important roles, including her part opposite Robert Redford in *The Natural.* and opposite Michael Keaton in *Batman.* Born into a family of five children, Bassinger grew up in Georgia. She played the piano and guitar and at fifteen, took ballet and singing lessons. When she moved to New York, she was an instant hit on the modeling scene. After five years, she was ready to take Hollywood by storm "I love comedy," Bassinger said, "and think it's the most powerful thing we have in the entertainment industry. I think people don't laugh enough and good humor is very seldom written. So I love it once I get something good. I love the ride along the way."

PARACELSUS (December 17)

Physician, philosopher, teacher, medical revolutionary.

Born Philippus Aureolus Theophrastus Bombast von Hohenheim in Einsiedeln, the Swiss place of pilgrimage, in 1493, Paracelsus was an only child. When he was nine, his mother died, and he moved with his father to Villach in Carinthia. Paracelsus's father was a physician. Paracelsus saw the comfort his father brought people and strove to emulate him. But he was restless, and driven by the desire to discover truth and acquire knowledge. Soon, he was traveling from village to village in his quest for learning. His formal education included time spent at the University of Vienna and a number of universities in Italy. However, firsthand experience would always be his greatest teacher. Nothing was insignificant to his eyes. He wrote "learn and learn, ask and ask, do not be ashamed." In spite of his inability to settle down, Paracelsus had an unshakable faith in the divine order of life. He believed that a doctor should remember that he is an instrument of God, and that his patients are also God's creatures. Everything—man, earth and the cosmos—was a part of the whole, a unified body ruled by God. Paracelsus is celebrated as the first modern medical scientist, a pioneer in microchemistry, antisepsis, modern wound surgery and homeopathy.

Sagittarius/*Nine* (November 27, December 9, December 18) Jupiter/Mars

PURPOSE: To present and protect your vision, creating it through the power of your being, influencing and convincing others to follow your path.

"Intelligence highly awakened is intuition which is the only true guide in life."—Krishnamurti. The Sagittarius/*Nine* should always listen to their instincts. Aggressive, stubborn and persistent, they love conflict and excitement. Their mind is keen, and they use it to avoid physical combat. Convinced they have a destiny to fulfill, they are anxious to manifest it. Capable of many emotions and multitalented, their problem is choosing one path. Sexy, charming, and magnetic, they have a passionate nature and a love for life. Nature itself calls them, and sports attract them. Gifted with unlimited energy, they are often their own worst enemy, chasing obsessively after someone or something that has aroused them. They demand loyalty. They want things their way, *right away.* A challenge attracts them to such a point that they often simply respond, instead of carefully choosing where to put their energy. The Sagittarius/*Nine* needs to slow down and look at the whole picture, only then will life cease to be a series of spurts with short-term rewards.

IF SPIRIT TAKES THE LEAD: If Spirit is in the lead, the Sagittarius/*Nines* are idealistic and desire to change the world. They feel they have a destiny. It may be true, but without patience, their progress is limited. Uncomfortable with asking for help, they choose huge challenges and try to solve them alone. Any cause that tugs at their heart, compels them. This is not good for relationships and completing a job. If they can't say no, nothing will ever get done and love won't last.

IF EGO TAKES THE LEAD: If Ego is ahead, then selfishness and pride are out front. These souls believe they are special and that their needs should come first. Aggressive and persistent, others often step aside. If they don't, they'd better be ready to fight. They can be abusive; they lack compassion for others. Stubborn and demanding, patience is not on their list of talents, but sex is.

JOHN MILTON (December 9)

Poet.

John Milton was born in London. His father was a moneylender and yet had high hopes his son would be a man of God. Gifted as a youth, Milton studied the classics and eventually attended Cambridge. There he abandoned the idea of a religious life, and retreated instead to the country, isolating himself with his studies. Politics attracted him and at various times throughout his career he fought for freedom and independence, both in his writing and in the political arena. As a poet, he transformed every genre. As a powerful prose writer, he argued for divorce and freedom of the press. He saw himself as chosen by God to glorify Him and to contribute to the public good. A true Sagittarius, he hated mediocrity. His aim was to master all learning, to become the ideal Renaissance humanist. *Paradise Lost,* an epic in 11,000 lines, was, according to Milton, divinely inspired. The monumental work was written after Milton had gone blind. Here, inner vision led to sublime truth and an encounter with the Almighty.

STEVEN SPIELBERG (December 18)

Director, producer.

From *Schindler's List* to *E.T., Jaws, Raiders of the Lost Ark* and *Indiana Jones and the Temple of Doom,* Spielberg's movies have been megahits. The divorce of Spielberg's parents left a profound impression on his psyche. He moved in with his father, an electrical engineer, who traveled all over the country. His mother was a concert pianist. Spielberg's brilliance did not surface in high school. In fact his grades were not good enough to gain him admittance to any leading film school. Instead he majored in English at California State College, and found a way to get into the studios where he watched directors such as Hitchcock in action. His first short film, *Amblin,* describes an "attack of crass commercialism." It won him awards at both the Atlanta and Venice Film Festivals and was distributed as a featured short with *Love Story.* At age twenty, Spielberg was signed to a seven-year contract with Universal Pictures. His first job was to direct Joan Crawford in Rod Serling's TV series *Night Gallery.* Spielberg also worked on *Marcus Welby, M.D., Columbo,* and *The Name of the Game.* His first full feature movie, shot in sixteen days for just $350,000 dollars, was called *Duel.* It starred Dennis Weaver as a traveling salesman. The movie grossed over $5 million dollars in Europe and Japan. The *Sugarland Express* came next, followed by his first megahit, *Jaws.* He is considered the most successful director/ producer in the world.

SUMMARY

As the soul tastes the newly earned freedom of emotional objectivity, it sees that fate is closing the door. Eager to retain its ability to create, it reaches to the heavens and to imagination. There, in the misty veil of the clouds, it reclaims its freedom and manifests the ethereal in its talents. Through the word, it inspires, unites and protects itself. Attached to the moment, the Sagittarius refuses to budge, defying fate, the enemy, and God. Of course,

Spirit returns to earth and heaven and earth are once more in alignment. This is the end of the crisis of faith. The soul has received the seed of self and knows nothing can harm it. With a positive attitude obstacles dissolve, problems are reduced to manageable parts, and the soul owns the moment. This is where everything comes together to create a man or woman of destiny. These are leaders and teachers. They are wise with wisdom gained through hard experience. They are versatile, resilient and multitalented. With the power of creation and communication, they enjoy the ecstasy of having their visions become real. Their reward for a job well-done is self-knowledge and full consciousness. In the next sign of Capricorn Ego and Spirit must work in harmony or the summit, the mid-point between heaven and earth, will not be reached.

SELECTED SOURCES

Clinton Cox   *Mark Twain: America's Humorist, Dreamer, Prophet A Biography*   Scholastic 1995

Benjamin DeCasseres   *Spinoza: Liberator of God and Men*   E.W. Sweetland 1932

Kirk Douglas   *The Ragman's Son: An Autobiography*   Pocket Books 1993

Jane Howard   *Margaret Mead: A Life*   Simon & Schuster 1984

Nikos Kazantzakis   *Saint Francis: A Novel*   Translated from the Greek by P.A. Bien   Simon & Schuster 1962

Manuel Komroff   *Beethoven and the World of Music*   Mead & Company 1961

Eric Lax   *Woody Allen: A Biography*   Knopf 1991

George Mair   *Bette: An Intimate Biography of Bette Midler*   Birch Lane 1995

William Manchester   *The Last Lion: Winston Spencer Churchill Alone 1932–1940*   Little Brown and Co. 1988

Bill Moyers   *Genesis: A Living Conversation*   Doubleday 1996

Paracelsus   *Selected Writings*   Edited by Jolande Jacobi   Princeton University Press 1951

Nadia Stancioff   *Maria Callas Remembered*   E.P. Dutton 1987

Henri Troyat   *Flaubert*   Translated by Joan Pinkham   Viking 1992

Cynthia Griffin Wolff   *Emily Dickinson*   Addison-Wesley 1988

PART IV
THE AWAKENING

*I*n **Capricorn, Aquarius,** and **Pisces,** the soul awakens to its true nature and chooses a spiritual ideal as its source of power. The heart becomes the center, forgiveness becomes possible, and unity is finally achieved. Ego and Spirit are balanced and in harmony, they work together to prepare to climb the summit, a height beyond worldly success, an impossible feat for a mere human. However, the divine is now present in the soul's consciousness, and when it acts with respect for both worlds anything is possible. This is the process, these souls are disciplined, versatile, and able to communicate with heaven as well as earth. In **Capricorn,** the soul must face its fears, its depression—all its weaknesses that have been previously ignored. By dancing with darkness, facing danger, it strengthens its spirit and prepares to conquer the summit. Once it has achieved the impossible, it must learn how to cope with success in **Aquarius.** Without a disciplined Ego and a strong Spirit, success can be destructive. When Ego and Spirit work together in harmony, then strength and success are used to help those who are lost and alone. The soul has gained the skill to divide from within, not without. Through embracing it all, it can choose instantly which part of itself must be called forth to achieve its goal. As the soul reinvents itself in the image of God, it begins to taste the blessings of harmony, peace, and freedom. Able to respond to the moment, in **Pisces,** the soul now has the emotional strength and the detachment to use suffering and grief to connect itself to all humanity and to drive the roots, that are anchored in the heart, deeper, into that of the soul. Once it is rooted in God, it has succeeded in its journey, it is whole and can now manifest its worldly and spiritual purpose, receiving the gifts of both heaven and earth.

Capricorn

(December 22 - January 20)

The quest of Capricorn is the natural way.
They're blessed with rhythm, and something to say.
Each soul has a message, uniquely its own,
This message it seems needs time to be shown.
Conformity, society, these are the threat
Whatever you do, don't get stuck or too set.
You need to uproot your spirit, your past.
Then the summit you'll climb, you'll be balanced at last.

Ruler: Saturn   **Symbol: Goat**
Element: Earth   **Number: Eight**

The soul, humbled by its unsuccessful quest to reach heaven in Sagittarius, now accepts its fate and prepares for another ascent. It has learned not to soar proudly ahead, but to pace itself alongside Ego in order to reach its goal. Transformed by the realization that it needs the practical world and must work within its limitations, it also knows that only at the point of exhaustion, despair, and hopelessness—the end of physical and spiritual boundaries—can the chains of limiting perceptions be crossed and transformed. This is done with God's grace. Without His help, you will never pass through the darkness and fear that keeps you rooted in the past and unable to move forward.

Capricorns are comfortable with their negative feelings, which keep them stuck and unable to grow. Everyone fears freedom; it's more frightening than the chains that bind. Responsibility, hard work, and discipline are the only remedies. A passion, a goal, a yearning to be the best is what will drive you forward and into a routine that will break through your fear. Once you've found your direction, nothing will stop you and the rewards are fit for a king. You get to walk your spiritual path and still live and interact in the world at the same time.

Capricorn is the process. Through the struggle to achieve, you learn to use despair and hopelessness as tools, instead of as emotional crutches. Nothing is wasted in God's world, not even your negativity. Capricorn is the disowned collective shadow that must be passed through before you can walk the path of self-mastery and perfection, giving birth to your spiritual self.

A new you is about to emerge, and you get to create it in your own image. To do this requires a loosening of your attachment to the past. You can't be invested in fulfilling your parents' motivations, or anyone else's for that matter. You need to give birth to that part of yourself that has remained pure and true to your nature. This is a second chance to become exactly what you were meant to be. Albert Schweitzer (January 14) said, "With consciousness and with volition I devote myself to Being. I become an imaginative force, like that which works mysteriously in nature, and thus I gave my existence a meaning from within outwards."

With this new beginning and connection to oneself, comes new insight. Every vision expresses an earthly quest and a spiritual goal. You may have ignored your spiritual path up until now, but as you reconnect with your true nature you feel a deep and powerful yearning to do something more than just succeed and achieve. As you commit yourself to the discovery of the spiritual, it unfolds before you. The stronger your desire to know it, the more it reveals itself to you.

Capricorns are challenged to walk two paths simultaneously. They've got to perform their earthly chores while keeping sight of their spiritual goals. As a Capricorn, you maintain your balance by centering yourself between Ego and Spirit, using their tension as a means to propel yourself forward. If Ego has a stronger grip on your soul, your pursuit of excellence may lead you to dominate events and others, to struggle to be in control, exhibiting only the shell of your potential, solidifying your ideas through repetition instead of growth.

If your spiritual path has precedence, then you will surrender your life to a higher cause. Yours will be the gift of sacrifice and your rewards, produced through your dedication and courage, will be reaped by others. Martin Luther King Jr. (January 15) gave his life for the cause of equal rights for all men and women.

The goal of Capricorn is unity; the challenge is the integration of all polarities through the heart. As you commit yourself to your spiritual path, and while you pursue your earthly goal, God's grace begins to work as a powerful force in your life. Conflict dissolves as differences complement, instead of oppose or detract. You cut through the negativity, fears, phobias, and resistance of others, because you have conquered them in yourself. The scientific and technical side of life is given the power of passion and intuition, bringing forth creative, new ideas that change the world. This is Sir Isaac Newton (December 25), the man who formulated the laws of gravity, and Louis Pasteur (December 27), whose vaccinations against polio and rabies continue to save millions of lives.

When your Spirit is great enough to embrace the two-dimensional world of the senses, then a third dimension rises—the third eye. Its position is the center of your forehead. Once it emerges you can travel into the far reaches of uncharted territory, and explore the secrets of the universe. The third eye—or, intuition—adds depth to your perceptions. Once intuition joins the team, a whole new world is yours. This cooperation between Ego and Spirit gives them each new powers and together, they do what alone they couldn't— transform their limitations and achieve even greater success than each imagined possible. In whomever intuition and practical technique unite, the mysteries of the universe reveal themselves.

Capricorn is the process, and Saturn, Capricorn's ruler, will show you the way, no matter what your chosen path. Aristotle Onassis (January 15) had the formula for wealth. Muhammad Ali (January 17) knew the way to become the toughest man alive. Martin Luther King Jr. fought to make the world a better place. William Masters (December 27), of the research team Masters and Johnson, discovered techniques to solve such sexual problems as frigidity, impotence, and premature ejaculation. Paramahansa Yogananda (January 5) offers Kriya Yoga and its eight steps to enlightenment and to God.

Every goal involves a process. All you have to do is learn the steps. Each of these steps is a world that must be mastered. Each world is embraced by a larger one. As each world is learned through repetition and experience, you expand your consciousness. When it encompasses the whole, you're automatically at the next level and the process begins again.

If you are impatient, you'll try to climb to the next level before you're ready. Being present in the moment is important. If you're always looking ahead instead of paying attention to what you need to do now, nothing gets done. Each new step brings confidence and a new set of skills, making the next set of challenges easier, until all that's left is the test, the initiation, and the victory.

Balance is the key to Capricorn and to achieve this you must remain centered. Only from this center, this totally subjective viewpoint, can you reach pure objectivity. This is a paradox. From your center you have access to everyone else's world; you feel connected to others and the universe. To maintain this unity you must keep yourself empty then spirit voice will be heard. The way to others is through the self.

Capricorn is repetition. Because of this, you'll have many opportunities to discard the old, the past, and the useless. However, with every pull to let go, there is a voice that demands you grasp a little tighter, and many Capricorns cling desperately to what is, instead of what could be. You get caught in the process of perfecting and forget your goal. The problem is compounded when you feel you are missing an important piece of information, a link in your chain of knowledge. If you seek this knowledge only from without, then the higher knowledge you need will never arrive. Higher knowledge cannot be communicated by words or figures. It is silent, and its message must be experienced, not told. You must feel the truth, and know without knowing how you got it.

Reversal and repetition. Capricorns are always going in two directions at once. Spirit's path zigzags; the worldly one is straight. You are totally committed to your goal, but how you get there is another story. You must be ready to change your directions and reverse your position.

The worldly path comes first. You need protection and security to really accomplish something in the world of Spirit. First learn to give to yourself, then, you'll be in position to do the most for others.

Your goal is your spiritual root, your direct line to nourishment. From this goal you gain everything—your new image, your spiritual path, your ability to overcome your fear, resistance, and despair. Once you have made a commitment, you magically attract what you need. Your challenge is to choose and discard. You know how to take pieces from here and there and weave them all into a blanket. Be careful what you throw away in the presence of a Capricorn. They take it and turn it into something great. Stealing someone's ideas and using them as your own, is plagiarism. Of course, when you take someone else's idea and give it your own personal twist, the idea changes. Then, the process in not stealing, but sharing and reinventing.

That's what Capricorns are all about. The danger for them lies in getting caught in a vicious circle. Without an all-encompassing goal, it's easy for them to perfect and criticize without reason, to waste time.

Capricorn is the unity of nuances and details, it is the bringing of all into line with a common thread or goal. That thread comes from the heart, the place where all differences disappear. The heart lies at the center of the self, and it is the center where all Capricorns want to be. They are attracted to authority and seek to be close to the inner circles of life. They are drawn to institutions and government; clubs with secret oaths and society status; the closed circles of winners and achievers; the private world of the rich and famous. They are the keepers of the secrets of the universe—the scientists, astrologers, gurus, saints, and spiritual leaders, who affect the lives of the masses through their knowledge and how they choose to share it. Capricorns are secretive, intriguing and mysterious. They love to uncover your secrets, so don't try to hide anything from them. They make great spies. During World War II, for example, Cary Grant (January 8) worked undercover for the government.

Capricorn is the highest point a soul can achieve as a human being. They're midway between heaven and earth, you see the whole picture in one sweeping, panoramic view. You see how every nuance, smile, tear, act and thought was necessary in order for you to reach this moment from the top of the mountain, the smile you give to a stranger has the same importance as winning an Olympic gold medal. From the top of the mountain, you know that every human being has value and that until our consciousness is great enough to include everyone, none of us will be truly free.

The climb to the summit demands balance, perfection, and a sacrifice. Balance is achieved through the power of love. Perfection is reached through the discipline of body and Spirit. The sacrifice is of the Ego. There is a moment when fate enters and throws your plans askew. You must move forward blindly, with only His grace and help. If you pass this test, Ego gets transcended.

Marked for extinction, Ego is capable of doing anything to avoid the end of its reign of power. If you're not disciplined, Ego will convince you to settle for the glamour of superficial success, empty praise, and adulation. Ego fills you with fear, tells you not to risk what you already have. If you listen and protect yourself from change through isolation, you're sacrificing your freedom. It's easy to get stuck in this phase of the process. As you become more disconnected from the world around you, you feel a loss of control, hope becomes nonexistent, and your world shrinks. Your need for control becomes greater. You trust nothing or no one. Nothing new enters without passing endless tests. To keep your world the same, you give up spontaneity, new ideas, and new friendships.

Ego has other ways of keeping its power. It can convince you to avoid the test altogether. However, success without work and without both a spiritual and earthly purpose, makes the summit a dangerous place. Without God's grace you're unprotected. Many great talents have died from an overdose of alcohol, drugs, or other forms of destructive living because they were spiritually unprepared for the pressure of fame. Elvis Presley (January 8) and Janis Joplin (January 19) are two such examples. Without the ability to set boundaries, without the strength to take in the love and adulation the public gives, use it for nourishment and return it to them twofold, you run the risk of feeling oppressed and controlled. Ask any big Lotto winner how he feels about his sudden success. For most, it has been a nightmare. Suddenly, everyone wants something from them. They become elevated in the eyes of many and their former best friends often abandon them. The fact that they haven't earned their fortune reinforces any poor self-worth issues they may have. If you prepare yourself mentally, physically, and spiritually for success, then you're ready to change the world, not be crushed by it.

Capricorn is winter, a cold and harsh environment which requires preparation in order to survive. Spirit is the source of strength, the link to a distant goal, that gets you through the cold and lonely time. You must believe in spring and its arrival. Then, the winter is only something to be endured, not endless punishment that promises no rewards.

Many Capricorns feel the despair of winter in their lives. Deprived of comfort, love, or nurturing, the absence of Spirit makes them feel disconnected and alone. One way to value something is to be deprived of it, for only when it is missing do we know how much we need it. Some Capricorns are blessed with a strong spiritual presence in the form of a parent. For these lucky souls, it doesn't matter what struggles they must encounter. They're connected to someone and through that connection, they are never alone.

For the Capricorn, life is about work and responsibility. Many never have a real childhood—at least, not until they grow up. Often, despair is all around them. At the age of thirteen, Jack London (January 12) worked in a pickle factory. "He knew that after a few years, he would become nothing more than a work beast, an animal with no hope, no ambition, and no future . . . Looking around, he was horrified at what he saw. Young men and old men stood side by side, bleary-eyed, their spirits crushed after years of toil; women of nineteen and twenty, were already hunched over, despair creasing their faces." London decided he would do anything to get out of that factory and change his life. Eventually, he became the highest-paid author in the world. His success was built on hard work. He worked a minimum of sixteen hours a day and every morning forced himself to write at least fifteen thousand words.

Cary Grant was working in a stage show at the age of six. Of course, unlike London and Grant, some Capricorns need to learn how to focus and stay on the path. They rely on their instincts to avoid anything that restricts their freedom. Responsibility is not high on their list. Sooner or later, they'll find themselves in a crisis that demands they embrace hard work.

Saturn is the challenge to bring the intuitive and the practical together. One side approaches a problem cautiously, scrutinizing every detail; the other jumps in and tries to fix it through its ability to adapt, adjust, and eliminate what is not important. If you can combine both techniques, you're on your way to the summit. No one will stop you when you can use both Ego and Spirit to advantage. A good scientist begins with intuition and then moves on to prove his ideas through detailed procedure. An artist must translate his ideas from vision to reality through hard work. Jack London approached writing like a science. ". . . London analyzed each short story, carefully studying its construction, its dialogue, its characters, its humor. What were its strengths? he asked himself. Its weaknesses? How could it be improved? He took copious notes, writing down every unfamiliar word. The next morning, while shaving he repeated these words to himself, forcing them to become a natural part of his vocabulary."

In Capricorn, there is no easy way to get ahead. The work must be done. Work keeps you centered and according to Pablo Casals (December 29), the famous cellist, "If you continue to work and to absorb the beauty in the world about you, you find that age does not necessarily mean getting old."

Capricorns do everything in reverse. Freedom is something they gain through accepting work and responsibility. Capricorn is the child and the man, both old young and young old. They are born too civilized and controlled.

As they reconnect with Spirit and their true nature, they feel their primal nature take hold, calling them to return to a spontaneous, natural way of living.

Facing despair and hopelessness is part of the journey. You can learn to use your fears and uncertainty, to make them your collaborators, not your enemies. They can strengthen you spiritually and physically. Nothing makes you more agile or cuts away the useless paraphernalia of life faster than performing a dance with danger. Think of the Cretan bull-rituals. "This direct contact with the Bull honed the strength of the Cretan, cultivated the flexibility and charm of his body, the flaming yet cool exactness of movement, the discipline of desire, and the hard-won virility to measure himself against the dark and powerful Bull Titan. And thus the Cretan transformed terror into a high game wherein man's virtue, in a direct contact with the beast, became tempered, and triumphed."

Don't be afraid to look into the abyss. It's freeing and will get you back to renewed hope and faith. If you prefer to be angry at life, then God will be your enemy, not a helping hand. Kipling's (December 30) biographer says that he lived in, ". . . fear of eternal damnation, arising from a sense of a God who could malignantly trap beings in a life they did not ask for." Guilt is great in Capricorn. After all, you're not perfect, and perfection is what you seek. Kipling's depressions seemed to overwhelm him; however, he found a way to dispel them. "I know of what I speak . . . but I can tell you for your comfort that the best cure for it is to interest yourself, to lose yourself, in some issue not personal to yourself—in another man's trouble . . ."

To do something for someone else makes you feel less lost and alone. The world is filled with good and evil, hope and hopelessness, faith and despair. It's up to you to choose what you want in your world. The choice for good now comes from having endured both good and bad. The return to goodness and to the heart is a reentry into nature and the simple, spontaneous and unstructured part of life.

Mastery over the self or others is a strong desire in Capricorn. The need to criticize and judge goes along with this nature. Racial issues are strong. Either your heart will have no boundaries, or you will desire racial "purity," which you see as one way of keeping things the same and everyone in neat little packages.

Those Capricorns who desire to change the world are the spiritual revolutionaries, gifted with a unique perspective. Kahlil Gibran (January 6) revolutionized Arabic poetry, both its language and its form, freeing it from its classical past. Howard Stern (January 12) changed radio, Muhammad Ali did the same for the world of boxing, and Elvis Presley revolutionized popular music forever. Capricorn is the spirit of revolt. It is not soft and prone to unconditional love. It's tough and demanding and doesn't give in to weaknesses. It's capable of making the tough choices that require radical change.

The past is a sensitive issue in this earth sign. If you stay attached to your past, your family, your old sense of security, you will not reach the limits of your potential. In Capricorn, the past is an anchor, not a place to measure yourself against. To create the new you, you need to feel detached from your background, unencumbered by legacy, tradition, and expectations. You can do this only if you remove yourself from the past and break the reflection that keeps you within your old limitations.

Some Capricorns have mysterious pasts and cannot own them. They're free, unless they're stuck in solving the mystery. Cary Grant suffered greatly from not knowing his real mother's identity. Biographers seem to agree that his mother was a Jewish seamstress who worked at the same clothing factory as his father, and was later institutionalized. The woman who raised him was cruel and indifferent to his needs. At the age of six, he left home to join an acting troupe called Pender's Little Dandies.

Since the mother often represents the spiritual connection in our life, she can be missing in the sign of Capricorn. Her absence or death creates a lack of nurturing that toughens the soul and provides the yearning for love that eventually leads to God. In Capricorn, the earth mother is replaced by the divine mother, and she is a tough woman who helps prepare you for the test you have to pass in order to reach the summit. Too much love and coddling are a hindrance. You need discipline and someone to guide you. The rewards and acclaim will come later, after you pass the test.

Sometimes in Capricorn, the spiritual connection is strong and the inner self has an opportunity to develop through love. Often one of the parents is religious or involved in metaphysical studies. From this strong spiritual parent the child learns how to trust himself and his own instincts. Pablo Casals said of his mother, ''She always acted on principle not on what others said but on what she herself knew to be right.'' She directed his career and knew what he needed to become a great cellist.

Capricorn parents often try to push their children toward worldly success. Jack London's mother encouraged him to enter a writing contest. Muhammad Ali said of his spiritual mother, ''She taught us to love people and treat everybody with kindness. She taught us it was wrong to be prejudiced or hate. I've changed my religion and some of my beliefs since then, but her God is still God. I just call him by a different name.''

Sometimes, strength is built on rejection. One summer, Rudyard Kipling and his sister were abandoned by their parents, who had paid a strange couple to take care of them. Without as much as a good-bye, the parents left the children to their new guardians. Years later, Kipling called the place, ''the house of desolation.''

Spirit is unity, but it can be used to exclude, as well as include. Sometimes, the Capricorn parents unite against the child. Sometimes, one parent doesn't protect the child from the other parent. This can be both good and bad. Ava

Gardner (December 24) describes a childhood memory. Her father spanked her and she ran to her mother who told her, "Daddy's right." Gardner later said, "It wasn't until years later that I really understood it fully, understood that right or wrong they backed each other to the hilt."

Sometimes, the child unites with one parent and then it's the other parent who is excluded. Pablo Casals's mother stood up against his father's wish for Pablo to become a carpenter instead of a musician. "Pablo is a musician. This is his nature. This is what he was made to be. He must go anywhere necessary. There is no other choice."

Whatever your situation, don't stay stuck. If you're not getting the love and acceptance you need, look elsewhere. If life was too comfortable, you might not know how to take the risks you need to follow your destiny. The past, tradition, habits, and the comfortable must be removed. As long as your physical being is rooted in comfort and love, you will not turn upward and strive for Him. The yearning created by desire must deepen; the simple flow of life must now encompass a deeper rhythm, one that includes it all. It is much easier to access Spirit, love and faith when you are lost, alone and left to search within.

One expression of the Capricorn need to uproot in order to move forward is the radical changes that can take place in their lives. Jack London got from his stepfather a need for adventure. Before turning thirty, Albert Schweitzer decided to leave his music and theology career behind. He began to study medicine and set off to work in Africa. As a young boy, Casals was sent to Barcelona to study the cello. Later, he was joined by his mother, and together they lived in different cities in Europe as he sought the best teachers. Paramahansa Yogananda left India and came to the United States to bring God's message of love. Aristotle Onassis left Greece, his family, and his father's business with only a hundred dollars in his pocket and took off for Argentina. Within one year, he was a millionaire. Eventually, he became the richest man in the world, and all because a serious break with his father forced him to leave home.

This severance from the past allows a Capricorn to reconnect with his or her true roots. Some begin by changing their name. Cassius Clay was the name of a black slave owner, and Muhammad Ali's birth name. Ali wanted to sever his tie with slavery and so he took an Islamic name which means *worthy of praise*.

Unconcerned with permanent roots, Capricorns must learn that home resides in the heart. No place of stone and mortar will ever provide the spiritual nourishment Capricorns receive when they connect with their true natures.

Everyone who attempts to climb the summit must pass the test of faith. Faith frees you from your shackles and gives you a taste of freedom. Early in his struggle for equal rights, Martin Luther King, Jr., learned to depend on faith. He prayed for faith and, "Almost at once my fears began to go, I was ready to face anything."

Total commitment is a must. Muhammad Ali's fight against Sonny Liston, for the HeavyWeight Championship of the world in 1964, is a perfect example. No one believed Ali could win. After the first round, he knew he could survive. By the second and third, he sensed he could win. It had all come together—his goal, his training, and his faith. All that stood between him and the championship was the test. Over twenty years later, Ali discovered that something had been put in his rinsing water, but at the time, all he knew was that suddenly, at the end of the fourth round, he couldn't see. "I can't see! My eyes!" he shouted at his trainer, Angelo Dundee. Dundee sent him back in the ring saying, "Stay away from him. Run!" Blinded, he obeyed. Ferdie Pacheco describes what happened. "Just going out for the fifth round was an incredibly brave thing to do. . . . Cassius can't see, and still Liston couldn't do anything with him. What can I say? Beethoven wrote some of his greatest symphonies when he was deaf. Why couldn't Cassius Clay fight when he was blind?"

Ali was just passing the Capricorn test. When you've done the work, instincts and grace will take you the rest of the way. Howard Stern passed a similar test by making it to WNBC radio in New York City with a big fat contract. This was the top of the mountain, but what Stern didn't know was that the top brass wanted him out. They hated his style and were dedicated to his destruction. Stern is a Capricorn/*Three*. That means the Sagittarius defiance is added to persistence. Stern wouldn't budge. In the end, his persecutors helped make him a star. Each time they set a limit, he found a creative way to overcome it. He became the voice of the disowned collective shadow.

The first real test of faith was given to Abraham when God commanded him to sacrifice his own son, Isaac. At the last minute, God intervened and prevented Isaac's death. But Abraham had to be willing to follow the will of God up to that point.

Capricorn is the sign of ultimate style. Cary Grant, Ava Gardner and Marlene Dietrich (December 27) are its perfect images. A problem arises when the image is disconnected from the real person. The driving need of the Capricorn to be perfect is transferred onto an image. The image is impeccable, and then, you don't have to be. Cary Grant was nothing like his movie image. In real life, he was stingy, demanding, abusive to his wives and attracted to both sexes. He was obsessive about details, holding up a production for hours or even days over something minor.

Sometimes, the image is worse than the reality. Janis Joplin worked hard to be everything everyone hated. Angry at being rejected for who she was, she made sure she became totally unacceptable. Her language and behavior repulsed her peers so much they threw things at her and called her "pig." However, within her was the Capricorn desire for excellence. She wanted to be the best, and she would settle for nothing less. Capricorns feel lost and alone until they find their style. Their style allows them to connect to their Spirit and create their new and unique image. Without this connection, nothing happens. Janis Joplin didn't bring down the house the first time she sang, and Elvis didn't impress anyone with his voice until he was accidentally overheard just hamming it up. Once Capricorns find their style, they go right to the top. Before that, they are ruled by self-consciousness and fear.

Civilization has separated man from his true nature, making him rely on things outside himself and forget his intuition or the instinctual side of his nature. If you have become too dependent on rules and regulations, knowledge, intellect and conformity, then what you need is some passion and spontaneity. If you have forgotten what it's like to feel the excitement of experiencing something new or out of the ordinary, then fate will enter your life and turn it upside down. Fate is there to remind you that you're not in control. It provides an opportunity through disruption to destroy your old patterns and come out with a more balanced way of life.

Another choice is the attachment to negativity and the perverseness of life. You are angry at those who offer you hope; you resist healing and remain an emotional invalid to punish others for having received more than you. You hold others back by holding your own growth at bay. Your revenge is an illness. Hope is a threat; it pulls you closer to the abyss, in which dwell your fears.

Albert Schweitzer recognized the primal desire within himself and tried to master it. "He recognized a force in himself over which he was in danger of losing control. He had to tame it, for his own peace of mind. His own violence now had to be penned into a corner and stopped from biting. His desire for mastery had to be turned onto himself."

The need to reintroduce nature with all its danger, cruelty, and unexpected happenings is a basic challenge of Capricorn. This can make the Capricorn attracted to violence, or to being the abusive one. This latter scenario occurs when they are angry at feeling disconnected and see life as unfair. Cary Grant would beat his wives and then deny having done so. Jealous, Howard Hughes (December 24) held Ava Gardner down and slapped her across the face over and over again. Being a Capricorn, she didn't stay down. "I threw [a heavy bronze bell] with all my strength—it hit him between the temple and cheek." Muhammad Ali's chosen profession is violent, and his father, an alcoholic, sometimes beat his mother. In *The Call of the Wild,* Jack London explores a tamed dog's return to nature. The dog's instinct yearned for "the old life within him." Finally, he gives in to his instincts and runs with the pack.

Love conquers the beast within and connects it to the whole. Kahlil Gibran felt that love could solve all the tensions of society. Louis Pasteur had a loving and generous father. ". . . generosity, self-sacrifice, kindliness even to unknown strangers cost not the least effort to the father and son, but seemed to them the most natural thing possible."

The struggle to love, to balance our civilized selves with the beast within, is a crucial Capricorn struggle. Western man sees nature as outside himself; he is in conflict with it because he is striving to control or master it. If he achieves his purpose, he loses himself. Torn between his desire to master his surroundings and unite with them, he must use the energy for self-mastery, and then he can have it all—civilization and the freedom to run naked through the forest.

Don't deny half of your existence. Open yourself to Spirit and let the dangerous and uncontrollable side of your nature in. When *you* invite it in, *you* make the rules; when it comes looking for you, there are no rules.

In Capricorn, the quest and thirst for knowledge can be an obsession. When Jack London decided to become a writer, he read day and night. "I read everything. I read mornings, afternoons, and nights. I read in bed, I read at the table, I read as I walked to and from school, and I read at recess while the other boys were playing."

The mind and intellect are challenged in Capricorn. Upon entry in to the instinctual world, words are replaced with abstract concepts and symbols. The telling of a story is a lesson, with both an apparent and a silent message. Capricorns are great storytellers. They gravitate toward places where stories are exchanged, such as bars, social events, or family gatherings. Their need to keep the story in alignment with Spirit leads them to change the facts. They know how to exaggerate in all the right places.

Intention is important. Misdemeanors don't matter to the Capricorn when intentions are based on the right goal. Morality in Capricorn is based on universal laws; it is not man-made. Spirit must be preserved. You become the master seer through the acknowledgement of only what validates the spiritual goal.

Communicating the true intent and direction is important. When Schweitzer relocated to Africa, he needed to learn new communication skills, his former style of thinking and communicating did not serve him with the Africans. Schweitzer said, "I have often thought how lucky I was not to be brilliant. It forced me to be profound." Schweitzer learned about universal thought, communication that reaches all people, not just intellectuals. When Casals's teacher, Count de Morphy, asked him to improvise, Casals often got carried away with a melody he fancied. Count de Morphy would say, "Pablito, in the language of everybody—yes? In the language of everybody."

The language of Capricorn is for all people. The intellect is freed and can return to *feeling* truth and not just describing it.

Capricorn separates the men from the boys. It's the initiation process. However, besides heralding adulthood or entry into a club or secret society, it also tends to have its women desire to hang out with the guys. Janis Joplin found her niche at school with the boys, not the girls. Capricorn women can be vulgar and swear like troopers. Some even dress and act like men. Marlene Dietrich made it stylish to dress like a man, and experimented with bisexuality.

Capricorns who succeed receive the gift of abundance. Whoever has heard the message from above has the responsibility to share it with others. This is the blending of your spiritual and earthly purpose. Community is the receiver of the Capricorn gifts. The individual and the community are inter-connected, like everything else in Capricorn. Casals formed an orchestra for the city of Barcelona. For seven years he supported it with his own money. Then, when it was established, he began providing concerts for the workers who couldn't afford the price of a ticket. He went to the unions and told them he would perform six concerts a year for its members if they would contribute six pesetas a year—the equivalent of about one dollar. He was smart enough to know that the pride of the average man was important and that requiring the fee preserved his dignity. The concerts were not only a success but led to the writing of a music newsletter, and the establishment of a music club and library, available to all its members. During World War II, Casals organized food and clothing to be donated and delivered to the refugees pouring into the European cities. He wrote personal letters of encour-agement and support, knowing all the time that what he was doing would make only a small difference, but a difference nonetheless, in the lives of those suffering poverty, hunger, loneliness, and the pain of losing a home.

For those who refuse a spiritual path, the gifts of fame and fortune will appear empty. Disillusionment will replace the thrill of success. Life is nothing without sharing what you have with others. Aristotle Onassis, the richest man in the world, died a lonely death. His only son had been lost to a plane crash. His daughter never found happiness with his money, and his wife, Jacqueline Kennedy Onassis, stayed by his side out of duty, not love. Jack London's story entitled ''Martin Eden'' expresses London's own disillusion-ment in life. ''In despair, Martin flees from society, sailing for the South Pacific, where he hopes to find a simpler more satisfying existence. By then, however, it is too late. Love, money, socialism, friendship, success, they are all worthless to Martin Eden because he lost his faith in mankind. He saw clear eyed, that he was in the valley of the Shadow.''

We all believe that achieving our goals will make us happy. We forget that it's the process or the journey that provides the rewards. At an early age, Gibran used to make sculptures. ''When I had finished a thing I'd bring it down to be shown [to the town]. But I liked them to look at it while I was not there. The pleasure was while I was doing the thing. The result was never what I wanted.''

Fate is the balancing factor for a Capricorn. It keeps control out of the hands of Ego or Spirit and places it in the court of divine justice, whose mission is to balance you. When you think you've got everything in place and that you understand the world, fate will play a hand. It rips the habits and patterns from life. And although the soul may feel insecure and lost for a while, there is also an excitement about newness. Fate enters to save or destroy. It takes us to a new place, it toughens our soul, reestablishes our link with a higher power, and returns to us a zest for life that too much civilization may have destroyed.

Art plays an important role in Capricorn. The artist desires freedom and a reconnection with nature. Color and all its passion is the Capricorn expression. Matisse (December 31) managed to bring the inner and outer worlds together in his paintings. He said "I desire an art of balance and purity which neither disturbs nor troubles. My wish is that the man who is tired, worn out, and overworked should taste peace and calm as he stands before one of my paintings."

For others, art is the product of labor. Casals knew that nothing could replace hard work and practice in the pursuit of excellence. "I could no longer lose myself in my music. I did not feel then—or have I ever felt—that music, or any form of art, can be an answer in itself. Music must serve a purpose; it must be a part of something larger than itself, a part of humanity."

Relationships for Capricorns are as different and varied as their talents. If the Capricorn is too civilized and intellectual, he may find himself attracted to a basic, childlike partner. This person could have a touch of something uncontrollable and uncivilized. If, however, the Capricorn is the adventurous type, she may seek a mate who's stable, someone who takes care of the responsibilities of life. Of course, a balance is best. Integrate your own dual nature and your partner will reflect that harmony.

Don't judge a Capricorn by his or her cover. You've got to go beyond their shell and pass the test of trust and loyalty. Then, they'll let you into their world. If your Capricorn appears self-centered, it's part of his or her need to keep focused on their goals. Remember, the two extremes of Capricorn mates are the wild one and the soul mate. Sometimes, they come in one person, and if your world is organized and neat, get ready for it to be turned upside down.

The summit gives you a view of the whole journey. You know where you're going and what you have to do. Your mission is clear; you must become the voice of the people. You know what they want and what they need. This is your gift. You belong to a larger world, not just the one you can see and touch. You are a part of the greater plan; you have and every other soul has something to offer to it. Discrimination is no longer possible, everyone counts. This is the message those who reach the top must carry home and share through the power of their lives. Capricorns feel they have a purpose. Muhammad Ali said, "I always felt like I was born to do something for my people. Some people have special resources inside, and when God blesses you to have more than others, you have a responsibility to use it right.'' To climb to the summit is not a journey for everyone. It is a test that requires balance of body and spirit, of confidence and faith; a will of steel; and a yearning so powerful that fear is left behind.

THE CAPRICORN ENVIRONMENT

The Capricorn environment either provides unity and love, or it rejects what you offer and gives you in return coldness and a feeling of being disconnected and alone. Unity between Spirit and Ego, between the form and essence, must take place. In Capricorn, balance can no longer be avoided. Attempting to build a fortress secure from fate and God is not possible. The more you repeat old patterns and ignore the events that could help you find your center, the balance between your inner world of Spirit and your outer, worldly goals, the more chaos you will invite into your life. Capricorn's environment is tough. You've got to begin the job of self-mastery and perfection. If you don't make the needed adjustments, you will encounter failure, rejection, and one problem after another. Open yourself up to grace. Listen to your inner voice and the peace and harmony you seek will be yours.

Capricorn/*One* (December 28, January 1, January 10, January 19) Saturn/Sun

PURPOSE: To not let discipline or your desire for perfection, make you forget that life is nothing without love.

"The never ending task of self improvement . . ."—Ralph Waldo Emerson. There is no other choice for the Capricorn/*One* than to be the best. Without a spiritual path, they may seek power over others instead of self-mastery. For true power, both a spiritual path and a worldly one are necessary. If the Capricorn/ *One* has high principles, he could be rigid and unyielding. They need to reclaim their lost sense of freedom and know that no one can diminish them. Capricorn/ *Ones* are gifted with charisma, charm and a passion for life. Some live too strongly and fail to find boundaries. If they have inner discipline and accept responsibility for where they are, success is assured. Happiness remains an issue of the heart. Capricorn/*Ones* must start listening to their inner voice, and learn to love and support themselves.

IF SPIRIT TAKES THE LEAD: If Spirit is in the lead, the Capricorn/*One* feels as if they have a purpose for being in this world. They want to change the world and they have the strength to do it. They are too demanding on others, however, and their personal life suffers. They have trouble accepting their flaws and this diminishes their desire to let someone else in. Remember, love is the ultimate goal of the Capricorn, the lesson is to love themselves.

IF EGO TAKES THE LEAD: If Ego takes the lead, the Capricorn/*One* could lack self-confidence and self-esteem, or they could be a dictator or a tyrant. Both experiences stem from the same problem—a feeling of being disconnected. They need to go beyond the acceptance of others and learn to recreate themselves in their own image. If they don't learn this lesson, abuse and deception could be issues.

JANIS JOPLIN (January 19)

Singer.

Janis Joplin did not have an easy time growing up. She was overweight, unattractive, and had a terrible acne problem that left her skin with deep scars. Because she didn't fit in, she rebelled. Her language was shocking, she dressed outrageously, and hung out with boys, even though they hated her and called her names. The experience left her scarred and constantly seeking the approval she never received as a youth. But Joplin had style. It took her time to find it, but once she had it down, the path to fame was paved. Eventually, she hooked up with a group called Big Brother and the Holding Company and an agent who could make a deal with the devil and win. Joplin's gift was her voice, and an incredible energy that could incite a crowd to riot. Joplin was very ambitious and had her heart set on being the best. Unfortunately, as with most Capricorns, fame would not change her into a happy person. In fact, it made her feel more alone. Joplin died of an accidental overdose of heroin, but her music lives on.

CEZANNE (January 19)

Artist.

Cezanne strove to fuse nature and the self in his work. To do this, he created a new method of painting. His work is a bridge between the old and the new, between representational and abstract art. He loosened the perspective system of traditional art by putting together successive perceptions, rather than depicting the perception of one moment. Born at Aix-en-Provence to a prosperous family, he decided at an early age that he wanted to become an artist. His father, a banker, tried to deter his son's goals, but Cezanne was a Capricorn and nothing changed his mind. At the age of twenty-three, he went to Paris to study painting. Cezanne's real love was for the country, and he spent the last twenty years of his life there, painting. The unity of a Capricorn gave him the talent to combine the rigorous, formal composition of the old masters with the new, naturalistic color techniques of the impressionist.

Capricorn/*Two* (December 29, January 2, January 11, January 20) Saturn/Moon

PURPOSE: To sever your attachment to the past and to self-pity so that you can reconnect with your spirit, go beyond your dark moods, recreate yourself, and achieve a goal that includes the help and healing of others.

"Every action we take, everything we do, is either a victory or defeat in the struggle to become what we want to be."—Anne Byrhhe. Capricorn/*Twos* have quite a task ahead of them. They are sensitive and loving and feel as though they are aliens in a world that cares only about achievement. Their mission is to forget what others think. Once they conquer the world, they can help everyone else. Their extra sensitivity makes life either a beautiful place or a living hell. They struggle with excessive mood swings. They need to remind themselves that they are the creators of their universe. They must work hard to achieve a passionate goal and through the discipline a new and stable self will emerge. Once it does they can begin a spiritual journey and return some of the gifts they were given. The Capricorn/*Two* should help others direct their lives and find their center. They have a great capacity to love and heal. If they don't connect with their feelings, they will feel very alone. Naturally a bit different, the difference will make the Capricorn/*Two* feel ugly and rejected instead of unique and natural. Without Spirit, they could feel like prisoners of their fears and emotions. They need to be careful of judging others. They need to share their feelings and their shyness will disappear.

IF SPIRIT TAKES THE LEAD: If Spirit takes the lead, the Capricorn/*Two* will either be a healer, turning their lives over to others, or, they will be strong, creative individuals who leave their mark on life. Gifted with psychic ability, they can be readers of the future or involved in the arts. Supportive and rebellious against injustice, they are willing to put themselves on the line for their beliefs no matter what the price. They are looking for a soul mate and nothing less will do. If anyone is capable of finding one, it's the Capricorn/*Two*.

IF EGO TAKES THE LEAD: If Ego is out front, these souls are selfish and insecure. They feel as if the world never gave them their fair share of love, and they're out to punish everyone else who may have gotten more. They do this by being a victim, and all those who want to help them get pulled under. They can be cruel and unforgiving. Self-conscious and shy, they feel very disconnected from others and the world around them. They need to find their spiritual mission and start giving instead of complaining.

PABLO CASALS (December 29)

Cellist.

Pablo Casals was born in San Salvador, Spain. His father was a piano teacher and played the organ in the church; his mother was the strength and moral leader of the family. She always acted on principle, on what she believed to be right. Casals showed early signs of musical talent. "Music was inside me and all about me; it was the air I breathed from the time I could walk." The first time he heard the cello, he knew he had found his instrument. Blessed with a mother who had the courage to believe in her son's talent in spite of the poverty of their existence, he was accepted at the music school in Barcelona. From there, he was given a letter of introduction to Count de Morphy, who would continue Casals's education and introduce him to the queen of Spain. The queen adored Casals and gave him a scholarship to study music with the count. His talent was so great that it was easily recognizable and Casals's career, although it had its ups and downs, eventually took him all over the world. Casals had a great compassion for humanity. He started an orchestra in Barcelona which he personally subsidized for seven years. During WWII, he raised food, collected clothing, and wrote letters to the refugees in the camps outside of town. He married late in life, but found great happiness. This is the story of man who used his talent as means to greater good. This is the true gift of Capricorn.

MARY TYLER MOORE (December 29)

Actress.

Mary Tyler Moore was born in Brooklyn, N.Y. Her mother was an alcoholic and her father, withdrawn and unloving. She was riddled with self-judgment and feelings of unspecialness; she thought there was something wrong with her because her parents couldn't show her love. But Mary Tyler Moore learned to face rejection by pursuing a career in acting. When she landed a lead role on *the Dick Van Dyke Show,* her life changed. She became "... a member, new, but still a member of the inner circle of comedians." But it wasn't until she starred in her own show that she reached her comedic prime. When the show went off the air after five seasons, she tackled the movies and won an Emmy for *Whose Life Is It Anyway? Ordinary People,* in which she starred, was filmed shortly after her son's accidental death. "I've grown to know myself better, to trust myself," she says. "I am still a person who enjoys having control. But I know there are some things over which you have no control, and you just have to accept that." She has been divorced twice and is presently married to Dr. Robert Levine, a man fifteen years her junior.

Capricorn/*Three* (December 30, January 3, January 12)
Saturn/Jupiter

PURPOSE: To break through the barriers of the mind and challenge the way others think through the originality of your thought and your ability to go beyond the accepted norm.

"Most powerful is he who has himself in his own power."—Lucius Annaeus Seneca, Roman author. Capricorn/*Threes* are strong and defiant. They either have no confidence in themselves and let others bully them or they stand up to the world and show the power of their strength and defiance. Capricorn/*Threes* are their own worst enemies. They need impossible odds to overcome their fears of uncertainty, their self-consciousness, and their resistance to success. Until they meet a formidable opponent, life will be a series of mishaps and failures. They need to access their spirit and sense of faith; when they do, nothing is impossible. Timing is their challenge. Without the ability to trust themselves, they're out of step with life and its rewards. Each time Capricorn/*Threes* change paths or careers, they discover something new and gain greater courage. If they have learned to control their emotions and to think independently they will succeed. They are resilient and resistant. They feel the suffering of others and can be tough and even cruel. Their goals are almost impossible but they are capable of reaching them.

IF SPIRIT TAKES THE LEAD: With Spirit strong, the Capricorn/*Three* is powerful, but they can get caught up in a struggle to overcome injustice. If they're not ready for the battle, it could mean their demise. This is difficult on a relationship. There's always something monumental going on, always an obstacle to overcome. Support and communication make the difference. They need to be open to readjusting their goals. Balance is the key and it needs to be altered each step of the way. They should keep their commitment to truth, and when they can live through the glory as well as the defeat, they're ready for true greatness.

IF EGO TAKES THE LEAD: If Ego is strong, then these souls know how to use the power of the public to gain their own end. If they are insecure, they may work under someone else's power, but their real mission is to take the lead. They can be self-conscious and awkward, and suffer from feelings of despair, darkness, and hopelessness. They only come alive when there is a problem. They don't believe they are getting what they deserve and are often angry. Once they take responsibility for their life, everything begins to change.

JACK LONDON (January 12)

Writer, journalist.

London, born John Griffith Chaney, was born out of wedlock and never knew the identity of his father. His mother married a man name Jack London, and for most of his life, he believed this man to be his father. In actuality, his birth father was an astrologer. London's early childhood was nomadic. The family was poor and London had to work to help them survive. At age thirteen, he made ten cents an hour working in a pickle factory, fifteen to eighteen hours a day. Surrounded by hopelessness, London made a commitment to break free. Borrowing three hundred dollars from his former wet nurse, he bought a boat and became an oyster pirate. He made twenty-five dollars the first day, more than he usually made in three weeks at the factory. His mother urged him to enter a writing contest sponsored by the newspaper. London won. London lacked an education, but the dedication and hard work of Capricorn allowed him to spend every waking hour studying, reading, and writing. He passed an equivalency exam for high school and entered college, which he found too slow and unrewarding. Caught up in the fever of the Klondike gold strike, he took off for the Yukon. The trip itself was a disaster, but he later used his experience in his novels. *The Call of the Wild* and *White Fang* became classics. He endured many rejections before a magazine gave him his break and bought a story. Once his name became known, it wasn't long before London was the highest paid writer in the world. He married twice and had two daughters. London lived his dreams but they did not make him happy. The success of Capricorn was not balanced with a well-defined spiritual purpose. He died at the young age of forty.

HOWARD STERN (January 12)

Radio jock, actor, writer.

Howard Stern's autobiography, *Private Parts,* was a hit in the bookstores and now the movie version is also a success. Stern's childhood, like that of most Capricorns, was a nightmare. His father called him a moron and his mother ignored his emotional needs. Unprotected, Stern faced a hostile world and it made him tough. He formed an early goal of being on the radio. To that end, he studied communications in college. His first few jobs were unrewarding and he showed little sign of his talent. Like all Capricorn/*Threes,* Stern was waiting for a challenge, a way to connect with his own personal style. Stern found a life mate who kept his heart open, and that's the key to a Capricorn's strength. The radio style that Stern created propelled him to fame and fortune and revolutionized radio. However outrageous and brazen he is before the mike, in person, he is shy and withdrawn. He loves his wife, and is faithful to her, despite his professional contact with raunchy women. He considers himself unexciting and somewhat childish. His fight with WNBC is famous and gave him a chance to hone his talents. He continues to amaze his enemies, surprise his fans, and rake in the abundance that Capricorn promises when you find balance in your life.

Capricorn/*Four* (December 31, January 4, January 13)
Saturn/Uranus

PURPOSE: To keep the precarious balance between your own needs and those of others while you face your fears, take responsibility, and keep your freedom in a world that demands nothing less than all of you.

"We improve ourselves by victories over ourselves. There must be contests, and we must win."—Edward Gibbon, British historian The life of the Capricorn/*Four* is filled with change and new directions, and they wouldn't have it any other way. Unique and different, they know how to stand alone and still get the job done. Attracted to tension and chaos, they try to bring people together, settle disputes, and heal old wounds. A list of their friends looks like the United Nations guest book. They like everything eclectic. The Capricorn/*Four* is a catalyst, stirring up the issues of others, and making them face themselves. The Capricorn/*Four* either takes on too much responsibility or walks away from it. *Fours* must build a bridge between their need to flee and their tendency to stay too long. If they have a dream, all they have to do is make a commitment to it and keep themselves open to new and different ways of completing the project. The Capricorn/*Four* is a great negotiator. They love to party, although there are times when they desire to be alone. They can be isolated and filled with a fear of self-examination. It's true they can be tough and critical, but self-reflection can help.

IF SPIRIT TAKES THE LEAD: With Spirit prominent, the Capricorn/*Four* has great sensitivity toward the suffering of others. Their attraction to the outcasts of society, those who are radically different and unique, often gets them in trouble. They can spend too much time saving those who want to remain wounded. They have charisma, but they need to recreate themselves from their own truth, strive toward moderation, and work toward a commitment. Without a strong purpose or goal, they may find themselves jumping from one cause to another, from hopeless soul to hopeless soul.

IF EGO TAKES THE LEAD: If Ego is strong, these souls will feel very isolated and alone. They are attracted to tense, tough situations and love being caught in the middle. They are intelligent and believe they have all the answers. Perhaps they do. But fate has a say and her hand will be felt whenever their control gets too strong. Radical, different, or just plain hard to reach, they may create powerful reactions in others by their lack of subtlety. They need to learn to see the world from the inside out.

DIANE VON FURSTENBERG (December 31)

Fashion designer

At age eleven Diane von Furstenberg told her mother, "I will always get what I want." At age thirteen, her parents divorced and she was sent off to boarding school. Within five years, she'd met and married Prince Egon von Furstenberg. Egon's father, Prince Tassil, didn't approve of his son's choice. His snub affected Von Furstenberg's entire life. "It made me feel small," she said. However, her father-in-law's snub didn't affect the couple's social life. In New York, she and her husband became the darlings of society. Then, with a simple idea, von Furstenberg changed the face of fashion and became a legend. Her unique creation was the plain, wrap dress. For $80 anyone could own a von Furstenberg and wear it anywhere—to the office or on a date. *Newsweek* called her, "the most marketable female in fashion since Coco Chanel."

BEN KINGSLEY (December 31)

Actor.

Kingsley's Oscar-winning performance in *Gandhi* changed his life. Virtually overnight, he went from being an unknown to being a star. "I knew that I was playing a star, and that I wasn't one. And the more I learned about Gandhi, the more I felt genuinely ennobled by my task," he says. Kingsley was born in a Yorkshire, England, village. He is the son of an Indian physician and was named Krishna Bhanji. He uprooted himself from South Africa and moved to England to study at the Royal Shakespeare Company. Playing Shakespeare is his real love. "If I play other parts," he says, "I get withdrawal symptoms—chemical longings in my veins." He has been married twice and lives in a village eight miles from Stratford-upon-Avon. His performance in Steven Spielberg's *Schindler's List* confirms that his career has many long years ahead.

Capricorn/*Five* (December 23, January 5, January 14) Saturn/Mercury

PURPOSE: To balance your extreme nature by learning flexibility and to blend your dual nature which is either too intellectual or totally uninhibited.

"Courage is doing what you're afraid to do. There can be no courage unless you are scared."—Edward Vernon. Fear may be an issue for Capricorn/*Fives,* but if they learn to take responsibility and make a commitment, they're halfway there. They may try to avoid anything that seems to limit them. However, until they choose a path, they'll never be free. The Capricorn/*Five* must rein in their gift of curiosity, desire for the truth, and their love of travel and choose a passionate purpose that will pull them past their fear and into the spotlight. They have a great deal of talent, but without a burning desire to achieve they can easily become their own worst enemies. Part of them wants to remain the innocent child; the other wants to become a man, to be greater than anyone else and to achieve perfection, no matter the cost. Capricorn/*Fives* are either too hard on themselves or not hard enough. They must learn to give themselves love and support. Then, the freedom they desire will be theirs.

IF SPIRIT TAKES THE LEAD: With Spirit strong, the critical, demanding side of this combination becomes evident. They are perfectionists and have trouble choosing one path or cause. Their lives are cluttered, which prevents the higher mind from being heard. They need to learn to meditate and let go. They have the ability to reach the masses and their leadership qualities are strong. They must learn balance.

IF EGO TAKES THE LEAD: If Ego is ahead, the Capricorn/*Five* either will be paralyzed because of responsibility, or have their fingers in a hundred different pies. Here resistance is met by more resistance, the only way to the other side is through hard work. They need to be focused, which means they'll have to give up running everyone else's life. They are doers, who often overdo. They are manipulators who know how to use the values and intentions of others for their own end. They are charming, but unreliable.

PARAMAHANSA YOGANANDA (January 5)

Spiritual yogi.

Born Mukunda Lal Ghosh, in Gorakhpur, in northern India near the Himalaya Mountains, Yogananda was the second son of eight children. His father was a mathematician and ruled by his mind; his mother helped the poor and was ruled by her heart. They comprised the perfect Capricorn parents. One year after his mother's death, his brother gave him an amulet with a message. He told Yogananda that after Yogananda was born, the guru had predicted both his mother's early death and the fact that he would be a yogi. Yogananda was not surprised. The call from God was strong. Several times he tried to run away from home to seek God or a guru, but his older brother always caught him and brought him home. It wasn't until he graduated from the University of Calcutta that he became a monk and took the name Yogananda, which means "bliss through divine union." He was told by his guru he would go to the West. For the yogi, the body and mind are disciplined so that gradually the soul can be liberated. Yoga is a method for restraining the natural turbulence of thoughts, which prevent one from glimpsing their true nature. In 1920, his yogi—Sri Yukteswar Giri—sent him to America as his emissary. A century after his birth, Yogananda has been recognized as one of the highest spiritual figures of our time. His influence and work continue to grow. His teachings are a spiritual legacy.

ALBERT SCHWEITZER (January 14)

Physician, missionary, organist.

Born midway between France and Germany, between Catholicism and Protestantism, between the mountains and the plains, Schweitzer learned how to balance the polarities of Capricorn with great skill. As a child, the son of a Lutheran pastor, Schweitzer was shy, sensitive and close to nature. A loner, he often felt left out. However, his separateness forced him to develop his own sense of inner morals by which he lived all his life. Like most Capricorns, Schweitzer was late coming into his own. By the time he was a young man, he was possessed of a great deal of magnetism, physical power, charm, and a responsiveness to everything around him. Before he was thirty, he became a controversial figure, achieving international renown for his theological writings. A respected piano and organ concert performer, he wrote an acclaimed paper on Bach. Suddenly, in 1905 he turned his life around. He enrolled in medical school and set off for Africa to establish a hospital in the tiny village of Lambaréné in 1913. ''It seemed to me a matter of course,'' he said, ''that we should all take our share of the burden of pain which is upon the world.'' His dedication to reducing the pain and suffering of the African villagers earned him the Nobel Peace Prize in 1952. *Time* magazine called him ''The Greatest Man in the World.'' Einstein said of him, ''He has not preached and he has not warned, and he never expected that his dream would become a comfort and a solace to innumerable others. He simply acted out of inner necessity.''

Capricorn/*Six* (December 24, January 6, January 15) Saturn/Venus

PURPOSE: To find your true identity, and have the courage to reveal it to the world in spite of the lure of luxury and pleasure and the expectations of others.

''To live is to change, and to be perfect is to have changed often.''—Cardinal Newman. Capricorn/*Sixes* are social but not easy to know. The truth is, they may not know themselves that well. They struggle between doing what they're supposed to do and wanting to return to a more basic existence. Work helps to center them, but a little self-reflection wouldn't hurt. If the Capricorn/*Sixes* are not disciplined, they will overdo everything. They must learn to set boundaries, embrace discipline, and create a moral base; otherwise, the world will drive them crazy with its ups and downs. Without a connection to the spiritual self, the Capricorn/*Six* will feel isolated and lost. They could be too self-critical and judgmental. Others choose to sit back and let life pass them by. Still others switch between the two habits. The Capricorn/*Six* loves beauty and longs for love, but may not let anyone in. They are seductive, creative, and charming but afraid to make a commitment that will limit their freedom. If they try to have it all, they'll end up with nothing. They must learn to say no as well as yes, and continue the process of elimination. There are two goals for a Capricorn, an earthly and a spiritual path. The Capricorn/*Six* needs to respect both.

IF SPIRIT TAKES THE LEAD: If Spirit takes the lead, the Capricorn/*Six* will drive themselves crazy trying to live up to lofty ideals. The love they seek will always be out of reach, unless they learn to live in the moment and give life their all. They have great discipline and the ability to endure. What they need is balance, and a way of protecting themselves from the world. A rebel by nature, they find that authority is an issue until they reconnect with their true nature and allow the beast within to emerge.

IF EGO TAKES THE LEAD: With Ego strong, these souls are led by desire which can get out of control. They struggle with the beast within. If it hasn't emerged, they'll be attracted to the uncivilized. If they've let their wild side come out, or found a place to express it, they're on the right track. Work is their savior. It provides the discipline and the boundaries needed to handle their erupting emotional self. They desire success and all the trimmings. It's lonely at the top if they don't take care of their spiritual nature first.

MARTIN LUTHER KING, JR. (January 15)

Civil rights leader, minister.

Martin Luther King, Jr. led the civil rights movement out of the dark ages and into the twentieth century. His ability to bring people together and his belief in nonviolence made him admired and loved by the world. His example of courage, dedication, and trust in God was powerful enough to unite the African-American community, both rich and poor, behind a movement for equality. When in 1955 Rosa Parks, a black woman, refused to give up her seat on a bus in Montgomery, Alabama, King was there to organize, to present the incident to the press, and to do it within the limits of the law. His handling of this turning point in the civil rights movement brought him national attention. His wife, Coretta Scott King, was his partner and his equal in support and courage. King was handsome, well dressed, and articulate. He learned the power of words from his father's sermons. He graduated from high school with an A average and was chosen Valedictorian. He went on to Boston University. The moral issue of Capricorn was always present in his speeches. He said to America, "Your moral progress outdistances your morality; your civilization outshines your culture." In 1963, he organized a march on Washington, in which 250,000 took part. At the rally following the march, King gave his most famous speech. "I have a dream," he said, "I have a dream that one day this nation will rise up and live out the true meaning of its creed: 'We hold these truths to be self-evident, that all men are created equal.' " In 1964, King won the Nobel Peace Prize. In 1963, King was arrested and jailed in Selma, Alabama while trying to publicize the black person's inability to register to vote. In 1968, King went to Memphis to lend his support to striking sanitation workers. There, he was fatally shot on the balcony of a motel. In his memorial, there is a Martin Luther King, Jr. Center for Nonviolent Social Change, established by his wife, Coretta Scott King. A bronze sculpture of Dr. King is on display in the U.S. Capitol. His birthday is officially celebrated as a national holiday.

AVA GARDNER (December 24)

Actress.

Ava Gardner was the seventh child of a poor sharecropper in North Carolina. When times were rough, the family moved to New York. Through some pictures her brother-in-law submitted, Gardner got a contract with MGM. Her sister accompanied her to Hollywood. Almost immediately, she caught Mickey Rooney's eye, the number one actor in the country. Their marriage lasted a little more than a year. Gardner then married Artie Shaw. That marriage also failed. Finally, she met the love of her life, Frank Sinatra. However, the timing wasn't right. Her career was on the rise and his was in the pits. Their relationship was volatile and didn't last. No producer could buy her. If she didn't want to do a script, it didn't matter how much money was involved. Gardner was beautiful and seductive but had her faults. She was demanding and self-conscious. She drank too much and loved to get revenge. Howard Hughes pursued her relentlessly for twenty years, but they remained platonic friends. Some of her classic films are *Show Boat, The Bible, The Night of the Iguana, The Snows of Kilimanjaro* and *The Barefoot Contessa*.

Capricorn/*Seven* (December 25, January 7, January 16) Saturn/Neptune

PURPOSE: To use your love of intrigue and your desire to know the secrets of the world to probe your own true nature and to reach for nothing less than enlightenment.

"The girl who can't dance says the band can't play."—Yiddish proverb. Capricorn/*Sevens* strive to do things just right. When things don't go their way, they're not the easiest people to live with. They switch between the role of victim or dictator with ease. They're critical and judgmental because of a desire to end chaos and be perfect. The Capricorn/*Seven* must learn to access faith and let go. Responsibility is an issue; they take on too much or none at all. They often are looked upon as an ideal, and must be careful not to get stuck on someone's pedestal. To live an ideal requires giving up the self. The Capricorn/*Seven* needs to access the moment and their own personal truth, and not be afraid of disappointing others, including God. Life is filled with trials and errors, and they need to learn to use their mistakes as building blocks to success. The Capricorn/*Seven* is gifted with intuition and psychic ability. This gift gives them the ability to communicate—often without words—with those unable to be understood, such as the handicapped. They have great ability to cross boundaries, reach the unreachable and do the impossible. The Capricorn/*Seven* must not settle for fear or insecurity. They have a great deal of creativity and talent to share with the world.

IF SPIRIT TAKES THE LEAD: If Spirit takes the lead, the Capricorn/*Seven* has a will of steel. Their desire for perfection is so powerful that they can drive themselves and everyone else crazy. They have an incredible ability to see nuances and small details everyone else has overlooked. This is a talent or a curse. Unreasonable and unbending in their principles, they need to learn that grace will carry them half of the way.

IF EGO TAKES THE LEAD: If Ego is strong with the *Seven,* then these souls can be either impossible dictators or hopeless victims. Afraid of being overwhelmed by life, they try to master it with power and will. If they've given in to their despair, they struggle with depression and dark moods. If their moods are too frequent, it's time to find their spiritual path.

CARLOS CASTANEDA (December 25)

Writer, seer.

In 1968, Carlos Castaneda's books took the world by storm. *The Teachings of Don Juan* sold millions of copies, and opened the eyes of the world to another reality, the strange and powerful world of the seer. An anthropologist, mystic, scholar, and gifted writer, Castaneda shares his own spiritual journey with the world. His leading character is Don Juan, a Yaqui Indian sorcerer who develops a pupil/teacher relationship with him. His stories, which take place in the desert of Sonora and the mountains of southern Mexico, provide a system of ethics, beliefs, and self-realizations that bring all the issues of Capricorn to their most powerful expression. The teachings are transmitted, Capricorn style, through stories. Even if the reader doesn't understand everything Castaneda says, he comes away with a new perspective. Don Juan convinces Castaneda that life is more than meets the eye. "Every warrior on the path of knowledge thinks, at one time or another, that he's learning sorcery, but all he's doing is allowing himself to be convinced of the power hidden in his being, and that he can reach it."

BARBARA MANDRELL (December 25)

Singer.

Mandrell's Capricorn goal is, "Always reach a little bit higher." She was born in Houston, Texas, where her father owned a music store. Her mother was a musician, and taught her daughter how to play the accordion. Mandrell learned how to read music before she could read the written word. Her musical debut came before the age of five when she played a gospel song at her uncle's church. When she was eleven, she accompanied her father to a trade show and helped him demonstrate different musical instruments. By that time, she was playing the accordion, steel guitar, and saxophone. From there, Mandrell was invited to join a show in Las Vegas. By age twelve, she was on TV. At thirteen, she toured with Johnny Cash and formed the Mandrells, a group consisting of Barbara, her parents, and three other family members. Ken Dudney was a member of the group and eventually became her husband. Mandrell settled down for a while and became a navy wife, but the nomad was too ingrained in her. Her next move was to sign a contract with CBS Records. Her first real hit was "Midnight Oil," and since then she has won over sixty awards. When she's not traveling, she lives in Tennessee with her husband and three children. A car crash involving herself and two of her children made her a spokeswoman for seat belts.

Capricorn/*Eight* (December 26, January 8, January 17) Saturn/Saturn

PURPOSE: To overcome your feelings of insecurity and despair; to use them to strengthen your soul. This in turn allows you to open your heart and receive the abundance of love that is yours.

"What a wonderful life I've had! I only wish I'd realized it sooner!"— Sidonie-Gabrielle Colette. Capricorn/*Eights* throw themselves into life and live it to the fullest, or live in a small world and strive hopelessly for control. Remember, in Capricorn there is no such thing as control. Fate plays an important role in the life, of the Capricorn/*Eight*. It's there to get them balanced; without fate, they could refuse to experience life. The Capricorn/*Eight* must not waste time avoiding a spiritual path. If they ignore Spirit, balance will ignore them. Without Spirit, they will never feel the security and power they seek. Capricorn/*Eights* must learn to give of themselves, giving alone will expand their consciousness and make them feel as if life is worth living. They are ambitious and jealous. They should remember that too much of anything can be destructive. They need to remember that the ability to handle outer pressure is only achieved through faith. With faith, the world will become a friend, not an enemy.

IF SPIRIT TAKES THE LEAD: If Spirit is strong, so is the heart. The Capricorn/ *Eight* senses the world's suffering and wants to make a difference. Once they toughen up, they're a strong leader, and their persistence will help them reach their goals. The danger is that they'll get stuck helping those who don't really want help. Capricorns teach by example. Find your center; then, your real work will begin.

IF EGO TAKES THE LEAD: If Ego is strong, the Capricorn/*Eight* may try to dominate or rule their environment. Driven by insecurity and incredible self-consciousness, they see the world as a threat. Jealous, stingy and selfish, they feel deprived and don't want others to have what they have missed. They either take on too much responsibility or avoid it at all cost. Either way, they are trapped in a place of limitation, repetition, and loneliness.

ELVIS PRESLEY (January 8)

Singer/Actor/Legend.

Elvis Aron Presley was magic on stage, but his success did not happen overnight. Like most Capricorns, he had to find his own unique expression. Once he did, the world was his and he became a legend in his own time. For a long time, it seemed as though the King would succeed at everything he attempted. But fame became Presley's burden and he died of an overdose of drugs at the age of forty-two. Presley lives on in the hearts of his fans.

MUHAMMAD ALI (January 17)

Heavyweight champion of the world.

Considered by some to be the most recognizable man in the world, Ali's experienced many of the reversals typical of Capricorn. Along the way, he won the hearts of even his greatest enemies, and commanded their respect. As a light heavyweight in 1960, he won a gold medal in boxing at the Olympics in Rome. His unprecedented speed, grace, and intelligence in the ring changed the way the world perceived a champion. Ali still uses his talents and his success for a higher purpose. All his life, he has been an unofficial ambassador of peace and faith. His embracing of the Black Muslim movement, and the changing of his name from Cassius Clay to Muhammad Ali, was the benchmark of his spiritual journey. At the 1996 Summer Olympics, he had the honor of lighting the Olympic flame. His honesty about his Parkinson's disease has helped others with the disease feel less ashamed.

Capricorn/*Nine* (December 27, January 9, January 18)
Saturn/Mars

PURPOSE: To use your drive and your ambition to break through outmoded ways of behavior and ideas, creating a new vision that will bring you success and happiness.

"The happiest people are those who seem to have no particular reason for being happy except that they are so."—William Inge. Love is what the Capricorn/*Nine* is all about. They must let an unbalanced sense of responsibility keep them from giving and receiving it. If they allow their insecurity to take the lead, they will be overworked. They must learn to go beyond their compassion and set limits. Capricorn is new spirit. It needs to be strong and demanding in order to deal with life. The Capricorn/*Nine* has a love of adventure and an attraction to violence. They need to love themselves. Only then will life begin to fall into place.

IF SPIRIT TAKES THE LEAD: If Spirit is in the lead, the Capricorn/*Nine* is idealistic and eager to change the world. They are capable of making others listen and setting a pace that others will follow. Boundaries are important. Without them, they could have a nervous breakdown. They are gifted with natural charisma, a strong, persistent nature, and an impatience that pushes them to do and want more. They must remind themselves that balance is important.

IF EGO TAKES THE LEAD: If Ego is ahead, then so is accomplishment. These souls know how to get a job done. Security is an issue and so is control. No matter how much they get, it's never enough. They lack faith and so fate will uproot whatever they plant. Their anger is strong; they either attract or give it. Love is the answer. Once they open their hearts and learn how to trust and give, everything they wanted will be theirs.

CARY GRANT (January 18)

Actor, spy.

Archibald Alexander Leach, better known as Cary Grant, was nothing like his suave, sophisticated image. Grant was a man of contradictions. He was generous and stingy, kind and cruel. He was driven by compulsive behavior. As an adult he finally learned that the woman who raised him—a tyrant who gave him very little love—was not his birth mother. Like many Capricorns, he started work at an early age. At the age of six, he joined an acting troupe and traveled through Europe and then to New York. Eventually, he returned to New York and began his stage career. Stardom came quickly once he got his break and found his style. Grant had an affair with Randolph Scott, as well as with many other Hollywood stars. He married several times but never found happiness. Jealous, abusive, and tight with money, he was known to hurt his partners physically. He sought therapy to help him struggle against mood swings and depression. His marriage to Dyan Cannon produced a daughter Jennifer, whom he loved. By some accounts, Grant got to play out a Capricorn fantasy by working as an undercover agent for the government during World War II. He loved vulgar humor and common food; sometimes, he ate with his hands. The baser instincts of the Capricorn were what made him sexy. Women found him irresistible, in spite of his conflicted feelings toward them. Grant will always be remembered for his grace, his charm, and his ability to make his audiences laugh.

WILLIAM MASTERS (December 27)

Writer, sex therapist.

William Masters and his wife, Virginia Johnson, broke new grounds with their research on sexuality and sexual behavior. Their landmark medical texts, *Human Sexual Response* (1966) and *Human Sexual Inadequacy* (1970) revolutionized the field of sex therapy. "If you can't communicate in bed, you probably can't communicate in marriage," says Masters. Masters was born in St. Louis and interned in obstetrics and gynecology. He realized that sex was the last frontier in biological research and set out to change that. With his wife as his partner, they have published more than nine books and one hundred scientific papers. Their monthly column in *Redbook* magazine was popular for many years. Masters and Johnson are presently divorced.

SUMMARY

Capricorn is the top of the mountain, the pinnacle of success in both the spiritual and the material world. If these worlds are not in balance, life is a series of tests which force the soul to try again and rearrange its priorities. This repetition can either provide the missing insight or keep you stuck and in a rut. What makes the difference is the goal. It must be strong enough to pull the soul through despair, disappointment, and hopelessness. Negative feelings exist to be overcome and to strengthen your body and Spirit. Once you face your fears, temptation is conquered, you can choose good over evil and you have the power to create your world. Until you have faced despair and chosen to live within conscious volition, you are not ready to recreate yourself in your own image. When this is accomplished, you are able to live your life to its full potential. Your greatest achievement is not reaching the summit, but staying strong and mindful of your path once the rewards of your efforts have arrived. If your struggle has reached your heart, you will proceed with love and generosity. You will know how to take from the collective world and how to give something back. You have recreated yourself in your own image and now you're ready to live life in your own unique way in the next sign of Aquarius.

SELECTED SOURCES

James Brabazon   *Albert Schweitzer: A Biography*   Putnam 1975

Pablo Casals   *Joys and Sorrows: Reflections*   Simon & Schuster 1970

Ava Gardner   *Ava: My Story*   Bantam 1990

Jean and Kalil Gibran   *Kalil Gibran: His Life and World*   Interlink Pub. 1991

Thomas Hauser   *Muhammad Ali: His Life and Times*   Touchstone 1992

Nikos Kazantzakis   *The Odyssey: A Modern Sequel*   Translation into English Verse, Introduction, Synopsis, and Notes by Kimon Friar   Simon & Schuster 1985

Lillie Patterson   *Martin Luther King, Jr. and the Freedom Movement*   Facts on File 1989

Rene Valery Radot   *Life of Pasteur*   West Richard 1923

Alan Schroeder   *Jack London*   Introductiory Essay by Vito Perrone   Chelsea House 1992

Marie Sellier   *Matisse from A to Z*   Peter Bedrick 1995

Martin Seymour Smith   *Rudyard Kipling: A Biography*   St. Martin's Press 1989

C H A P T E R   T W E L V E

Aquarius

(January 21–February 18)

Progress is the Aquarius quest.
They link what's missing, they are the best.
Strong in their purpose, their mission is clear,
Limitations and dangers are nothing to fear.
Against injustice they make a stand,
For unity and truth they'll lend a hand.
Ego and Spirit have joined through the heart;
Reality and vision are no longer apart.

Ruler: Uranus   **Element: Air**
Symbol: Waterbearer   **Number: Four**

The roots of Aquarius are anchored deep within the heart, and with love as
its primary source of nourishment, you have greater courage and strength
than ever before. In fact, it seems there is nothing you can't do. The impossible
is your favorite pastime. Danger, pain, or sorrow do not interfere with your
purpose; your mission is unity, and you are the warriors who patrol the limits
of the known. You walk the dark and dangerous corridors of life, bringing
light to those who've lost their way. You are attracted to the outcast, the
odd, the different, the lepers of society. Unafraid of the shadow you have
faced and survived, you are ready to help others do the same.

You have gained freedom and power from facing your fears and turning
them into strengths. Your most valued possession is your freedom. It took
every ounce of your courage to pass through your feelings of nothingness
and hopelessness and survive. Now, you know the importance of wholeness
and to keep yourself from sinking back into the comfort of separateness, you
have discovered a way to maintain Spirit's presence in almost every moment.
You embrace adventure and leap from one new and exciting experience to
another. You take risks and push your boundaries beyond the point of safety.
When you do this, Spirit comes alive. It lives to be tested and to overcome
great odds. Charles Lindbergh (February 4) said, ''The best way to cope
with danger [is] to keep in continuous, intimate contact with it.''

Danger is found at the extremes of life. Being an Aquarius is like being
a cartoon character walking across a mine field. When a mine goes off and

you're blown into the sky, you shatter and fall apart; but by the time you land, you're all together again. Amazing? Not when you know your destiny and have the ability to invent whatever you need along the way.

You're a master creator, taking what is and changing it into what's new and needed. Thomas Edison (February 11) invented the lightbulb. For Aquarius, the unknown is not a problem. You have a well-developed third eye. Your instincts guide you, phantoms instruct you, and there is no place you cannot go. Your vision reaches into the future. Over one hundred years ago, Jules Verne (February 8) wrote about submarines, diving suits and fax machines in imaginative science-fiction stories.

Aquarius is the sign of the prophet, the healer, and the psychic, the person who knows how to call forth the divine spark to perform miracles. Rasputin (January 23), the healer to Czar Nicholas II and his hemophilic son, possessed these magical qualities as a child. Through the power of prayer, he could lay his hands on a wounded person and reunite the torn flesh. Rasputin first noticed his powers when he realized he could read the thoughts of animals and heal their wounds.

As a mystical creature you entered this world either spectacularly, or cautiously. Your first challenge is to align your will with God's. Once you do this, nothing will stand in your way. The Aquarian starts slow, then, with lightning speed, races toward the finish line. The obstacle is choosing the right path, testing it for a few steps, and if it doesn't feel right, making a change. That's why you often seem indecisive; you're just trying to find your life purpose. Once you know it, you're on your way.

With one foot in heaven and the other on earth, you have two worlds from which to draw your strength. You've done the hard work (remember Capricorn) and now there's time to play. Spirit can do this both when you're conscious and unconscious. At night, through dreams, Spirit gets a chance to soar above physical limitations. It plays with symbols and what it says to you at night can help you during the day. It's how your unconscious unites or speaks to your conscious mind. During the day, imagination is how Spirit plays. Once you call it forth, it leads you beyond your boundaries, taking you from the impossible to the possible. A good imagination builds the invisible bridge that is the first step to accomplishing a goal.

Through dreams and the imagination, reality is presented without rules or regulations. What is said is not as important as the emotional impact it brings. Nonsense begins to make sense when you allow the power of symbols to tell the story.

Ego gets to play by testing fate. It knows that the end is near, so why not challenge destiny? This is the sign in which God gets to play and so do you. Don't be surprised to learn that God is waiting to set you up. He loves to offer you whatever you want, and then intertwine it with something more, something that arouses your curiosity. This is how we discover our purpose, disguised in an adventure. The universe interweaves what we need to discover and refuse to see, in an adventure, something that excites our whole being.

The love of adventure is inherent in all Aquarians. The wanderer, the navigator, and the nomad are images associated with this sign. Charles Darwin (February 12) was approached by a Captain Fitzroy, who was looking for a naturalist to share his experiences of wild lands and refute the scientists who were challenging religion with their discoveries of petrified plants and animals. At the time, Darwin was a young man who had recently failed in the field of medicine and was thinking about becoming a country person. In short, he had no direction. Fate presented him an opportunity which took him to the Galapagos Islands, directly on the equator. There he found, ''A little world in itself with inhabitants such as are found nowhere else.'' His discoveries led to his writing *The Origin of Species,* a book that changed the scientific world forever.

Fate is the pawn. You move it and whatever happens is the test. You must find something useful in the event. You've got to see the gifts that come with sorrow, the dangers that accompany success. You have to be able to change directions in a blink of an eye, or invent a new solution when the old one is destroyed. When you can juggle light and shadow with equal confidence, choose what you want from chaos, and hold the rest at bay, you're ready to play.

Aquarius is the sign of forgiveness and reconciliation. Forgiveness is the perfect interweaving of joy and sorrow. Forgiveness gives you grace and a chance to rise above your fate. Together with your acts of goodness, forgiveness builds an invisible shield that protects you from the world. With this shield you have freedom—the Aquarian dream. Without this shield of grace, the world is a truly dangerous place. Take the time to forgive yourself and your enemies, to give up hate and revenge, and to know that you and everyone else are equally loved and welcomed by God.

In Aquarius, *you* must choose to start your destiny. Your full presence is required for God to give you his divine spark. If you choose to start too soon, your fears and your lack of boundaries may destroy you. If you wait too long, you're wasting time, and time is of the essence. Timing is the key to success, and Aquarians have the best reactions and instincts. Everyone has seen Michael Jordan (February 17) hesitate in midair, as if supported by an invisible force. In that hesitation, he divides the moment and chooses when and how he will make the basket. Jack Benny (February 14) was the undisputed master of comic timing. He knew how to hold a pause to draw every laugh possible from a joke.

Aquarius deals with human legacy, not inheritance, with something of yourself rather than a big bank account. With the end so near, worldly possessions are less important. What you begin to value is the part of yourself that you *can* leave behind—your love, experiences, knowledge, and truth.

These gifts will determine your true greatness. Talent and resources are not enough. What you produce with them is what is important.

Aquarians are prolific and multitalented. Franz Schubert (January 31) wrote over six hundred songs and was a master of many different types of music. Thomas Edison holds the record of patenting more inventions than any other man alive—he is responsible for inventing the lightbulb, the phonograph, and the movie projector, to name just a few. In Aquarius, the soul must manifest its dream and Ego and Spirit work together to make it happen. Success in the world will provide the shield that allows Spirit to begin her work.

In Aquarius, the mind has finally learned to listen to the heart. The heart of the Aquarian hears the silent sounds of fear, the words of loneliness, the voices of the lost and the abandoned. In a production called *A Grapefruit in the World of Park,* Yoko Ono (February 18) tried to invoke the silent sounds of people's fears. "I set up everything and then made the stage very dim, so you had to strain your eyes—because life is like that," she said. "And then it went into complete darkness. I thought that if everything was set up in a lighted room and suddenly the light was turned off, you might start to see things beyond the shapes. Or hear the kind of sounds that you hear in silence. You would start to feel the environment and tension and people's vibrations. Those were the sounds that I wanted to deal with, the sound of fear and of darkness, like a child's fear that someone is behind him, but he can't speak and communicate this."

The voice of Aquarius is a song with its own special melody. It includes both spoken and unspoken words, joy and sorrow. In Aquarius, you are asked to sing your song and add your voice to the collective.

Aquarians are social reformers, the rebels who fight for equality. Your mission is to force society to look at the shadow she tries to hide. Seldom mainstream, the Aquarian is contrary and loves to use shock to wake people up. You've got to rearrange your thinking just to interact with them. They don't care who stares when they dye their hair blue, or wear eighteen lip rings, or date the only African-American Mexican with a Portuguese/French father in your school. If you're the Aquarius, you get your pets from the Humane Society. You wear what you like in spite of the fashion. When what you do becomes mainstream, you give it up. It's time to move on and find value in something the masses have overlooked. You have a great eye for value and can pick the Limoges china from the imposters any day. You can cut through the superfluous and get to the heart of a matter more quickly than any other sign.

Without a clear sense of self, however, the Aquarian will feel torn between wanting approval and rejecting it when it's offered. Neither being alone nor with others will make you happy. These people need to stop looking to others for their self-worth or their decisions. They've got to dare to be themselves and believe that others will love them for it.

Friends are important to the Aquarian. They come from all walks of life and they remain friends for life. You give and demand loyalty; you have good friends because you are one. You are able to step back and let a friend take a fall. Then, you extend a helping hand. You give great advice when asked, and, in an emergency, you take charge.

Love is the driving force in Aquarius. The heart rules, but it has lost its innocence. Having endured pain and sorrow, it has developed depth and patience. This is the universal heart and its capacity is immense. In Aquarius, love is never stagnant; nor does it wallow in pity. It takes action and makes choices which lead to change and wholeness. Its goal is unity through tolerance of differences, the forming of ''one mind,'' driven by a common destiny or dream.

When that dream is rooted in the heart, you become the center of your world, the calm of the eye of a hurricane. Sometimes you cause the air around you to swirl. You enter a room and things start to fly and laughter fills the air. But more often than not, you are drawn to tension and chaos, eager to unify division. This is the sign of the great negotiator, or the child born of two parents of different religions, races, or cultures, united through love. The child learns to relate to both worlds through feelings—not exterior appearances—and to take that gift and teach it to the world.

Reversed, the child feels torn between its parents, both of whom he loves. Unable to unify them, he seeks situations or people that keep the tension and feelings of separation alive. That child needs to learn self-acceptance. He must heal the part of him that feels responsible for the split, forgive himself, and his world will begin to change.

In Aquarius, you must not be afraid of the negative feelings that surround you. Even the fear of death must be faced and accepted. Let everything pass through your forgiving heart. The flame of purification will transform all into strength and light. Your mission is unity. Whether fighting for an heroic cause, or just hanging out with five friends, each of whom wants to go in a different direction, you'll be the one everyone turns to to bring them together in harmonious agreement. You'll have to make the decisions and make them with the kind of power no one will question.

Aquarians get this power from being centered and aligned with Spirit. The Leo's need to be the focal point of a group has been deepened; you are your center, you don't need to seek it. You pull everyone and everything into your influence. You're a catalyst.

Your power is not diminished when it is driven by hate; however, instead of unity, division and destruction will result. This is the cold and calculating Aquarius, who uses the emotions of others for his own ends. This is the rabble-rouser and the leader of the mob, driven by hatred and an unconcern for consequences.

Thus, the genius of Aquarius can be used to heal or destroy. If you choose the way of love, your talent lies in your ability to embrace both sides, and keep that embrace while the old order is destroyed and the new order instituted. You must be careful not to use this magnificent energy randomly to break apart the old order, to challenge and topple authority, or to crush your opponent simply because his views are different from yours. Aquarius destroys with the intention of rebuilding. If you have to knock someone down, lend him a hand to help him up. Show him through your actions that you're ready and willing to tolerate his perspective, if he gives you the same respect. Forgive, and you will receive the blessings of peace and harmony.

The ability to manipulate boundaries is the essence of the Aquarian strength. The ability to divide without separation allows you to love others for their wit, their brilliance, their kindness, and still refuse to accept their judgments. The Aquarius mind can choose goodness and keep evil at a distance. You have the power to select. Aquarians are capable of great intimacy because of this factor. Yoko Ono's interactive art attempted to enhance this ability in others. The Aquarian teaches by instructing and inter-acting with you.

The ability to separate what you like and don't like from an experience or a person is the key to your ability to accept them and yourself, too. What you highlight and accept grows. Abraham Lincoln (February 12) sought to stop the spread of slavery while accepting its presence in those states in which it was established. His ability to separate his own beliefs from what was agreed upon by the collective, made him a great leader.

Aquarius is the ability to separate thought from action. You nourish your ideal but wait until the right time to implement it. The collective action of Aquarius can only be achieved through compromise. To do this you must know yourself and each side must sacrifice something. This is the individual in unity and in conflict with the collective. Aquarius knows that we are all connected and need each other, and so it is willing to make the compromise.

Unity only works when there is a central idea, a cause that everyone can unite behind. Lincoln chose unity between the Union and the Confederacy as the nation's most important goal and what didn't go along with that goal was excluded. By doing this, he cleared the road to action. Action in Aquarius has gained patience because it has passed through the heart. The Aquarian mind can separate and unite. Action and thought are divided while emotions and ideas come together. Abraham Lincoln said, "Some things right can be wrong to perpetrate, and some things wrong can be right to do. Each must be recognized in its own time and place and be properly adjudged." Now more than ever the intention behind an action is important, and only experience can give the wisdom needed to act appropriately.

Aquarians have the common touch. When they're not eccentric, they're simple and direct. They seek truth with a humanitarian heart. When Ego stops fighting unity, it allows the soul to remain centered in modesty. From this place it can rise to an occasion of grandeur, take to the spotlight, or relax and appreciate the quiet moments. Lindbergh sought privacy all his life, but he knew how to use the spotlight to bring attention to his causes, namely, preservation of the environment and animals threatened by extinction. Abraham Lincoln cut a humble appearance in his simple black suits and top hat. He seemed unsuited for the job of president when he arrived in Washington, D.C., but it didn't take his colleagues and adversaries long to learn to respect the man without pretension. Only from a position of modesty can Spirit seek the truth and learn. When you start believing in your own greatness, your growth stops.

Lincoln used the Aquarian talent of being able to invoke emotional unity through a collective cause. His fight for human rights was echoed throughout Europe because he had the wisdom to share his struggle. His ambassadors included self-made millionaires, Negroes, the clergy, men of letters who wrote articles on the cause, and men of leisure who spoke to the gentry. He carried on a personal correspondence with workers in England who suffered greatly from the loss of the American south's cotton. He embraced their struggle and they joined him in his fight for the freedom for all men. Men and women all over the world felt a part of America's Civil War, because Lincoln spoke to their hearts and included them in his. When he died, the world mourned. Lincoln had become a symbol of hope. Biographies surfaced around the world after his death. Printed on cheap paper, they accompanied the overthrow of tyranny in Russia, Turkey, and even Japan. In China, Sun Yat-sen was influenced by Lincoln during the long years of planning and working toward the establishment of a Chinese republic.

Ego and Spirit, united at birth through the union of heaven and earth, are about to part. The journey is almost over. Aquarius is the next to the last sign of the zodiac. As in any long and lasting relationship, Ego and Spirit have fought, competed, supported and loved each other, creating a bond and a trust based on experience. What has been forged between them is a friendship. They share both joy and sorrow, intertwining them through the process of love. These two energies, one descending from heaven, mythical, and symbolic, one rising from earth, wild and instinctive, have shared the same path while trying to balance their opposing points of view. Their tension has centered the soul on its path. They have learned to respect and honor their differences, realizing that only with each other's support can the journey be completed.

As the end nears, Spirit and Ego join forces in Aquarius to manifest a worldly dream, something *real* that the world can use for progress. From this worldly success will come the spiritual dream which will manifest in the next and last sign of Pisces.

With their union comes the end. The body must die and Spirit must rise. Ego and the body are old and weary from battles and losses; their victories, too, have taken a toll. As Ego's strength diminishes, Spirit begins to soar. It's been reborn, and now appears younger than ever, enjoying the curiosity and magic of a child. It sees the world as new and exciting, and is ready for adventure.

Aquarius is both young and old, child and aging parent. It is filled with imagination and the desire to play, but it is wiser than the Aries child. It knows that life is both pain and sorrow and that commitment to a goal is what will carry it to the end. Its joy is laced with melancholy as it prepares to say good-bye to its lifelong friend. Joy and despair, beauty and sorrow are intricately woven in Aquarius.

This child/adult that inhabits the body of an Aquarian makes him or her experience life a little upside down. Often, Aquarians are very mature when they're young and playful as adults. The older they get, the younger they feel. The key to their freedom and lust for life is the way they deal with responsibility. Charles Lindbergh's father gave him as much freedom as he showed he was capable of handling. "He'd let me walk behind him with a loaded gun at seven, use an axe as soon as I had strength enough to swing it, drive his Ford car anywhere at twelve. Age seemed to make no difference to him. My freedom was complete. All he asked for was responsibility in turn."

Adventure fills Aquarians' spirit, but responsibility keeps them from becoming the vagabond they so desire to be. With a strong purpose they are able to mix their high ideals with practical habits, their sense of timing, with their impatience, their wisdom with the ability to see the world from fresh and youthful eyes. Old age is not limiting when Spirit is well intertwined with Ego. Lindbergh said . . . "with health, one is still close enough to life to feel its surging and close enough to death to see beyond one's passions."

The thought of death seeps into the mind and the fear must be faced. If Ego is still in charge, fear will turn into terror. With no place to escape the soul will feel as if it's being buried alive. However, if Spirit has its proper place, death will be looked upon as natural and its presence will be used to keep the soul striving and achieving as it hurries to accomplish everything it desires before time runs out.

When Spirit is strong, pain and the fear of death are not problems. Once, Lindbergh was duck hunting with a group of men on a very cold day. The ducks they shot had fallen into the icy water of the lake and the hounds refused to retrieve them. Lindbergh removed his clothes and jumped in to retrieve the birds. On another occasion, during a political campaign, someone fired a gun at Lindbergh's car. The driver quickly accelerated and Lindbergh said, "Don't go too fast. They'll think we're afraid of them." On his flight over the Atlantic, he kept telling himself the worst that could happen to him was death or failure. He put death, the less shameful alternative, first.

Death is not feared because love is present. When love is missing, death might actually be sought. Deprived of love, the soul chooses to hate. When you can see the consequences of your hate, guilt is born. Guilt creates the need to make reparation. Guilt also causes depression. To end depression, you can remedy the harm you have caused. If your attempt comes from the heart, you will gain forgiveness and something good will have come from something bad.

Aquarius is the dark horse, the hero who bursts onto the scene, invoking a sense of mystery, representing a link to symbol and a mythological past. George Balanchine (January 22), the famous ballet choreographer, was born in the Caucasus, the mountains that separate the Black Sea from the Caspian. The ancient Greeks believed it was on Georgia's Mount Kaybek that Zeus chained Prometheus as punishment for stealing fire from heaven, and it was to the western coast of Georgia that Jason sailed with his Argonauts in search of the Golden Fleece.

In order to maintain its power in both worlds, Aquarius must root itself in its mythological past. The myths hold ancient truths that speak to everyone in his own language. Able to transcend time, myths and symbols reconnect the soul with its godly strength. The inheritance of Aquarius is not possessions, but emotions, memories, and symbols that have the power to invoke passion in others.

Aquarians have the power to meet any challenge, often surprising themselves and others with the scope of their talents. Aquarius comes from the shadow. They are slow starters but are waiting for the right moment to make their move. They know that a good start carries them most of the way and so they spend time getting everything in place. Since the world is quick to judge, Aquarians make special efforts to make an impact on the first encounter. The process to success learned in Capricorn has been absorbed, and now the soul can play. Aquarians can take more than one challenge at a time, rush ahead, change directions whenever the moment requires. They are hyper. Their minds race ahead of their bodies, mouths and words. They finish other people's sentences because they're way ahead and have trouble staying in the now.

The Aquarian mind is acrobatic. It can handle more than one thought at one time. Aquarians love to work on several projects or read three or four books at once. However, to do this requires a strong center and sense of self. If this is missing, your timing is off. Your instincts are the key and you need a good relationship with them. meditation or reaching out to help someone else is a sure way to hone your instincts.

Aquarians usually rise when something else is falling. They bring hope and new solutions to old problems. Franklin Delano Roosevelt (January 30) became president as America entered the Great Depression and then World War II. Lincoln came to office when the nation was ready to go to war. Yoko Ono bears the burden of being known as the person who destroyed the Beatles. Her own success came when she was invited to join the "Destruction in Art" symposium. Aquarians have an attachment to decay and the destruction of something beautiful. They are drawn to transition and the passing away of an old order. The object of Lord Byron's (January 22) affection was his inheritance, a beautiful home in the process of decay. Until he could take care of it himself, it was rented to a Lord Grey. Lord Grey ". . . [he] let everything go to pieces, but in the very fact of the desolation of something beautiful, there was a melancholy that delighted Byron's heart."

The father plays a central role, an obstacle for the Aquarian to overcome. In order to align one's mind and will with the Divine Father, the Aquarian must go beyond his earthly father. The father can be reminiscent of the Leo father, strong and dictatorial, but his strength is seen as that of a merely mortal man. Earthly power is not impressive; however, if the Aquarian makes a break in order to follow his own path, he will seek forgiveness and reconciliation.

The father can be missing—emotionally or physically. Sometimes, this leads to combining the Divine and earthly fathers. When this occurs, you can feel a spiritual connection between yourself and your father, one that doesn't require words to tell you that you are important in his life. Schubert was alienated from his father for years because he wanted Franz to remain a teacher, instead of pursuing a musical career. Babe Ruth (February 6) was raised by his father, who paid absolutely no attention to him. He let his son roam the streets, never sent him to school, and allowed him to hang out in the bar that he owned. Lord Byron didn't know his father and neither did Germaine Greer (January 29), who yearned all her life to understand the man who came back from the war a different person than when he left.

The earthly father appears weak compared to the Divine Father. In Aquarius, it's time to reclaim your true origin, your divine inheritance. To do this, you must not be attached to your earthly family, its legacies, rituals, and traditions. The hopes and dreams of your parents must be transcended before you can possess your own dreams the process goes like this. You reach upward and claim your hopes and dreams, then, look back and realign everything with this purpose. In short, you get to retell your story from your own perspective, making yourself the hero. From above you can see that your pain and struggles were nothing more than tests that made you strong. With a little creative rearranging of your old perspective you can suddenly see your heroic nature. You were never a victim. You overcame the odds and survived the challenges. They made you stronger, more sure of yourself and your journey. So what if you faltered and fell? You always picked yourself up and kept going.

It's time to claim your heritage. Truth, beauty, and love are yours. Freedom and the right to be whoever you desire is your true birthright. Claim it, fight for it, help others do the same. This is your story, from point of view of the son, not the father. In Norman Mailer's new book, *The Gospel According to the Son,* Mailer (January 31) reviews the Bible from the point of view of Jesus. Jesus says of his encounter with the devil, "I had been tested, had proved loyal, and now my tongue began to feel clean. . . . I was obliged to wonder. Why had the Lord left me alone with Satan? Was it to scourge me of an excess of piety? Before long I would learn that there might be truth in this. There was work to do, and it could not be accomplished on one's knees."

When we can look back on our pain and sorrow it gives us moral strength. Charles Dickens's famous Ebenezer Scrooge begins to be converted once he faces painful scenes from his past. In Aquarius, you desire the opportunity to rise above the conditions you were born in too. Lincoln said, "There is no permanent class of hired laborer." This is the power to shape your own destiny. You can turn one minute into a turning point, or you can condense ten years into a meaningless passage. It's up to you. Charles Lindbergh wrote in his *Wartime Journals,* "A great tradition can be inherited, but greatness itself must be won." Forget that you felt lost and abandoned. Look what you did with that meager beginning. You created a life from your own vision, talents, and mind. Your past is in alignment with your vision, which summons you into the now and onto a new and powerful course. With heaven and earth working with you, the impossible is just a matter of choice.

The search for your true origin, the haunting memory of happier days, innocence and youth—this is your memory of Eden and paradise. Darwin shocked and divided the world when he declared that men and apes had a common ancestor. His findings challenged the biblical origin story. The truth is that both origin stories are correct. We come from both heaven and earth. Heaven provides our mythical and symbolic origin. Evolution is what happens to us on earth—we evolve and grow and transform. The two are not in conflict.

In Aquarius, the mother, the female, or Spirit has a dual nature. She is usually strong and more powerful than the men, because Spirit, symbolically represented here, has accessed her full power and reconnected with her true nature. The male has taken on Spirit's ways—he is reflective and concedes when confronted. On the other hand, Spirit has yang energy. She has become selfish and outwardly strong. Yoko Ono's father was a pianist, her mother's family was wealthy and would not bless the marriage unless their future son-in-law gave up his musical career and went to work in their family's bank. He did just that. Music is Spirit's realm, and Spirit gave in to the world of finance. Spirit allows Ego to use it to achieve a goal. When it taps into Spirit's source, Ego gains Spirit's power as it loses its earthly vitality.

The female Aquarian feels her strength and at the same time, desires to serve. If she serves the wrong person for the wrong reason, she will be used. If, however, she has a strong will, she will choose well whom and how she serves. When Spirit is missing for the Aquarian woman, she can be a threatening, selfish and unnurturing woman, who tries to control all men. Yoko Ono's mother was very beautiful but emotionally abandoned her child. When a doctor made a sexual advance on Yoko at the age of nine, her mother, instead of supporting her daughter, told her she "must have invited it." Then she went off to a party and left Yoko alone.

The male Aquarian can feel impotent and overwhelmed by females unless he can learn to harness Spirit's force for his own purpose. He must know that through uniting he will not lose himself, that when he owns his own destiny and spiritual strength, surrendering will only add to his power. The man without a sense of service or Spirit, will avoid relationships with women, feeling the need to protect himself from being kept from his purpose. Fearing the urge to surrender, the only way he stays strong is by keeping his distance.

Both Ego and Spirit long for lost innocence and unconditional love. Lewis Carroll (January 27) found joy in photographing innocent young girls. He is as much recognized for his photographs of children as he is for his stories. Carroll profoundly felt the Aquarian dilemma, the innocent child having to survive in the world of the adult. He wondered how someone could maneuver through the endless rules and regulations of adult life that are really nothing but nonsense. Changing common sense to nonsense is one of Aquarius's greatest achievements. They know how to laugh at life, making the serious ridiculous. They use humor to objectify an event. Once objectified, they can laugh at the event and use it for their own end. Nonsense is Ego's way of defying death. Spirit laughs for a different reason. She knows the "real" is totally nonsense. Nonsense gives meaning and order. It allows you to separate from words, events and appearances, and then the true voice, all the things that can't be said, the silent fears and joys are spoken through the emotional impact of the story or situation. Lewis Carroll's *Alice's Adventure in Wonderland* describes birthday parties that go on forever, a Cheshire cat who speaks in riddles, and playing cards that play croquet. Realities switch in Aquarius. The real loses its power, and the supernatural, the nonsensical, and the dream state become empowered.

The Aquarius mind needs to know where it's going or thought becomes its worst enemy. Without direction it jumps from topic to topic, never finding satisfaction with its discoveries. Once the goal of Capricorn has been transformed into a purpose, your whole being begins to participate and work toward its fulfillment. A powerful purpose demands unity of mind, emotions, heart, conscious and unconscious thoughts. The uniting of the unconscious and the conscious is what gives the Aquarian access to the secrets of the universe. They can reach into the past, present, or future and possess the jewels of higher knowledge. Pose a question with your conscious mind. Then the unconscious goes to work. It digs within and finds a symbol that allows you to snatch the truth you need from its image. You are connected to everyone, living and dead. Spirits speak to you, angels appear, the ancients reveal all.

On Charles Lindbergh's thirty-three and a half hour flight across the Atlantic, he had a personal experience with spirits. The fuselage behind him became filled with the silhouettes of phantoms. He could see them because his head had become "a single large eye, capable of seeing everywhere at once." Then, the spirits spoke to him. "First one and then another presses forward to my shoulder to speak above the engine's noise, and then draws back among the group behind. At times, voices come out of the air itself, clear yet far away, traveling through distances that can't be measured by the scale of human miles; familiar voices, conversing and advising on my flight, discussing problems of my navigation, reassuring me, giving me messages of importance unattainable in ordinary life." The years did not diminish Lindbergh's memory of those spirits. "My visions are easily explained away through reason, but the longer I live, the more limited I believe rationality to be . . . Certainly my vision in the *Spirit of St. Louis* entered into the reality of my life, for they stimulated thought along new lines; thought enters into both the creation and the definition of reality . . . I recognized that vision and reality interchange, like energy and matter."

In Aquarius, visions are common. While working in the fields, Rasputin had a vision of the Virgin Mary. "And as the Virgin, radiating her divine love, faded from his sight, and the celestial choir from his hearing, he remained on his knees in wonder. What was her purpose for him? In what way did she want him to serve her?"

In Aquarius, purpose is important. Do your work, get your earthly life on track, then ask for your divine purpose to be revealed. Rasputin ". . . knew that he would be told in time and that the time would be chosen by God . . . In describing this golden moment . . . he called it his 'Awakening,' or his 'Spiritual Rebirth.'"

Aquarius is a reawakening to a world beyond the earthly reality on which we have based so much of our thoughts and actions. Experiences with the supernatural give us insight to the fact that there is so much more than what can be seen and touched. In *A Christmas Carol* Charles Dickens used phantoms to teach necessary lessons to old, stingy Scrooge. The Ghost of Christmas Past takes Scrooge on a journey through his childhood. This reflection allows him to "see" how he came to be who he is and sets the stage for change. The Ghost of Christmas Present makes him look at his life as it is now. The Ghost of Christmases to Come reveals the frightening truth, that if Scrooge continues on the path he has chosen, the rest of his life will be miserable and his death will go unmourned. The combination of past, present, and future insight is what changes his attitude forever.

In Aquarius, you start with the future and work backwards. Take your dream and, from it, rearrange your perceptions. You are now a product of your own destiny. Events, parents, friends, and lovers are no longer the central figures in your drama. You are.

Your mind is a problem solver. Give it a challenge and then ask, demand, plead, and pray for your answer. The tension unites your conscious and unconscious. Then, as if from nowhere, the solution to the problem emerges. It may seem like a sudden insight, but the problem-solving process has been going on for a while.

If you're having trouble identifying with the Aquarian I have been describing, then you have work to do. It's easy to get stuck along the journey. A common trap for Aquarians is the challenge directly related to Capricorn, the previous sign. If you haven't found the courage to look into the darkness of your soul, then you'll be living that darkness now. The shadow must be faced before you can move on. You must own all your negative thoughts, your guilt, anger, primal desires, and feelings of nothingness. You must face your fear that you have nothing to offer, that what lies at the core of your being is an ugly, worthless cad. This is your Ego speaking. It knows that it has nothing to offer beyond the illusion. But Spirit has everything to offer. Awaken to your true self. You are a creature of divinity and once you realize that, your whole world changes. Remember, you must ask for help, you must choose to know, you must participate in this drama or it will not happen.

If you refuse to acknowledge your true origin, then you will face depression, darkness, and nightmares. Within you is a living hell; without you, there is no escape. You feel suffocated as the demands of others are imposed upon you. You rebel but it changes nothing. You travel here and there; you refuse to participate. You are unable to set boundaries, inward or outward, and so you isolate yourself. You offer this phantom shell to the world. You feel as though you are a ghost without worldly impact. You're a misfit, lost and abandoned. That is, until you discover your true origin. This is Dickens's Oliver Twist. Twist is not safe in the world of thieves, or in the world of society. It is not until he discovers his *real* origin, his parents, that he is brought back into life and given a new beginning.

The dangers of not owning your divine self are many. For one, success can destroy you. Without a purpose, temptation is too easily embraced. Once you know who you are and where you are going, no one can lure you off your path. Charles Lindbergh faced this dilemma when he became an international hero, one the world wanted to use as an ideal. In 1927, William Randolph Hearst, one of the richest and most powerful men alive, offered him a half-million-dollar movie contract. Lindbergh turned him down saying it would take him away from his purpose, which was to advance aviation and protect the environment. In Aquarius, money is not important other than to provide the means by which to reach your dreams. It has no purpose of its own. What it is used for determines its value. What you allow yourself to be used for determines your value.

Passion, the soul's desire to be united with God, is the driving force of an Aquarius. This passion can be used to change the world. If your goal is less lofty, you can be the rabble-rouser who leads the mob to violence. On a more personal level, human passion leads to the desire to be intimate with another. When this passion is not understood or resolved it can tear the soul apart. Rasputin struggled terribly with his strong sexuality. He found he could not meditate or worship God when he was burning with passion. He joined a group of religious seekers who believed in fornication before worship. The decision was a poor one and gave him a terrible reputation.

In Aquarius, a love relationship serves a multitude of purposes. Your mate must be everything: friend, lover, confidant. John Lennon said about Yoko Ono that he had found someone he, "could go and get pissed with, and have exactly the same relationship as any mate in Liverpool you'd ever had. But you could go to bed with it, and it could stroke your head when you felt tired, or sick, or depressed. It could also be mother."

Marriage and commitment are not a priority in Aquarius. These are independent souls who carry their home in their heart, giving themselves the freedom to be and go wherever they need to in order to fulfill their destiny. However, Aquarians do take commitment seriously, and many make the perfect mate, once they surrender. The problem is that they are very much aware of the consequences of commitment and fear the emotional and physical limitations that may ensue from the union. They often marry late, or take their time in popping the question. Franz Schubert was said to have an "almost frantic desire for freedom, a wish to remain emotionally unencumbered. He was fond of many people, but he did not love—love wholeheartedly and with the complete dedication of his being—anyone." Schubert was what we would call an "emotional drifter." Aquarians have the ability to have the ideal relationship, if they understand themselves and their needs.

Good and evil are intricately interwoven in Aquarius. It's up to you to decide how much space to allow each one inside you. The Aquarius point of view is that everyone is born good and pure; it's the environment that is filled with evil. You must be able to preserve your goodness in spite of what happens around you. Temptation must be conquered, and this is only possible when you know who you are and where you are going. Others may feel deceived by you when you choose your own path and decide to fulfill your spiritual purpose. Your values now conflict with the values of others. If you don't show off, if you can't be bought, you let down those ruled by Ego. You make them feel their smallness. Some will grow from your example and others will blame you for their faults. Don't pay attention to praise or attacks. Listen to yourself.

Deception can be used by Spirit, too. In the Bible, Rebecca used deception to fulfill God's prophecy. When she was pregnant with twins, God spoke to her and said, "Two nations are in your womb, and two peoples born of you shall be divided; the one shall be stronger than the other, the elder shall serve the younger." What happens next can be called Abel's revenge. The younger must now take back the destiny that was denied him by his innocence. Isaac, Rebecca's husband, calls to him his favorite son, the older Esau. Isaac by this time blind, tells Esau that he is dying. Esau is a hunter. Isaac sends him out to bring and prepare game, so that Isaac can bless him. Rebecca hears this and sends Jacob, the younger son and her favorite, in place of Esau to receive the blessing of his father. She dresses Jacob in Esau's clothes, and to make sure Isaac doesn't discover the deception, she ties sheepskin to Jacob's hands and neck to resemble the hairiness of his older brother. The deception works, and the younger child gains the inheritance. In Aquarius you must reach for what you want. You must participate in your destiny.

Rasputin lost his older brother, Mischa, to pneumonia. He carried the sorrow of that death with him always. Sometimes, the birth of a new child takes the attention away from the older, creating jealousy or a sense of abandonment. Charles Dickens felt this way at the age of two, when a younger brother deposed him. In Aquarius, the younger sibling often represents Spirit, and is now stronger than its older sibling, Ego. Ego works through deception, lies and pride. Spirit is not attached to these things, and uses them for her own purpose. The intention is what makes the difference. The spirit of the law is what must be upheld.

In Aquarius, God is no distant stranger. He dwells within. To reach him, all you have to do is meditate or pray and His presence will be felt. Rasputin's life was changed when he first heard these word in church: "The kingdom of God cometh not with observation: Neither shall they say, Lo here! or, Lo there! for, behold, the kingdom of God is within you." The tension of Ego and Spirit is gone. In its place is the divine spark. This divine spark manifests through fate, visions, voices and good old-fashioned luck, which is nothing more than the hand of God manifesting in our lives. The life of an Aquarius is fraught with events that dramatically alter the path. They never end up where they start out, instead, they are asked to take one leap of faith after another. Each time they are backed up against a wall, they are forced to ask for help. As soon as they do, the divine spark manifests and a way out emerges. This creates an attitude that there is always a solution or a different choice. To the Aquarius, there is no such thing as impossibility. They need to know that they have the power to evoke God's presence. This is the awakening of Spirit to its true destiny. Heaven awakens the Aquarian soul, and the Aquarian awakens the world to new ideas.

Aquarians are independent and don't deal well with authority. Many are self-taught. Arthur Rubinstein (January 28) said, ''The butterfly flies from flower to flower and tries to find the best mixture in creating her honey— so try to make your musical honey the same way.'' The creative process is never about discovering something new; it's about arranging what already is. Goethe said, ''The most original men are not so much original because they tell us something absolutely new, but because they know how to tell us things in a way in which they were never told before.''

In Aquarius, the barrier between art and the artist is removed. This is pop and interactive art, and it takes you beyond where you've been before. It jolts your perceptions and forces your mind to recognize its thoughts. For example, with *Painting to Be Stepped On,* Yoko Ono instructed the audience to put an empty canvas on the floor and wait for someone to walk on it. Art now goes beyond the shape of things into what cannot be communicated except through experience.

In Aquarius, the individual has reached his or her full power and the powers are supernatural. Aquarians add a touch of magic to everything they do. Thomas Edison literally lit up the world when he invented the lightbulb. Imagine that magical moment when he pulled the master switch and in lower Manhattan, four hundred lamps lit up the sky. ''In a twinkling,'' said the *New York Herald,* ''the area bounded by Spruce, Wall, Nassau and Pearl Streets was in a glow.'' Aquarians are dedicated to the advancement of the human race, spiritually as well as economically. They lead the way, holding high their lamp that burns on the oil of faith and truth. They are unafraid of death, danger, or the phantoms that lurk in realm of the unknown. In order for the individual to reconnect with the collective, bringing his unique skills and lessons, he must feel strong and whole enough to walk his path alone. This is Aquarius.

THE AQUARIUS ENVIRONMENT

The Aquarius environment either embraces your individuality and honors you for your difference and originality or it rejects you for this difference and keeps trying to direct you into the mainstream. Without a spiritual purpose, fate will change your plans and your direction every time you get it set in place. Spirit will play, too. She will give you the gifts of imagination, but you must provide the courage and the voice to make it happen. Without a song, you are lost in the crowd. With a song, your unique voice blends with those of others and creates a greater song for the whole world.

Aquarius/*One* (January 28, February 1, February 10, February 19) Uranus/Sun

PURPOSE: To be able to maintain your individuality and goals in spite of the endless changes and crises that cross your path.

"Familiar things happen, and mankind does not bother about them. It requires a very unusual mind to undertake the analysis of the obvious."—Alfred North Whitehead, British philosopher. The Aquarius/*One* has a great mind, but it can be unbending. Their principles are strong and their nature perfectionist. They want things right and according to their vision. Loners by nature, Aquarius/*Ones* don't let others in easily. Authority or father issues are strong. They may have had to break away from home in order to pursue their own dream. Aquarius is about forgiveness and reconciliation. These come easily once Aquarius/*Ones* access their higher purpose. The heart has a great capacity to love; they should not be afraid of losing their identity as the right union will empower them. Relationships can be difficult because they value their freedom with a passion. They need to be careful they don't go through people too quickly, ending the relationship as soon as their partner starts making demands. They have a strong sense of justice and will reach out to help friends in need. When they're generous, they give everything. When they pull back, they pull back completely. They must learn inner discipline and build a bridge between these two extremes. They either reject responsibility or take on too much. Although adventure and faraway places are constantly calling them, they need to manifest a talent or become the best at a skill the world will value. Once they have achieved their fame, they must use their position to open the hearts of others.

IF SPIRIT TAKES THE LEAD: With Spirit strong, Aquarius/*Ones* can be passionate crusaders. Equal rights, the environment, and racial discrimination are some of their favorite causes. They need to learn discrimination, or their desire to serve will hold them back. Refining their purpose is the key. If they are too gentle, they could be attracted to tough individuals, even abusive tyrants. They must learn to protect themselves and choose wisely.

IF EGO TAKES THE LEAD: With Ego in the lead, so is strength. These souls don't take no easily. They may have had a tough father. They either imitate his actions or withdraw within themselves. If they are a man, they are attracted to very strong women and can be abused. If they are a woman, they need to watch how they use their strength. They are loners. They avoid anything mainstream, then wonder why they feel left out. They must learn to give and compromise, and life will become a safe haven instead of a war zone.

ALAN ALDA (January 28)

Actor, director, writer.

Alda is known best for his starring role as Dr. Hawkeye Pierce on M*A*S*H, for which he won several Emmy Awards. Alda was born in New York City, the son of an actor. He worked with his father in summer stock, and sometimes entertained the soldiers at the Hollywood Canteen. He graduated from Fordham University. With a three-year Ford Foundation grant, he performed off-Broadway and made a few guest appearances on television. His first Broadway hit was *The Owl and the Pussycat*. Two years later, he received a Tony nomination for his performance in *The Apple Tree*. Married to Arlene Weiss, a classical clarinetist, Alda has three daughters and prefers to live in a small, New Jersey town, rather than in the limelight. "To me work is love," Alda says. "Work is at the heart of health."

ROBERTA FLACK (February 10)

Pianist, singer.

"To live is to suffer; to survive is to find some meaning in that suffering," says Roberta Flack. Her love of music can be traced to the moment her father found a piano in a junkyard and had it restored. Flack was nine years old at the time; her mother taught her to play. At the age of fifteen, she went to Howard University on a scholarship and graduated with a B.A. in music education. After her father's death, she taught music in Farmville, N.C., for a while. Flack said, "Let me tell you, it's damn tough for a black woman hanging out there [in the music business] on her own. It takes enormous strength." She was discovered by the jazz pianist Les McCann, who heard her play in a Washington, D.C., nightclub. He arranged for an audition with Atlantic Records. From that point on, it was a straight climb to the top. Like many Aquarians, Flack did not hesitate to marry interracially. But commitment doesn't come easy to this sign. She married twice before she decided to "avoid combining marriage and the pursuit of a career."

Aquarius/*Two* (January 29, February 2, February 11) Uranus/Moon

PURPOSE: To integrate your extreme nature which keeps you either isolated and alone or losing yourself in your quest to right injustice and save lost souls.

"Only a life lived in the service to others is worth living."—Albert Einstein. Loners by heart, Aquarius/*Twos* still manage to do their share of giving. They need to learn to open up a little more and trust their instincts to tell them whom to love, whom to help, and whom to leave alone. They project their own feelings onto the wounded. They need to heal themselves first. Aquarius/*Twos* struggle with mood swings and depression. They are attracted to the eccentric and have a strange sense of humor. They are defiant, a bit rebellious, and very persistent. The danger here lies in attaching themselves to the wrong person. They need to use discrimination before letting their passionate nature rule. They are sensitive and psychic. They need to trust their inner voice and direct their obsessive nature toward something positive.

IF SPIRIT TAKES THE LEAD: When Spirit is strong, then so is heart. The Aquarius/*Two* tends to surrender too easily to those who are lost and in need. A good cause gets them going faster than a winning Lotto ticket. They want to change the world and are brilliant and persistent enough to do it. Family and personal life tend to be sacrificed. They prefer to dedicate themselves to larger, more lofty goals. They're obsessive and need to be careful who they choose to save.

IF EGO TAKES THE LEAD: If Ego is powerful, then so are isolation, independence, and deep feelings of hurt. These souls may have to deal with depression, moodiness, and fear. They feel abandoned by life and have trouble connecting with others. They don't take orders well. Instead, they feel sorry for themselves. They need to put a little Spirit in their life; dedicate some time to someone else, and they'll be surprised how much better they'll feel.

OPRAH WINFREY (January 29)

Talk show hostess, actress, producer.

Oprah Winfrey is one of the richest women in America, and she got there all by herself. Born in Kosciusko, Mississippi, Winfrey was raised by her grandmother when her parents left to seek their fortune and their dreams. At age six, Winfrey left her sheltered farm life to live with her mother, Vernita Lee, in Milwaukee. There, she was sexually abused by an older cousin and later, by a friend of the family. The pain she suffered eventually gave her the compassion needed to heal others. Before she learned to turn tragedy to triumph, she became a rebel and ran away from home. But it wasn't until she went to live with her father, Vernon, in Nashville, Tennessee, that Winfrey received the structure and security she needed to blossom. Eventually, she became an honor student and joined the drama club. At sixteen, she won an oratorical contest and a thousand-dollar scholarship which helped pay her tuition to Tennessee State University. In college, Winfrey landed a job on WTVF-TV. This led to a position as feature reporter and coanchor of the six o'clock news on a Baltimore station. Today, her talk show has the highest ratings, and Winfrey is an accomplished actress. Her part in Steven Spielberg's film *The Color Purple* won her an Academy Award nomination for Best Supporting Actress. Her own company, Harpo Productions, has produced many award-winning shows. Winfrey is the first woman in history to own and produce her own show. She says, "My mission is to use this position, power and money to create opportunities for other people."

THOMAS EDISON (February 11)

Inventor.

Thomas Edison is responsible for inventing the phonograph, the motion-picture projector, and the electric lightbulb. During his lifetime, he registered more patents than anyone else alive. Edison was born inquisitive. Growing up he was called "the question box." Gifted with incredible powers of observation and retention, Edison believed in the direct experience over learned scholastic studies. His mother played an important part in his life, giving him guidance and love. Edison's first job was selling magazines, peanuts, and candy on a train. He mastered the Morse code and the telegraph, which led to his first important invention—the quadruplex wire for Western Union. The quadruplex wire enabled more than one signal to be sent at a time and in more than one direction. Edison was also a shrewd businessman and fought to protect his ideas and inventions in the marketplace. Many of his inventions were triggered by other people's ideas or by information from various sources. In the Aquarius way, he reinvented the thing and made it unique. Edison's family life was plagued with depression and alcoholism. He neglected his wives and the six children from his two marriages. With all his faults, there is no doubt that Edison's ability to manifest his ideas allowed him to be a catalyst for change. The *New York Times* named him "The Greatest Living American."

Aquarius/*Three* (January 30, February 3, February 12) Uranus/Jupiter

PURPOSE: To take that inner voice that says you are special and have a calling, and unite it with your earthly voice in order to manifest a dream.

"Many a man has found the acquisition of wealth only a change, not an end, of miseries."—Lucius Annaeus Seneca, Roman author. Aquarius/*Threes* are born with a great deal of strength and a strong sense of purpose. Their job is to activate their strength through learning to believe in themselves and to discover their spiritual path, that will bring them happiness and reward beyond earthly success. Although they may feel like orphans, the roots of Aquarius/*Threes* are anchored both deep in the earth and high above in heaven. Nothing seems impossible. The greater the challenge, the more they're interested. This can be dangerous if they take on too much before they're old enough to handle it. Early failure can cause a lack of trust in their own ability. Aquarius/*Threes* have a love of freedom, a fear of commitment and a desire to be the boss. They run their own business or work independently. They have the ability to influence and make others see their point of view. They might be gurus, super salesmen, actors or inventors. They should remember that their mission is not to control others but to help them become strong and secure in their own opinions.

IF SPIRIT TAKES THE LEAD: If Spirit has the weight, the Aquarius/*Three* may feel as if they are chosen for a very special purpose. They feel that their destiny is already determined. They must remember that although they feel a calling, they need to remain modest and allow themselves to be guided by their inner voice. They are meant to manifest something great in the world and from that success, give something back to mankind.

IF EGO TAKES THE LEAD: If Ego is ahead here, these souls feel as if they are meant to rule the world, to have others serve them and listen to their every word. They get annoyed when they don't get the respect they feel they deserve and the attention they demand. They are restless and attracted to impossible feats. They want control over everything they do, but if they get it, they are unhappy. The rebel in them is looking for the Divine Father who will set limits.

ABRAHAM LINCOLN (February 12)

Lawyer, legislator, sixteenth president of the United States.

Abraham Lincoln remained a man of the people, even after he became the sixteenth president of the United States. His early acquaintance with poverty and hardship gave him an understanding and sympathy for the needy and the oppressed. Lincoln had only one year of formal schooling, yet his common sense and natural intelligence enabled him to lead America through the Civil War. Lincoln held the Aquarius vision of unity before any other. He believed it was better to get something done than to do it perfectly. He married Mary Todd and had four sons, two of whom died. Lincoln carried a melancholy that reflected his humanitarian soul. Yet, he loved life and could laugh and joke. Lincoln was a great statesman and military strategist. He believed in the opportunity for everyone to climb the ladder of success. He was assassinated in 1865 while attending a performance of *Our American Cousin* at Ford's Theater in Washington, D.C.

CHARLES DARWIN (February 12)

Scientist.

Charles Darwin, discoverer of the theory of evolution by natural selection, reorganized man's view of the world and his place in it. In 1831, Darwin embarked on a five-year voyage with Robert Fitzroy, a sea captain, naturalist and religious man, who declared himself against the "new-fangled geology" and wanted to refute it. At the time, Darwin, who had failed at medicine, had no direction and agreed to accompany Fitzroy. As they headed down the South American coast, Darwin noted the differences in species from place to place, the fossils, and the environment. While in the Galapagos Islands, Darwin realized that each island was a world unto itself. Though the islands were close to one another, many species of animals had developed differently on each. For example, the finches found on each island exhibited variations in their beaks. Over time, each species had developed modifications suited to its particular island home. On his return to England, Darwin married his cousin Emma Wedgwood and isolated himself with his family in a little village called Down, in Kent. For twenty-two years Darwin didn't publish a word about his findings. Instead, he worked on compiling a large book, well documented and persuasive, regarding his beliefs on evolution. At one point, a comparatively unknown naturalist named Alfred Russel Wallace sent Darwin his ideas on evolution. Shaken, Darwin submitted Wallace's paper and a short summary of his own work to the Linnean Society. Darwin immediately went to work explaining his views in a book called *An Abstract of an Essay on the Origin of Species,* promising that a "real" book would follow. He never had to write the second book. *The Origin of Species* sold out in a single day. Although it created a religious and scientific storm, it was also readily received by most scientists and by much of the public. Within ten years, Darwin was known all over the world, and his theory of evolution had become a guiding principle in all biological studies.

Aquarius/*Four* (January 22, January 31, February 4, February 13) Uranus/Uranus

PURPOSE: To stay on your path and not get attached to the excitement of change and transformation, as events, upsets and unexpected happenings bring you to new levels of understanding.

"You have your way. I have my way. As for the right way, the correct way, and the only way, it does not exist."—Friedrich Nietzsche. Aquarius/*Fours* are always taking on more than they should. They cross boundaries as soon as they reach them. Sometimes this is good. At other times, it gets them into trouble. Good discrimination is a must. They have an adventuresome spirit and are not afraid to try anything new. If their heart is open, they will care about others and want to make the world a better place. If they are stuck in fear, then they will stay on the outskirts of life, feeling lost and alone. Courage is necessary, and it comes from taking responsibility for one's own actions. Once Aquarius/*Fours* trust their instincts and act on their conscience, all obstacles will turn into stepping-stones.

IF SPIRIT TAKES THE LEAD: Spirit and the number *Four* are friends—they like excitement and making things happen. These souls are always in a state of crisis, taking on more than they should, pushing boundaries and people to make changes in their lives. They are catalysts. Whatever they decide to do becomes undone and is then put back together in a new way. Relationships are hard because they're always off on a new adventure, feeling their freedom and making a difference.

IF EGO TAKES THE LEAD: Ego with the number *Four* creates a loner. The Aquarius/*Four* is hard to reach, loves to take risks, and lives by themselves. They don't like to compromise. Money is not as important as is their independence. They desire their freedom more than anything and may spend their life exploring the most remote corners of existence. They're inventors. They love a challenge, and as soon as they've conquered it, they move on.

CHARLES LINDBERGH (February 4)

Aviator.

Charles Lindbergh was an American hero. He represented the spirit of America—the youth, courage and daring to break new ground. As a child, Lindbergh was close to both his parents. Their divorce devastated him. His father taught him how to fish, hunt, and drive a car, long before most boys were allowed those privileges. Lindbergh received freedom in return for responsibility. The ability to take charge and the faith he had in himself, were the guiding principles of his success. When Lindbergh was dismissed from college, he chose the field of aviation, in which he would excel. Lindbergh became the first man to cross the Atlantic on a solo, nonstop flight and became an instant hero. The world wanted a piece of him, but Lindbergh had inner strength and direction. He turned down a half-million-dollar movie contract from William Randolph Hearst because his primary goal was not money. He became a strong supporter of efforts to save the whales, and the forests. Lindbergh was happily married to the writer Anne Morrow Lindbergh. In March 1932, their two-year-old son was kidnapped and killed. Lindbergh tried to live a private life, and when he couldn't, he used the press to help advance his causes.

GEORGE BALANCHINE (January 22)

Ballet master.

George Balanchine is often considered one of the three creative geniuses of the twentieth century. As a choreographer, he was innovative, always stretching himself and his dancers to their limits. Born in the Caucasus, Russia, Balanchine was a child who liked to scrutinize the world from the sidelines. Piano was his first musical connection. However, when his older sister auditioned for the Imperial School of Ballet, it was suggested that he audition, too. They were both accepted, but his sister dropped out shortly after her admission. Once Balanchine discovered the beauty and power of dance, he was committed. Early in his career, he defected with a group of dancers. His talents took him to Broadway where he choreographed four movies and nineteen Broadway musicals, including *On Your Toes,* In this stage production he was the first to work the dancers into the plot. In *Peter's Journey* he created the first dream sequence. Balanchine went on to choreograph sequences for movies as well as for the Metropolitan Opera. He helped establish the School of American Ballet and eventually formed his own ballet company. Balanchine had a gift for seeing the potential in a dancer. He worked at high speed and could perform work for several different companies simultaneously. The "speed and economy" of his work reflects the spirit of the twentieth century. Balanchine liberated dance from the story and showed the world the divine possibilities of the human body.

Aquarius/*Five* (January 23, February 5, February 14) Uranus/Mercury

PURPOSE: To use your great mind and your unlimited strength to set inner boundaries, preventing you from diminishing your power by taking on the responsibility of the world, which will prevent you from manifesting your own wonderful dream.

"Whatever you can do, or dream you can, begin it. Boldness has genius, power, and magic in it."—Johann Wolfgang von Goethe. The Aquarius/*Fives* are brilliant and are capable of solving almost any problem. Their problem is that they take on too much. They can't say no to responsibility. They feel too sorry for others, know they can do a better job, and so volunteer. This kind of action keeps them from manifesting something truly wonderful in the world. They need to find their purpose and then watch the doors open. Aquarius/*Fives* desperately need boundaries. They need to learn how to be in a relationship and to face the fact that they are not perfect and bound occasionally to disappoint their partners. They hide from relationships until they learn not to lose themselves in one. Aquarius/*Fives* need some assertiveness training when it comes to their emotions. Once they truly understand they're entitled to a life of their own, they're on their way.

IF SPIRIT TAKES THE LEAD: If Spirit is ahead, they are likely to have a nervous breakdown. They are capable of everything and try to do it all. This does terrible things to their body and sense of self. They need to remember they can't help others if they're incapacitated. Their personal life suffers if they don't learn to accept their whole self. Versatility is a burden if the soul is without a purpose or central theme.

IF EGO TAKES THE LEAD: If Ego is strong, the Aquarius/*Five* may be a genius. They are great manipulators; they know how to get what they want from others. When their conscience is missing, they can play any game and become anything they want. They are never satisfied.

RASPUTIN (January 23)

Healer.

Born Grigory Yefimovich Novykh, Rasputin is and has been a controversial figure. His great gift of healing was often clouded by his strong, sensual desires. What brought him to international prominence was his connection with the czar and czarina of Russia—a connection which began in 1905. Their son and only male heir to the throne was a hemophiliac, and they believed that only Rasputin could heal him. Their allegiance to Rasputin allowed their enemies room for trouble. As a child, Rasputin could communicate with animals and predict who was coming to the house hours before they arrived. His powers were first temporarily lost when his brother died of pneumonia, which they both caught when they almost drowned in a river. Always religious, at age thirty Rasputin had a vision from the Virgin Mary. He knew he had a mission, but struggled desperately to overcome his desires. Eventually, he joined a group that practiced group sex before meditation. However, his debauchery only led to the loss of his powers, which came and went with his struggle to stay on the spiritual path. Rasputin spent several years in a monastery; he also was married and had several children. His most profound belief was that the kingdom of God was found within each person.

JACK BENNY (February 14)

Comedian, violinist, actor.

Jack Benny was born Benny Kubelsky. Like any true Aquarius, he was different. He had very little in common with his parents, who focused their interest on the family store. Benny wanted to be a concert violin player. During his freshman year at Central High School, he got a job at the local vaudeville theater, playing in the evening performances and occasionally doubling as an usher. At age sixteen, Benny formed an act with a piano player and almost immediately they were booked and on the road. He experienced no great setbacks, on his path to the top. Both onstage and off his timing was perfect. During World War II, Benny enlisted in the navy at Great Lakes. He joined the Great Lakes Review. One night, one of the acts needed someone to read three comedy lines. Benny volunteered. His delivery was so different—so flat and understated—the audience roared and a comedian was born. Benny went on to develop a career in radio, television, and the movies. Like a true Aquarius, Benny knew it's how you start that counts. He would work hours on his opening lines. "Once you get rolling," he said, "and get the attention of the audience, it's not important how you finish." Benny contributed time and money to many charitable causes. He died of cancer, a legend in his own time.

Aquarius/*Six* (January 24, February 6, February 15) Uranus/Venus

PURPOSE: To gain strength and discrimination from within so that you can manifest something wonderful in the world and slow down enough to enjoy your success.

"Blessed is he who makes his companions laugh."—the Koran. Aquarius/ *Sixes* have a love of truth and beauty and a natural social nature that makes them easy to get along with. Their date books are always filled because of their charisma and knowledge of how to treat others. But Aquarius/*Sixes* need discipline. Their hearts are either too big, or they are loners who keeps their distance from others. They are excellent manipulators. They sense what people want and like and know how to give it to them. They can be obsessive, and desire to be spoiled and seen as special. Aquarius/*Sixes* must find their spiritual purpose and then, if they can learn to say no to themselves and others, they're on their way. They are hidden rebels. They love truth and will fight for justice. They know how to surrender to love, or how to not give it at all.

IF SPIRIT TAKES THE LEAD: If Spirit is strong, these souls will have trouble with affairs of the heart. They give too much, expect too much, and are never happy. Divine discontent is definitely their partner for life, so they need to learn to use it to their advantage. They need a spiritual goal.

IF EGO TAKES THE LEAD: Ego and the number *Six* go very well together. They like lots of everything and all of it the finest money can buy. These souls are seductive and know what you want and how to get it. They are charming and manipulative. Their instincts are great. Able to sell anyone anything anytime, they know how to reach others. If they live alone, it's because they prefer it that way.

NEIL DIAMOND (January 24)

Singer, actor composer.

Born the son of Polish and Russian Jews, Neil Diamond grew up in the Coney Island section of Brooklyn, New York. Diamond was drawn to music at an early age. In high school, he sang in the choral group. He attended college on a fencing scholarship but dropped out in his senior year to take a job writing songs with Sunbeam Music. After only sixteen weeks, he was let go. Diamond made a commitment to his spiritual journey by renting a piano and an office where he could compose songs for himself. "It wasn't until I began to sing my own songs that I had real success,'' he says. In addition to his own hits, such as "Kentucky Women," "Cracklin' Rose," and "He Ain't Heavy, He's My Brother," he wrote for the pop group The Monkees. Diamond won a Grammy Award and an Oscar nomination for his music for the movie *Jonathan Livingston Seagull,* and his concerts are always sold out. Diamond has been married twice and is the father of four children.

NATALIE COLE (February 6)

Singer.

Natalie Cole is the famous daughter of the famous, late singer Nat King Cole. Cole attributes her success to a great deal of love, not just the love from her audience but God's love, as well. Aquarius is the sign where the heart is open. "My father was as natural a man as you could ever meet," she says. "If God gives me success, I hope I can handle it with as much grace and humility as he did. That would be my greatest gift." Cole grew up in Los Angeles, where she was surrounded by great singers and recording artists. At age eleven, she sang on stage with her father. Not long after that, she formed a combo, just for fun. Only after college did Cole begin to sing at clubs. She has won Grammys, American Music Awards and Soul Train Awards. Her concerts have brought her great acclaim. Cole gives her time to many humanitarian causes, including the American Cancer Society and N.O.W., Neighbors of Watts, an organization which raises funds for children's centers in the L.A. ghetto.

Aquarius/*Seven* (January 25, February 7, February 16) Uranus/Neptune

PURPOSE: To align your will with His, using your faith to protect you so that you can manifest your dreams without becoming hurt or being destroyed.

"He that is discontented in one place will seldom be content in another."— Aesop, Greek storyteller. Aquarius/*Sevens* are gifted, but that gift can lead to destruction unless they have developed from within. They need faith, a belief in themselves and in something greater. They will live with divine discontent until they accept a spiritual path. Others will take advantage of them if they remain innocent and unable to protect themselves. If they are street-smart, they could take advantage of everyone else. Aquarius/*Sevens* are incredibly intuitive and struggle with depression and mood swings. They are creative and able to pass through doors closed to others.

IF SPIRIT TAKES THE LEAD: If Spirit leads the way, the Aquarius/*Seven* will have an unrelenting will. They are perfectionists and dictators. They can be judgmental. They have a big heart but need to learn to let Him lead the way. They must learn compromise so that they can enjoy life.

IF EGO TAKES THE LEAD: If Ego is ahead, these souls are perfectionists and control oriented. They doubt themselves and don't want anyone to find out. They can be incredibly successful in their profession. Music or the creative industries may attract them. Without Spirit they could be abused or give abuse, they have no sense of boundaries. They only achieve balance when they find their center and open their heart.

CHARLES DICKENS (February 7)

Writer.

Charles Dickens is the author of such classics of Western literature as *A Christmas Carol, Oliver Twist, Great Expectations,* and *A Tale of Two Cities.* Born in Landport Portsea, England, Dickens was the second of eight children. When his parents were sent to debtor's prison in London, Dickens was removed from school and sent to work in a factory, where he pasted labels on bottles of blacking. He saw his parents only after work and for breakfast. The horrible years during which Dickens experienced the effects of child labor are explored in *David Copperfield.* "I was not beaten or starved; but the wrong that was done to me had no intervals of relenting, and was done in a systematic, passionless manner," Dickens wrote. "Day after day, week after week, month after month, I was coldly rejected." Fortunately, Dickens received a legacy which provided for two years of formal schooling at Willington House Academy. After that he worked as an attorney's clerk and newspaper reporter until he sold his first story and became an almost instant success. Dickens's marriage to Catherine Hogarth was unhappy, though it did produce many children. For many years, he had a secret affair with a young actress named Ellen Ternan. Dickens died at the age of fifty-eight.

SONNY BONO (February 16)

Singer.

Sonny Bono was born in Detroit, Michigan. His family was not wealthy. When he was seven, they moved to Los Angeles and his parents divorced. Bono found strength in writing songs, rather than doing his homework, and made money at odd jobs. Bono hit the jackpot at age twenty-two when he was hired as songwriter producer for Sam Cooke, Little Richard, and Larry Williams. "Koko Joe" was his first hit. It was performed by the Righteous Brothers in 1964. While working his way up the ladder, Bono met a singer named Cherilyn Sarkisian LaPiere, better known as Cher. "I thought Cher was a natural star immediately," Bono said. "She was a real generator for me." They were married almost immediately. At first, they billed themselves as "Caesar and Cleo"; later, they called themselves simply Sonny & Cher. Their song entitled "Baby Don't Go" went right to the top of the charts. "I've Got You Babe" followed and success was assured. The *Sonny and*

Cher Comedy Hour was a huge success, until the couple split in 1974. Bono went into the restaurant business. He owns the Bono Restaurant in Hollywood, and another restaurant in Houston. With Cher, Bono had a daughter named Chastity. In 1981, he remarried to model/actress Susie Coelho. The marriage didn't last and in 1986, he married again. In 1994 he was elected to Congress.

Aquarius/Eight (January 26, February 8, February 17) Uranus/Saturn

PURPOSE: To use your great observational skills to get ahead, gain complete understanding of yourself, so that you lose your fear of change and then to use your success to contribute something to your community.

"Fate gives us the hand, and we play the cards."—Arthur Schopenhauer. No matter what Aquarius/*Eights* decide to do with their lives, they will feel as though someone else has had a hand in the decision. Don't worry. He knows what He's doing. They have incredible observational skills. They also have great psychological understanding; this gives them insight into themselves and an edge in the world. They can be too self-critical and too tough on others. Aquarius/*Eights* take on too much responsibility and deal with depression. They need courage to face their dark side and own it. Once they look at all the things that make them feel unworthy, they get strong. Then, success will come at a steady pace. They must listen to their inner voice and open up their world. Aquarius/*Eights* must learn to use the power of the collective force to their advantage. They prefer being their own boss and should stay free of situations in which they have to take orders. They value their freedom and are driven to succeed.

IF SPIRIT TAKES THE LEAD: If Spirit is strong, then the Aquarius/*Eight* will have a strong need to give to their community and help others. The *Eight* is the teacher, and they want to instruct others on how to improve their lives. They can be so self-demanding they get stuck in their own perfectionism. They need to access faith and allow things to happen.

IF EGO TAKES THE LEAD: If Ego takes the lead, these souls will want to achieve and be in control. They feel as if they are better than others and that life owes them something. Success goes to their head, and they can become abusive and demanding. They are tough and strong, but inside, they're insecure. They are haunted by nightmares and feelings of abandonment. They may struggle with depression and dark feelings. These must be owned and faced in order for them to reach the light.

MICHAEL JORDAN (February 17)

Basketball player.

Michael Jordan has elevated the game of basketball. Gifted with the Aquarius speed and timing, he is a one-man team, known to score more than fifty points a game. He helped his team, the Chicago Bulls, win the NBA Championship three years in a row, and five years out of seven. Jordan has made millions of dollars, not only as a player but as spokesperson for Nike shoes. His own line of shoes, Air Jordans, has outsold the entire stock of other companies. Jordan's popularity with the youth of America is incredible, for which he has run into criticism. Some say he has not used his talent or his success to make a difference by encouraging good values and education. Jordan's talent was not evident early. In fact he was once cut from his high-school team. However, being intense and competitive, Jordan rose to the challenge of being the best. Today, his is one of the most recognizable faces on the planet. In 1992, Jordan was a part of the Olympic Dream Team sent to compete in Barcelona. Jordan's father was shot to death in 1993. Two months later on October 6, 1993, Jordan retired from basketball and entered the sport of baseball. At the age of thirty, he was ready to try something new. Jordan said, "My father used to say that you never know what you can accomplish until you try." Today, Jordan once again plays basketball, but with his talent and the Aquarius desire to break new grounds, who knows what his future will bring?

PAUL NEWMAN (January 26)

Actor.

Paul Newman, like any true Aquarian, is a very private person. He grew up in Cleveland Heights, a suburb of Cleveland. Though his mother is Catholic, he considers himself Jewish. He spent World War II as a radioman in bombers in the Pacific Campaign. Marriage and the family business came before Yale Drama School. "I wasn't driven to acting by any inner compulsion," Newman said. "I was just running away from the sporting-goods business." Within a few months, Newman was on television and on his way to becoming one of the hottest box-office draws of all times. He received his first Oscar nomination for his part in *Cat on a Hot Tin Roof.* He was also nominated for his performances in *The Hustler, Hud,* and *Cool Hand Luke.* Newman loves to run and fish. At the request of his family, he gave up auto racing. Newman has spoken on various issues, including civil rights, gay rights, and the use of seat belts. He established the Scott Newman Foundation, in honor of his son, who died of an overdose of painkillers and alcohol at age twenty-eight. Newman has his own brand of salad dressings, spaghetti sauces, and popcorn. The money earned from these products goes to charity.

Aquarius/*Nine* (January 27, February 9, February 18)
Uranus/Mars

PURPOSE: To work all your talents and skills around your spiritual goal, instructing others by imposing your views and ideas on the collective conscious.

''The crowd gives the leader new strength''—Evenius, Roman scholar. Aquarius/*Nines* are meant to lead. They have their own unique way of handling things and get others to go along. Their mission is to succeed and to use their success to make a difference in the world. The problem is they're too talented and are pulled in too many directions. It's important for them to have a strong spiritual goal around which to focus their lives. Action-oriented, they move more quickly than most people can handle. They need to be able to relax and let themselves be led by instinct. Aquarius/*Nines* are psychic, intuitive, and creative. Their minds are sharp and go right to the heart of a problem. They need to master patience. Their hearts are big and they want to help everyone. They need to learn how to give and still keep something for themselves.

IF SPIRIT TAKES THE LEAD: If Spirit is strong, the Aquarius/*Nine* will use their uniqueness and talent to make a difference. The danger is that they'll be attracted to lost and abandoned souls. They are idealistic and see things as they would like them to be. They need to learn to be in the moment, not to expect so much from themselves, and learn that letting someone fall is sometimes the best way to help them grow.

IF EGO TAKES THE LEAD: If Ego is strong, they can be cruel. They want what they want, and quickly. They are strange and different and like the unusual. They look for excitement. If they haven't received love, they could be filled with hate. They are always in a crisis and affect the lives of those they encounter in a powerful way. They seek those who are self-sacrificing but happiness will elude them until they learn to give.

YOKO ONO (February 18)

Artist, singer.

Yoko Ono was born in Japan to wealthy parents. Her father gave up his career as a musician to marry her mother and work in the family's bank. Ono showed signs of musical talent, too, but her father didn't want her to achieve where he had failed. Her mother was a beauty who spent her time attending social functions. Consequently, Ono was raised by servants. During World War II, her mother was forced to flee to a small village south of Karuizawa. Her father was working in another town. For the rest of the war the family almost starved, selling off whatever they owned for food. In 1952, with her parents reunited, Yoko went to Sarah Lawrence College and even in this progressive setting, she felt like a misfit and was attracted to those on the cutting edge. Ono fell in love with a Japanese musician named Toshi. Her parents were against the union but finally agreed when Yoko packed up and left. Their marriage was anything but traditional. They lived in a loft in the early 60s in New York City and hung out with the avant-garde artists of the day. Ono put on shows and exhibits that forced new perceptions on her audiences. The critics were not kind. It was in London that her talent was finally acknowledged. In 1966, Ono was invited to participate in the "Destruction in Art" symposium. She arrived with copies of her book, *Grapefruit,* and it was a big success. At an art show, Ono met John Lennon, but it wasn't love at first sight. Like any good Aquarius, Ono pursued him. She sent him a copy of her book and she bombarded him with funny and unique cards. When they finally wed in 1969, they seemed like reflections of each other. Their union is blamed for the dissolving of the Beatles. Together, Ono and Lennon tried to emphasize the necessity for peace and love through art and events many people thought shocking. "In 1980, Lennon was murdered by a fan. Ono and their son, Sean, were left to carry on John's message. Ono continues to create with her own, unique voice.

MIKHAIL BARYSHNIKOV (January 27)

Ballet dancer.

Mikhail Baryshnikov was born in Riga, Latvia, to Russian parents. He didn't start to study dance until he was twelve and joined the Latvian Opera Ballet School. He says that he was "a very normal schoolboy. It was only after I began my ballet training that I became abnormal. I became obsessed with dancing." It all started when he entered the Latvian Opera Ballet School. Three years later, he passed the necessary tests and was accepted by the Kirov Training Institute. After another three years of study under the famous Aleksandr Pushkin, Baryshnikov joined the parent company as a soloist. "I did not have the look of a *premier* dancer," he said. "I was short, I was very young, and I looked it. . . . I did not have that princely look." Nevertheless, Baryshnikov did manage to win a slew of awards which brought him a great deal of attention. His London debut was a huge success. Clive Barnes of the *New York Times* wrote, "Mr. Baryshnikov is technically the most gifted and the most stylish male dancer in the world today." By the time he became a principal dancer at the Kirov, he already had decided to defect to the West. Russia offered little opportunity to try new things, so important to the Aquarius. Once in the United States Baryshnikov had several headline romances with stars such as Gelsey Kirkland and Jessica Lange, with whom he had a daughter. From 1980 to 1989, he was artistic director at the American Ballet Theatre. Since then he has tried making movies and acting on Broadway.

SUMMARY

The soul has aligned its will with a collective ideal and God. It has tasted the power and seen the incredible feats that can be done when heaven and earth work together. With this wisdom Aquarians try to unite division in the world, take care of the isolated, the lost, and the abandoned. Their huge hearts are capable of endless love, and once they find their spiritual path they share their wisdom with others. Once they identify with their godly selves and not just their earthly bodies, they are read to play with fate, enjoy life, and laugh at the absurdity of events that throw mere mortals into a state of crisis. The restlessness and tension that is constantly with them will pass when they accept their new being and allow His will to function in every aspect of their lives. This peace and harmony, this ability to let heaven rule will be the challenge of Pisces, the last sign of the zodiac.

SELECTED SOURCES

Neil Baldwin   *Edison: Inventing the Century, Vol I*   Hyperion 1995

Loren Eiseley   *Darwin and the Mysterious Mr. X: New Light on the Evolutionists*   Marlboro 1979

Brendan Gill   *Lindbergh Alone*   Harcourt Brace 1980

Jerry Hopkins   *Yoko Ono*   MacMillan 1987

Henry B. Kranz, editor   *Abraham Lincoln: A New Portrait*   G.P. Putnam's Sons 1959

Norman Mailer   *The Gospel According to the Son*   Random House 1997

George R. Marek   *Schubert*   Viking 1985

Bill Moyers   *Genesis: A Living Conversation*   Doubleday 1996

Maria Rasputin and Patte Barham   *Rasputin, The Man Behind the Myth: A Personal Memoir*   Warner 1981

Harvey Sachs   *Rubinstein: A Life*   Grove 1995

Paul G. Trueblood   *Lord Byron*   Twayne Publishers 1977

Pisces

(February 19–March 20)

Pisces are the kings of kings,
The lost souls, the enlightened beings,
A purpose to life is what they seek.
Their song, their silence is what they speak.
Fate picks them up, it turns them around.
Within the chaos, they hear a sound,
It's their own voice, it holds them near.
Love is its gift, it shatters all fear.
Now they can see and know The One,
In the sign of Pisces, the work is done.

Ruler: Neptune　　　　　　　　　　　　　　　**Symbol: Fishes**
Element: Water　　　　　　　　　　　　　　　**Number: Seven**

Pisces is the last sign of the zodiac and the ultimate challenge is reserved for it—the moment. The Pisces must stay balanced in this precarious place of change and transformation, juggling mind, body, and soul, which now work as one. In the moment, everything comes and goes as quickly as money at a blackjack table. If the Pisces still believes in *reality* and *things,* if they haven't experienced their power to create, they're in for quite a ride.

Pisces is like no other sign. Pisces are ultrasensitive and resilient souls. They feel like misfits because they see the world from a unique and personal perspective. They operate from their souls, and don't need anyone but themselves to fulfill their needs. They live on the pipeline of life, the artery that leads to God and the universe. What they think or want magically manifests. Their mission is to unite the disowned collective emotions.

The danger is that many Pisces are not aware of the power of their thoughts. Fate and others get blamed for what is nothing more than a manifestation of their negativity. If self-worth has been acquired through struggle and self-awareness, it is a precious gift. Confidence is theirs. With this potent attitude as a weapon, they are able to act in a world whose feedback has become meaningless because their reality is nowhere close to the norm. However, if the world of others still attracts them and they seek its luxuries and advice, Pisces may find that nothing happens as they want it to, and the success they achieve leaves them feeling empty and numb. Nothing in the ''real'' world makes the emptiness go away, so they reach for drugs and alcohol. When consciousness returns, so does the void.

Discipline is the key; it's a necessity, not a choice. Pisces must be able to control their thoughts and desires and unite them behind a central purpose. This is mind, body, and Spirit unified in the heart and anchored in the soul. When this happens, they no longer need to look outside themselves for support. All answers are found within. Perfected, this is a spiritual state, and anyone who reaches it is enlightened and rooted in God. In this state or place, renunciation is chosen over possessions, desires, joys and fears. With expectations gone, Pisceans are free to enjoy it all.

The inner journey is filled with excitement and passion; everything they have experienced and achieved in the world is there, and more. To gain this state requires work and personal discipline. The Pisces must be able to set limits and boundaries, depend only on himself, be able to say no to temptation, and know himself so well that he can allow his instincts to decide even major decisions because body, mind, and Spirit now work as one.

That's a tall order, but in the last sign of the zodiac, there's no more time to put it right. Without discipline or a spiritual purpose, the self-centeredness of this sign can inflate the Ego and the Pisces will become narcissistic and selfish to an amazing extreme. Commitment will be there only as long as needs are fulfilled. These are the con men of the universe. With Ego strong, they live for the moment, not to master it and make it their own, but to take from it whatever they can to fulfill their obsessive nature.

If the Ego is deflated through a sense of failure and emptiness, feelings of nothingness and hopelessness will prevail.

The difference between a happy and a hopeless Pisces is a purpose. Without a central theme around which to weave the emotions and nuances of their lives they will feel lost and alone. Their minds are the builders of their worlds. They must use their minds with precision and then what they build will be strong and bring rewards. According to Edgar Cayce's (March 18) teachings, as interpreted by Herbert B. Puryear, we ''are co-creators with God, that which we think and experience not only happens to us, but also becomes a part of us.''

In other words, attitude is the key. With confidence, the world is theirs. Without it, the world imposes whatever it chooses, uplifting or destroying. Jackie Gleason (February 26) called being funny a ''con game'' one plays on oneself, but the concept works with life, too. ''Everything works as long as one avoids even considering that there might be a problem,'' he said. ''Once one starts to worry—everything stops functioning and that fear becomes a self-fulfilling prophecy.''

Albert Einstein (March 14), Edgar Cayce, Frederic Chopin (February 22), George Harrison (February 25), and Yitzhak Rabin (March 1) are Pisces who have changed the world with their talents. Whether making war or peace, uniting the universe under one theory, accessing the Akashic records, a concept similar to Jung's "collective unconscious, or holding an audience under the spell of music or song, they believed in themselves. Gentle, delicate, and graceful in physique, a Pisceans's slender and aristocratic frame can be deceiving. Within that sensitive exterior is a strength and a will that are invincible, precisely because they are flexible and committed to whatever they do.

A Pisces in touch with his soul has learned the secrets of the universe, and what he has discovered is that there are no secrets at all. He realizes that he has free will and that his power is in his spirit, the response he gives to life. Without Spirit that response becomes totally unreliable and instead of commitment the Pisces forgets, changes his mind and is notoriously late. When he faces problems and finds something of value from every experience, God's grace will help him through. When he sees problems as problems, they stay problems. When he learns to mold life to his purpose, he raises his consciousness.

Attitude determines limits and possibilities. Change your thoughts and you change your world. When considering a new perspective, the first require-ment is a beginner's mind, the open mind of a child. Every moment must be entered without preconceived ideas or judgments. Without an open mind, life becomes a monotonous repetition.

Once attitude has been mastered, it's time to work on disciplining your thoughts. The enemy lies within and that enemy is comprised of doubt and negativity. The mind must be centered on honesty, integrity and strength of conviction. There are no secrets, just will and commitment, getting from one moment to the next.

Pisces is the sign of the process. It is not about results or achievements, but about an ongoing lifelong relationship with perfection. When he was dying, Chopin begged his sister to burn his inferior compositions. He said, "I owe it to the public and to myself to publish only good things. I kept this resolution all my life; I wish to keep to it now." Pisces must keep learning and growing and perfecting themselves. Through self-knowledge and mental discipline, their goals will be achieved.

A great way to train the mind is by taking risks. Risks force your thoughts into the moment because something new is being confronted. The more practice you get adjusting yourself to the unexpected, the more centered and flexible you become and the closer you get to your natural rhythm and true nature. When you can meet the moment without resistance, you can mold it to your inner will and shape it to your purpose. The more you do something, the less self-conscious you become and the more your body gains an intelli-gence all its own.

Spontaneity is the ability to play with life and allow it to play with you.

Jackie Gleason got his first emcee job in vaudeville because he could play with the moment. Someone had spilled seltzer on the stage. Gleason purposely skidded on it for his entrance, taking a graceful pratfall that got him a laugh and a job for the next two weeks. The ability to play is your way of inviting the divine spark to join in and make the magic happen. Spontaneity brought Dean Martin and Jerry Lewis (March 16) together in the most unusual and successful comedy team ever to hit stage and film. Martin was everything Lewis was not—handsome, cool, controlled, and indifferent. They first became friends while working together at the same nightclub. Months later, Lewis was playing a gig at the 500 Club in Atlantic City when the lead singer got sick. Lewis called Martin's agent, and Martin was hired. Unbeknownst to them both, the agent told the owner of the club about the funny stuff Martin and Lewis did between them. After a few nights, the owner of the club became disenchanted with Lewis's solo performance and demanded the two men come up with some of their "funny stuff" if they wanted to keep their jobs. In their dressing room, before the show, they worked out the act, the Playboy and the Putz, cool, removed Martin and wild, emotional Lewis. The result was phenomenal. The team took America by storm.

Jerry Lewis spoke with his body what the tongue could never convey. He was a master at body intelligence and expressed emotions the collective had disowned. Pisces is the sign of unspoken communication; here, the unconscious and the superconscious get a voice. Pisces is about the power of silence used to highlight words and actions. This is the art of pantomime. Gleason could get as much response from his audience by slamming a window on his hand, as he could from bemoaning a lost dream.

The world around and inside us is in a constant state of flux. To balance this flux requires the ability to adjust instantly and spontaneously to the moment, which means our bodies must have their own intelligences. Only through self-awareness can we change habits and transform them into new responses. This is true freedom, to meet the moment without fear, knowing we can bend it to our will.

In Aquarius, you reframed your past by aligning it with your spiritual ideal. Now you're asked to add tone, texture, and emotional emphasis to your story. This is highlighting: shading, refining, polishing, and finishing your creation. Caruso struggled with this concept in developing his voice. His teacher, Guglielmo Vergine, had been too restrictive and had prevented his spirit from reaching full expression and joy. Speaking about Vergine, Caruso said, "He restrained all my inclination to color a note, deprived me of all power of emphasis. For the years I studied against my grain, repressing nature in order to become a Vergine product." Once Caruso started to shape his singing, he became an international star. "A great light shone upon me, and never again did I sing against nature. There after I always sang with all the voice I had when the right moment came, and always with the color that my heart told me should envelope my poet's words.''

The key is to remain close to your true nature; learning what to emphasize in your life is how you shape your story. Chopin was known for his ethereal images. He invoked ''small fairy voices sighing under silver bells.'' His style was not the loud and grand style of the times. His uniqueness made him question his own style. ''One instinctively doesn't want to be thought of as a miniaturist . . . I was looking for something bigger. I was looking to gain a more heroic style, more epic. I made the mistake of thinking it could be gained through loudness. I had to learn my lesson, that I wasn't being true to myself.'' Your song must come from your soul, unconcerned with what you will get in return.

A purpose, a central theme around which to hang your dreams, is essential for you to express yourself with total freedom. The worldly path comes first. Without being able to maneuver in the world, spiritual work cannot be done. Find your Ego purpose, seek success in the world, and then ask for your spiritual path to be revealed. Commitment and faith are necessary because steps are revealed one at a time. Direction can change as Spirit finds a better way to work from the moment and your abilities.

Without a worldly or spiritual purpose, you become a lost soul. Lee Radziwill (March 3) led a life filled with parties and social events, but no direction. ''What I'm seeking is self-expression. I need some kind of personal satisfaction. I want to be evolved in something I have passion for, rather than to just go on existing.'' Passion comes from your purpose, from connecting with your soul. Elizabeth Taylor (February 27) has said that on her tombstone she wants engraved the phrase, ''She Lived.''

Pisces is unity, within and without. It's the colors black and white; black is the void; white contains the all. It's the yin and yang symbol, which shows how one energy can flow into another and still remain itself. The total interrelatedness of everything is apparent even when the ''moment'' is examined. Einstein said, ''There is no such thing as a 'now' that is independent of some system of reference. . . . that all our judgements in which time plays a part are always judgements of simultaneous events.'' A train arriving at seven o'clock creates time because there are two variables—the train and the clock. Without one or the other, time does not exist. Time is relative. Within each moment is the past, present and future.

Consider what the Buddha said. ''If you want to know what you did in your past life, observe your present condition; if you want to now what your future condition will be, observe your present actions.'' This moment, the one you have occupied since the day you were born, represents your point of view, which determines your reality. Einstein said, ''One's relative position in the universe controls viewpoint.'' How you express this ''viewpoint,'' whether you use it to serve mankind or yourself, will determine your fate and your happiness. Seek your divine purpose, and, instead of feeling lost and abandoned, you will find that life does have meaning and you do have passion, the kind that makes it all worthwhile.

Since the moment is so important in Pisces sometimes Pisces have a moment that changes their lives, a moment of ephiphany. It all comes together in a flash and they know what they are meant to do. Sometimes, Spirit plays with a person and challenges him to risk and try something new. From that risk, the person finds his destiny. Nat King Cole (March 27) switched from being a jazz musician to being a singer when a drunk from the crowd demanded he sing "Sweet Lorraine." Jackie Gleason was seated in the audience at the Halsey Theater when his moment came. Intermission was announced. The audience rose and he joined them in applause. Suddenly, he had an urge to turn around and look behind him. "No," he thought, "this is the way to see it. I want to be up there and look out at them applauding for me. That is what will feel the most natural." Pisces is about returning to your true nature, becoming whatever it is that rises from your soul and speaks to you.

From your soul center the whole universe becomes your playground. Through proper alignment, you can access the Akashic records, that place where all information is stored. This is a direct line to the infinite, and to reside here demands that the lower self be put aside. The Ego must be under your will and that will should be aligned with God. All is recorded in the soul. Your past, your future, your thoughts and actions. The truth is, you can access these records without being a spiritual person. However, to misuse God's way of communicating with souls is to ask to be taught a grave lesson. Misuse is occultism, witchery and black magic. It is psychics who are not spiritually trained to use their powers for enlightenment.

The ability to access the feelings, thoughts, and soul of another is what makes Pisces great healers and humanitarians. They can feel the pain of a single soul and the emotional collective cry for help. They're the ones at the forefront of a crusade to save mankind. George Harrison helped raise millions of dollars with the song "We Are The World." Elizabeth Taylor took up the unpopular cause of AIDS and brought public attention to the plight of those infected.

In order to heal, you must have suffered. Without a resonance to pain, there is only intellectual identification. Suffering should never be avoided or sought, merely faced. Pisces use their suffering to take them deeper into themselves so that they can access their soul. Darkness and grief are tools used to enlarge the ability to feel and express compassion. Depth is never developed through joy. Happiness makes your soul soar and reach toward heaven; suffering anchors you to the world and connects you to mankind. The hero of Pisces is the man or woman who quietly accepts failure, grief and pain. In the Christian faith, Christ suffered on the cross and gave us eternal life. Our suffering unites us with God's love and that of all people. Pisces is the recognition that the journey is not complete if we do not give something back to the world.

Pisces is the end of the road and because of this, death is not a distant stranger. In fact, it can occupy a great deal of the Piscean's thoughts. Death is a part of life, but to the ultrasensitive Pisces, it can be devastating. Their need for love and their ability to connect with the souls of those they love make them feel as if a piece of them is missing when whomever they care about dies. However, their unconscious knows that their lesson is to stand alone, to go on after the physical has decayed, keeping the Spirit alive through love. Death creates feelings of abandonment and that ignites an anger at God and the universe for forcing a separation the soul does not want. This is the final test of the zodiac, to love and lose and go on living. Ego must die with the body, and Spirit must return to heaven to prepare to repeat the process. Elizabeth Barrett Browning (March 6) lost her mother and her beloved brother. Her grief was great, and her already secluded life became more monastic. But fate forced her back into the world when her father had to move the family to London. This act of fate led her to her soul mate, Robert Browning, the man she would marry at the age of forty. Jackie Gleason endured the abandonment of a father who disappeared one day after work and never came home. By the time he was twenty, Gleason was an orphan. The need of the soul to walk alone, to find strength within itself and not with others, is the Pisces path.

Feelings of separation and loss, either because your path leads you elsewhere or someone else's path has come to an end, is symbolic of the relationship between Ego and Spirit. Pisces is the end of the journey, and these two antagonists have traveled together through sunny days and terrible storms. They know each other in any disguise. They can recognize each other in a crowd, in the role of pauper or king, thief or saint. Together they have played all the parts, challenged each other's goals and ideals, fought for and against each other's dreams, shared each other's joys and sorrows, triumphs and failures. Their commitment to the journey has bonded them through shared experiences, and now their differences seem unimportant and small. Theirs is a true relationship, one tested and sure, one based on an earned respect. Now, when they have put aside their differences and learned how to play, it's time to part. Love has awakened through the impending separation. Ego is old and must face death. Spirit is young. Having been reborn to a new strength, she can now defend herself and move forward, taking Ego's memory into her heart and soul. Along the path he has protected her, allowing her to do her work. His devious ways and masterful disguises have honed her ability to see and discriminate. He has been her warrior, fighting her dragons; her enemy vying for position and power; her lover, embracing her with desire and will, trying to control her every breath. He has put her on a pedestal and he has abandoned her for fruitless dreams. But through it all they have remained together. Forgiveness came in Aquarius and the true meaning of love will come with separation. For without loss one does not know what one once had. They are soul mates and the song they sing has finally become one. Ego will surrender into the soul of Spirit, ending their separation forever. Their love defies death because they are children of heaven and earth, who through their magical relationship have been able to bring one person closer to his or her true nature, to enlightenment, and to God.

The drama of Ego and Spirit is symbolically represented in many different ways in Pisces. First, there is the longing for a soul mate. Pisces intuitively know a perfect partner exists. Pisces are idealistic when it comes to love. However, the Pisces should remember that a soul mate is not a gift, but the result of a committed struggle, something earned. If they can endure and learn in a relationship, they can grow to love each other beyond the physical and the exterior, beyond their own needs and desires. Because a Pisces knows how to connect spiritually, it is often the differences, the things of the world, that give him a problem. What is necessary is the commitment to the journey, not to each other. There must be a higher ideal each can work toward. No two people can sustain the direct demands and expectations that occur in any relationship without a common goal, a central purpose that makes it all happen. Anyone can have a soul mate if he or she is willing to do the work.

Differences attract a Pisces, because Ego and Spirit come from two different worlds. Thus, a person with a different background, religion or lifestyle may catch the Pisces' eye. They can be attracted to the unattainable, to a relationship where separation is inevitable, because what they are learning is to love and go on, embodying that love within their soul, knowing that their physical presence is not needed for it to be real. Elizabeth Taylor had to go on when Mike Todd died in a plane crash. Richard Burton also died, and she had been married to him twice. Elizabeth Barrett Browning had given up on love, accepted its absence in her life. When it unexpectedly appeared in the form of Robert Browning, a man six years her junior, she seized the opportunity. Rex Harrison (March 6) loved Kay Kendall and lost her to leukemia.

Separations are part of life. You must learn to love and to let go. Don't let the search for a perfect partner keep you hopping from one relationship to another. You should be looking for an equal partner, someone who can stand up to you and put you in your place. Elizabeth Taylor knew she needed strength. "I knew I wanted more than anything else in the world a man who could control me. Mike [Todd] was strong, which was very good for me, [and] I loved it when he would lose his temper and dominate me." Pisces need confrontation. Sometimes, this translates in an attachment to a good fight. Rex Harrison enjoyed fighting with Kay Kendall, the love of his life. "When Rex and Kay had a row, it was with great humor and with tremendous style. It was like a contest to see who could be the most outrageously nasty, but with an undercurrent of such amusement with it all and tremendous fun. It was not lethal venom—but theatrical venom.''

In Pisces, relationships are idealistic or wrought with hostility and disappointment. Jackie Gleason put ''women on a pedestal and treated the hardest of them with deferential respect.'' If Pisces can't have a perfect relationship, they don't want one at all. If the obsessive quality of Pisces is not balanced with inner discipline, a relationship can be destructive, even if there is love. Elizabeth Taylor and Richard Burton ''fed each other's weaknesses and demanded little of their strength, and the unquenchable thirst for excitement and the ceaseless desire to acquire things exemplified other desire to avoid being bored.'' Elizabeth Barrett found her soul mate after years of searching. Pisces are unconcerned about age difference; what counts is the spiritual connection. With the absorption of one into the other, there is often a confusion about sexual identity. When Pisces connects at a soul level, sex and sexual difference doesn't exist.

Pisces often feel abandoned. People don't support them, emotionally and otherwise. What they need to know is that they are meant to stand alone. They are meant to be independent and in charge of their own destiny. Still, the anger Pisces carry is strong. Jackie Gleason ''suffered a lifelong rage that energized his art and frequently poisoned his personal relations.''

Anger can drive you to new heights or it can stand in the way of success and love. The key is to channel it creatively.

The opposite of abandonment is overprotection. Some Pisces have lived charmed lives. The danger here is that fate will offer a balancing experience. In the last sign of the zodiac you've got to learn it all. If you've missed any of the lessons along the way, you'll learn them now. Patty Hearst (February 20) lived a charmed, protected life until she was kidnapped for three years. Elizabeth Barrett was ill as a child and spent most of her youth studying, reading, or writing poetry. It was only fate that forced her out of her shell and into the arms of the man she would love with all her heart.

When it comes to sad stories and abandonment, Pisces have little competition. Jackie Gleason grew up in an apartment much worse than the one Ralph and Alice Kramden shared in *The Honeymooners*. As a child, Jerry Lewis was shuttled between friends and relatives while his show business parents were on the road. Albert Einstein was placed in a boardinghouse in Germany when his father took a job in Italy. He was only a teenager, but the German government wouldn't let him leave the country without fulfilling his military obligations. Einstein renounced his citizenship.

Abandonment also occurs when the Pisces is ready to take his or her own path. The world is not going to support them. They've got to believe in themselves and their own purpose. Pisces has a will that is matched by no other sign. Jerry Lewis's parents didn't want him to go into the entertainment business. Enrico Caruso was kicked out because his father wouldn't accept his son's wanting to be a singer. Michelangelo (di Ludovico Buonarroti Simoni (March 6) broke with family tradition when he became a painter and a sculptor. His father considered his son's work below the family's social status. Schopenhauer's father opposed his desire to pursue a literary career and bribed him with a trip to England and France. He wanted his son to follow in his footsteps and have a mercantile career. Schopenhauer (February 22) accepted the bribe and suffered, finding his own path only after his father died. The father of George Frideric Handel (February 23), the famous German composer, wanted his son to be a lawyer. He would never have given his child a piano lesson if the Duke Johann Adolf had not ordered it.

Pisces often feel as if they don't fit in. When you live within your own truth, the challenge is to mold that truth to the world and learn how to make it work. When you're young, with no one to help you out, it's a difficult challenge. Often, the Pisceans' environment contributes to their feelings of alienation. For the first few years of his life, Einstein was taught at home. When he finally joined other children, he didn't feel as if he belonged. He was shy and the other children had friendships already. Pisces often feel either superior or inferior to others. They have trouble with equal relationships.

Health can be a problem. Pisces children seem to contract every illness being passed around, and a few that no one else has. Elizabeth Barrett Browning suffered all her life from ill health. It is estimated that from 1947–94, Elizabeth Taylor has had seventy-three illnesses, injuries, and accidents requiring hospitalization.

Pisces have a great need to be alone. They absorb the emotions of others and often need space in order to feel good about themselves. Their ability to create a world within a world is also an issue. Without boundaries or limits, Pisces need to know how to protect themselves. Solitude is a popular choice. How small or large your world is depends on your consciousness and your confidence in dealing with the moment. Negativity is not kept away through isolation. Pisces must learn how to deal with life, rather than hide from it. Once again, consider Elizabeth Barrett Browning, who lived the first part of her life secluded in her home. She used poor health as an excuse to live the contemplative life. Once he was successful, Jerry Lewis had a self-enclosed apartment built within his house. It became his sanctuary.

Pisces also rules imprisonment and imposed isolation. These states occur when the boundaries of society are not acknowledged and the law is broken. Pisces often find themselves playing the scapegoat, being blamed for things they never did.

Pisces is having all or nothing. Pisces presents you with a compressed experience of your entire journey. The challenge is to taste it all. Balance is a necessity. Light and dark, love and hate must be accepted and embodied. If you're ignoring an experience, fate will create a way for you to experience it. As heir to one of the largest fortunes in America, Patty Hearst lived a protected life. When she was kidnapped, she was locked in a closet for months on end. To survive, she had to join her kidnappers and live in their world, one fueled by anger and resentment at everything she previously had represented. Hearst survived, and her experience placed her on a new path. Before her flight into the unknown, she was about to marry a man she didn't really love and embark on a life that didn't meet her needs. If nothing else, Hearts's journey forced her to get in touch with herself.

In Pisces, confidence is the difference between success and failure. This thin thread has the power to lift you up and pull all your talents together, allowing you to risk yourself at the right moment and ride the road to success with the least amount of resistance. Jackie Gleason said, "Look around this room. Probably twelve people here are as funny as I am. The difference is that I have the nerve to get up and do it in public." Gleason began his life with less than his most famous character, Ralph Kramden, ever had. Eventually, he became one of the highest-paid entertainers in America. The common denominator between Gleason and Kramden is their will to survive, their ability to adapt to circumstances without confusing temporary conditions with their true natures. Their greatness lies within their souls, not their environments.

Patty Hearst's fortune was impotent to save her life. What did make a difference under stress was her flexibility and her intelligence. Pisces represents the extreme highs and lows of life which force you to find your center and constantly adjust it in accordance with inner and outer necessity. If you've developed the right discipline and skills, the challenges of Pisces present the ultimate game. If you're not competitive, if you don't like to play or risk your protective space, you won't win; nor will you have any fun. The champion chess player of all time is Bobby Fischer (March 9), a Pisces. He brought the game of chess to a new popular high. "Chess is like war on a board," he said. "The object is to crush the other man's mind . . . I like to see 'em squirm."

In Pisces, the sakes are high, the game is mental, and only those willing to take a risk will win. These are the kings and queens of the zodiac, those who have gained their position not by birthright or family legacy, but because they've earned it. Pisces claims "The Great One" (Jackie Gleason); "The King of Comedy" (Jerry Lewis); "The King of Opera" (Caruso); and the crooner and jazz pianist, Nat King Cole.

In Pisces, life is reduced to one choice. What will rule you, love or fear? Whichever one you choose creates your path. Love is fraught with excitement and drama and is a path with an open end. Fear leads you down a smooth, monotonous, road where control is the most important factor and the end is very much in view. Fear represents a linear point of view. Everything you have fought for has no meaning when the journey is over. Death is all that life has to offer, so why raise your hopes when the end offers nothing but loss and despair? However, love sees life as cyclic and everlasting. What you have gained along the way is yours forever and every moment is precious and filled with exciting discoveries.

Schopenhauer chose the path of fear. His philosophy is known for its pessimism. "You can . . . look upon our life as an episode unprofitably disturbing the blessed calm of nothingness. In any case, even he who has found life tolerably bearable will, the longer he lives, feel the more clearly that on the whole it is a disappointment, nay a cheat." On the path of love, the results are drastically different. Love unites and brings fulfillment; it gives courage that takes you beyond the limits set by others. Life calls you to explore, discover, and create. Life is one exciting challenge after another. Elizabeth Taylor exemplifies the choice of love. "In my life, I have never, God knows, done anything by half-measures. I believe people are like rocks formed by the weather. We're formed by experience, by heartache, by grief, by mistakes, by guilt, by shame . . . I am glad that in my life I have never cut short my emotions. The most awful thing is to be numb . . . As for life and death. I think there is more to it all than we are aware."

Love may be the better choice, but it's not necessarily the easier. To love with strength requires discipline of mind, body and spirit. Edgar Cayce said, "To be sure patience, long suffering, and endurance are, in their respective manners, urges that would lead to virtues, but they cease to be a virtue when the individual entity allows self merely to be imposed upon, and to take second place merely because someone else of a more aggressive nature imposes."

The need to be and to have the best is a Pisces concern. For Lee Radziwill, "Quality was very important to her. Lee loved quality things—handmade shoes, beautiful fabrics. If she could only have one chair in her home, that chair would have to be the best and have the best fabric on it." Jackie Gleason found the good things in life impossible to be without. "Throughout his life he loved empty, costly pomp, from custom made pool cues to a special-order limousine that he boasted was the longest in America." Pisces often are wonderful dressers. Gleason kept a bowl of carnations just offstage in case the one in his lapel dropped a petal. Chopin dressed in high style. He loved ". . . costly attire and was very correct in the matter of studs, walking stick and cravats."

If your mind is occupied with solving the riddles of the universe, possessions will not hold any lure. Albert Einstein presented a disheveled appearance. His pants were too short, his shirts wrinkled, and his hair, uncombed. But once he spoke, his listeners were mesmerized. However, when quality is not important, quantity and excess take over. Jackie Gleason's motto was, "Three elephants are better than one." He had little if any self-discipline.

When he sat down to eat, he ate everything on the table, no matter how much there was.

To be the best means others envy the Pisces. And if the Pisces dares to think he is special, there is always someone to remind him he is not. Once Einstein became famous, his home was surrounded by hostile people who condemned and were afraid of his theories. A woman attempted to kill him. Michelangelo di Lodovico Buonarroti Simoni and Leonardo da Vinci were jealous of each other. Envy is big in Pisces. If you have chosen fear as your path, you'll be concerned only with what others think, afraid to trust your own opinions. Lee Radziwill struggled with this. "Always insecure about how people might perceive her, when Lee sought the counsel of others who usually ended up taking the advice of the person who spoke the loudest, rather than ultimately doing things on her own." Lee Radziwill envied her popular, older sister, Jacqueline Kennedy Onassis. "Lee always felt Jackie had something she didn't have, something that she wanted. It was true all her life."

Pisces is about winners and losers. If you see yourself as special, you may believe you are better than the masses and shouldn't have to associate with those who are less important, smart or successful. This attitude creates isolation and separateness. Never forget you can learn from everyone. When you are in touch with yourself, everyone is the same and you treat the common man or the king as one. Einstein, "spoke in the same way to everybody. The tone with which he talked to the leading officials of the university was the same as that with which he spoke to his grocer or to the scrub women in the laboratory."

If you haven't found confidence, you run the danger of becoming a victim of life. Jackie Gleason performed a skit called the Poor Soul. A typical episode went like this. The Poor Soul wants to elope. "To arouse his beloved, he throws a heavy object through a window—the wrong window. An angry man throws it back and brains him. As he reaches the right window . . . an alarm clock inside his suitcase goes off, rousing the neighbors and even the police. . . . he pushes a ladder up against the house front and the alarm goes off again. Finally reaching the window, he takes his girlfriend's suitcase, her second and even bigger trunk, really—and helps her down. At that moment a robber on the lam races by and drops his swag bag. Of course the police arrive and arrest the Poor Soul, who sadly hands his fiancée her ticket so that she can elope alone while he heads, as usual, off to jail." Attracting the punishment of others occurs when you haven't learned how to protect yourself. Montaigne said, "The soul that has no established aim loses itself. He who lives everywhere lives nowhere."

An audience with God is the highest achievement anyone can expect in life. Some Pisces actually receive this gift. Handel says he saw God when he wrote *Messiah*. "I did think I did see all heaven before me, and the Great

God Himself.'' Einstein said he had tapped ''God's thoughts'' when he discovered the master plan of the universe. In the Bible, Jacob sees God face to face when he wrestles with him during the night. Often the encounter with God happens in a dream state or just before or after waking. Einstein found his answers to the theory of relativity in the waking hours of the morning, after a difficult night of tossing and turning. In our sleep and through our dreams, spirits or angels can enter our consciousness, teach us, unite with us or take us on a journey. Pisces make wonderful channelers, for their spirits know how to leave their bodies and let another spirit take over and speak through them.

Pisces is selective intelligence. They can concentrate only on what interests them and forget the rest. Einstein was considered mentally retarded when he was young because he didn't fit into the norm. He only got good grades in science and physics, because those were the subjects he enjoyed. Jackie Gleason was obsessive about and smart in the things he enjoyed. ''Everything to do with the craft, from lighting, to makeup to costumes to choreography, Jackie would study intently, grasp at once and keep sharp in memory. Everything else, every other branch of learning from calculus to common sense, he had no use for and would forget at his earliest opportunity.''

The mind has learned to select what it wants to see. If your purpose is strong, this talent will be helpful, removing distractions from your path. If you don't have a purpose, you can use this ability to ignore things you don't want to see. One way Pisces prevent themselves from getting too lost in their worlds is through criticism. They invite it into their lives. Criticism helps them balance their opinions and test themselves against the viewpoints of others. But finding good criticism is difficult. Don't confuse it with control. Good criticism forces Pisces to interact with others by demanding they listen and respond to the critic.

Pisces can be geniuses. Their minds accept no boundaries, limitations, or authority. They reach into the unknown. Einstein said of his theory of relativity, ''There is not a logical path to these . . . laws. They can only be reached by intuition, based on something like intellectual love of the objects of experience.'' Edgar Cayce used his mind to read the souls of others. In a trance state he could see the past lives, the present challenges, and the future of a soul. The Pisces mind fuses with imagination and intuition and goes beyond logic to the truth that lies outside the realm of the known.

As far as a career is concerned, Pisces can be anything and everything. They make great scientists and artists. Sensitive yet strong, they have an eye for the best and so they can see the gem in the pile of junk, which makes them wonderful with antiques, decorating, fashion, or art. Because they can be spontaneous, they make great announcers and entertainers, onstage or before the camera. Pisces should direct their thoughts and actions toward their personal passions.

Pisces love mystery and intrigue. They need excitement to keep them from getting bored and if it's not around, they're great at instant chaos. They keep their past a mystery; it makes them feel important and special. They like to weave plots and will choose the most difficult path just for the fun of it. Elizabeth Barrett Browning chose to elope rather than face her father. Spirit likes to play. It is much more romantic.

Pisces is the end of the journey, and only when you're close to the finish can you look back and see the chain of events that have led you to the moment. Each thought and choice along the way played its part in the whole. The path is narrow and one wrong choice can lead you astray. The mind must be trained to obey the will so that you can journey into the unknown and meet each moment without fear. Pisces is the final test. Here, you must prove to be totally self-sufficient, sure of yourself, your thoughts and your purpose. As you pull within and center yourself in the soul, you root yourself in God. Then, although you still participate in life, your nourishment and inspiration come from above. To stand alone against the world takes confidence and the willingness to make mistakes. You cannot be afraid of loss or negative results, for you must focus on the process. Pisces is the vision, the ability to go beyond logic and knowledge to truth of a divine nature. By becoming the best person you know how to be, you become a shining example to others. Then, you will have achieved true harmony and peace and completed the final lessons of your journey.

THE PISCES ENVIRONMENT

The Pisces environment is either unsupportive, distant and indifferent, or critical, controlling, and demanding. Either way, you are forced to look within yourself, decide on your purpose and proceed on your own, without help or support from others. It's not an easy environment when it's out of harmony with your inner nature. The challenge is to be yourself, regardless what others do and think. To be the best, you've got to be able to do it all and without a moment's hesitation. This is spontaneity at its finest, the ability to play with mistakes and failures and turn them into triumphs. Fate plays a hand here by throwing in your face anything you've tried to avoid. Just when you think everything is in a neat little package and under control, something happens to throw you off-center and make you risk yourself one more time. If you try to escape life, you'll succeed for a while. Without opposition or limitations from others, excess and self-destruction is easily achieved. With no one but yourself to blame, you must look within and awaken to the message of your soul.

Pisces/*One* (February 28, March 1, March 10, March 19)
Neptune/ Sun

PURPOSE: To achieve the confidence and discipline necessary to be fully independent and turn your excess charm into eternal rewards.

"The undertaking of a new action brings new strength."—Evenius, Roman writer. Pisces/*Ones* have the ability to be physically, mentally, and spiritually strong, but if they hide from life; they may suffer from physical ailments, confusion, and chaos. They need a purpose and lots of discipline. Competitive, Pisces/*Ones* can drive themselves relentlessly to be the best, along the way acquiring luxuries that suit their exquisite taste. If Neptune is strong, Pisces/*Ones* may suffer from a series of annoying illnesses, feel as if they are victims of circumstances, and shun possessions and beautiful things because they prefer the spiritual path. Masters at creating the world according to their vision, the Pisces/*One* needs self-confidence. They must learn to be spontaneous and adaptable. They must learn not to let fear make them rigid or control keep their world small and isolated; Many exhibit both extremes; an over-confidence that hides a deep rooted insecurity. Pisces/*Ones* have big, generous hearts. They demand respect and seek soul mates. Pisces/*Ones* can have trouble with relationships because they hate restraint and tend to see a partner idealistically. They must learn to let go of fear and risk. Pisces/*Ones* are meant to experience life with zest and passion, not pessimism and doubt.

IF SPIRIT TAKES THE LEAD: When Spirit is strong, the soul uses its position in life to pave the way for others less fortunate. They are strong-willed and desire to make a difference through the power of their careers and personality. Caution is needed when it comes to challenges. They find it difficult to walk away, even when it may be to their benefit. If they are not careful, they can be abusive to their body.

IF EGO TAKES THE LEAD: If Ego rules, the Pisces/*One* are either a dictator or a victim. If discipline is strong, and the will is forged, then they will pursue their goals with a strength that can be frightening. They are unrelenting in their quest for fame and fortune. If they are weak and insecure, the danger will come from others who are strong. They can be abused and suffer greatly, either from sickness or from the force of others acting against their soul.

MARIO ANDRETTI (March 10)

Race car driver.

If there ever was a sport where being in the moment is essential, race car driving is it. Andretti is the only man to win the Indy 500, Daytona 500, and Formula 1 World Championship. "I've always wanted to be an all-around driver, to be able to handle any car on any surface." Born in Montona,

Trieste, Andretti came to America in 1955 and learned to speak English working in his uncle's gas station in Nazareth, Pennsylvania. As a child, Andretti's idol was the car racing champion Alberto Ascari. Andretti says, "The race I remember best of all was the 1954 Grand Prix of Monza. It was Ascari versus (Juan) Frangio, wheel to wheel in those big-front-engine giants. That race at Monza crystallized my thinking. Before that race I wanted to be a racing driver. After that race I had to be a driver." Andretti is a member of the Automobile Hall of Fame, was awarded the ABC-TV's Athlete of the Year (1969), and won the World Grand Prix Championship in 1978. He lives in Nazareth, Pennsylvania with his wife, Dee Ann, the mother of his children, Jeffrey and Barbara Dee.

HARRY BELAFONTE (March 1)

Singer.

Harry Belafonte was born in the Harlem section of New York City. When he was eight years old, his parents returned to Jamaica and took their son with them. He returned to the U.S. to attend high school. In 1944, he joined the Navy. Belafonte's moment of decision and purpose came when someone gave him tickets to see the American Negro Theater. It was then he decided to become an actor. But when he auditioned for a part, he was hired instead as a singer. Eventually, Belafonte bought into his own restaurant, discovered folk music, and became known as "The Calypso King." After he became a sensation as a singer, Belafonte returned to acting both in films and on Broadway, and to producing his own films. He has always been committed to helping African-Americans by providing opportunities and speaking out on civil rights. "I fully believed in the civil-rights movement," Belafonte says. "I had a personal commitment to it, and I had my personal breakthroughs. I felt that if we could just turn the nation around, things would fall into place. And it actually happened." Belafonte was a major force in the making of the record "We Are the World," which raised millions for African famine relief.

Pisces/*Two* (February 20, March 2, March 11, March 20) Neptune/Moon

PURPOSE: To harness your excessive compassion and learn how to say "no" and set boundaries so that you can experience intimacy without fear and allow your creativity to blossom.

"Many a man fails to become a great thinker only because his memory is too good."—Friedrich Wilhelm Nietzsche. Pisces/*Twos* need to learn how to empty themselves and let go of the past. Their memories are strong and so are their anger and feelings of abandonment. They have had to learn how to nurture themselves and stand on their own two feet. Pisces/*Twos* yearn for a soul mate either because they have never had the intimacy and closeness they desire, or because they have once felt very connected to someone and are eager to experience that again. Either way, the Pisces/*Two* needs to know that being on the earth plane means living with divine discontent. Nothing will ever be perfect. Pisces/*Twos* are exceptionally sensitive, psychic, and creative. Their will and resistance gets them into trouble. They must learn to be flexible and forgive those who have hurt them. Music may delight the Pisces/*Two*. They could be talented artists, or at least appreciate the works of geniuses. Pisces/*Twos* are extreme in nature. They are loners and need space because they absorb the energy around them. They must learn to mediate and set up boundaries without having to remove themselves from life. Others come to them for advice; they have great depth and big hearts.

IF SPIRIT TAKES THE LEAD: If Spirit is ahead, their ability to heal is strong. They know how to connect to those who are lost or alone. They have high ideals and long for intimacy, but may be too afraid to bring it into their lives. Protection is important, for abuse or emotional abandonment could be strong. They need to be careful of spiritual manipulation and avoid connecting with others through a cult that confines and limits instead of teaching them how to grow.

IF EGO TAKES THE LEAD: If Ego rules, they are hard to reach, mysterious and very manipulative. They are creative, but use their creativity for their own ends. Obsessive, they should guard against alcohol and drug abuse. The desire to escape reality is strong. They have an indomitable will and a tendency for self-destruction. They need a reason for living besides acquiring and collecting the best things money can buy.

DR. SEUSS (March 2)

Children's book writer.

Born Theodore Gelsel, Dr. Seuss is the author of *The Cat in the Hat, How the Grinch Stole Christmas* and *Green Eggs and Ham.* Dr. Seuss's rhyming stories have delighted children and adults for years. "You can fool an adult audience with persiflage or purple prose," he said, "but a kid can tell if you're faking immediately." During his lifetime, Dr. Seuss published more than forty-four books with sales topping a hundred million dollars worldwide. Born in Springfield, Massachusetts, he enjoyed sketching animals on his trips to the zoo with his father, a city superintendent in charge of running the zoo. He graduated from Dartmouth in 1925; later, he studied literature at Oxford. His first job was in advertising and he created an ad campaign for an insecticide called Flit. His wife Helen was his chief critic. When she died in 1967, he married Audrey Stone. Surprisingly, Dr. Seuss had no children of his own. Still, he always knew what children did and didn't want. "They don't want to feel you're trying to push something down their throats. So when I have a moral, I try to tell it sideways." Dr. Seuss received a special Pulitzer Prize for his work in 1984.

CARL REINER (March 20)

Comedian, writer, producer, director.

Carl Reiner's career was launched on the television series, *Your Show of Shows,* also starring Imogene Coca and Sid Caesar. From there, Reiner went on to create the popular sitcom *The Dick Van Dyke Show.* Born in the Bronx, Reiner learned to used laughter as a means of self-defense. "I was what I call a charming coward," he said. "It was one of those neighborhoods where if you fought back, you had to be good. So to get attention I'd turn to comedy. I'm more and more convinced that all comedians are charming cowards." During World War II, Reiner entertained the troops in the South Pacific with Major Maurice Evans's Special Services Unit. Later, as an actor, Reiner made *It's a Mad, Mad, Mad, Mad World* and *The Russians Are Coming,* among other films. He directed *Enter Laughing, The Comic, Where's Poppa?, The Jerk* and *Dead Men Don't Wear Plaid.* He is married to the former Estelle Lobost and the father of three children. His son Rob Reiner has followed in his footsteps and is best known for his role as Meathead on *All in the Family* and as the director of the hit movies *When Harry Met Sally* and *A Few Good Men.*

Pisces/*Three* (February 21, March 3, March 12)
Neptune/Jupiter

PURPOSE: To use your generosity and strength to live by your own rules, acquiring confidence and a belief in yourself.

"No statement should be believed because it is made by an authority." —Hans Reichenbach. Authority is the enemy of new ideas and creativity. But Pisces/*Threes* never listen to anyone but themselves. They are attracted to impossible odds. They have a great need to be the best and are capable of achieving their goals. Their ideals are high. They dream of the perfect relationship. However, intimacy is not easy for Pisces/*Threes*. They love their freedom and hate restrictions of any kind. If they are rigid, they are also critical and judgmental. Pisces/*Threes* are gifted with great minds. They are inventive, intuitive and courageous. Good with words, they can be attracted to the profession of writing, and may find travel and foreign places intriguing. In fact, anything different and out of the ordinary attracts them. When they discover their purpose, they can transform themselves into more than just powerful intellectuals.

IF SPIRIT TAKES THE LEAD: If Spirit is strong, the Pisces/*Three* will seek to do the impossible. They have a strong will, a desire to know God, and to live in the world of knowledge, imagination, or Spirit. Their minds are sharp, but they need to be discriminating enough not to get lost in the mystique of a superhuman leader who promises them everything they want to hear. They are either great leaders or perfect disciples. They should follow what they feel. Pisces is about standing on your own two feet.

IF EGO TAKES THE LEAD: With Ego powerful, they like to show off and be the best. They have the power to convince and persuade. They are creative, manipulative and seem larger than life in all they do. If they are a victim, they may fluctuate between great hope and despair.

EDWARD ALBEE (March 12)

Playwright.

Born in Washington D.C., Albee was adopted at the age of two. His parents owned a theater chain called the Keith-Albee Theaters. Albee was a member of the privileged class. He attended three prep schools and got himself discharged from Trinity College, in Hartford, Connecticut. His trust fund of $100,000 may have given him courage to be a rebel. Albee's first years as a writer were uneventful or, as he called them, a "haze." It wasn't until he wrote *Zoo Story,* which was first produced in Berlin and then in New York, that he received recognition as a playwright. In 1962, Albee wrote *Who's Afraid of Virginia Woolf?* That was followed by *Tiny Alice, A Delicate Balance, Everything in the Garden* and *The Ballad of the Sad Café.* Harold Clurman says of him, "He is frozen fire . . . No one else in our theatre writes in this particular way." Albee writes and lectures. He lives between Manhattan and Montauk Long Island. In 1997, he was elected to the Theatre Hall of Fame.

LIZA MINNELLI (March 12)

Singer, actress.

Liza Minnelli is the daughter of Judy Garland and director Vincent Minnelli. By the time she was sixteen, Minnelli had been to at least as many schools. She does not look upon her childhood as unhappy, but as the child of superstar parents, it certainly was not the norm. At the age of seven she made her first public appearance, dancing on stage where her mother was performing. At sixteen, she left home with a ticket and one hundred dollars. Before her money ran out she was performing off-Broadway and had cut her first record. With an invitation from her mother to share billing at the London Palladium, Minnelli made her British debut. In the course of her career she has won three Tony awards and on Oscar. Unfortunately, love and relationships haven't been easy. She has been involved with Martin Scorsese, Desi Arnaz, Jr. and Peter Sellers and has been married several times. Still, Minnelli says, "I believe in grabbing at happiness ... if you have to pay later for a decision you've made, that's all right ..."

Pisces/*Four* (February 22, March 4, March 13)
Neptune/Uranus

PURPOSE: To organize your life over and over again, always raising your awareness, gaining new insight into yourself and others, and leaving whomever you meet a little bit changed.

"To spend life for something which outlasts it."—William James. Pisces/*Fours* must pursue goals greater than the things of the world. They have the imagination, genius, and the creativity to change the world around. However, self-knowledge is the prerequisite to all success. Pisces/*Fours* are perfectionists, but they get bored easily and jump from one thing to the next. Others may think the Pisces/*Four* critical and judgmental because they don't share the high goals of this combination. Pisces/*Fours* can find peace if they seek the spiritual path and learn how to meditate. If they're engaged solely in worldly pursuits, they will never have any peace. They can be either too responsible, taking on other people's tasks and problems, or they are overwhelmed by life and afraid to take a risk. If the Pisces/*Four* is fearful, fate will turn plans upside down. Pisces/*Fours* may be psychic and intuitive. It's important they listen to their inner voices. Whatever they do, they bring about change, so they must learn to choose wisely.

IF SPIRIT TAKES THE LEAD: Spirit and the number *Four* work well together, at least when it comes to breaking through old patterns and habits. They bring change. They are great humanitarians and tend to take on too much responsibility. There is little they can't do and do well. They tend to offer help to others, rather than wait for others to get things done. They have no patience. Tension is the result of such overloading, and relaxation will elude them if they don't learn how to say no.

IF EGO TAKES THE LEAD: Ego demands attention and wants everything done its way. They are loners and don't take orders well. They are skilled, versatile, and manipulative. They know how to get what they want. Without limits, they could be their own worst enemy. They could eventually get caught and punished for their greed.

FREDERIC CHOPIN (February 22)

Composer.

As a child, Chopin was very sensitive and could not hear music without crying. The famous pianist Arthur Rubinstein said of Chopin "The piano bard, the piano rhapsodist, the piano mind, the piano soul is Chopin . . . Tragic, romantic, lyric, heroic, dramatic, fantastic, soulful, sweet, dreary, brilliant, grand, simple all possible expressions are found in his compositions and all are sung by him upon his instrument.'' Chopin had excellent taste in clothes and carried a walking stick. He was known for his ''shades of sound.'' The nuances of his playing created a ''new language of the soul.'' Before his death, Chopin's desire for excellence made him plead his sister burn his inferior compositions. ''I owe it to the public and to myself to publish only good things. I kept this resolution all my life; I wish to keep to it now.''

JULIUS ERVING (February 22)

Basketball star.

''I get up in the air and do whatever comes into my mind to make a play. I don't make moves for effect, although I love to hear the crowd enjoy them.'' Julius Erving was born in Hempstead, Long Island, New York. He has a sister and a brother. His father deserted the family and his mother worked as a domestic to support the family. After three years, she remarried. School was easy for Erving and at the age of ten he found basketball. With an average of twenty-seven points and twenty rebounds a game in his sophomore year at the University of Massachusetts, Erving gained recognition. He was chosen for the U.S. Collegiate Team and toured Europe and the USSR. After three years, Erving left college, lured by a half-million-dollar contract with the Virginia Squires. By his second year, he was a star, leading the circuit with a 31.9 scoring average. He has played for the New Jersey Nets and Philadelphia and made millions in the process. Erving believes his life is predestined by God. ''I've tried to stay on the right side of The Man,'' he says, ''and I've been blessed.''

Pisces/*Five* (February 23, March 5, March 14) Neptune/Mercury

PURPOSE: *To balance your feelings of superiority with those of little self-worth and realize that the intention behind a thought or action is what counts.*

''Fate gives us the hand, and we play the cards.''—Arthur Schopenhauer. Pisces/*Fives* are spontaneous and versatile beyond belief. With too many choices, and too much talent, they've got to have a purpose to make life worth while. They must learn that without self-awareness, nothing is clear. Pisces/*Fives* must learn from others, but not allow themselves to take another's path instead of their own. If relationships give them trouble, they are idealists who dream about the perfect mate but run away from intimacy. They must learn to work toward intimacy, to build up trust. Pisces/*Fives* have everything they need to be successful, if they don't let fear get in the way.

IF SPIRIT TAKES THE LEAD: With Spirit strong, so is the connection to the public and the masses. These souls are attracted to the things of everyday existence and the simplicity of a spiritual path. They take on too much responsibility and overload their lives with the problems of others. This prevents them from following their own path and learning about their own needs. They teach through inspiration.

IF EGO TAKES THE LEAD: Ego and the number *Five* may create a person who avoids responsibility and seeks to escape life. They are creative but without discipline, that creativity can be lost. They need to grow up and leave behind anger, fear, drugs, and alcohol. If they can turn their energy inward, they can manifest their talents and achieve something great.

QUINCY JONES (March 14)

Composer, musician.

Quincy Jones is one of the most prolific, successful, and versatile personalities in jazz and pop music. He has created scores for TV productions and movies, including Michael Jackson's best-selling album *Thriller.* Born on the South Side of Chicago, he moved to Seattle in 1943. It was none other than Ray Charles who introduced Jones to the world of jazz. "I learned a lot from him about the world and particularly about music," Jones said, describing the Pisces moment if enlightenment. "I remember once we were listening to a Billy Eckstine recording. I asked Ray how was it that band members are playing different notes and melodies, but it all fits. Well, he sat down at the piano and showed me. It was like a light came alive in my head. I guess that's what really got me interested in writing, that one little incident." Jones graduated from Berklee College of Music in Boston, then took off on a tour with Dizzy Gillespie, playing the trumpet. After this experience, Jones formed his own band and toured Europe and America. In 1961, he become vice president of Mercury Records. He continued to compose for films such as *The Pawnbroker* and *In Cold Blood.* His song "Miss Celie's Blues" from the film *The Color Purple,* won him an Academy Award nomination. Jones has also recorded several albums, including *Body Heat, I Heard That, Sounds . . . and Stuff Like That,* and *The Dude.*

ALBERT EINSTEIN (March 14)

Scientist.

In the words of Max Born, Einstein achieved the "greatest feat of human thinking about nature, the most amazing combination of philosophical penetration, physical intuition, and mathematical skill." Einstein's mind went beyond logic into the realm of the unknown; according to him, his ideas came straight from God. Like most geniuses, early in life Einstein didn't feel as if he fit in. At school, he was thought to be retarded because he expressed interest only in science and physics. He was known to have an eye for women and married twice. When his theories of relativity were first published, little attention was paid to them. He was nominated many times for the Nobel Prize, but it took the committee years to recognize his genius. However, once his theories were accepted, Einstein was forced to accept the highs and lows of fame, including threats on his life. He was called a crazy scientist, a radical, and a Red. Some tried to stop him from coming to the United States. Einstein's legacy is inexpressible. He changed our concept of the universe. Einstein's letter to Franklin Roosevelt in 1939 about the German research into splitting the atom led directly to the Manhattan Project which created the atomic bomb.

Pisces/*Six* (February 24, March 6, March 15) Neptune/Venus

PURPOSE: To achieve inner discipline so that your great spirit and charm can manifest in a talent or a spiritual quest instead of an obsessive addiction.

"Happiness is not best achieved by those who seek it directly."—Bertrand Russell. This is good advice for any *Six* who seeks love, pleasure, and the good things in life—often to excess. Pisces/*Sixes* have a need for truth, beauty, and love. If they can translate some of that need into a spiritual path, they'll find true happiness, because no human being will fulfill their needs or desires. Pisces/*Sixes* must learn how to give with discrimination and discipline. Once they do, they'll get back everything they want. The soul mate they are seeking is possible, but they must first know how to stand alone. Pisces/*Sixes* have powerful feelings. Their ability to charm and influence others is a great talent. The pursuit of truth and justice can turn them into rebels. They despise boredom and prefer their own company to that of the common folk. Either they feel they are special and better than others, or they play the part of the victim, who needs others in order to be whole. They must learn to set boundaries. Only then will life will be a joy, instead of an overwhelming burden.

IF SPIRIT TAKES THE LEAD: Spirit and the number *Six* are close companions; they both seek perfection and the truth at all cost. They will not settle for anything less than their dreams. They inspire us all to reach for more. They suffer isolation and loneliness because their standards are so high. They are not only brilliant but charming, and can leave their mark wherever they put their heart and soul.

IF EGO TAKES THE LEAD: If Ego is strong, then they are great manipulators. They are charming and know how to get what they want by being whatever it is someone wants them to be. Flexible and conniving, they are very ambitious and desire the whole pie. They tend to take over whatever they become involved in, and their talents allow them to do it with ease. If their motivation is in the right place, their rewards could include love.

ELIZABETH BARRETT BROWNING (March 6)

Poet.

Born Elizabeth Moulton in County Durham, England, Elizabeth Barrett Browning was gifted with a strong intellect. Secluded in a beautiful country home called Hope End, she studied Italian, Greek, and Hebrew. One of eleven children, Elizabeth's primary source of love was her mother and when she died, Elizabeth was devastated. With the end of slavery, her father, who had made his money from Jamaican slave wealth, was forced to sell his mansion. They moved to London. Elizabeth was not a well woman. She suffered from a back injury as well as a constant cough. Her father was overprotective and sheltered her, and himself, from life. Elizabeth Barrett (her father changed his last name to Barrett after her birth) was almost forty when she eloped with Robert Browning and fled to Italy. A published and acknowledged poet before her marriage to Browning, she helped support them with her writing. She blossomed in Italy's sunshine and with the love she had always dreamed about. Her love sonnets to her husband are still much admired. Barrett Browning suffered several miscarriages, but finally gave birth to a son. She died young, but only after having manifested her dreams.

ED McMAHON (March 6)

TV personality.

Ed McMahon will always be best known as Johnny Carson's sidekick on *The Tonight Show*. Their relationship demonstrates the Piscean ability to find a soul mate, even in a business partner. McMahon's father had a minstrel-show, and later turned fund-raiser. McMahon sold pots and pans door-to-door to put himself through college. He hooked up with Carson on a daytime quiz show called *Who Do You Trust?* When Jack Paar quit *The Tonight Show* in 1962, McMahon and Carson became the show's new hosting team. In 1992, McMahon and Carson taped their last episode of the show they made famous. McMahon has hosted and cohosted several television programs, such as *Star Search* and *TV Bloopers and Practical Jokes*. With Jerry Lewis, McMahon has cohosted the Muscular Dystrophy Telethon. In 1976, he married a much younger woman and together, they had a baby girl. They separated in 1989. McMahon is the father of four children by his first marriage. McMahon has published two books, *The Art of Public Speaking* and *Selling*.

Pisces/*Seven* (February 25, March 7, March 16)
Neptune/Neptune

PURPOSE: To develop confidence and discipline enough to allow you to use your genius to create the world the way you want it to be.

"My hopes are not always realized, but I always hope."—Ovid, Roman poet. Pisces/*Sevens* must learn not to give up or give in. They are the cocreators of their worlds and their test is to survive and be happy no matter what life offers. When they are connected to their soul, when they know how to help and inspire others, when they keep their passion for life close to the surface, then nothing will stop them from growing. Others may not support the Pisces/*Sevens*, or give help, because their mission is to stand alone and do it well. Pisces/*Sevens* are versatile and talented, psychic, and sensitive. They must not let their perfectionism keep them from taking risks and opening their hearts. They must be careful that their fear and need to be protected do not keep them isolated.

IF SPIRIT TAKES THE LEAD: If Spirit is strong, then these souls will be able to accomplish the impossible. They struggle with extremes and must learn to set boundaries from within. If they are disciplined they will play with life and leave it a better place. Intimacy is difficult. They prefer to be alone. Meditation, yoga, or any other mental or spiritual practices are good for them. They need to help others feel good about themselves, but without limitations, they could lose their sense of self.

IF EGO TAKES THE LEAD: If Ego gets inflated, there is no one around to stop them from their excessive nature and ability to self-destruct. Their emotions are powerful. Their strong desire to be loved and protected can make them neurotic. They can be narcissistic and a loner someone whom others view as strange or different. They can feel removed from life. Extremely talented, they are capable of achieving great things. The key here is to help others and not become self-obsessed.

JERRY LEWIS (March 16)

Actor, comedian.

Jerry Lewis was born into a showbiz family. As a child, he suffered from the fact that his parents were never home and he was shuffled between friends and relatives. Like most children, Lewis thought there must be something wrong with him. "If I could make people laugh," he said, "I thought they'd like me and let me be with them. I had to do it in self-defense because I felt I couldn't compete for their attention with my brains." Lewis hooked up with Martin by chance. In 1946, they were performing in the Catskills and Catrin in Atlantic City when they were pressured into performing together in order to keep their jobs. They created the ad lib act in the dressing room and were an instant sensation. Together they made sixteen movies, and Lewis became the first actor who debuted in talkies to direct himself. The Lewis and Martin team, which stayed together eleven years, was the most successful comedy duo of all times. Lewis became the highest-paid performer in the history of film, on television, and on Broadway. When Lewis and Martin split, it was international news. Envy, their totally different styles, and Lewis's obsession with work each played a part in the separation. Lewis, who thought he could go it alone, found that his type of humor didn't work without a straight man. Still, Lewis has spent a good deal of time contributing to charities, and raising over one billion dollars. He has been nominated for the Nobel Peace Prize.

GEORGE HARRISON (February 25)

Musician.

George Harrison was born in Liverpool, the son of a bus driver. When he was around twelve years old, he bought a guitar from a schoolmate but studied to become an electrician's assistant, not a musician. However, in 1958, when he was fifteen years old, he joined Paul McCartney and John Lennon in a band that came to be known as the Beatles. The band's success made Harrison an international star. But Harrison felt the need to pursue his own spiritual quest. He became interested in Eastern philosophy and was inspired by Maharishi Mahesh Yogi. He studied the sitar with Ravi Shankar and then introduced the sound into the Beatles' music. Once the Beatles broke up, Harrison produced several albums of his own. In 1971 he organized top rock performers for a benefit to help poverty-stricken Bangladesh. Harrison has backed several films, including *Monty Python's Life of Brian, Time Bandits,* and *Brazil.* He is divorced from his first wife, Patti Boyd. With his second wife, Oliva Arias, he has a son.

Pisces/*Eight* (February 26, March 8, March 17) Neptune/Saturn

PURPOSE: To reach the unreachable and do the impossible knowing you have the gift of communication and that with confidence and discipline your path is paved in gold.

"The desire for safety stands against every great and noble enterprise."— Publius Cornelius Tacitus. Pisces/*Eights* need to learn to take risks and be spontaneous. They must call on their courage and choose the paths, they know they should be walking. Pisces/*Eights* are either very rigid and critical, afraid of opening up and letting others in, or they extend a hand to others in need and help them become strong and independent. They may be psychic and are certainly sensitive, but could appear to have a tough shell. They have the gift of communication, and are wonderful working with the handicapped or anyone who has trouble communicating feelings. They must not let the selfish and self-critical side of this dynamic take over. If it does, they will be very ambitious and difficult to get along with. They have their own unique way of looking at the world and no one can change their point of view. They need inner discipline. Pisces/*Eights* must watch out for their idealistic nature; they want things perfect and don't care about the cost to themselves and others. They are strong and like to be the authority. In fact, it is hard for them to take orders from anyone but themselves and God. Pisces/*Eights* should choose a profession that allows some freedom.

IF SPIRIT TAKES THE LEAD: If Spirit is powerful, so is their ability to achieve great things. They are idealists who strive to be perfect no matter who they hurt along the way. They are attracted to anyone who is tough and gives them good criticism. Unafraid of difficulties, they can take on too much responsibility and need to consider their boundaries. Their problem is their extreme nature. Either they give too much, or not at all.

IF EGO TAKES THE LEAD: If Ego is strong, they are ambitious and want to achieve. They struggle with control and authority issues; They need to be at the top or they're not happy. Without confidence, they can be shy and afraid of fulfilling their dreams. Then, they may be used by others and never get the credit they deserve. Obsession is common, and so is their ability to enter the worlds of others no matter how strange and different. They need to access their faith and find their purpose.

JACKIE GLEASON (February 26)

Actor, comedian.

Years after his death, Jackie Gleason still finds his way into the homes of millions of Americans. "The Great One" created the most successful sitcom in history, *The Honeymooners.* Gleason's character, Ralph Kramden, is still so popular because he speaks to that part of each of us that continues to hope, in spite of all the odds against us. Gleason was born in New York to poor parents. His father deserted the family and by the age of twenty, Gleason was an orphan. Gleason, had a goal—to be onstage. His rise to the top was driven by confidence, courage, and an ability to be spontaneous. He was a great reactor and could say more with silence than any other comic. Gleason made a great deal of money, but always said he needed two fortunes, "one to enjoy and one to save for his old age." He spent thousands on gambling debts, loved treating his friends and strangers, and had an eye for women. A lousy husband by his own admission, he married twice and had two daughters who rarely saw him. Gleason was a workaholic, obsessive in everything he did. Television could not contain him. He tried Broadway and conquered that, too. His movie career boasted moments of genius. His portrayal of the pool shark in *The Hustler,* with Paul Newman, won him an Academy Award.

NAT KING COLE (March 17)

Singer, Jazz Pianist.

Nat King Cole's laid-back style and smooth, satiny voice was unique and instantly recognizable. Born Nathaniel Adams Coles, he was one of the few African-American superstars of his time. However, he couldn't avoid heavy discrimination. His gift of personality helped him get ahead when others were left behind. By the time he reached his thirties, Cole was a millionaire. He is remembered for such hits as "Mona Lisa," "Nature Boy," "Route 66," and "Unforgettable."

Nat King Cole was born in Alabama when segregation was the only way of life. In high school, he put together a band. Eventually, he dropped out of school. One night, a drunk asked him to sing "Sweet Lorraine." Even though he thought he had a terrible voice, he sang the song and a new career was born. Cole had less than a two-octave range but his delivery had great depth and intimacy. Cole's personal life and his career were one. He married more than once and somehow managed to avoid any scandals in the press. His shyness hid his ambition. A key to his success was his belief in himself. His second wife, Maria Ellington, was a beautiful and intelligent woman who managed his career. She helped polish his image and encouraged him to become a stand-up singer. Cole's philosophy was love. He believed that being loved as a musician and as a man where the most important values in the world. A heavy smoker, Cole died of lung cancer in 1965, at the age of forty-six.

Pisces/*Nine* (February 27, March 9, March 18)
Neptune/Mars

PURPOSE: To jump into life and live it to the utmost, manifesting a dream and never forgetting that what you do and how you do it, will be an example to others.

"We should consider every day lost in which we have not danced at least once."—Friedrich Wilhelm Nietzsche. The Pisces*Nine* has a passion for life. They are here to live and love and no one or nothing should stand in their way. Their true challenge is found in how they conduct themselves, face their challenges, and treat others who have less courage. They must balance a strong Ego and a tendency toward selfishness, with the desire to give and serve. Pisces/*Nines* must throw their whole beings into whatever they do. People are attracted to their beauty and charm. They are psychic and intuitive. They can be shy. Without a purpose or sense of self, others could overwhelm them. With a purpose, they must be careful not to misuse their powerful will to dominate others. Pisces/ *Nines* can be narcissistic and demanding. They struggle with anger and need to channel it creatively. Obsession is not a distant stranger; they must work on inner discipline, practice patience, and use their brilliant minds for a great purpose.

IF SPIRIT TAKES THE LEAD: If Spirit is strong, then these souls will dedicate themselves to a great humanitarian cause. They are warriors of the Spirit and have incredible courage to overcome whatever life throws in their path. Their will is a problem. It dominates others and the temptation to misuse it is strong. They need to stay centered and remind themselves that they are here not to do things their way but His.

IF EGO TAKES THE LEAD: If Ego is strong, the Pisces/*Nine* may be dangerous. They can be abusive, angry, and domineering. The world is there to satisfy their needs alone. They are also hard workers, versatile and talented. They need to balance compassion with strength.

ELIZABETH TAYLOR (February 27)

Actress, humanitarian.

Elizabeth Taylor was born in England. Her violet eyes and her beautiful face got her into the movies as a child. When she landed her first big part in *Lassie Come Home,* her parents moved to Hollywood. Fame came with her starring role in *National Velvet.* Taylor has been married eight times, twice to her greatest love, Richard Burton. Taylor's courageous fight against AIDS when it wasn't a popular cause has earned her the respect of many. Her life exhibits the extremes that are so prevalent in Pisces. She has loved and lost, lived life with a passion, and experienced both great pain and joy. This is Pisces. This is the journey.

EDGAR CAYCE (March 18)

Psychic.

Edgar Cayce was America's greatest mystic. While in a sleeplike state, he could read people's physical conditions, their futures and their pasts. His skill in diagnosing illnesses and describing remedies, many of them ancient, astounded doctors. Cayce's readings were transcribed, and because of this, he is the most documented psychic. Edgar Cayce believed he received his gift from an angel. The night after the vision, he placed his schoolbook under his pillow and the next morning, he knew it by heart. Still, Cayce went only to the eighth grade. Always a plain and simple man, he read the Bible every day of his life. He was as amazed as others at his gift and tried always to use it in alignment with God's will. Cayce had an honest desire to help others. Whenever he deviated from the spiritual path, his gift failed him. He believed in the oneness of all life, and the power of love. His believed we were all spiritual beings, children of God, and that life has continuity beyond the end of time. He believed in reincarnation, karma, and grace. He encouraged others to trust in their spirit for guidance, information, and healing. The body of Cayce's works are in Virginia Beach, available to anyone who wants to study them. Cayce published numerous books on his philosophy and his life.

SUMMARY

Pisces is the last sign of the zodiac and the challenges are great. You must stand alone, believe in yourself, and stay centered in God and your soul while you walk the path of temptation. Pisces will test you wherever you lack experience and confidence. You must be able to create spontaneously, adjust to anything, and remain focused on your goal. Fear is a thing of the past. Life is eternal, and you're here to learn and grow. You are master of yourself, and you can use pain and sorrow, joy and passion to help you accomplish your purpose. Heaven and earth have lost their sense of separateness. Your friends are spirit guides, not just the man next door. You talk with angels, hear messages from fairies, and your mind blends with your imagination, creating fantasies and illusions that delight the Spirit and the soul. Reality is the changing moment, and just this knowledge makes you different. You have learned to let go of exterior control and have directed your power inward, harnessing your mind and its desires behind your will. Heaven and earth are eager to share their fruits and gifts, but have waited for you, knowing that to taste the nectar without truth and discipline is dangerous indeed. The honey has an addictive flavor. In Pisces, you are the enemy when you are not the master of yourself. With discipline you can travel on light beams, dance with angels, and experience the bliss and joys of heaven and earth as no other sign can. Once you have experienced it all, you can look back and see what you could have done to make the journey perfect. Excited, you beseech heaven to give you one more chance. Of course, the gods give you the nod, and you're off once again, eager to change the world and mold it to your vision. When the planets are aligned to reflect your karma, you make your reentry to earth and meet the trauma of being born with all the fire and passion of a true Aries.

SELECTED SOURCES

Earl Blackwell *Celebrity Register, 1990 (50th Anniversary Edition)* Gale Research 1990

Denis Brian *Einstein: A life* John Wiley & Sons, Inc. 1996

Diana DuBois *In Her Sister's Shadow: An Intimate Biography of Lee Radziwill* St. Martin's 1997

Salvatore Fucito and Barnet J. Beyer   *Caruso and the Art of Singing: including Caruso's Vocal Exercises and His Practical Advice to Students and Teachers of Singing*   Dover 1995

William A. Henry   *The Great One: The Life and Legend of Jackie Gleason*   Doubleday 1992

James Huneker   *Chopin: The Man and His Music*   Dover 1966

Jeffrey Kallberg   *Chopin at the Boundaries: Sex, History and Musical Genre*   Harvard University Press 1996

Shawn Levy   *King of Comedy: The Life and Art of Jerry Lewis*   St. Martin's 1997

Roy Moseley with Philip and Martin Masheter   *Rex Harrison: A Biography*   St. Martin's 1987

Chogyal Namkhai Norbu   *Dzogchen: The Self-Perfected State*   Edited by Adriano Clemente   Translated from the Italian by John Shane   Routledge 1990

Herbert B. Puryear, Ph.D   *The Edgar Cayce Primer: Discovering The Path to Self-Transformation*   Bantam 1994

Arthur Schopenhauer   *Essays and Aphorisms*   Selected and Translated with an introduction by R.J. Hollingdale   Viking 1973

Donald Spoto   *A Passion for Life: The Biography of Elizabeth Taylor*   Harper Collins 1995

Herbert Weinstock   *Handel*   Alfred A. Knopf 1946

CHAPTER FOURTEEN

Moving Toward Change and Transformation

Change is a process and the gasoline needed to drive its engine is desire. Without it there is no force or passion to propel you forward past the obstacles and personal resistance you will certainly meet along the way. Change will unfold when you see yourself and the world from a new perspective. Do not try to impose change on others; if you take care of your own growth, you will inspire others to do the same. Information is like a seed; if you're not ready to receive it, it will wait until the soil is fertile and the soul is eager to blossom. As the old saying goes, "When the student is ready, the teacher appears." As you gather new ideas, remember, nothing should be accepted that does not "feel" right. You are the sole authority on yourself and your life. Don't let anyone tell you who you are or what you should be; that must come from within. Learn to hold information that you don't understand to the side, without judging it, but waiting for it to be either further confirmed or denied. There are certain basic skills that I can only touch on in this book, that once you understand, make almost any new situation less frightening and easy to tackle. Confidence in yourself is the key, and to achieve this you must develop a relationship with yourself and your instincts. Without a relationship with the self, you become dependent on others—their advice, their ideas, and their support. If a crisis happens and you're alone—you're in trouble. Learning to be self-sufficient—responsible for your life, your decisions, your actions—is the key to worldly and spiritual happiness. Balance must be strived for. That means you need a strong Ego and Spirit to overcome life's obstacles and to feel protected and secure. If the word God is not comfortable, then think of Spirit as an energy that connects you to all things, an harmonious state that is reached when you have the courage to go beyond yourself, when you can risk yourself for someone else, when you can use your strength to help others. Then you're on your way. This ability to go beyond the Ego is the key to happiness. As long as you stay imprisoned in your own small world of personal desires, you invite the devil and its demons to torment your soul. For desires of the earthly kind are never satisfying. The more you feed them, the bigger their appetite becomes. It is only when you can begin to turn your back on these earthly temptations that a true sense of power and optimism begins to surface. By becoming master of yourself you become master of the world. Holding someone else down, controlling others, only ends up imprisoning the controller. For to guard another is to limit your own freedom.

The search for truth is an endless quest, and truth itself seems to change with one's state of consciousness. It is not found in one particular place— the halls of ancient and renowned universities do not have a monopoly on the secrets of the universe. Truth and knowledge is in everything that exists, in all experiences and in all persons, rich or poor, smart or dumb. Truth is available to all who seek it. The only way to see it is to summon it forth with the heart and an open mind. Remember, truth "feels right," it rings clear, and it's applicable to more than one situation. To know how something feels requires that you be in touch with your feelings. If you haven't learned how to listen to your own inner voice, it will be almost impossible to know the truth. True power requires a centeredness in truth, a direct relationship with the self. This doesn't happen on its own, not in today's world of information. You can't turn around without being assaulted with knowledge and advice on how to live your life. You are told on the TV, in the movies, on the internet what to eat, wear, think, and do. As soon as you embrace one idea, it's invalidated by another. This breeds insecurity and uncertainty. The ability to select what is useful from around you and use it to improve your life is a primary challenge of survival. You must not be afraid to express who you are, while at the same time respecting the beliefs and feelings of others. This simple quest to hold your own space, while interacting in the space of others, is the most challenging thing you will have to learn in your life. Put the time and effort into a few simple truths, spend some time on self-reflection, and your world will unfold without effort, and the fruits of life will be within your reach.

Learning To Confront Others And Protect Your Space

If you can't confront and express yourself without fear, you will spend your life either running away or being dominated by someone who believes that their opinion is the only way. Without being able to take a stand for what you believe in, you will never get the chance to sing your song. The ability to confront another person is important, and those who are too aggressive and angry and those who are passive both need to stand up and look at what is preventing their free expression. Anger makes most souls afraid because when they expressed anger they felt a loss of love. Abandonment is associated with anger because the whole process was never completed. When you first stand up for yourself, others turn their back. But if you can be consistent, without high expectations, or an obsession with results, then you can begin to change your life and how others treat you. The universe will test you until you make a total commitment to what you are doing, something which would not happen without resistance. The first thing to remember when speaking up or trying something out is not to worry about doing it perfectly. You can't learn if you're afraid of making mistakes. If you overstep your boundaries in the beginning, apologize, but don't stop. You can't get good without practice, and if you're truthful and don't intentionally want to hurt someone, then the damage you will do will be far less than if you repress your feelings. When you let others hurt you without saying anything, you give them permission to do it again. Speak up, even if you can't change the situation. First of all, *you* will feel better, and the person doing the misdemeanor will have to think about your words when they commit their improper act. If your husband comes home and doesn't spend any time with the children, and it makes you angry, don't nag him, don't yell. No one listens when they're attacked. State it! Present what you want. And better yet, present it in a way that is possible to be achieved. Don't ask for too much too soon. Start small, then add to your list as things improve. Suggest that twice a week he reserve some special time. Don't let him off the hook because he complains or has excuses. Be consistent and, once again, don't accuse or attack. Don't make him have to defend his position. Maybe his father never spent time with him, and he doesn't know how. Communication is the key; it prevents anger. When you can't communicate, you hold things in. Then the silent communication becomes a powerful negative force in your relationship. Speaking up sets boundaries. It tells others what you will accept and what you won't. Don't rely on the fact that *they should know*. They don't, not if you don't tell them.

There is nothing wrong with anger. It's a natural response to many things in life. Holding on to anger is destructive. Hurting someone because you're angry is not good. But having the feelings are normal. Learn to accept your anger, and speak up when something happens. Repressed anger finds a way of retaliating. No one escapes unscathed. Even a child knows how to get even when she feels unjustly hurt. That new sofa will have a spill, or your freshly washed floor will get dirtied but they'll get even, and so will you. So learn how to express *all* your feelings, they are what teaches us to set our boundaries, to stand up for ourselves, and to make sure that others know that's our space. Our sense of justice is operating and we are aware of what is going on.

Taking Responsibility

You and no one else but you can change your life or make it happen. Others can extend a helping hand, but without your participation, nothing lasting will manifest. In order to grow and be successful, in order to take your place in the world, you must take responsibility for your life. I don't care what has happened to you before this moment. If you were a child and not capable of taking action, you are capable now. Do not deny the pain of the past, but don't get stuck there. Until you get off the spot that hurts you can't heal it. If you're constantly licking your wounds, they stay open and have a chance to get reinfected. To move forward requires that you take responsibility. All that means is you stop blaming the world, or others for your predicament, and start investigating what *you* can do to get out of it. The world does not owe you an existence. You must make things happen yourself. The sooner you learn how to use the world for your own end, the sooner you will feel confident, strong, and in charge. Once you are in control of your own life you can reach out and help others. If you try to save someone else when you yourself are drowning, then you both will go under. Learn how to swim, then teach someone else. It's not as difficult and as frightening as it seems. One step in front of the other, one day, one challenge at a time. If you don't know what to do, ask the universe to send you the information. Keep an open mind, struggle for the truth, this creates the tension needed for you to access your unconscious which is in touch with all information. And at an unexpected moment the answer will come. Have the courage to try, and you'll be amazed at what you can do. Remember, shortcuts don't work. Get rich quick schemes usually take your money, they don't give it to you. Hard work is the only thing you can count on. When you do the work, no one can take your rewards. There is a process and a way to improve everything in your life.

Taking Risks

To break out of any pattern or habit, to change or grow, requires one to step into the unknown. A risk must be taken. I'm not talking about the gambling tables or putting your life in danger, I'm talking about doing something without a guarantee. If you don't take a chance, you don't invite the magic in. Go to the art opening alone. Take that job you were offered even though you've never done that kind of work before. Meet the demands of the moment with confidence and creativity, when you put yourself on the line it's amazing how creative even the most insecure and frightened person can become. Practice putting yourself at risk with simple things, where the results don't matter. Do something you normally wouldn't do. Change the habits and patterns of your life, and you'll see a change come over you.

Move the furniture around, try a new color on your nails, take a weekend workshop on Eastern philosophy, learn a new skill, expose yourself to new ideas, and life will become a place of opportunity and possibilities instead of the same old thing.

Get Out Of Yourself And Help Someone Else

The key to happiness is getting out of yourself. If you are totally self-involved then you will never feel rewarded by life, whatever you do will leave you empty, isolated, and alone. When you can get out of yourself, you invite Spirit in. The good feelings that you gain from sharing or helping someone in need, stays with you, makes you feel connected to the world, and makes life worthwhile. Loneliness, emptiness, unhappiness are always found in those who are cut off from the world. Everyone has something to give. If you have time, volunteer it. If you don't, then let the moment show you how to help. If someone drops something in a store, help them pick it up. Put yourself out in the world. Risk yourself by extending yourself to someone else, and you will begin to realize just what life is all about. The good deeds you do are the best protection you can have. Buy stolen goods, and you invite thieves into your home. Ignore a cry for help, and when you're in need, you'll be ignored, too. What you do, what you think, and what you hold dear are what you manifest. You are the creator of your world—make it one where giving and receiving is commonplace.

Keep Good Attitudes And They'll Keep You

Thoughts are powerful; they are the building blocks of the universe. Negativity holds you back, keeps you down, and prevents confidence, a needed ingredient for spontaneity to exist. When you tell yourself you can't do something, chances are you won't. You're already defeated. Live your life as an open road; keep hope and all possibilities before you. If you're not good at positive thinking, buy yourself one of the many wonderful affirmation books that are on the market and read one a day. You have to train your mind to think the way you want it to. Take charge of your thoughts, and you're on your way to creating your world around your point of view.

Step Back And Analyze Yourself And The Situation

The ability to be objective is easier for some than others. If it's hard for you to separate things from your emotions, then learn about your emotions and what sets them off. The more you understand yourself, the easier it is to make positive changes. With distance and an overview, you can see what is wrong, what needs work, and what must be let go of. It's important to get away from the situation, so take a trip, don't be available, give yourself that space. A tried-and-true way of being objective is the list. Put on a sheet of paper all the facts—what you like, what you don't, what you need to discover. You are objectifying the problem, and now you can use it instead of it using you.

Don't Ask For Advice Until You Are Clear On Your Position

Other people usually confuse you more than help you. If you get too many opinions before you've thought the problem through, you're going to be more confused than when you started out. Find your own perspective, then ask opinions, and only from people whom you respect. If you don't like how someone is raising their kids, don't ask their advice on yours. If you don't like the way someone dresses, don't ask them to help you choose between two outfits. Go to yourself first, then go to someone you look up to on the issue. Weigh the information, don't give a quick answer. Let things settle within you, and then you'll know what to do.

Creative Visualization

Last but not least, is a little technique I learned that is very powerful. Review the events of the day, anything that didn't work out the way you wanted it to, and replay it in your mind the way you would want it to have happened. Rethink what you said, what they said, and change it. You are programming your mind to respond differently to a certain situation, and when it occurs again you will be ready and in a different position because now you'll have another option.

Change does not have to be a frightening thing, you will welcome it in your life when you see the benefits it brings. Life requires a response, not control. That can only be accomplished from within. Self-mastery is the key to happiness. Never forget you are the cocreator of your world. You can re-create it anytime you choose. *The Day You Were Born* has given you basic insight into yourself, but it's up to you to make it happen. Don't waste another moment. Don't be afraid to begin life again. Recreate yourself anew, this time in the image of your soul.